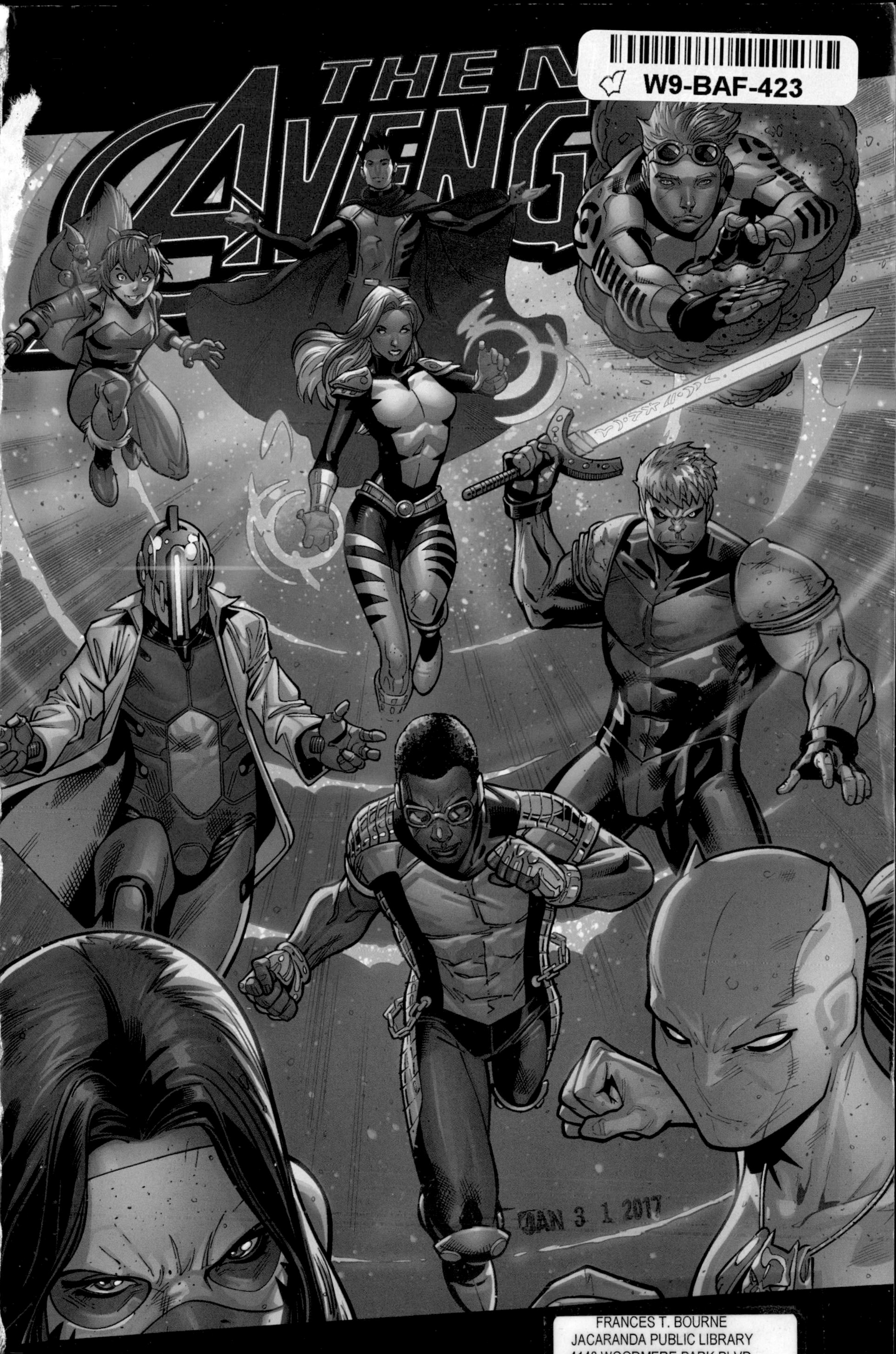
THE N
AVENG

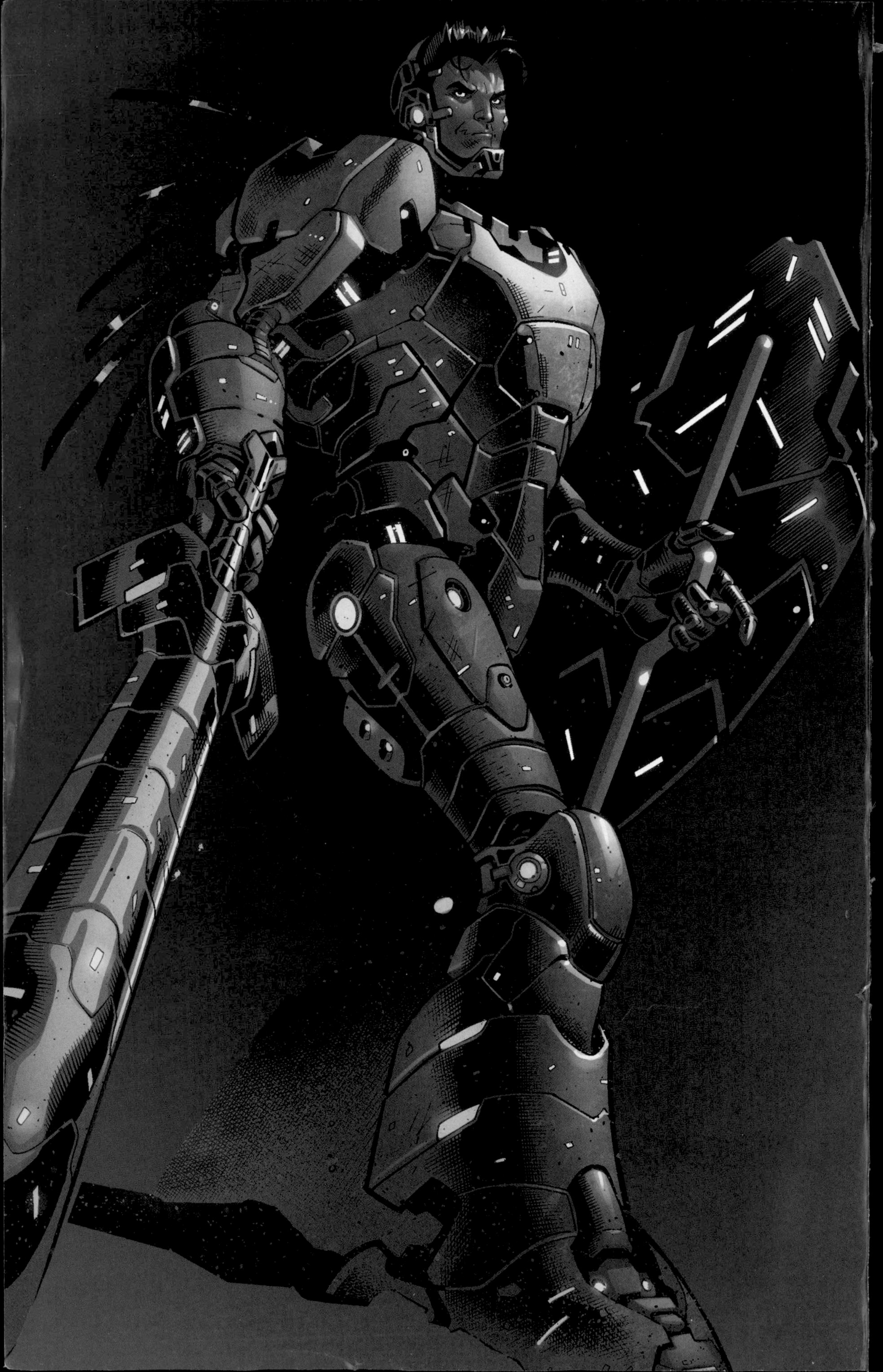

NEW TECH.
NEW IDEAS.
NEW MISSION.
THEY ARE...

THE NEW AVENGERS

CIVIL WAR II

WRITER: AL EWING

NEW AVENGERS #12-17

PENCILER: PACO MEDINA

INKER: JUAN VLASCO

COLOR ARTISTS: JESUS ABURTOV
WITH DONO SÁNCHEZ-ALMARA (#9)

LETTERERS: VC'S JOE CARAMAGNA (#12-13),
TRAVIS LANHAM (#14) & CLAYTON COWLES (#15-17)

COVER ARTIST: JULIAN TOTINO TEDESCO

NEW AVENGERS #18

ARTIST: CARLO BARBERI

COLOR ARTIST: JESUS ABURTOV

LETTERER: VC'S CLAYTON COWLES

COVER ARTIST: JULIAN TOTINO TEDESCO

ASSISTANT EDITOR: ALANNA SMITH

EDITORS: TOM BREVOORT with WIL MOSS

AVENGERS CREATED BY **STAN LEE** & **JACK KIRBY**

COLLECTION EDITOR:
JENNIFER GRÜNWALD
ASSOCIATE MANAGING EDITOR:
KATERI WOODY
ASSOCIATE EDITOR:
SARAH BRUNSTAD
EDITOR, SPECIAL PROJECTS:
MARK D. BEAZLEY

VP PRODUCTION & SPECIAL PROJECTS:
JEFF YOUNGQUIST
SVP PRINT, SALES & MARKETING:
DAVID GABRIEL
BOOK DESIGN:
ADAM DEL RE

EDITOR IN CHIEF:
AXEL ALONSO
CHIEF CREATIVE OFFICER:
JOE QUESADA
PUBLISHER:
DAN BUCKLEY
EXECUTIVE PRODUCER:
ALAN FINE

NEW AVENGERS: A.I.M. VOL. 3 — CIVIL WAR II. Contains material originally published in magazine form as NEW AVENGERS #12-18. First printing 2016. ISBN# 978-1-302-90235-3. Published by MARVEL WORLDWIDE, INC., a subsidiary of MARVEL ENTERTAINMENT, LLC. OFFICE OF PUBLICATION: 135 West 50th Street, New York, NY 10020. Copyright © 2016 MARVEL No similarity between any of the names, characters, persons, and/or institutions in this magazine with those of any living or dead person or institution is intended, and any such similarity which may exist is purely coincidental. **Printed in the U.S.A.** ALAN FINE, President, Marvel Entertainment; DAN BUCKLEY, President, TV, Publishing & Brand Management; JOE QUESADA, Chief Creative Officer; TOM BREVOORT, SVP of Publishing; DAVID BOGART, SVP of Business Affairs & Operations, Publishing & Partnership; C.B. CEBULSKI, VP of Brand Management & Development, Asia; DAVID GABRIEL, SVP of Sales & Marketing, Publishing; JEFF YOUNGQUIST, VP of Production & Special Projects; DAN CARR, Executive Director of Publishing Technology; ALEX MORALES, Director of Publishing Operations; SUSAN CRESPI, Production Manager; STAN LEE, Chairman Emeritus. For information regarding advertising in Marvel Comics or on Marvel.com, please contact Vit DeBellis, Integrated Sales Manager, at vdebellis@marvel.com. For Marvel subscription inquiries, please call 888-511-5480. **Manufactured between 9/30/2016 and 11/7/2016 by LSC COMMUNICATIONS INC., SALEM, VA, USA.**

10 9 8 7 6 5 4 3 2 1

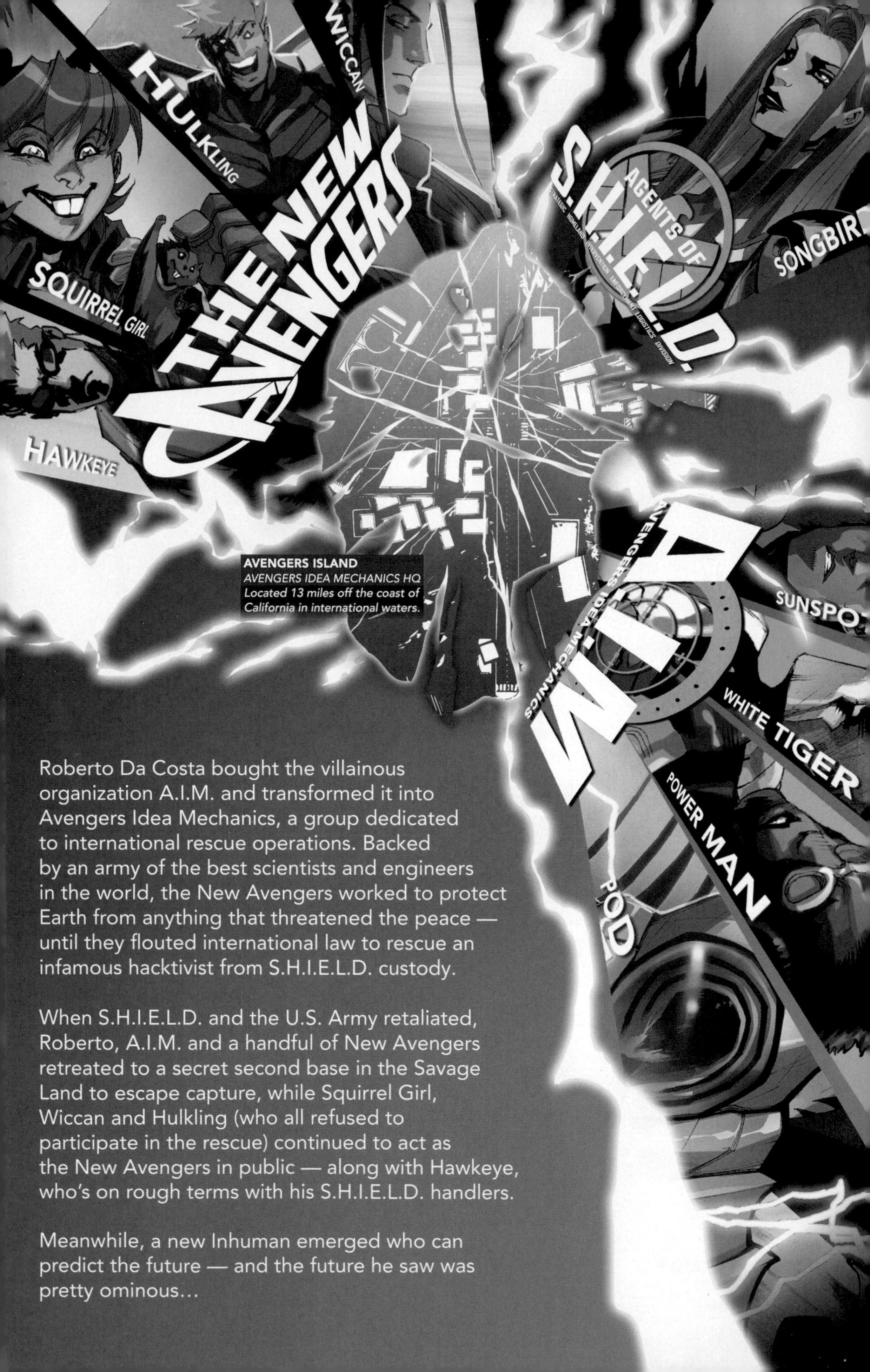
HULKLING
WICCAN
SQUIRREL GIRL
HAWKEYE
THE NEW AVENGERS
AGENTS OF S.H.I.E.L.D.
STRATEGIC HOMELAND INTERVENTION ENFORCEMENT LOGISTICS DIVISION
SONGBIR
AVENGERS ISLAND
AVENGERS IDEA MECHANICS HQ
Located 13 miles off the coast of California in international waters.
A.I.M.
AVENGERS IDEA MECHANICS
SUNSPO
WHITE TIGER
POWER MAN
POD

Roberto Da Costa bought the villainous organization A.I.M. and transformed it into Avengers Idea Mechanics, a group dedicated to international rescue operations. Backed by an army of the best scientists and engineers in the world, the New Avengers worked to protect Earth from anything that threatened the peace — until they flouted international law to rescue an infamous hacktivist from S.H.I.E.L.D. custody.

When S.H.I.E.L.D. and the U.S. Army retaliated, Roberto, A.I.M. and a handful of New Avengers retreated to a secret second base in the Savage Land to escape capture, while Squirrel Girl, Wiccan and Hulkling (who all refused to participate in the rescue) continued to act as the New Avengers in public — along with Hawkeye, who's on rough terms with his S.H.I.E.L.D. handlers.

Meanwhile, a new Inhuman emerged who can predict the future — and the future he saw was pretty ominous…

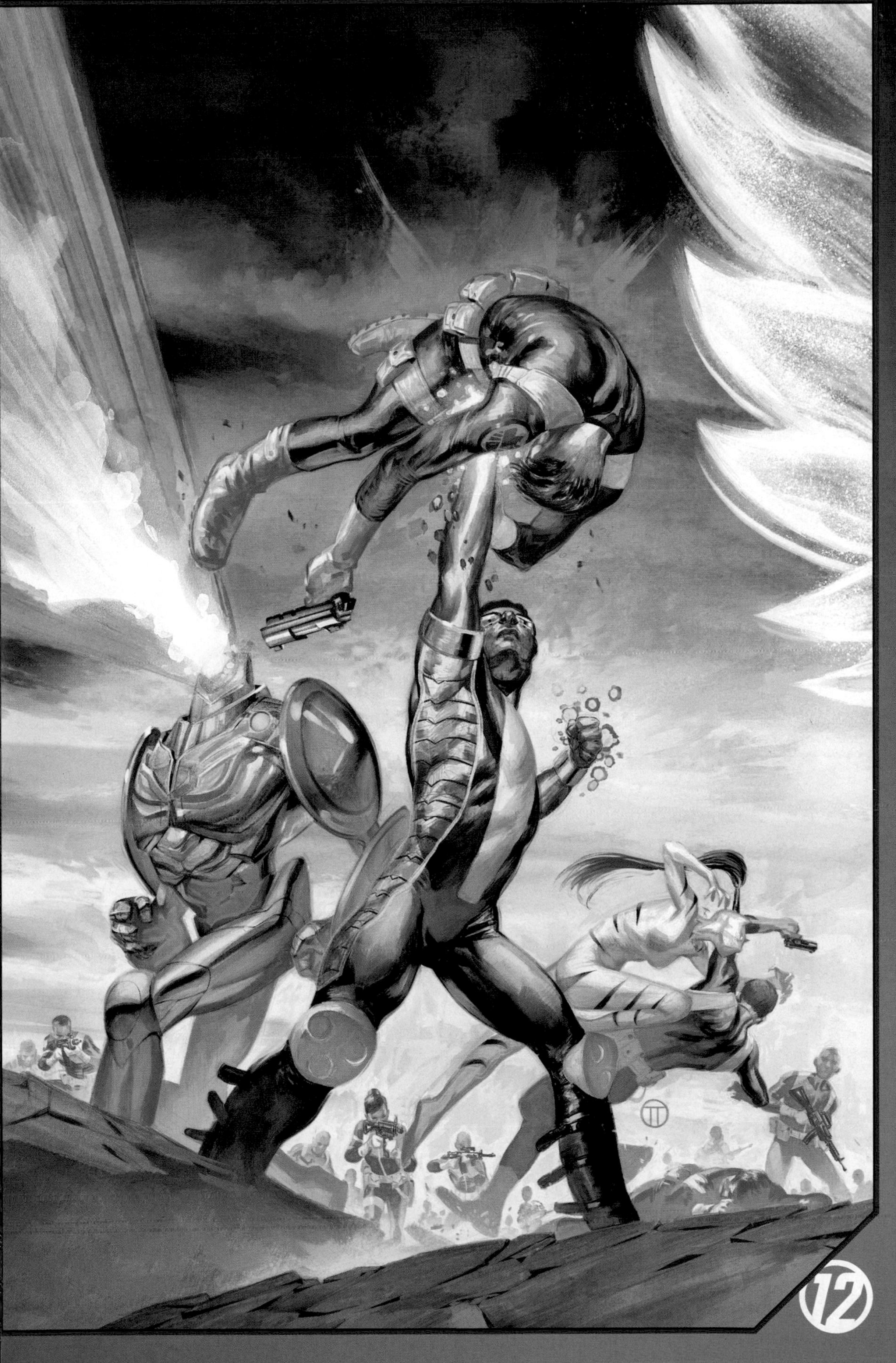
12

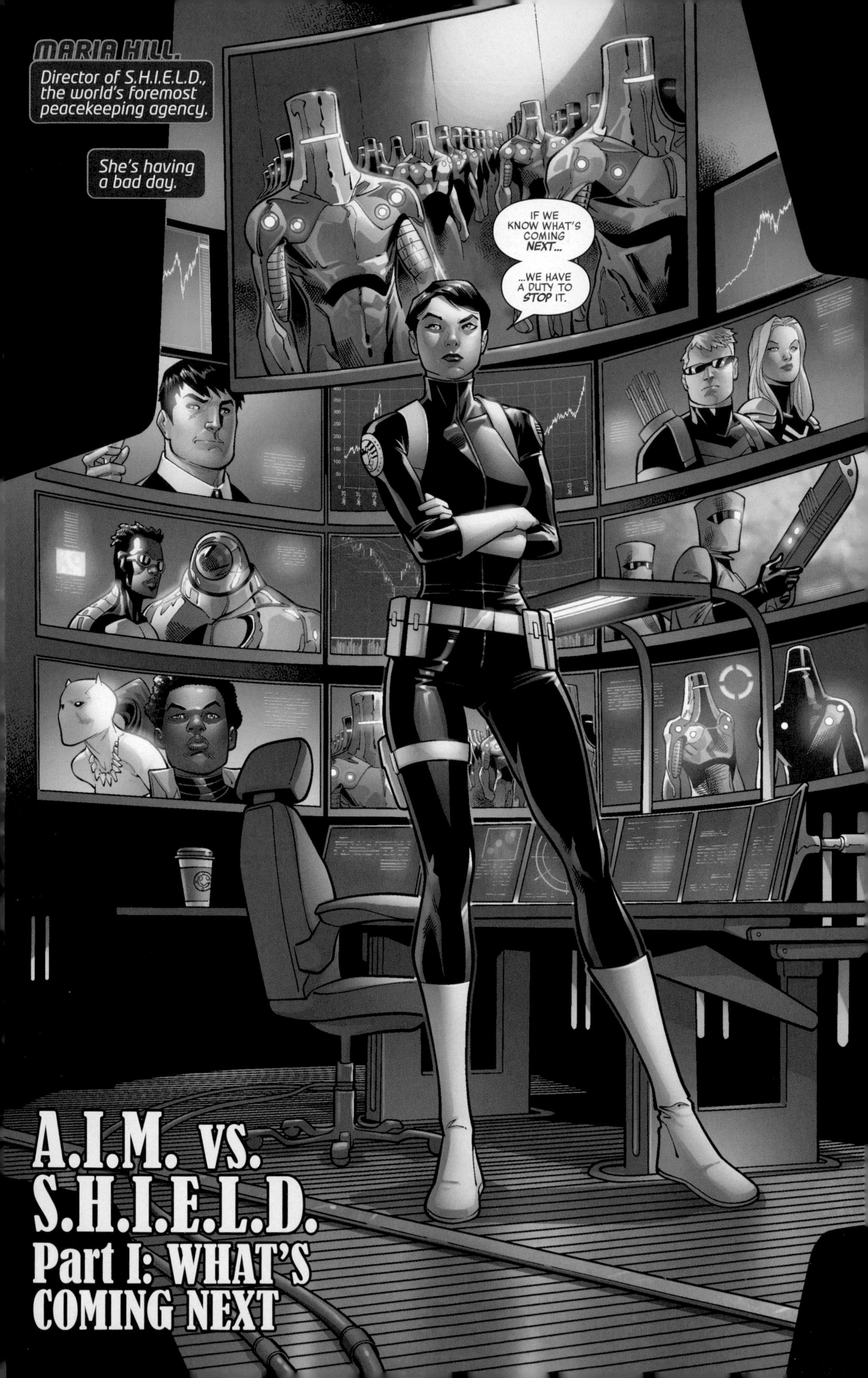

MARIA HILL.
Director of S.H.I.E.L.D., the world's foremost peacekeeping agency.
She's having a bad day.
IF WE KNOW WHAT'S COMING NEXT...
...WE HAVE A DUTY TO STOP IT.
A.I.M. VS. S.H.I.E.L.D.
Part I: WHAT'S COMING NEXT

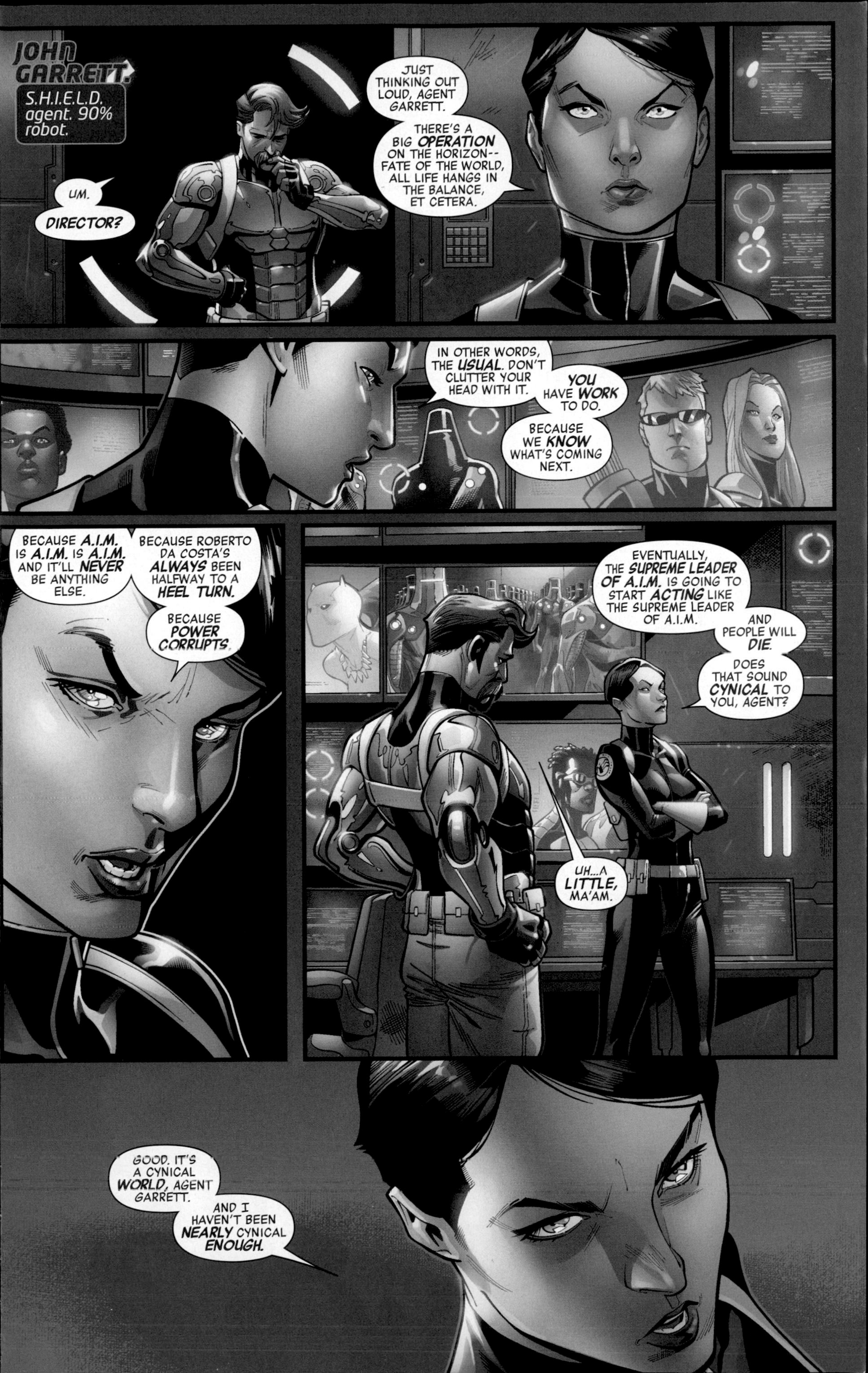
JOHN GARRETT.
S.H.I.E.L.D. agent. 90% robot.
UM. DIRECTOR?
JUST THINKING OUT LOUD, AGENT GARRETT.
THERE'S A BIG OPERATION ON THE HORIZON-- FATE OF THE WORLD, ALL LIFE HANGS IN THE BALANCE, ET CETERA.
IN OTHER WORDS, THE USUAL. DON'T CLUTTER YOUR HEAD WITH IT.
YOU HAVE WORK TO DO.
BECAUSE WE KNOW WHAT'S COMING NEXT.
BECAUSE A.I.M. IS A.I.M. IS A.I.M. AND IT'LL NEVER BE ANYTHING ELSE.
BECAUSE ROBERTO DA COSTA'S ALWAYS BEEN HALFWAY TO A HEEL TURN.
BECAUSE POWER CORRUPTS.
EVENTUALLY, THE SUPREME LEADER OF A.I.M. IS GOING TO START ACTING LIKE THE SUPREME LEADER OF A.I.M.
AND PEOPLE WILL DIE.
DOES THAT SOUND CYNICAL TO YOU, AGENT?
UH...A LITTLE, MA'AM.
GOOD. IT'S A CYNICAL WORLD, AGENT GARRETT.
AND I HAVEN'T BEEN NEARLY CYNICAL ENOUGH.

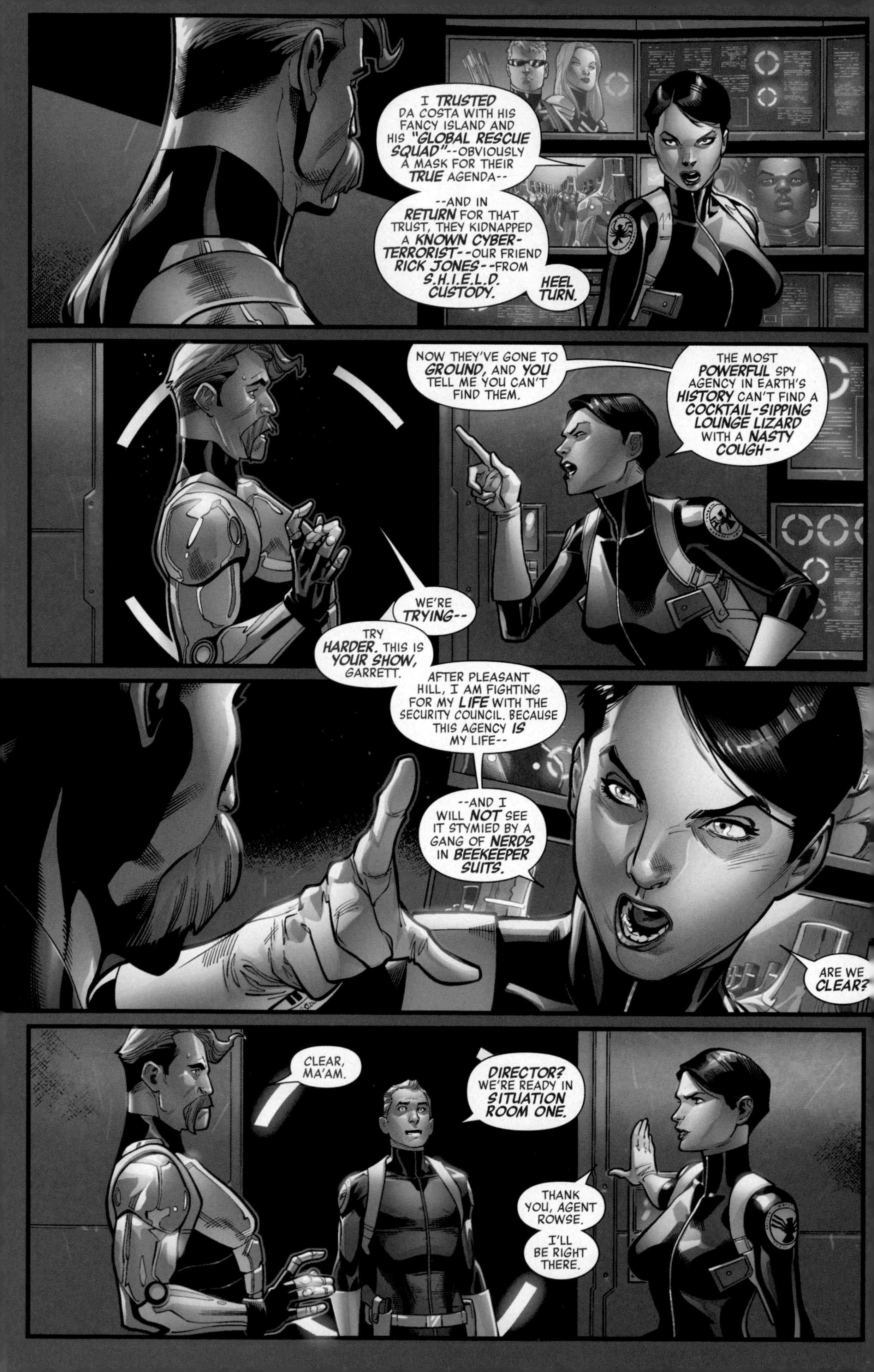
I TRUSTED DA COSTA WITH HIS FANCY ISLAND AND HIS "GLOBAL RESCUE SQUAD"--OBVIOUSLY A MASK FOR THEIR TRUE AGENDA--
--AND IN RETURN FOR THAT TRUST, THEY KIDNAPPED A KNOWN CYBER-TERRORIST--OUR FRIEND RICK JONES--FROM S.H.I.E.L.D. CUSTODY.
HEEL TURN.
NOW THEY'VE GONE TO GROUND, AND YOU TELL ME YOU CAN'T FIND THEM.
THE MOST POWERFUL SPY AGENCY IN EARTH'S HISTORY CAN'T FIND A COCKTAIL-SIPPING LOUNGE LIZARD WITH A NASTY COUGH--
WE'RE TRYING--
TRY HARDER. THIS IS YOUR SHOW, GARRETT.
AFTER PLEASANT HILL, I AM FIGHTING FOR MY LIFE WITH THE SECURITY COUNCIL. BECAUSE THIS AGENCY IS MY LIFE--
--AND I WILL NOT SEE IT STYMIED BY A GANG OF NERDS IN BEEKEEPER SUITS.
ARE WE CLEAR?
CLEAR, MA'AM.
DIRECTOR? WE'RE READY IN SITUATION ROOM ONE.
THANK YOU, AGENT ROWSE.
I'LL BE RIGHT THERE.

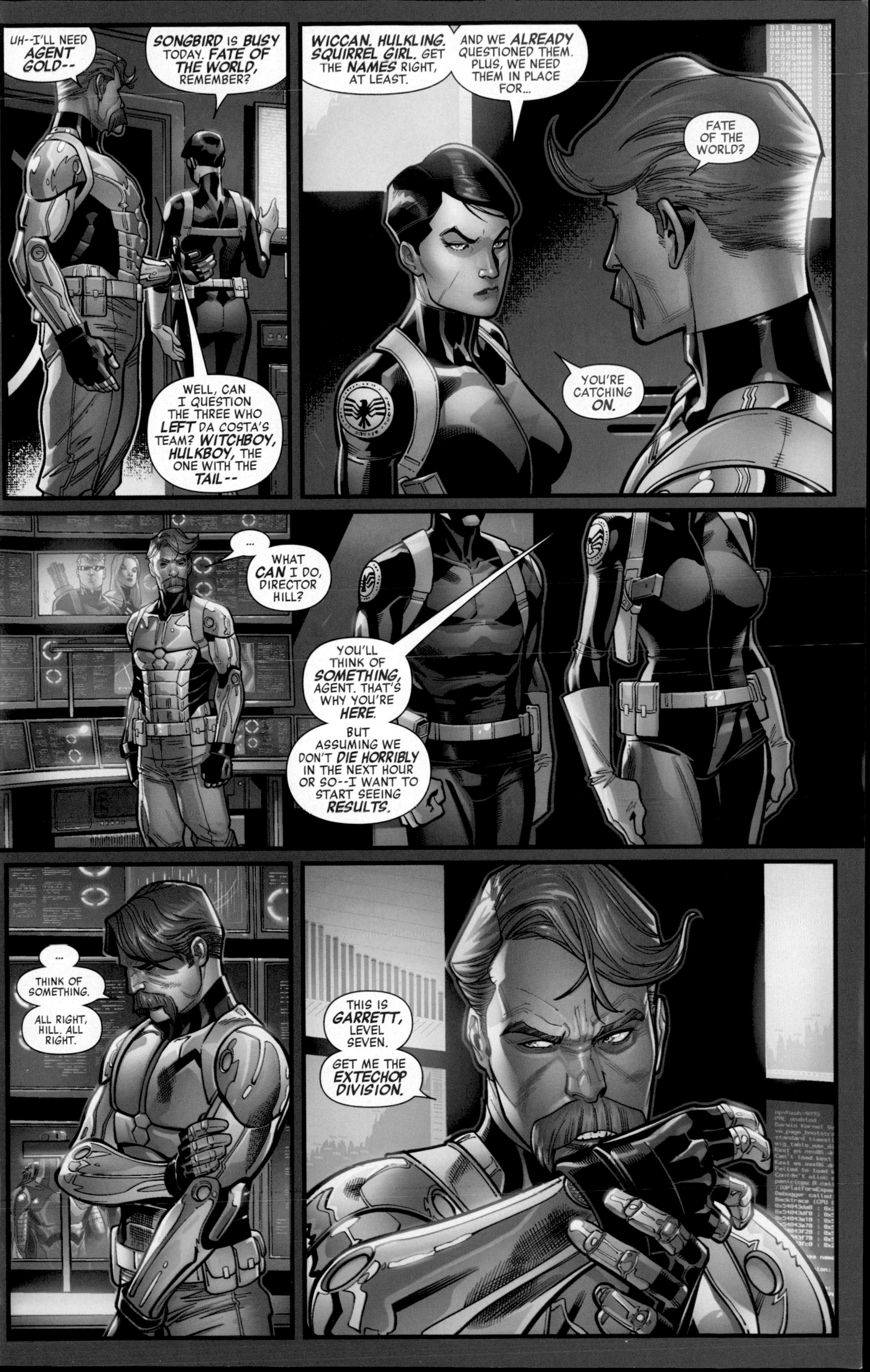

UH--I'LL NEED AGENT GOLD--
SONGBIRD IS BUSY TODAY. FATE OF THE WORLD, REMEMBER?
WELL, CAN I QUESTION THE THREE WHO LEFT DA COSTA'S TEAM? WITCHBOY, HULKBOY, THE ONE WITH THE TAIL--
WICCAN. HULKLING. SQUIRREL GIRL. GET THE NAMES RIGHT, AT LEAST.
AND WE ALREADY QUESTIONED THEM. PLUS, WE NEED THEM IN PLACE FOR...
FATE OF THE WORLD?
YOU'RE CATCHING ON.
...
WHAT CAN I DO, DIRECTOR HILL?
YOU'LL THINK OF SOMETHING, AGENT. THAT'S WHY YOU'RE HERE.
BUT ASSUMING WE DON'T DIE HORRIBLY IN THE NEXT HOUR OR SO--I WANT TO START SEEING RESULTS.
...
THINK OF SOMETHING.
ALL RIGHT, HILL. ALL RIGHT.
THIS IS GARRETT, LEVEL SEVEN.
GET ME THE EXTECHOP DIVISION.

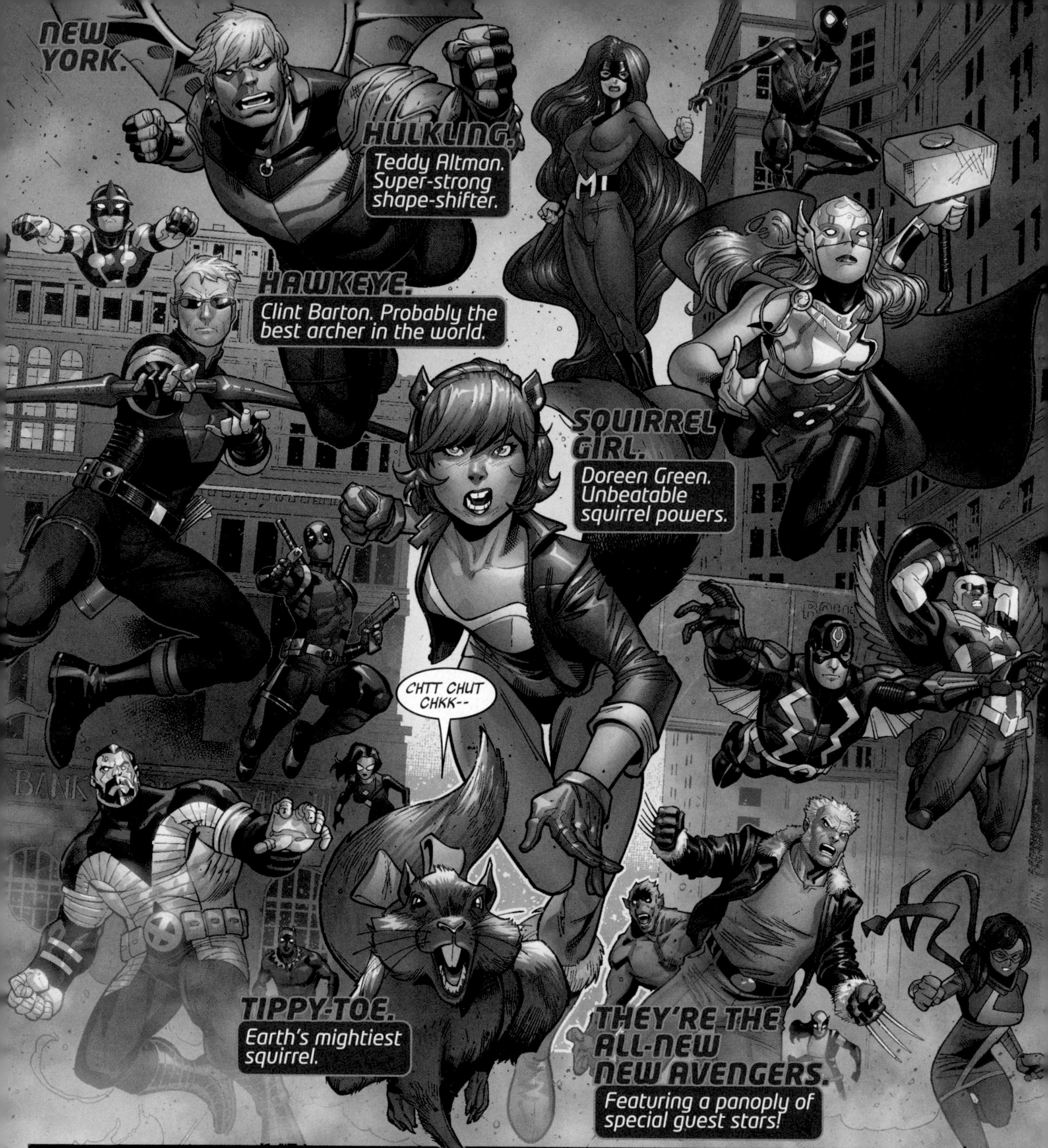
NEW YORK.
HULKLING.
Teddy Altman. Super-strong shape-shifter.
HAWKEYE.
Clint Barton. Probably the best archer in the world.
SQUIRREL GIRL.
Doreen Green. Unbeatable squirrel powers.
CHTT CHUT CHKK--
TIPPY-TOE.
Earth's mightiest squirrel.
THEY'RE THE ALL-NEW NEW AVENGERS.
Featuring a panoply of special guest stars!

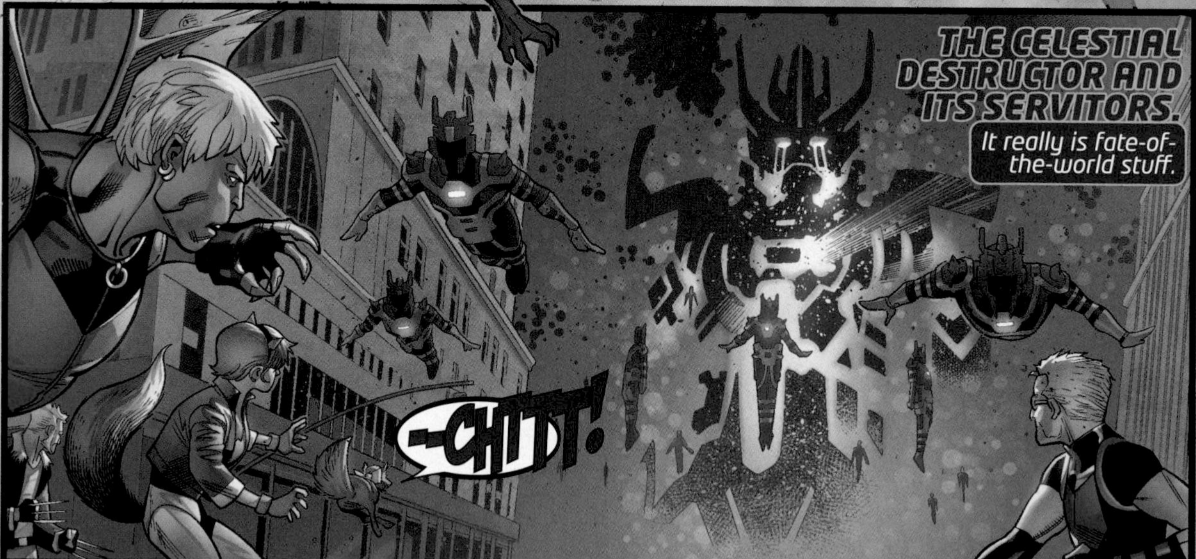
THE CELESTIAL DESTRUCTOR AND ITS SERVITORS.
It really is fate-of-the-world stuff.
-CHUT!

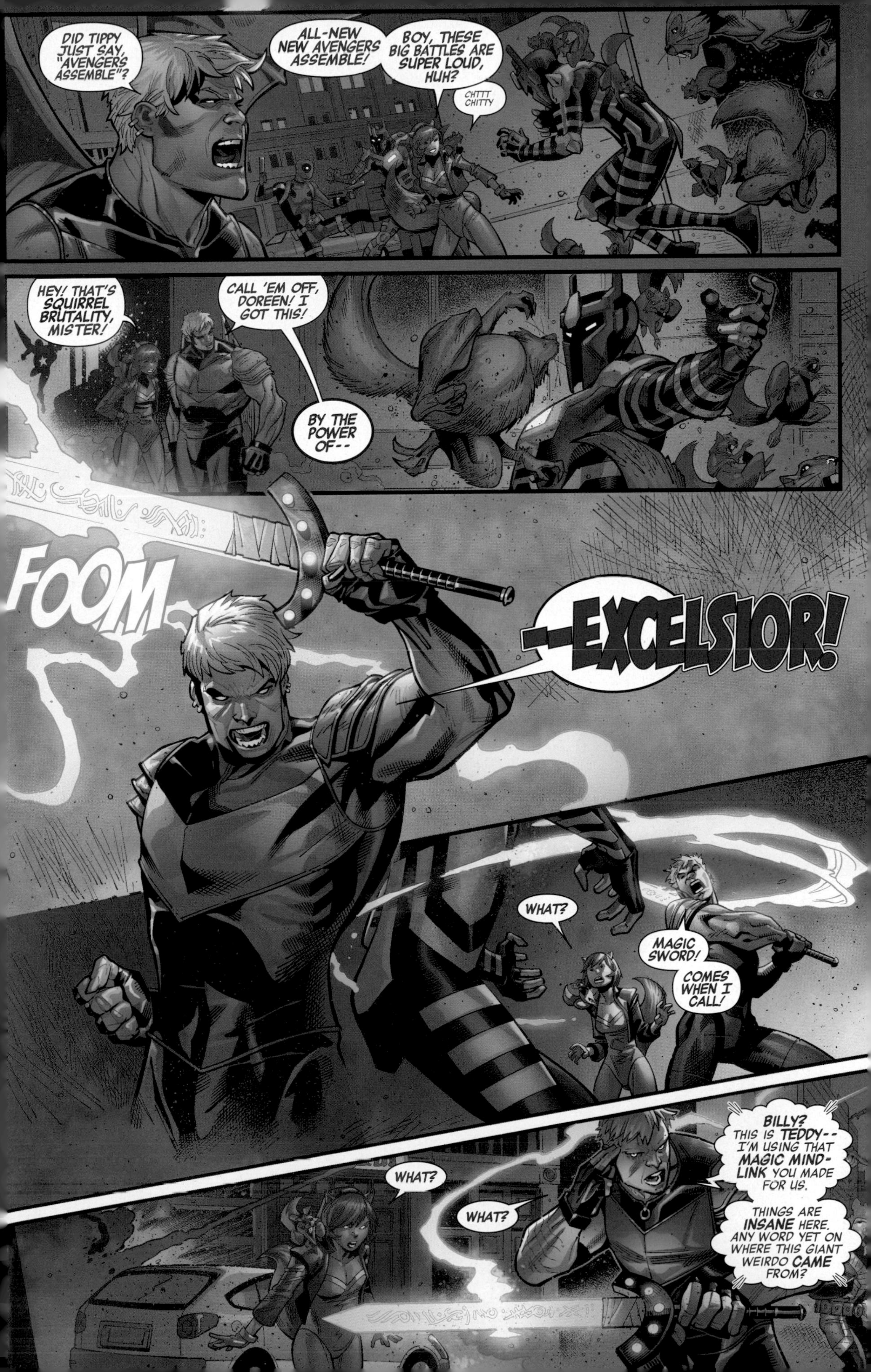

DID TIPPY JUST SAY, "AVENGERS ASSEMBLE"?
ALL-NEW NEW AVENGERS ASSEMBLE!
BOY, THESE BIG BATTLES ARE SUPER LOUD, HUH?
CHTTT CHITTY
HEY! THAT'S SQUIRREL BRUTALITY, MISTER!
CALL 'EM OFF, DOREEN! I GOT THIS!
BY THE POWER OF--
FOOM
--EXCELSIOR!
WHAT?
MAGIC SWORD!
COMES WHEN I CALL!
WHAT?
WHAT?
BILLY? THIS IS TEDDY-- I'M USING THAT MAGIC MIND-LINK YOU MADE FOR US.
THINGS ARE INSANE HERE. ANY WORD YET ON WHERE THIS GIANT WEIRDO CAME FROM?

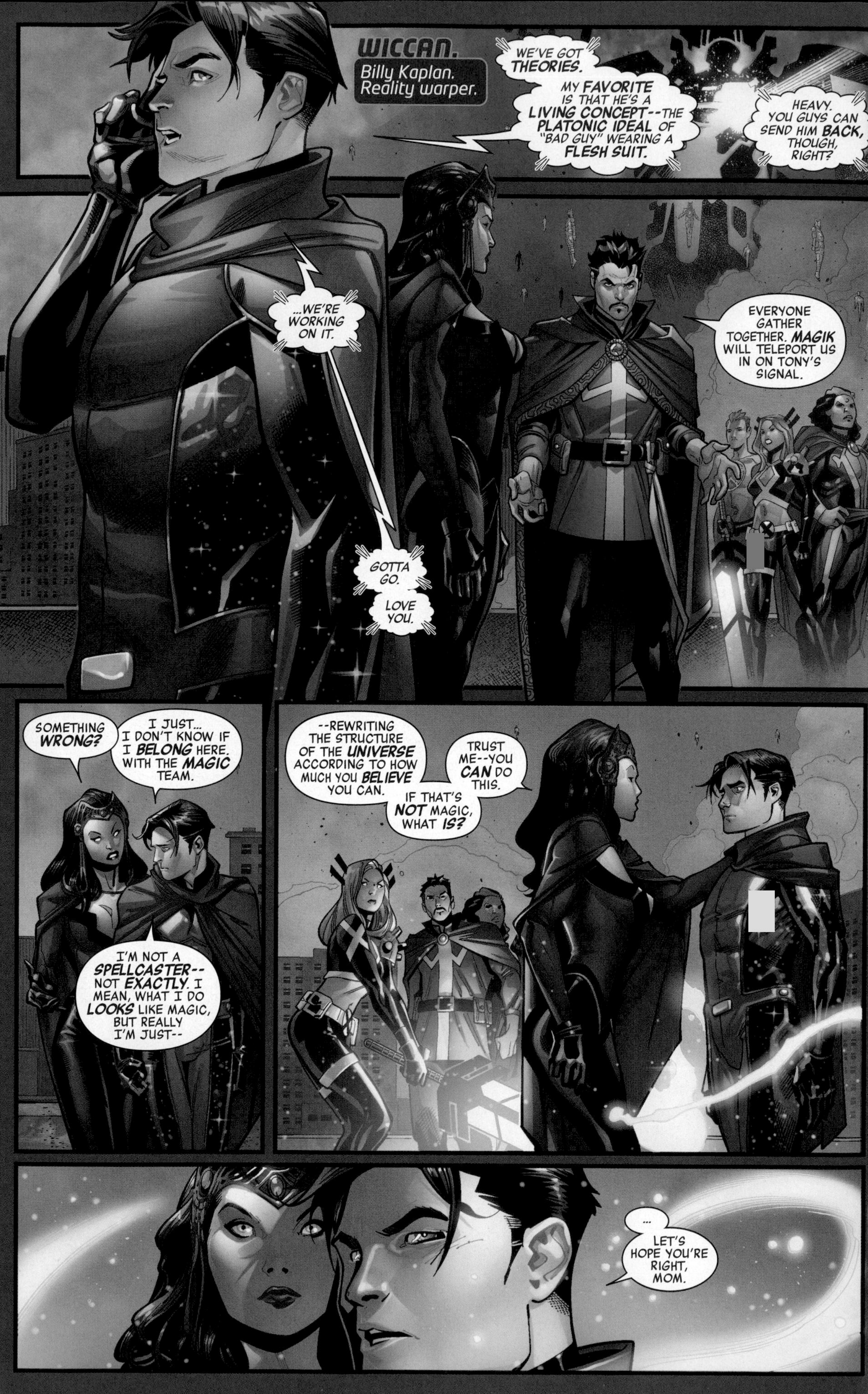
WICCAN.
Billy Kaplan. Reality warper.
WE'VE GOT THEORIES.
MY FAVORITE IS THAT HE'S A LIVING CONCEPT--THE PLATONIC IDEAL OF "BAD GUY" WEARING A FLESH SUIT.
HEAVY. YOU GUYS CAN SEND HIM BACK, THOUGH, RIGHT?
...WE'RE WORKING ON IT.
GOTTA GO.
LOVE YOU.
EVERYONE GATHER TOGETHER. MAGIK WILL TELEPORT US IN ON TONY'S SIGNAL.
SOMETHING WRONG?
I JUST... I DON'T KNOW IF I BELONG HERE. WITH THE MAGIC TEAM.
I'M NOT A SPELLCASTER--NOT EXACTLY. I MEAN, WHAT I DO LOOKS LIKE MAGIC, BUT REALLY I'M JUST--
--REWRITING THE STRUCTURE OF THE UNIVERSE ACCORDING TO HOW MUCH YOU BELIEVE YOU CAN.
IF THAT'S NOT MAGIC, WHAT IS?
TRUST ME--YOU CAN DO THIS.
... LET'S HOPE YOU'RE RIGHT, MOM.

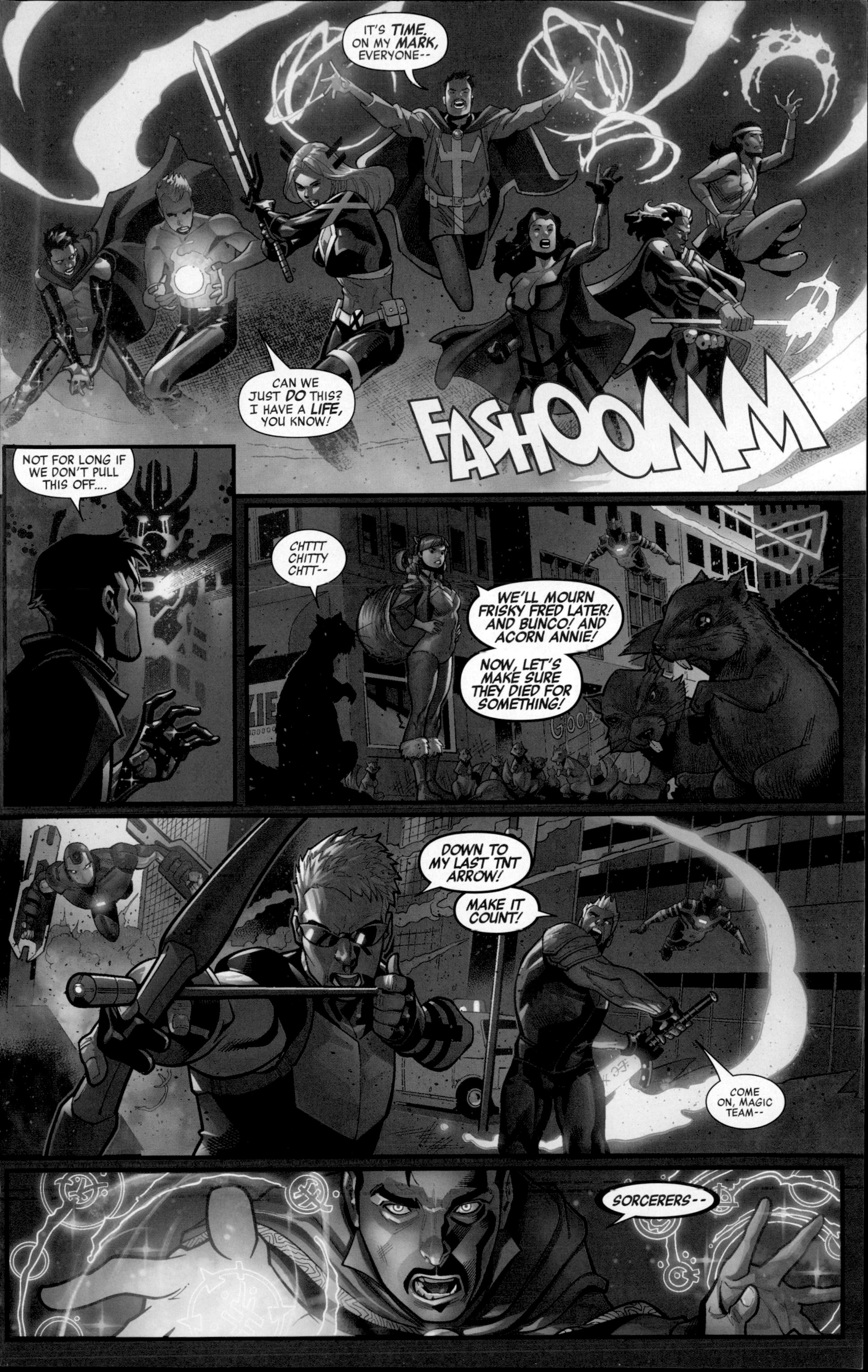
IT'S TIME. ON MY MARK, EVERYONE--
CAN WE JUST DO THIS? I HAVE A LIFE, YOU KNOW!
FASHOOMM
NOT FOR LONG IF WE DON'T PULL THIS OFF....
CHTTT CHITTY CHTT--
WE'LL MOURN FRISKY FRED LATER! AND BUNCO! AND ACORN ANNIE!
NOW, LET'S MAKE SURE THEY DIED FOR SOMETHING!
DOWN TO MY LAST TNT ARROW!
MAKE IT COUNT!
COME ON, MAGIC TEAM--
SORCERERS--

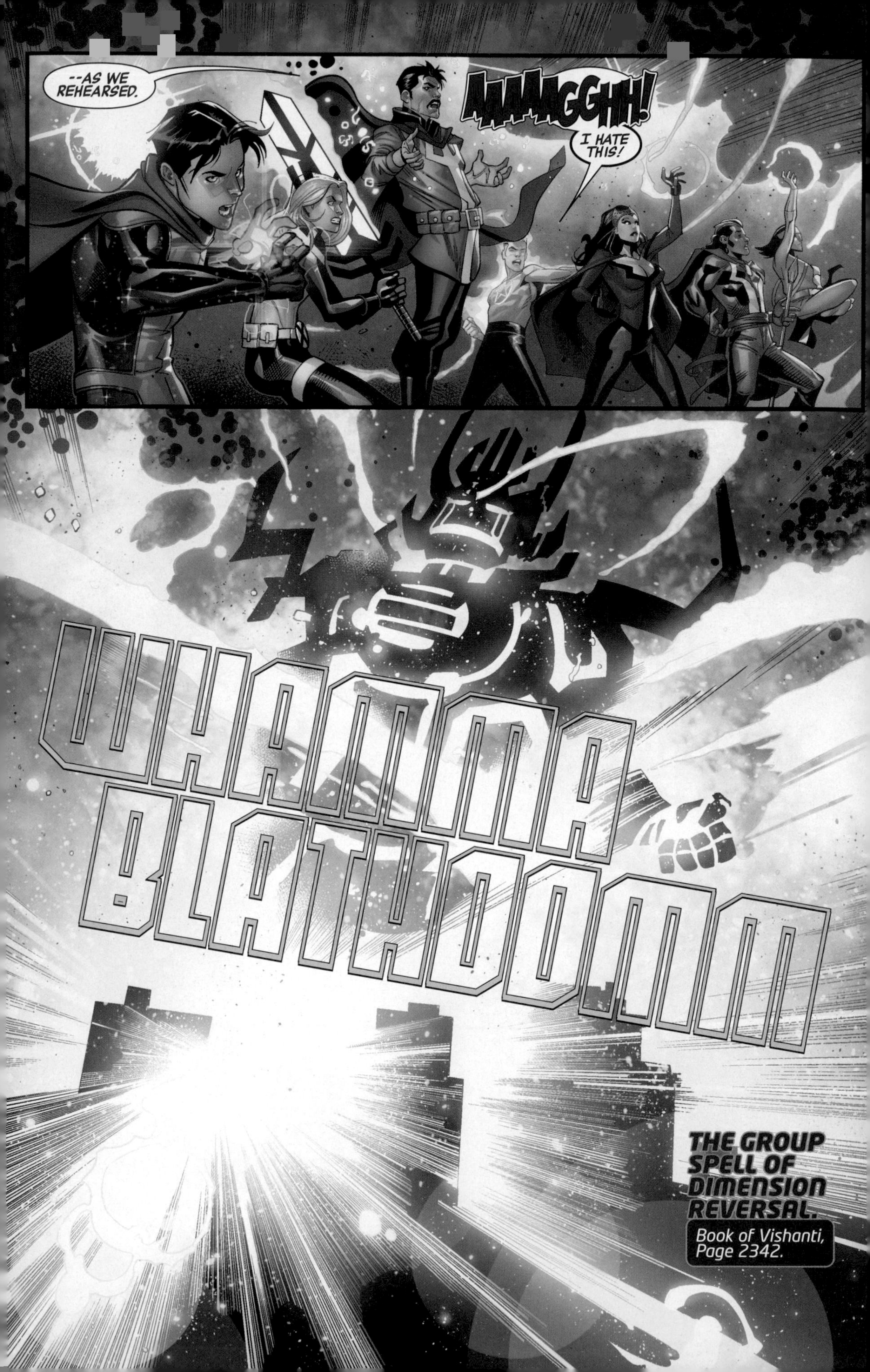
--AS WE REHEARSED.
AAAAAGGHH!
I HATE THIS!
WHAMMA BLATHOOMM
THE GROUP SPELL OF DIMENSION REVERSAL.
Book of Vishanti, Page 2342.

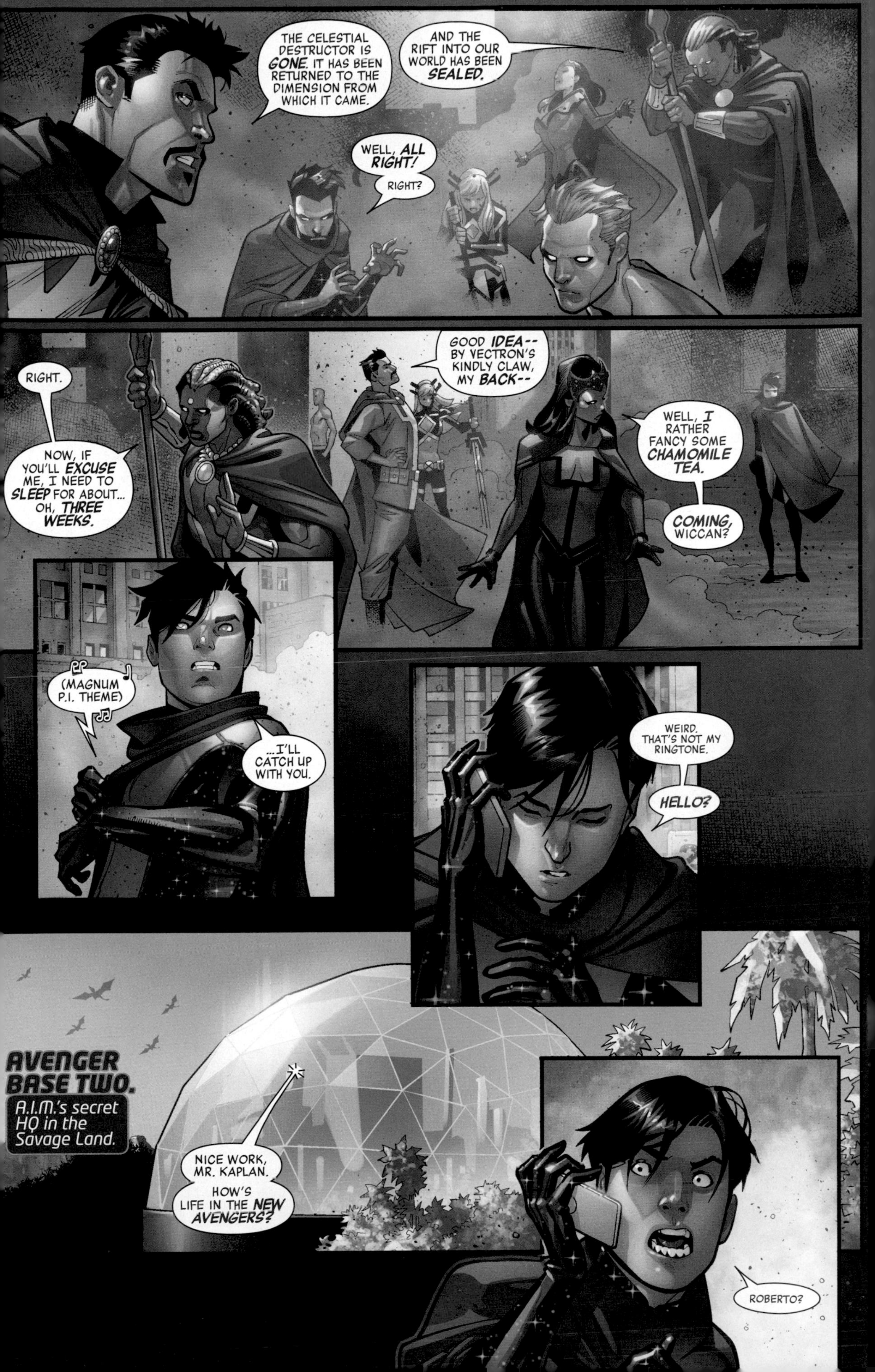
THE CELESTIAL DESTRUCTOR IS GONE. IT HAS BEEN RETURNED TO THE DIMENSION FROM WHICH IT CAME.
AND THE RIFT INTO OUR WORLD HAS BEEN SEALED.
WELL, ALL RIGHT!
RIGHT?
RIGHT.
NOW, IF YOU'LL EXCUSE ME, I NEED TO SLEEP FOR ABOUT... OH, THREE WEEKS.
GOOD IDEA-- BY VECTRON'S KINDLY CLAW, MY BACK--
WELL, I RATHER FANCY SOME CHAMOMILE TEA.
COMING, WICCAN?
(MAGNUM P.I. THEME)
...I'LL CATCH UP WITH YOU.
WEIRD. THAT'S NOT MY RINGTONE.
HELLO?
AVENGER BASE TWO.
A.I.M.'s secret HQ in the Savage Land.
NICE WORK, MR. KAPLAN.
HOW'S LIFE IN THE NEW AVENGERS?
ROBERTO?

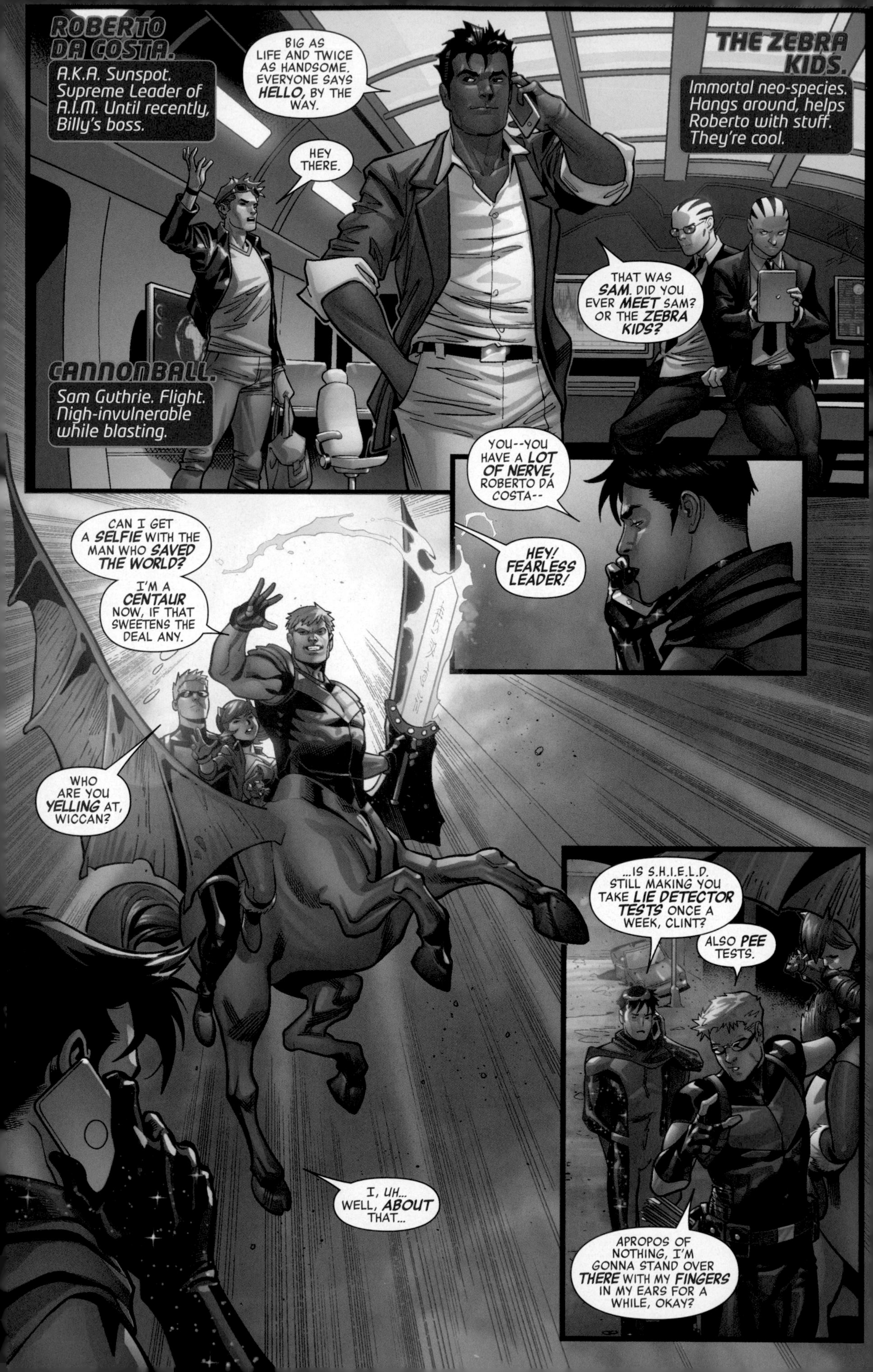

ROBERTO DA COSTA.
A.K.A. Sunspot. Supreme Leader of A.I.M. Until recently, Billy's boss.
BIG AS LIFE AND TWICE AS HANDSOME. EVERYONE SAYS HELLO, BY THE WAY.
THE ZEBRA KIDS.
Immortal neo-species. Hangs around, helps Roberto with stuff. They're cool.
HEY THERE.
THAT WAS SAM. DID YOU EVER MEET SAM? OR THE ZEBRA KIDS?
CANNONBALL.
Sam Guthrie. Flight. Nigh-invulnerable while blasting.
YOU--YOU HAVE A LOT OF NERVE, ROBERTO DA COSTA--
HEY! FEARLESS LEADER!
CAN I GET A SELFIE WITH THE MAN WHO SAVED THE WORLD?
I'M A CENTAUR NOW, IF THAT SWEETENS THE DEAL ANY.
WHO ARE YOU YELLING AT, WICCAN?
I, UH... WELL, ABOUT THAT...
...IS S.H.I.E.L.D. STILL MAKING YOU TAKE LIE DETECTOR TESTS ONCE A WEEK, CLINT?
ALSO PEE TESTS.
APROPOS OF NOTHING, I'M GONNA STAND OVER THERE WITH MY FINGERS IN MY EARS FOR A WHILE, OKAY?

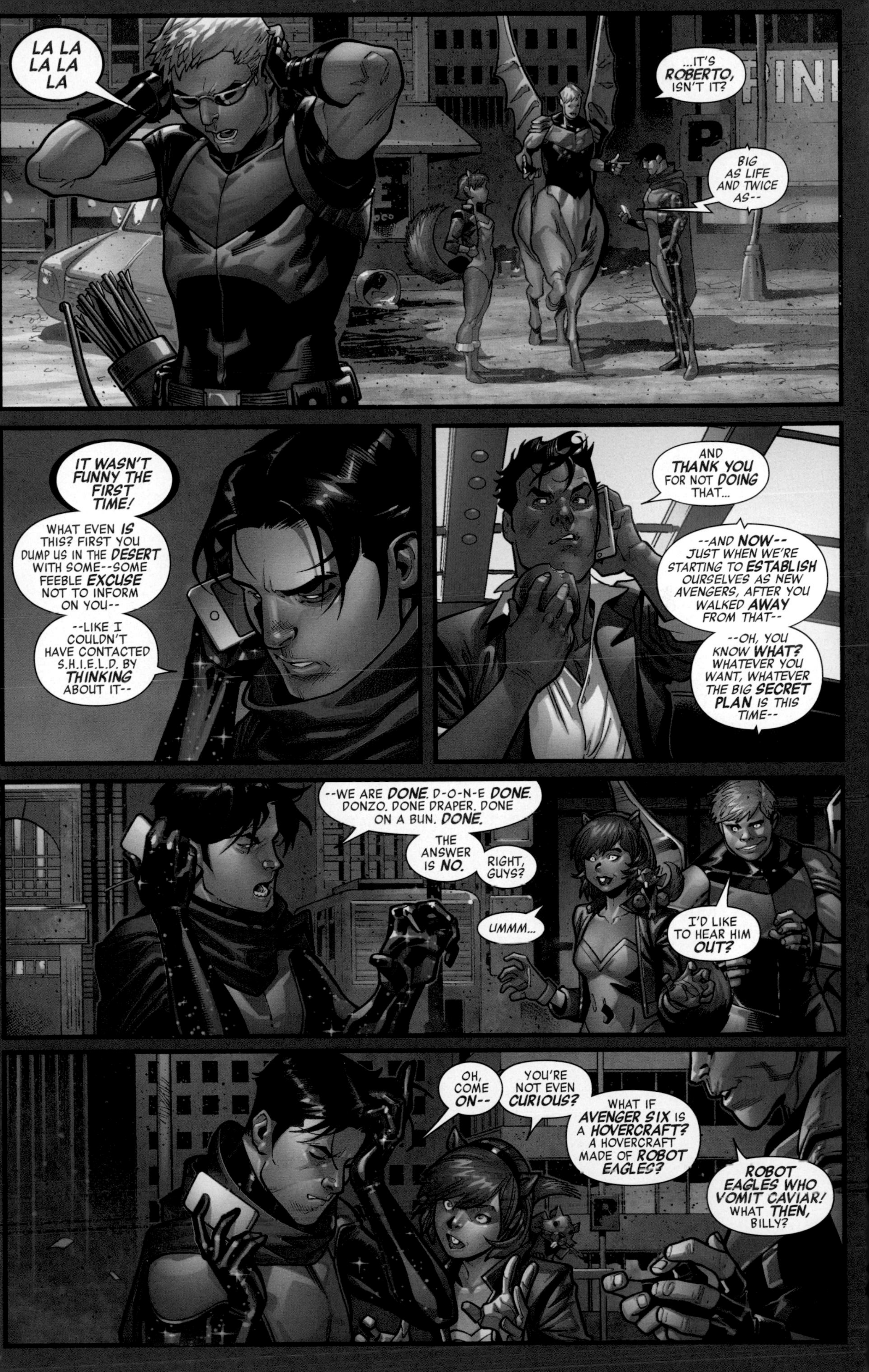
LA LA LA LA LA
...IT'S ROBERTO, ISN'T IT?
BIG AS LIFE AND TWICE AS--
IT WASN'T FUNNY THE FIRST TIME!
WHAT EVEN IS THIS? FIRST YOU DUMP US IN THE DESERT WITH SOME--SOME FEEBLE EXCUSE NOT TO INFORM ON YOU--
--LIKE I COULDN'T HAVE CONTACTED S.H.I.E.L.D. BY THINKING ABOUT IT--
AND THANK YOU FOR NOT DOING THAT...
--AND NOW-- JUST WHEN WE'RE STARTING TO ESTABLISH OURSELVES AS NEW AVENGERS, AFTER YOU WALKED AWAY FROM THAT--
--OH, YOU KNOW WHAT? WHATEVER YOU WANT, WHATEVER THE BIG SECRET PLAN IS THIS TIME--
--WE ARE DONE. D-O-N-E DONE. DONZO. DONE DRAPER. DONE ON A BUN. DONE.
THE ANSWER IS NO.
RIGHT, GUYS?
UMMM...
I'D LIKE TO HEAR HIM OUT?
OH, COME ON--
YOU'RE NOT EVEN CURIOUS?
WHAT IF AVENGER SIX IS A HOVERCRAFT? A HOVERCRAFT MADE OF ROBOT EAGLES?
ROBOT EAGLES WHO VOMIT CAVIAR! WHAT THEN, BILLY?

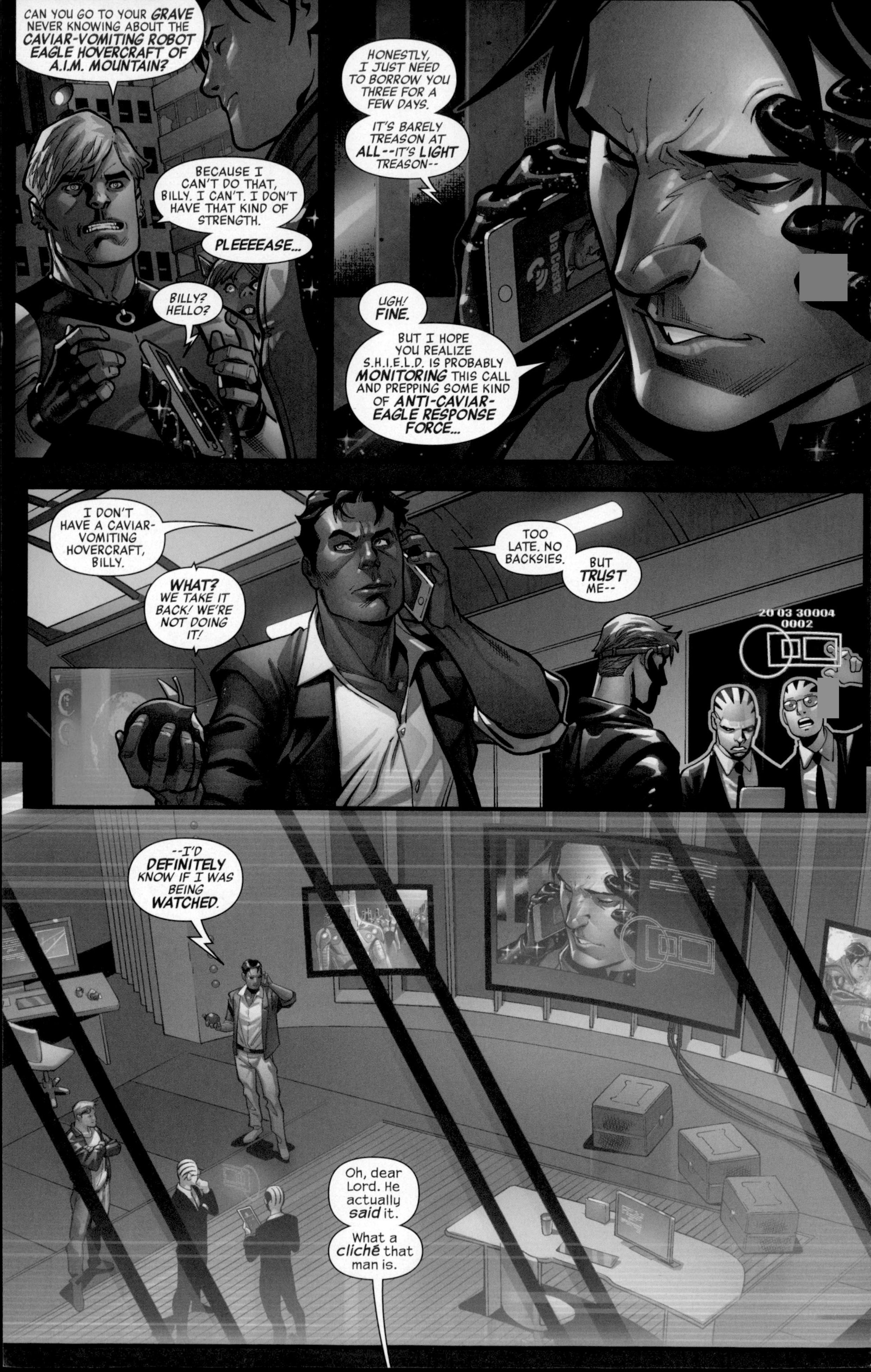
CAN YOU GO TO YOUR GRAVE NEVER KNOWING ABOUT THE CAVIAR-VOMITING ROBOT EAGLE HOVERCRAFT OF A.I.M. MOUNTAIN?
BECAUSE I CAN'T DO THAT, BILLY. I CAN'T. I DON'T HAVE THAT KIND OF STRENGTH.
PLEEEEASE...
BILLY? HELLO?
HONESTLY, I JUST NEED TO BORROW YOU THREE FOR A FEW DAYS.
IT'S BARELY TREASON AT ALL--IT'S LIGHT TREASON--
UGH! FINE.
BUT I HOPE YOU REALIZE S.H.I.E.L.D. IS PROBABLY MONITORING THIS CALL AND PREPPING SOME KIND OF ANTI-CAVIAR-EAGLE RESPONSE FORCE...
I DON'T HAVE A CAVIAR-VOMITING HOVERCRAFT, BILLY.
WHAT? WE TAKE IT BACK! WE'RE NOT DOING IT!
TOO LATE. NO BACKSIES.
BUT TRUST ME--
20 03 30004 0002
--I'D DEFINITELY KNOW IF I WAS BEING WATCHED.
Oh, dear Lord. He actually said it.
What a cliché that man is.

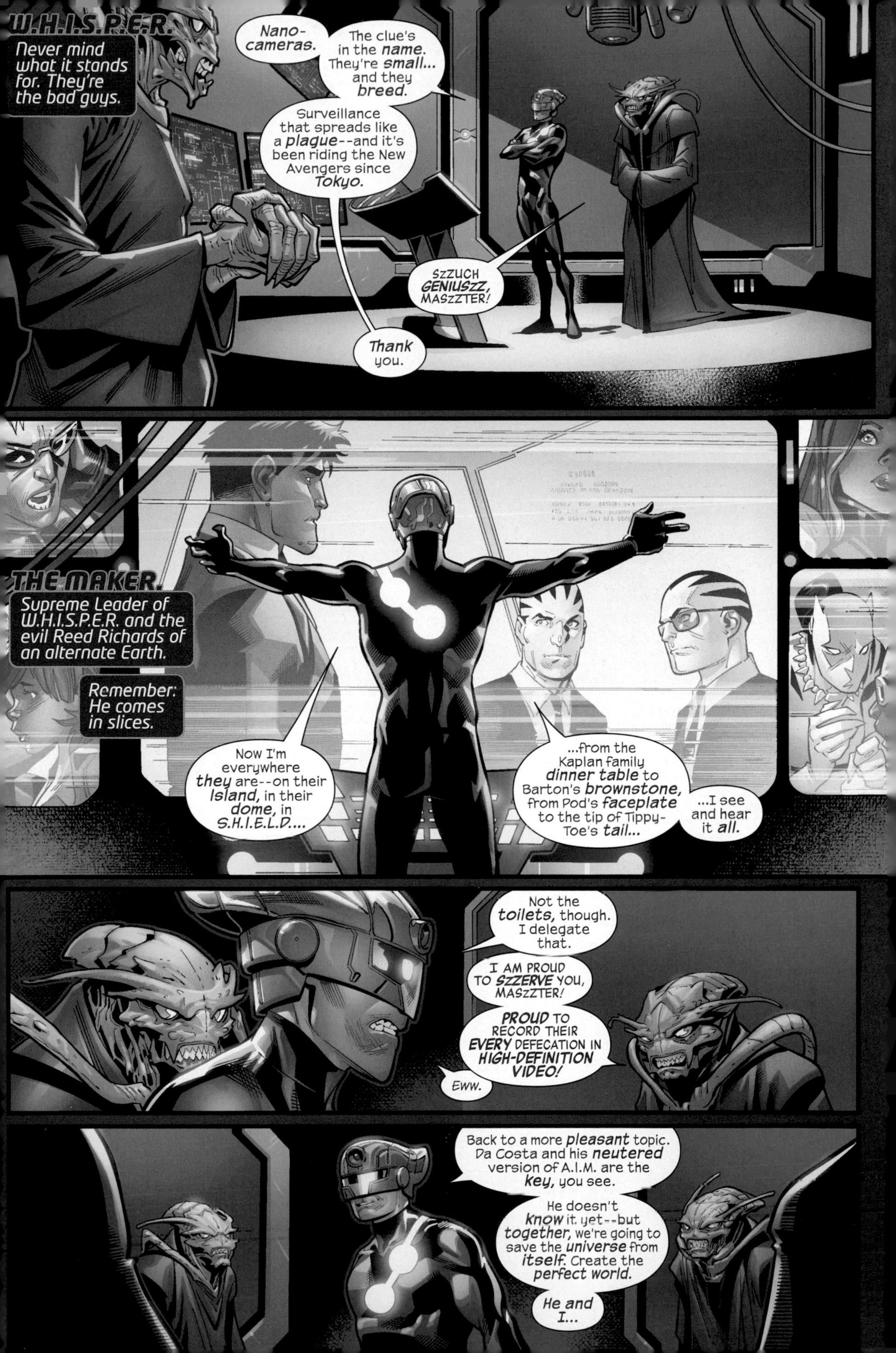
W.H.I.S.P.E.R.
Never mind what it stands for. They're the bad guys.
Nano-cameras.
The clue's in the name. They're small... and they breed.
Surveillance that spreads like a plague--and it's been riding the New Avengers since Tokyo.
SZZUCH GENIUSZZ, MASZZTER!
Thank you.
THE MAKER.
Supreme Leader of W.H.I.S.P.E.R. and the evil Reed Richards of an alternate Earth.
Remember: He comes in slices.
Now I'm everywhere they are--on their Island, in their dome, in S.H.I.E.L.D....
...from the Kaplan family dinner table to Barton's brownstone, from Pod's faceplate to the tip of Tippy-Toe's tail...
...I see and hear it all.
Not the toilets, though. I delegate that.
I AM PROUD TO SZZERVE YOU, MASZZTER!
PROUD TO RECORD THEIR EVERY DEFECATION IN HIGH-DEFINITION VIDEO!
Eww.
Back to a more pleasant topic. Da Costa and his neutered version of A.I.M. are the key, you see.
He doesn't know it yet--but together, we're going to save the universe from itself. Create the perfect world.
He and I...

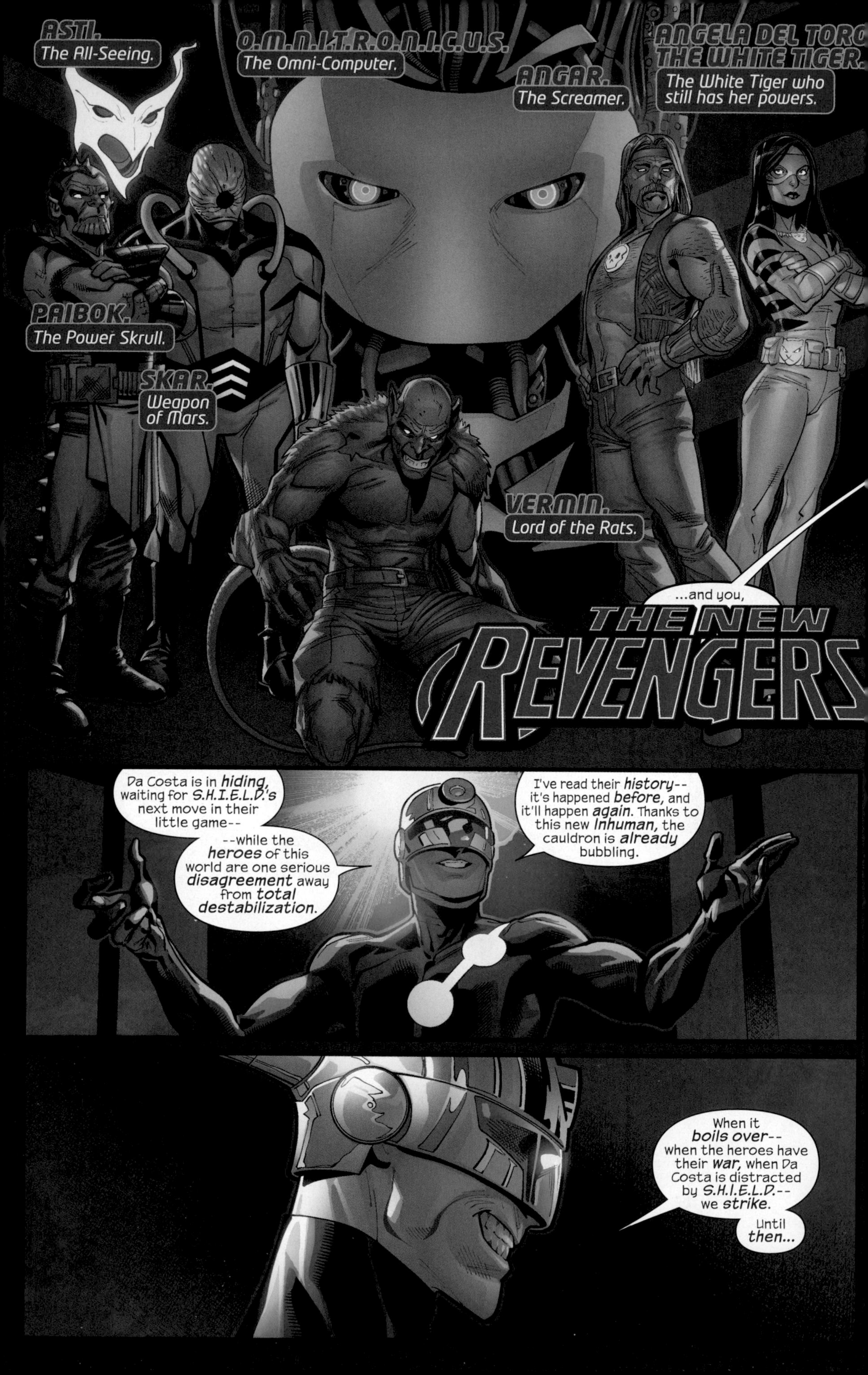
ASTI.
The All-Seeing.
O.M.N.I.T.R.O.N.I.C.U.S.
The Omni-Computer.
ANGAR.
The Screamer.
ANGELA DEL TORO THE WHITE TIGER.
The White Tiger who still has her powers.
PAIBOK.
The Power Skrull.
SKAR.
Weapon of Mars.
VERMIN.
Lord of the Rats.
...and you,
THE NEW REVENGERS
Da Costa is in hiding, waiting for S.H.I.E.L.D.'s next move in their little game--
--while the heroes of this world are one serious disagreement away from total destabilization.
I've read their history-- it's happened before, and it'll happen again. Thanks to this new Inhuman, the cauldron is already bubbling.
When it boils over-- when the heroes have their war, when Da Costa is distracted by S.H.I.E.L.D.-- we strike.
Until then...

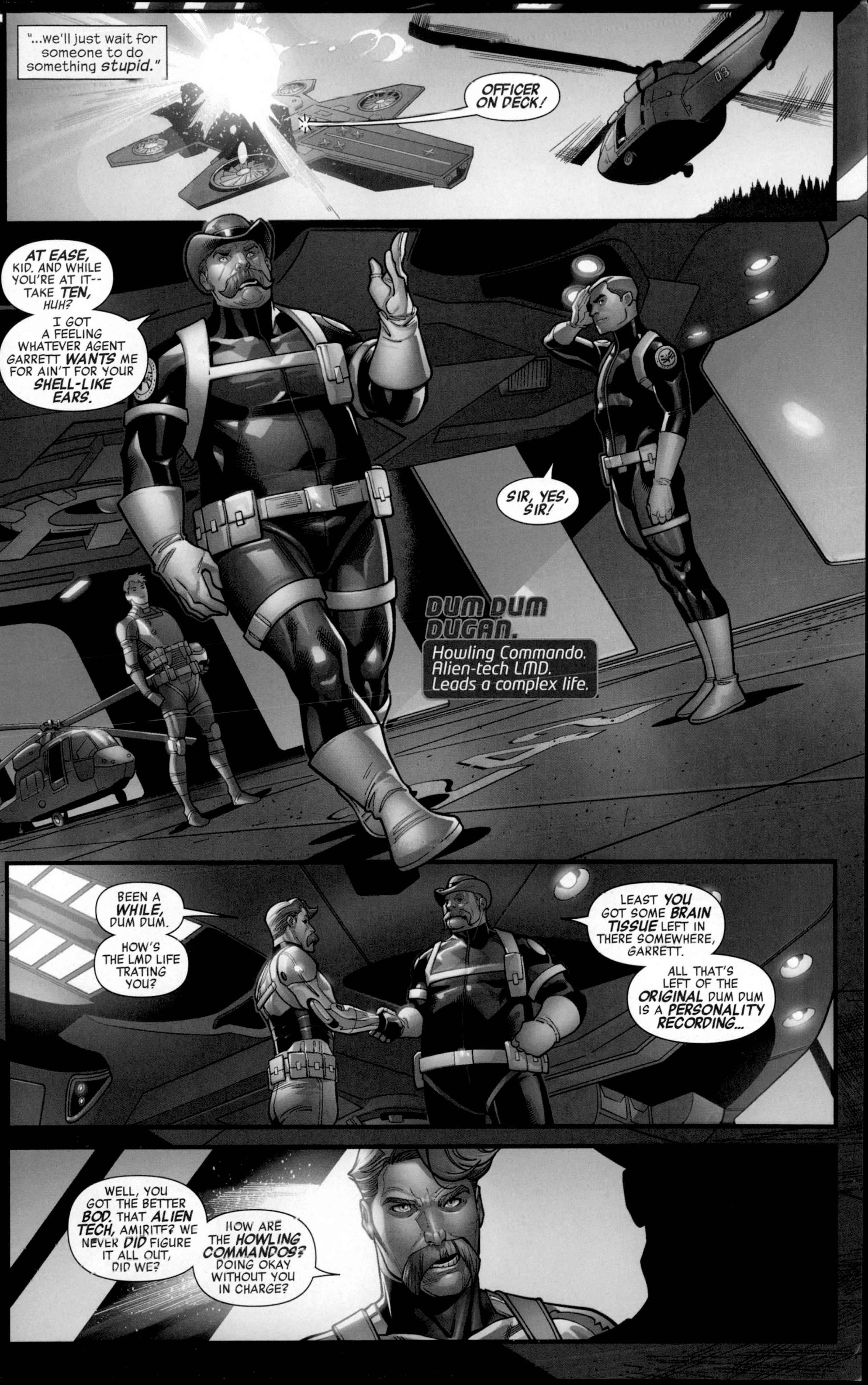
"...we'll just wait for someone to do something stupid."
OFFICER ON DECK!
AT EASE, KID. AND WHILE YOU'RE AT IT-- TAKE TEN, HUH?
I GOT A FEELING WHATEVER AGENT GARRETT WANTS ME FOR AIN'T FOR YOUR SHELL-LIKE EARS.
SIR, YES, SIR!
DUM DUM DUGAN.
Howling Commando. Alien-tech LMD. Leads a complex life.
BEEN A WHILE, DUM DUM.
HOW'S THE LMD LIFE TRATING YOU?
LEAST YOU GOT SOME BRAIN TISSUE LEFT IN THERE SOMEWHERE, GARRETT.
ALL THAT'S LEFT OF THE ORIGINAL DUM DUM IS A PERSONALITY RECORDING...
WELL, YOU GOT THE BETTER BOD. THAT ALIEN TECH, AMIRITE? WE NEVER DID FIGURE IT ALL OUT, DID WE?
HOW ARE THE HOWLING COMMANDOS? DOING OKAY WITHOUT YOU IN CHARGE?

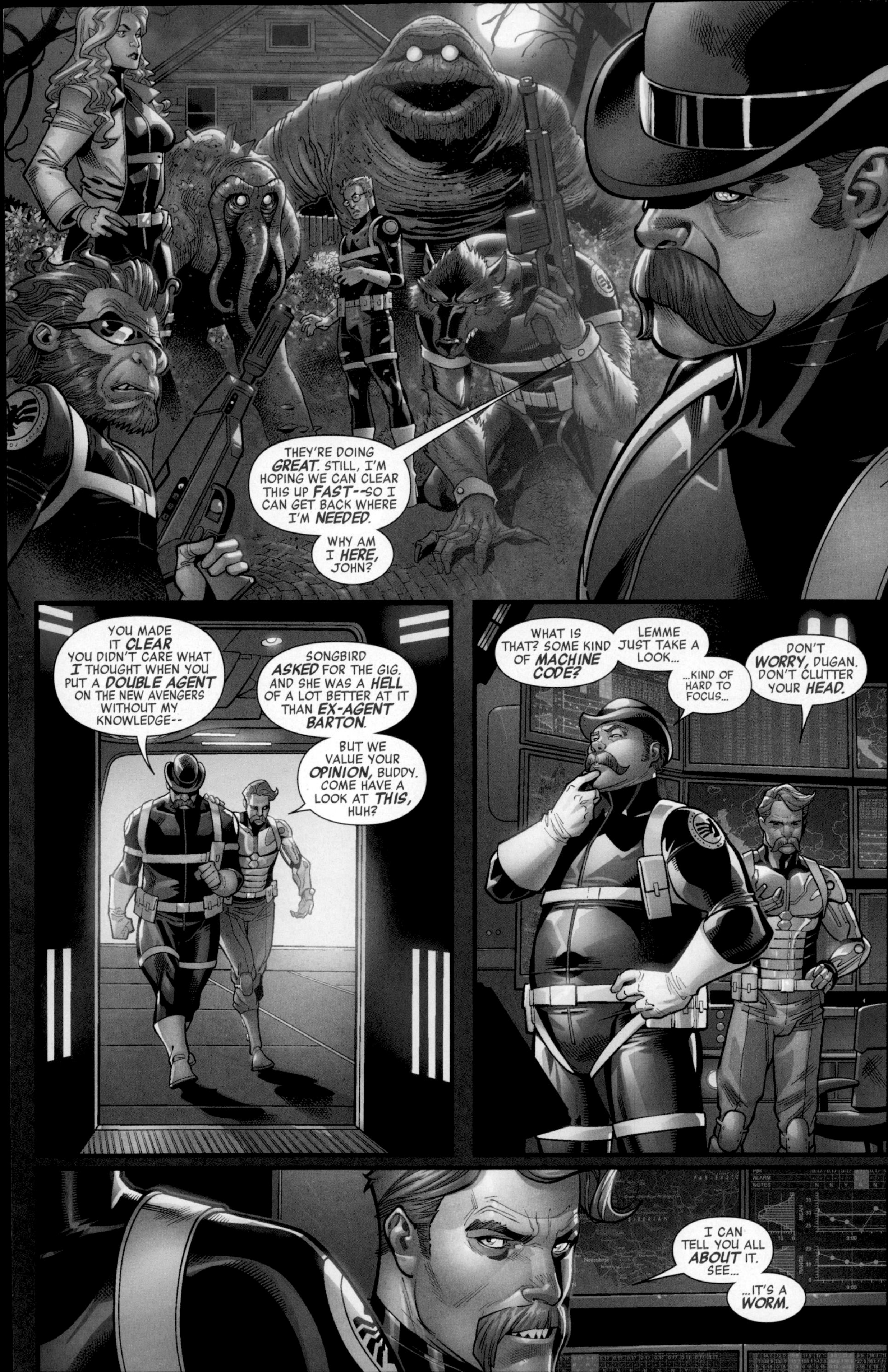
THEY'RE DOING GREAT. STILL, I'M HOPING WE CAN CLEAR THIS UP FAST--SO I CAN GET BACK WHERE I'M NEEDED.
WHY AM I HERE, JOHN?
YOU MADE IT CLEAR YOU DIDN'T CARE WHAT I THOUGHT WHEN YOU PUT A DOUBLE AGENT ON THE NEW AVENGERS WITHOUT MY KNOWLEDGE--
SONGBIRD ASKED FOR THE GIG. AND SHE WAS A HELL OF A LOT BETTER AT IT THAN EX-AGENT BARTON.
BUT WE VALUE YOUR OPINION, BUDDY. COME HAVE A LOOK AT THIS, HUH?
WHAT IS THAT? SOME KIND OF MACHINE CODE?
LEMME JUST TAKE A LOOK...
...KIND OF HARD TO FOCUS...
DON'T WORRY, DUGAN. DON'T CLUTTER YOUR HEAD.
I CAN TELL YOU ALL ABOUT IT. SEE...
...IT'S A WORM.

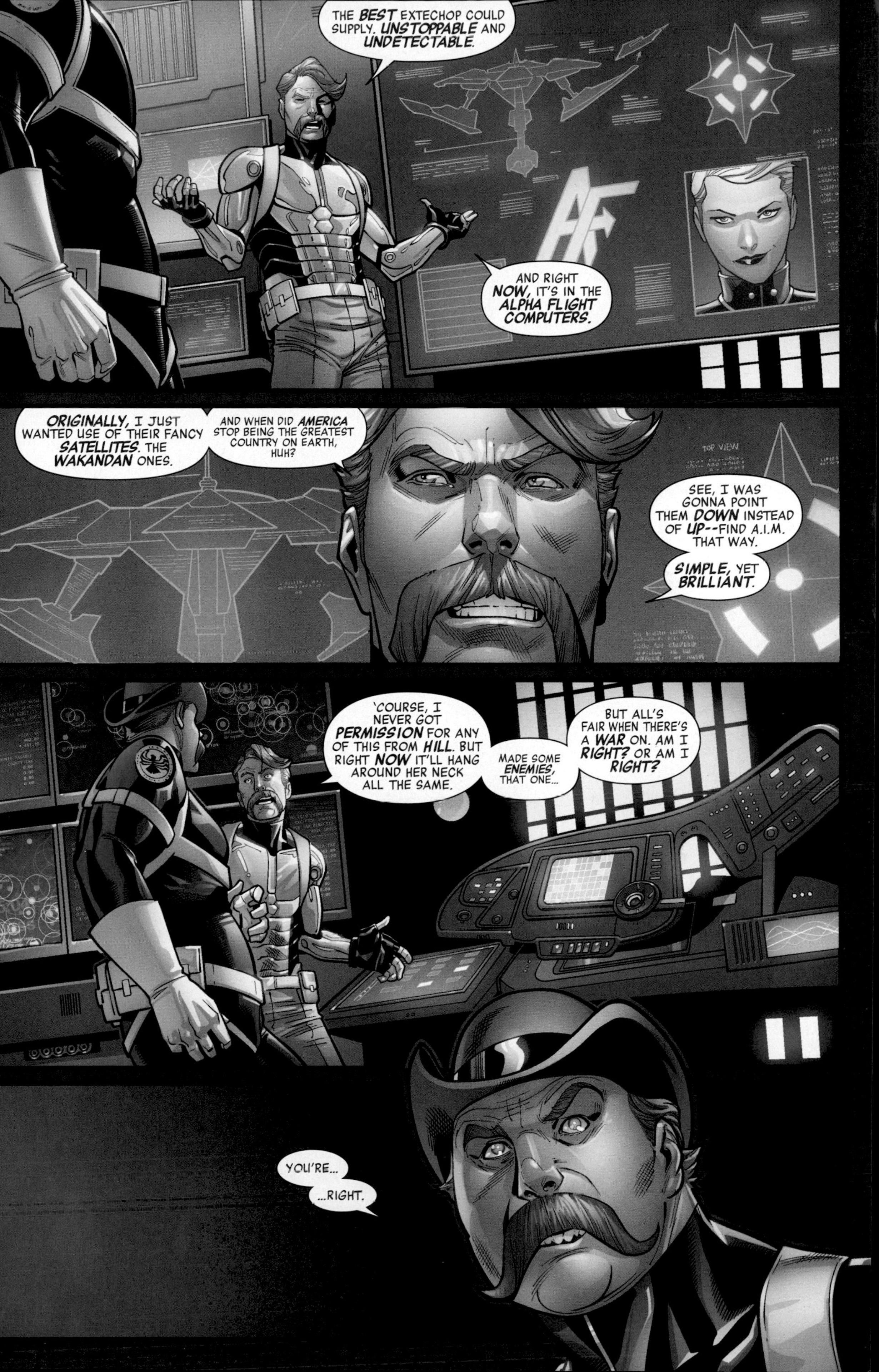
THE BEST EXTECHOP COULD SUPPLY. UNSTOPPABLE AND UNDETECTABLE.
AND RIGHT NOW, IT'S IN THE ALPHA FLIGHT COMPUTERS.
ORIGINALLY, I JUST WANTED USE OF THEIR FANCY SATELLITES. THE WAKANDAN ONES.
AND WHEN DID AMERICA STOP BEING THE GREATEST COUNTRY ON EARTH, HUH?
TOP VIEW
SEE, I WAS GONNA POINT THEM DOWN INSTEAD OF UP--FIND A.I.M. THAT WAY.
SIMPLE, YET BRILLIANT.
'COURSE, I NEVER GOT PERMISSION FOR ANY OF THIS FROM HILL. BUT RIGHT NOW IT'LL HANG AROUND HER NECK ALL THE SAME.
MADE SOME ENEMIES, THAT ONE...
BUT ALL'S FAIR WHEN THERE'S A WAR ON. AM I RIGHT? OR AM I RIGHT?
YOU'RE...
...RIGHT.

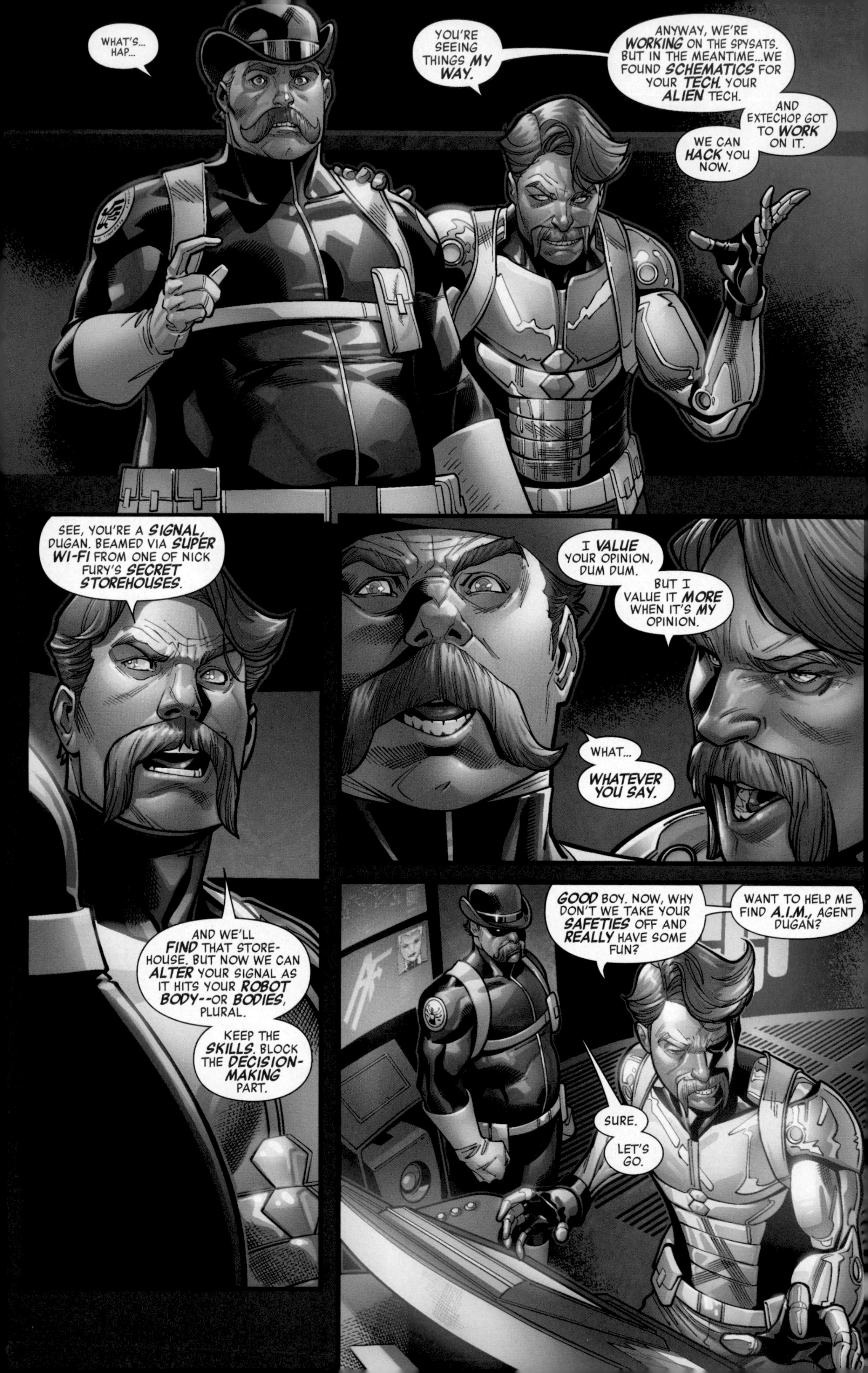
WHAT'S... HAP...
YOU'RE SEEING THINGS MY WAY.
ANYWAY, WE'RE WORKING ON THE SPYSATS. BUT IN THE MEANTIME...WE FOUND SCHEMATICS FOR YOUR TECH. YOUR ALIEN TECH.
AND EXTECHOP GOT TO WORK ON IT.
WE CAN HACK YOU NOW.
SEE, YOU'RE A SIGNAL, DUGAN. BEAMED VIA SUPER WI-FI FROM ONE OF NICK FURY'S SECRET STOREHOUSES.
AND WE'LL FIND THAT STORE-HOUSE. BUT NOW WE CAN ALTER YOUR SIGNAL AS IT HITS YOUR ROBOT BODY--OR BODIES, PLURAL.
KEEP THE SKILLS. BLOCK THE DECISION-MAKING PART.
I VALUE YOUR OPINION, DUM DUM.
BUT I VALUE IT MORE WHEN IT'S MY OPINION.
WHAT... WHATEVER YOU SAY.
GOOD BOY. NOW, WHY DON'T WE TAKE YOUR SAFETIES OFF AND REALLY HAVE SOME FUN?
WANT TO HELP ME FIND A.I.M., AGENT DUGAN?
SURE.
LET'S GO.

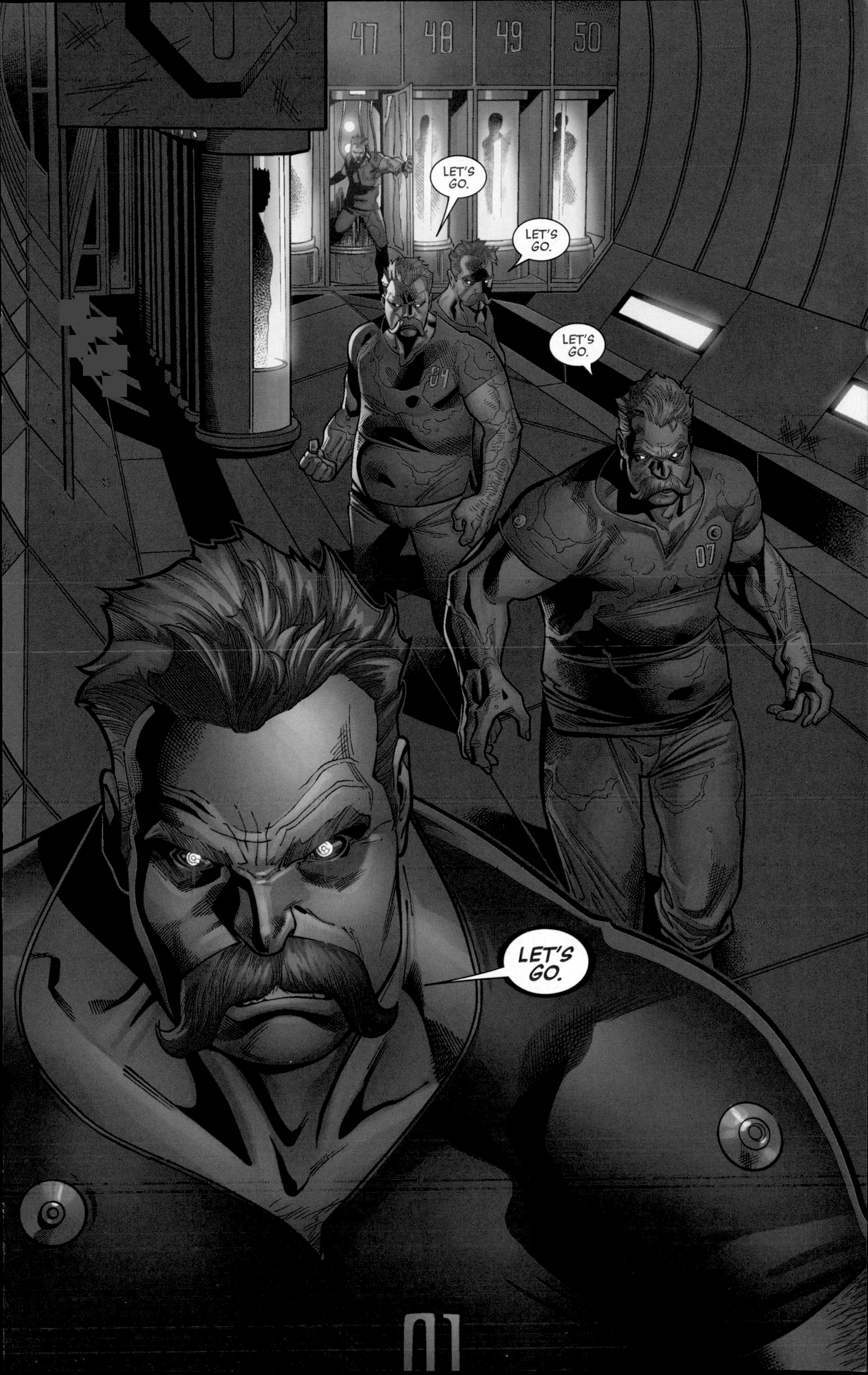
47
48
49
50
LET'S GO.
LET'S GO.
LET'S GO.
04
07
LET'S GO.
01

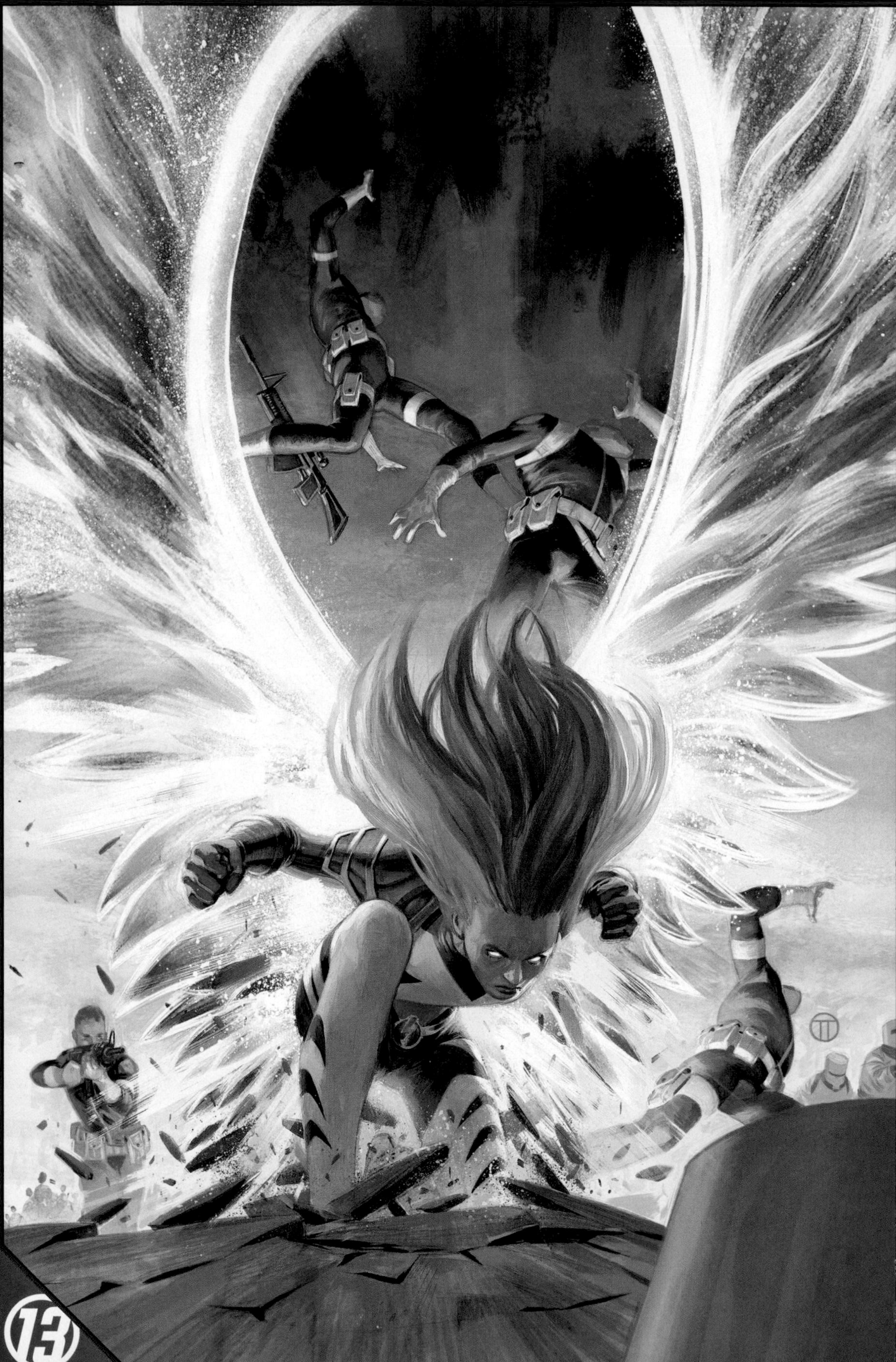
13

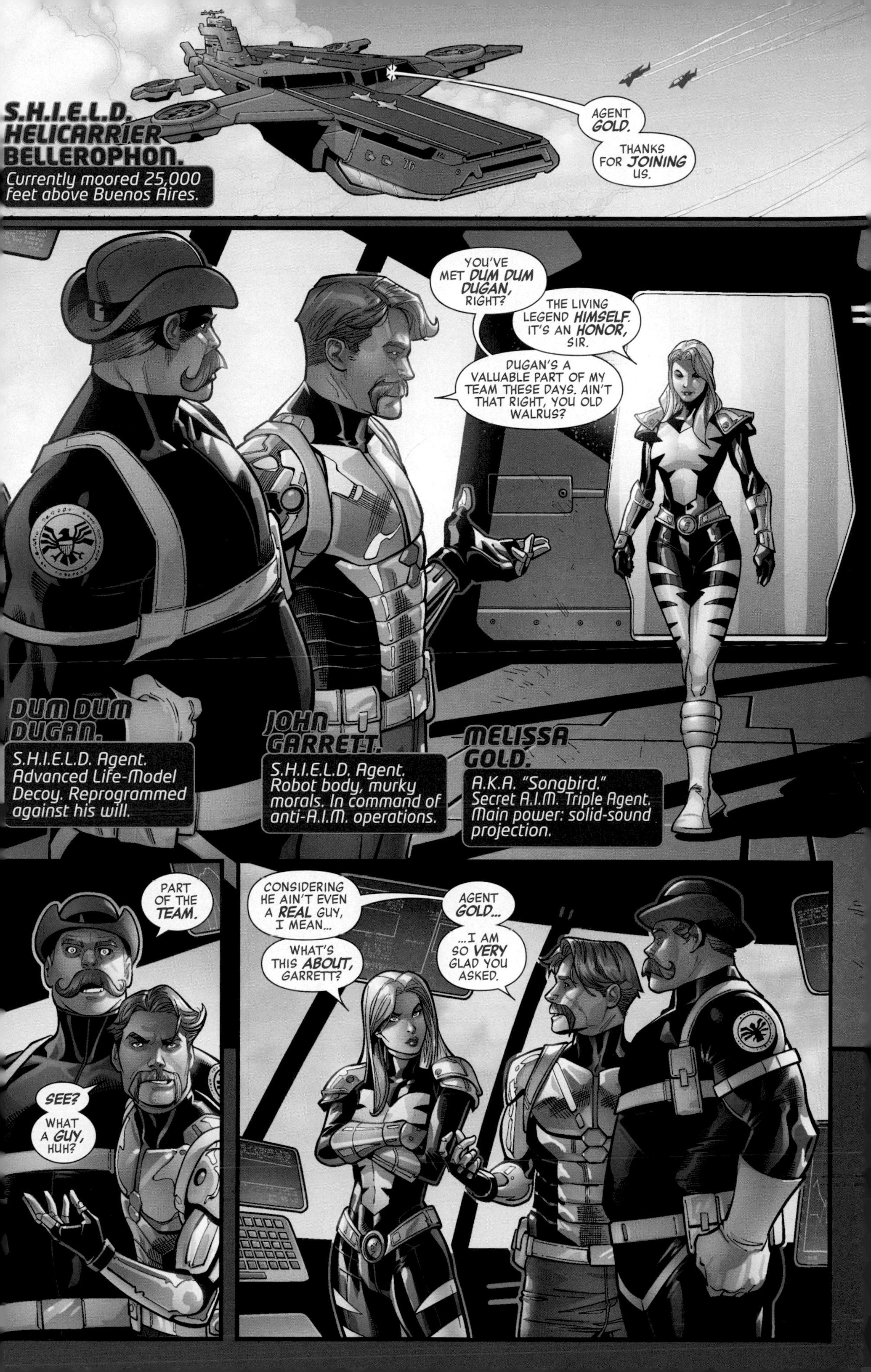
S.H.I.E.L.D. HELICARRIER BELLEROPHON.
Currently moored 25,000 feet above Buenos Aires.
AGENT GOLD.
THANKS FOR JOINING US.
YOU'VE MET DUM DUM DUGAN, RIGHT?
THE LIVING LEGEND HIMSELF. IT'S AN HONOR, SIR.
DUGAN'S A VALUABLE PART OF MY TEAM THESE DAYS. AIN'T THAT RIGHT, YOU OLD WALRUS?
DUM DUM DUGAN.
S.H.I.E.L.D. Agent. Advanced Life-Model Decoy. Reprogrammed against his will.
JOHN GARRETT.
S.H.I.E.L.D. Agent. Robot body, murky morals. In command of anti-A.I.M. operations.
MELISSA GOLD.
A.K.A. "Songbird." Secret A.I.M. Triple Agent. Main power: solid-sound projection.
PART OF THE TEAM.
SEE?
WHAT A GUY, HUH?
CONSIDERING HE AIN'T EVEN A REAL GUY, I MEAN...
WHAT'S THIS ABOUT, GARRETT?
AGENT GOLD...
...I AM SO VERY GLAD YOU ASKED.

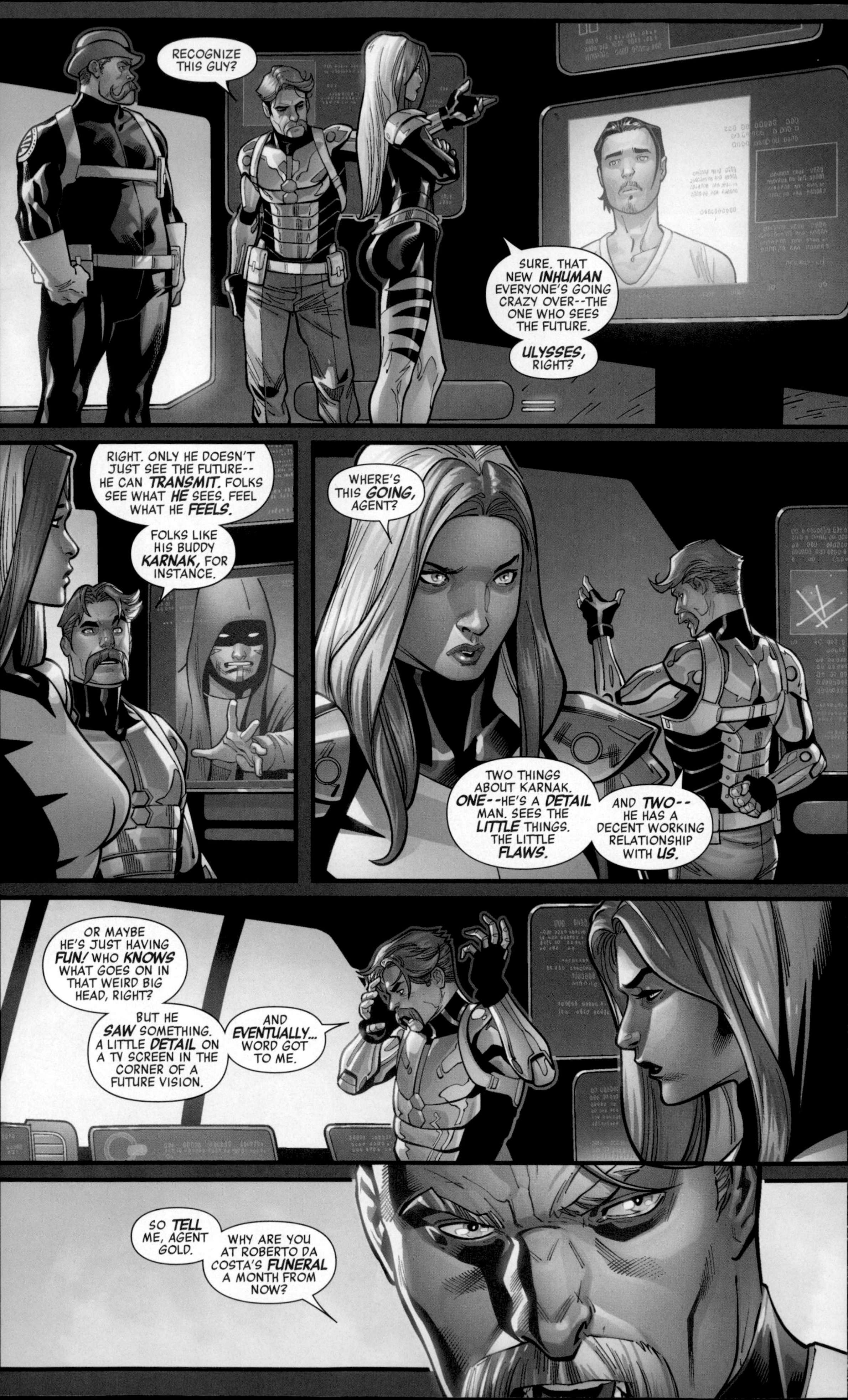
RECOGNIZE THIS GUY?
SURE. THAT NEW INHUMAN EVERYONE'S GOING CRAZY OVER--THE ONE WHO SEES THE FUTURE.
ULYSSES, RIGHT?
RIGHT. ONLY HE DOESN'T JUST SEE THE FUTURE-- HE CAN TRANSMIT. FOLKS SEE WHAT HE SEES. FEEL WHAT HE FEELS.
FOLKS LIKE HIS BUDDY KARNAK, FOR INSTANCE.
WHERE'S THIS GOING, AGENT?
TWO THINGS ABOUT KARNAK. ONE--HE'S A DETAIL MAN. SEES THE LITTLE THINGS. THE LITTLE FLAWS.
AND TWO-- HE HAS A DECENT WORKING RELATIONSHIP WITH US.
OR MAYBE HE'S JUST HAVING FUN! WHO KNOWS WHAT GOES ON IN THAT WEIRD BIG HEAD, RIGHT?
BUT HE SAW SOMETHING. A LITTLE DETAIL ON A TV SCREEN IN THE CORNER OF A FUTURE VISION.
AND EVENTUALLY... WORD GOT TO ME.
SO TELL ME, AGENT GOLD.
WHY ARE YOU AT ROBERTO DA COSTA'S FUNERAL A MONTH FROM NOW?

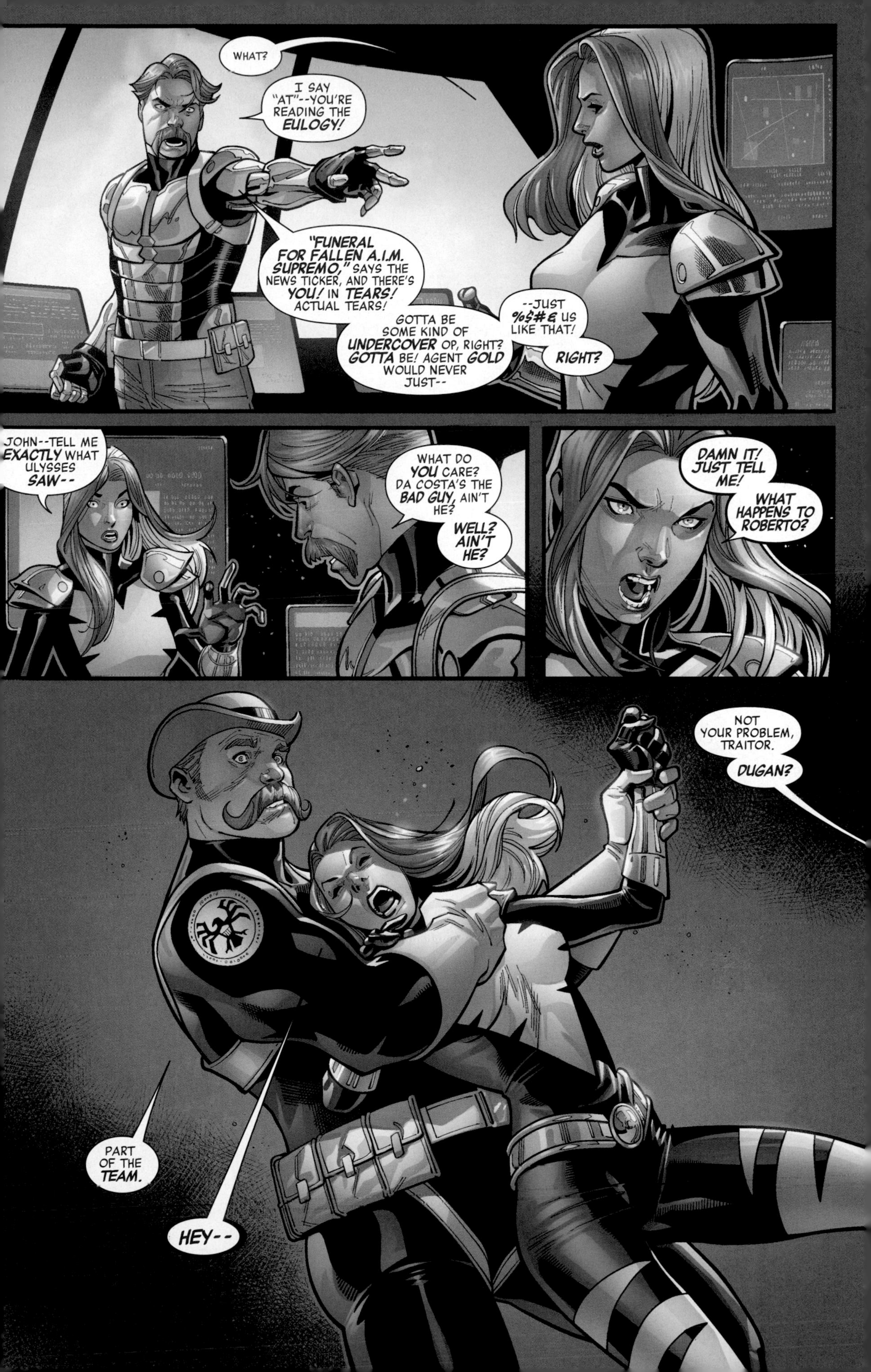
WHAT?
I SAY "AT"--YOU'RE READING THE EULOGY!
"FUNERAL FOR FALLEN A.I.M. SUPREMO," SAYS THE NEWS TICKER, AND THERE'S YOU! IN TEARS! ACTUAL TEARS!
GOTTA BE SOME KIND OF UNDERCOVER OP, RIGHT? GOTTA BE! AGENT GOLD WOULD NEVER JUST--
--JUST %$#€ US LIKE THAT!
RIGHT?
JOHN--TELL ME EXACTLY WHAT ULYSSES SAW--
WHAT DO YOU CARE? DA COSTA'S THE BAD GUY, AIN'T HE?
WELL? AIN'T HE?
DAMN IT! JUST TELL ME!
WHAT HAPPENS TO ROBERTO?
NOT YOUR PROBLEM, TRAITOR.
DUGAN?
PART OF THE TEAM.
HEY--

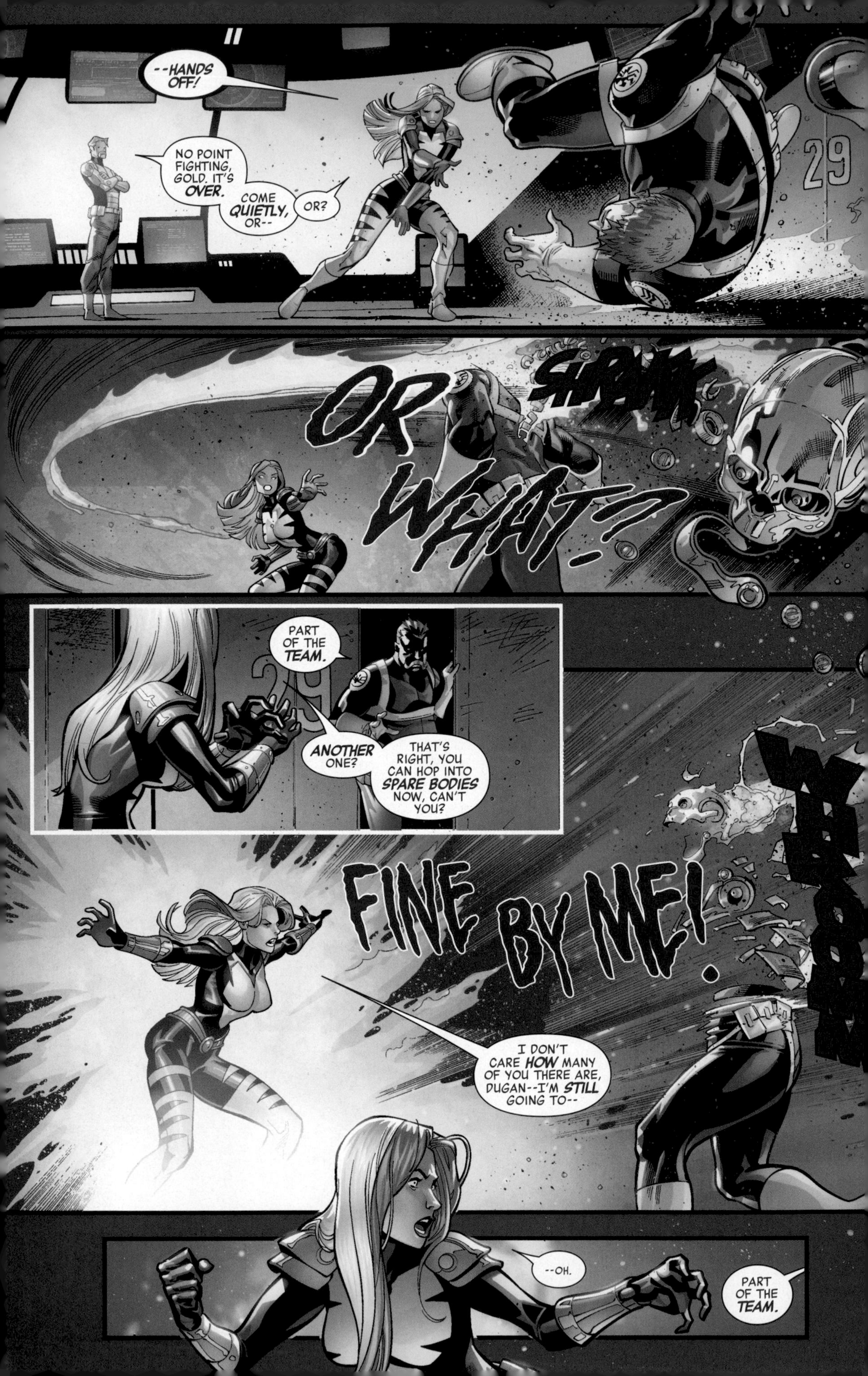
--HANDS OFF!
NO POINT FIGHTING, GOLD. IT'S OVER.
COME QUIETLY, OR--
OR?
OR WHAT--?!
PART OF THE TEAM.
ANOTHER ONE?
THAT'S RIGHT, YOU CAN HOP INTO SPARE BODIES NOW, CAN'T YOU?
FINE BY ME!
I DON'T CARE HOW MANY OF YOU THERE ARE, DUGAN--I'M STILL GOING TO--
--OH.
PART OF THE TEAM.

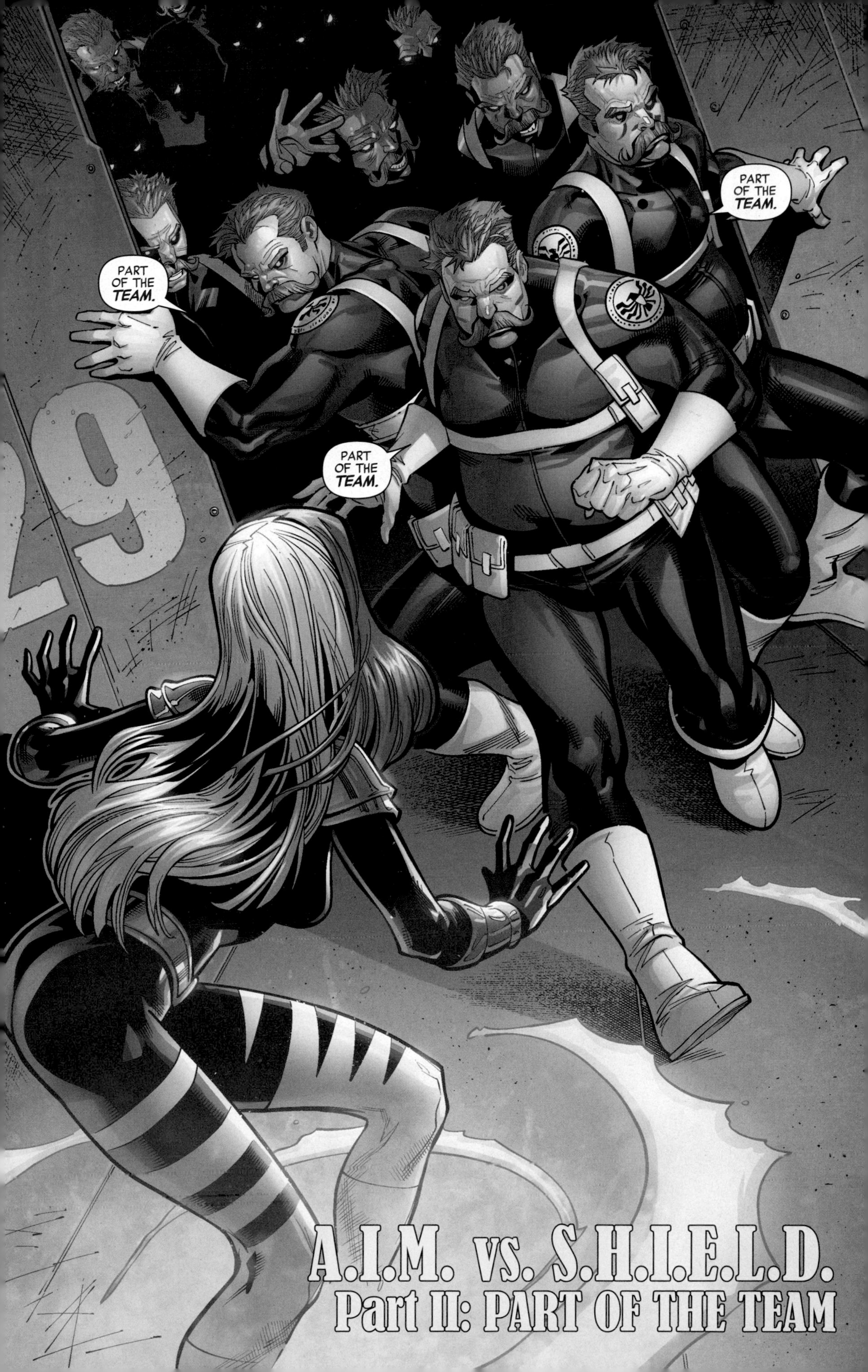
PART OF THE TEAM.
PART OF THE TEAM.
PART OF THE TEAM.
A.I.M. vs. S.H.I.E.L.D.
Part II: PART OF THE TEAM

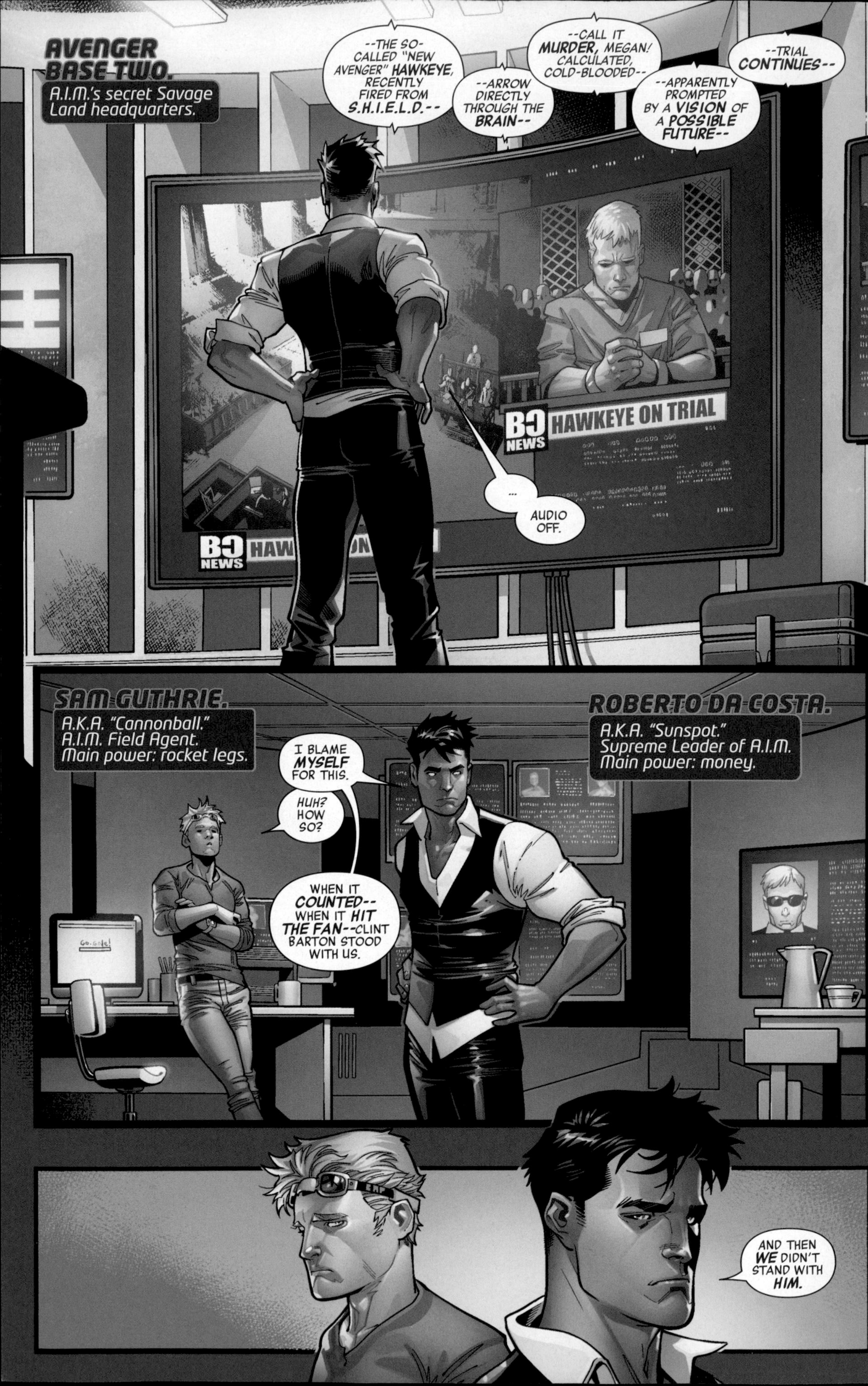
AVENGER BASE TWO.
A.I.M.'s secret Savage Land headquarters.
--THE SO-CALLED "NEW AVENGER" HAWKEYE, RECENTLY FIRED FROM S.H.I.E.L.D.--
--ARROW DIRECTLY THROUGH THE BRAIN--
--CALL IT MURDER, MEGAN! CALCULATED, COLD-BLOODED--
--APPARENTLY PROMPTED BY A VISION OF A POSSIBLE FUTURE--
--TRIAL CONTINUES--
BC NEWS HAWKEYE ON TRIAL
... AUDIO OFF.
SAM GUTHRIE.
A.K.A. "Cannonball." A.I.M. Field Agent. Main power: rocket legs.
ROBERTO DA COSTA.
A.K.A. "Sunspot." Supreme Leader of A.I.M. Main power: money.
I BLAME MYSELF FOR THIS.
HUH? HOW SO?
WHEN IT COUNTED-- WHEN IT HIT THE FAN--CLINT BARTON STOOD WITH US.
AND THEN WE DIDN'T STAND WITH HIM.

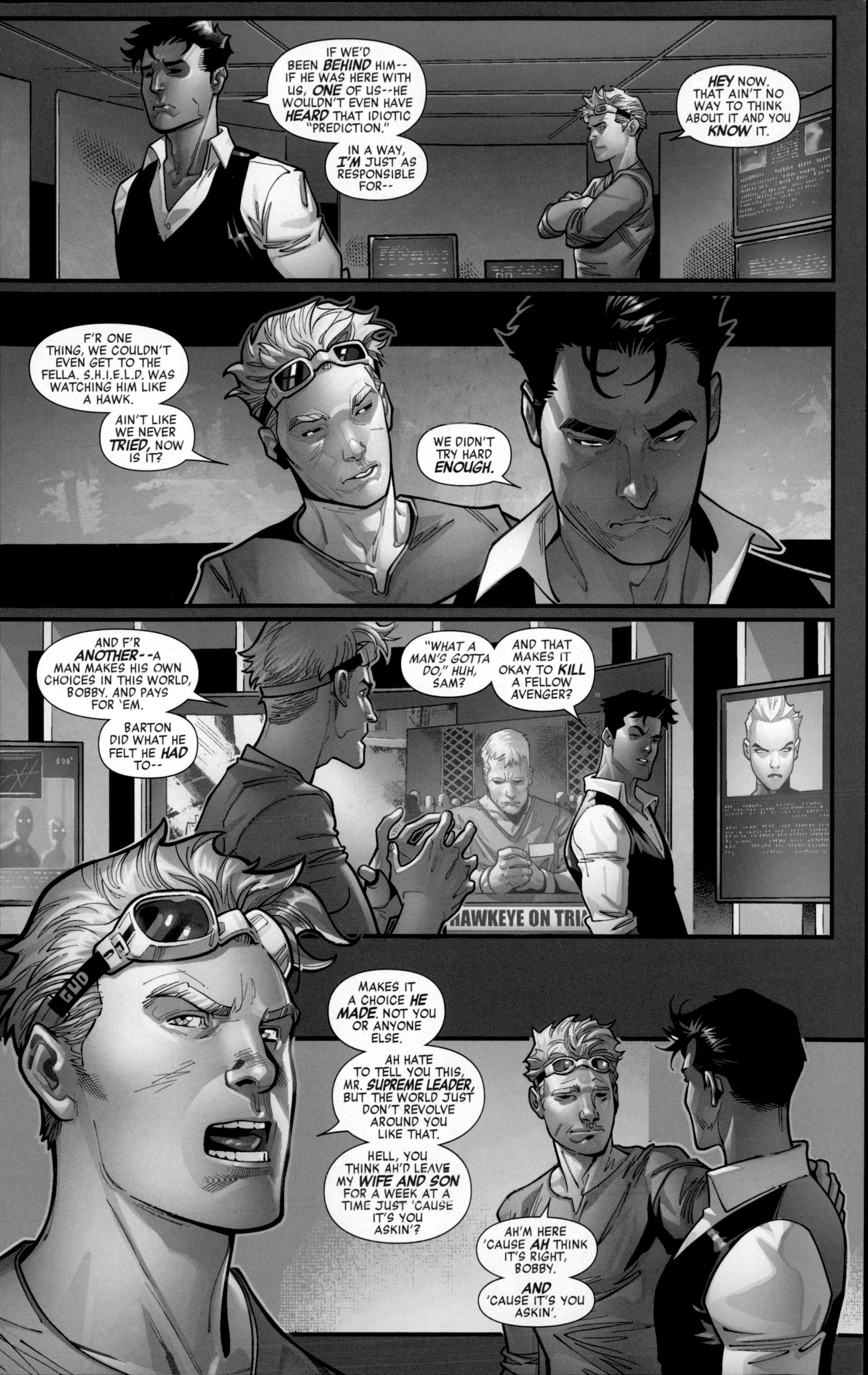
IF WE'D BEEN BEHIND HIM-- IF HE WAS HERE WITH US, ONE OF US--HE WOULDN'T EVEN HAVE HEARD THAT IDIOTIC "PREDICTION."
IN A WAY, I'M JUST AS RESPONSIBLE FOR--
HEY NOW. THAT AIN'T NO WAY TO THINK ABOUT IT AND YOU KNOW IT.
F'R ONE THING, WE COULDN'T EVEN GET TO THE FELLA. S.H.I.E.L.D. WAS WATCHING HIM LIKE A HAWK.
AIN'T LIKE WE NEVER TRIED, NOW IS IT?
WE DIDN'T TRY HARD ENOUGH.
AND F'R ANOTHER--A MAN MAKES HIS OWN CHOICES IN THIS WORLD, BOBBY. AND PAYS FOR 'EM.
BARTON DID WHAT HE FELT HE HAD TO--
"WHAT A MAN'S GOTTA DO," HUH, SAM?
AND THAT MAKES IT OKAY TO KILL A FELLOW AVENGER?
HAWKEYE ON TRI
MAKES IT A CHOICE HE MADE. NOT YOU OR ANYONE ELSE.
AH HATE TO TELL YOU THIS, MR. SUPREME LEADER, BUT THE WORLD JUST DON'T REVOLVE AROUND YOU LIKE THAT.
HELL, YOU THINK AH'D LEAVE MY WIFE AND SON FOR A WEEK AT A TIME JUST 'CAUSE IT'S YOU ASKIN'?
AH'M HERE 'CAUSE AH THINK IT'S RIGHT, BOBBY.
AND 'CAUSE IT'S YOU ASKIN'.

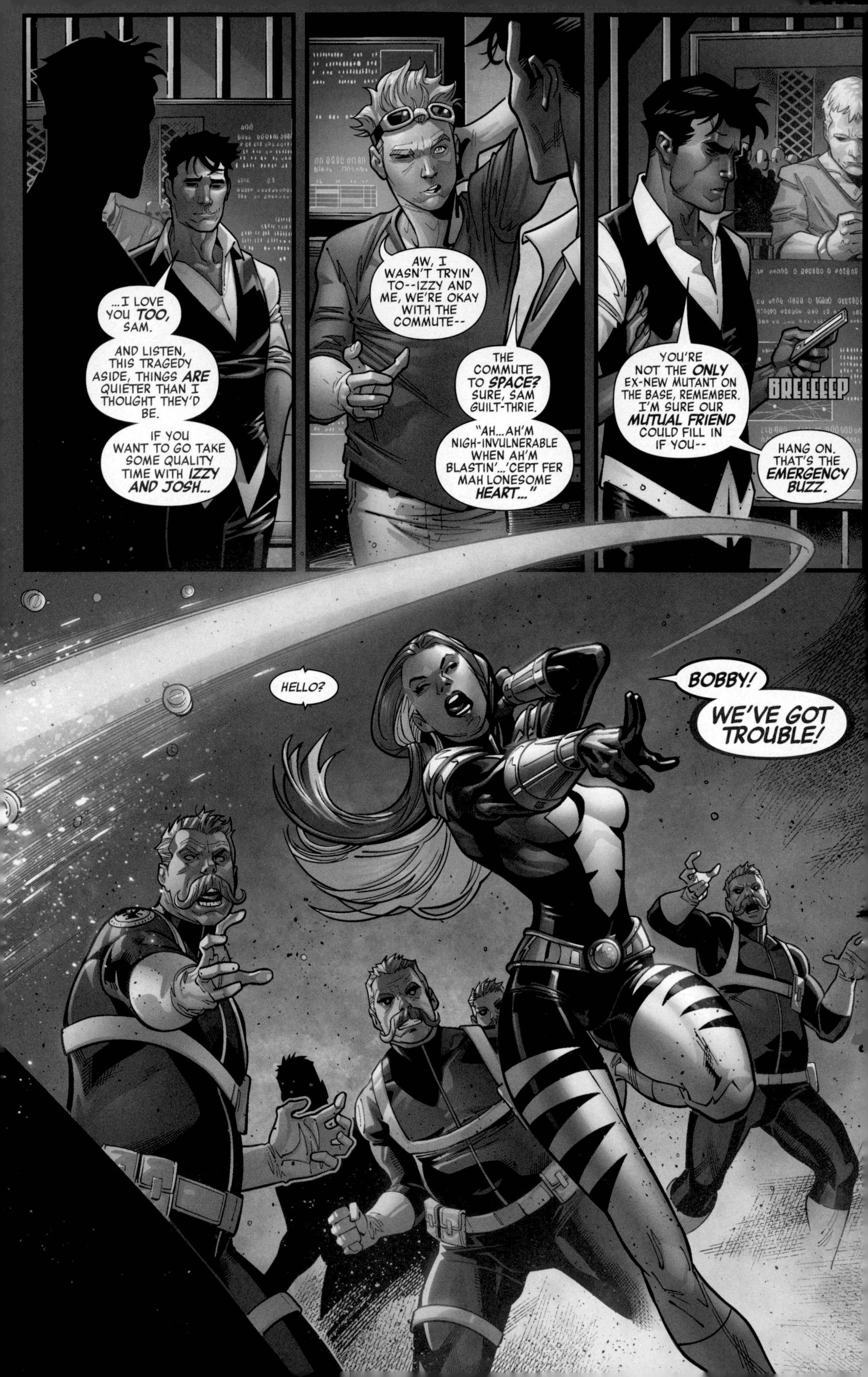

...I LOVE YOU TOO, SAM.
AND LISTEN, THIS TRAGEDY ASIDE, THINGS ARE QUIETER THAN I THOUGHT THEY'D BE.
IF YOU WANT TO GO TAKE SOME QUALITY TIME WITH IZZY AND JOSH...
AW, I WASN'T TRYIN' TO--IZZY AND ME, WE'RE OKAY WITH THE COMMUTE--
THE COMMUTE TO SPACE? SURE, SAM GUILT-THRIE.
"AH...AH'M NIGH-INVULNERABLE WHEN AH'M BLASTIN'...'CEPT FER MAH LONESOME HEART..."
YOU'RE NOT THE ONLY EX-NEW MUTANT ON THE BASE, REMEMBER. I'M SURE OUR MUTUAL FRIEND COULD FILL IN IF YOU--
BREEEEEP
HANG ON. THAT'S THE EMERGENCY BUZZ.
HELLO?
BOBBY!
WE'VE GOT TROUBLE!

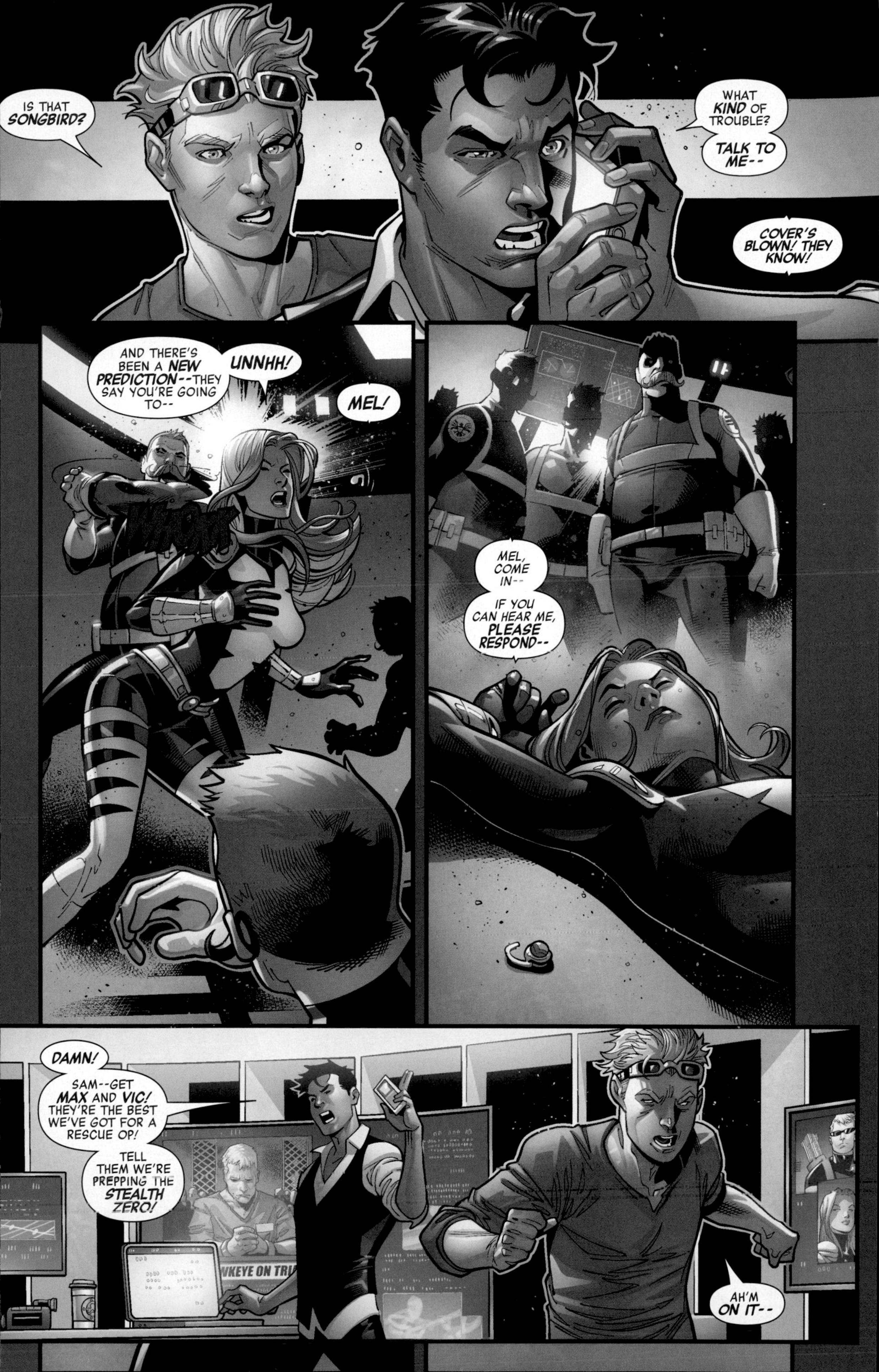

IS THAT SONGBIRD?
WHAT KIND OF TROUBLE?
TALK TO ME--
COVER'S BLOWN! THEY KNOW!
AND THERE'S BEEN A NEW PREDICTION--THEY SAY YOU'RE GOING TO--
UNNHH!
MEL!
MEL, COME IN--
IF YOU CAN HEAR ME, PLEASE RESPOND--
DAMN!
SAM--GET MAX AND VIC! THEY'RE THE BEST WE'VE GOT FOR A RESCUE OP!
TELL THEM WE'RE PREPPING THE STEALTH ZERO!
AH'M ON IT--

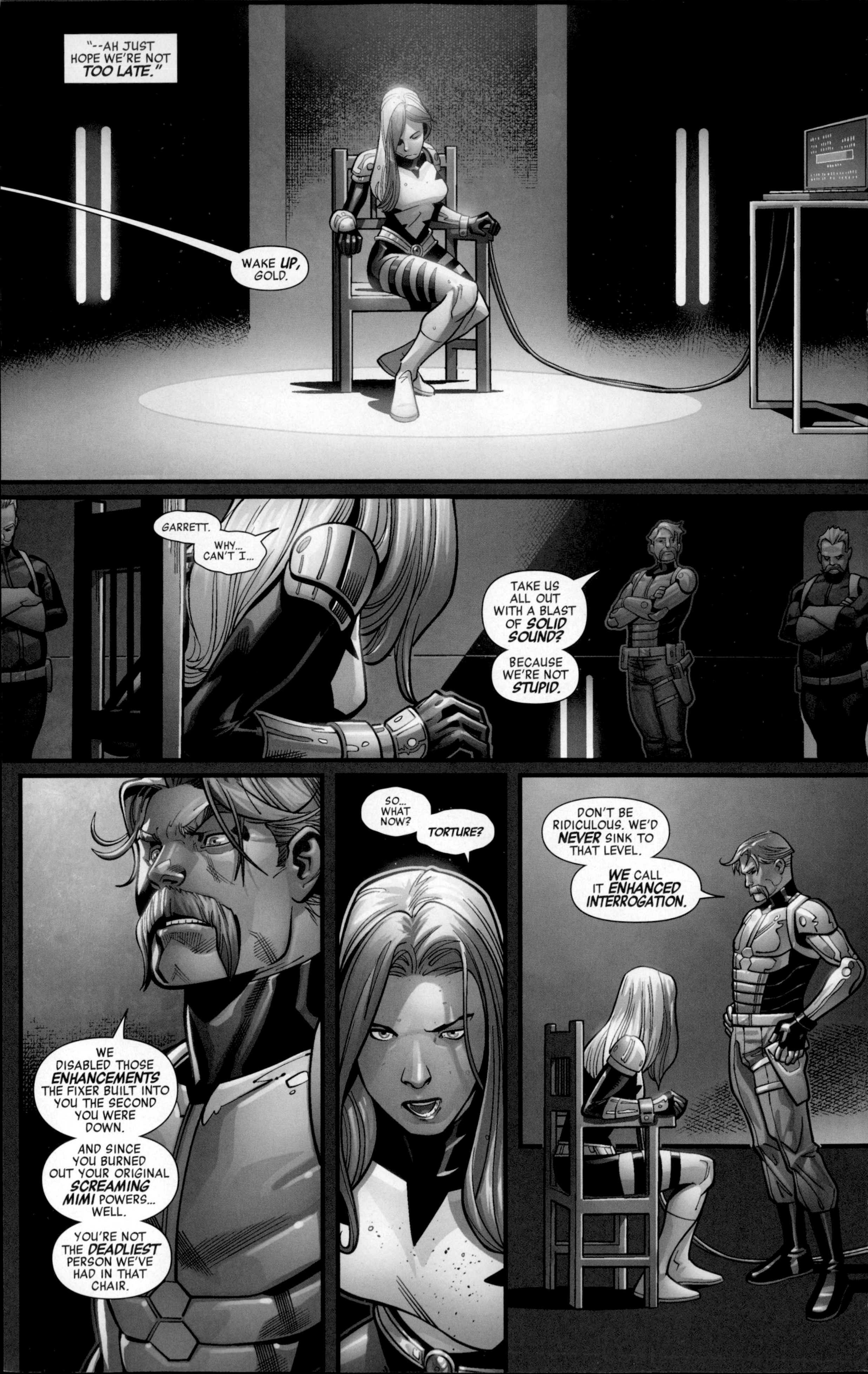
"--AH JUST HOPE WE'RE NOT TOO LATE."
WAKE UP, GOLD.
GARRETT.
WHY... CAN'T I...
TAKE US ALL OUT WITH A BLAST OF SOLID SOUND?
BECAUSE WE'RE NOT STUPID.
WE DISABLED THOSE ENHANCEMENTS THE FIXER BUILT INTO YOU THE SECOND YOU WERE DOWN.
AND SINCE YOU BURNED OUT YOUR ORIGINAL SCREAMING MIMI POWERS... WELL.
YOU'RE NOT THE DEADLIEST PERSON WE'VE HAD IN THAT CHAIR.
SO... WHAT NOW?
TORTURE?
DON'T BE RIDICULOUS. WE'D NEVER SINK TO THAT LEVEL.
WE CALL IT ENHANCED INTERROGATION.

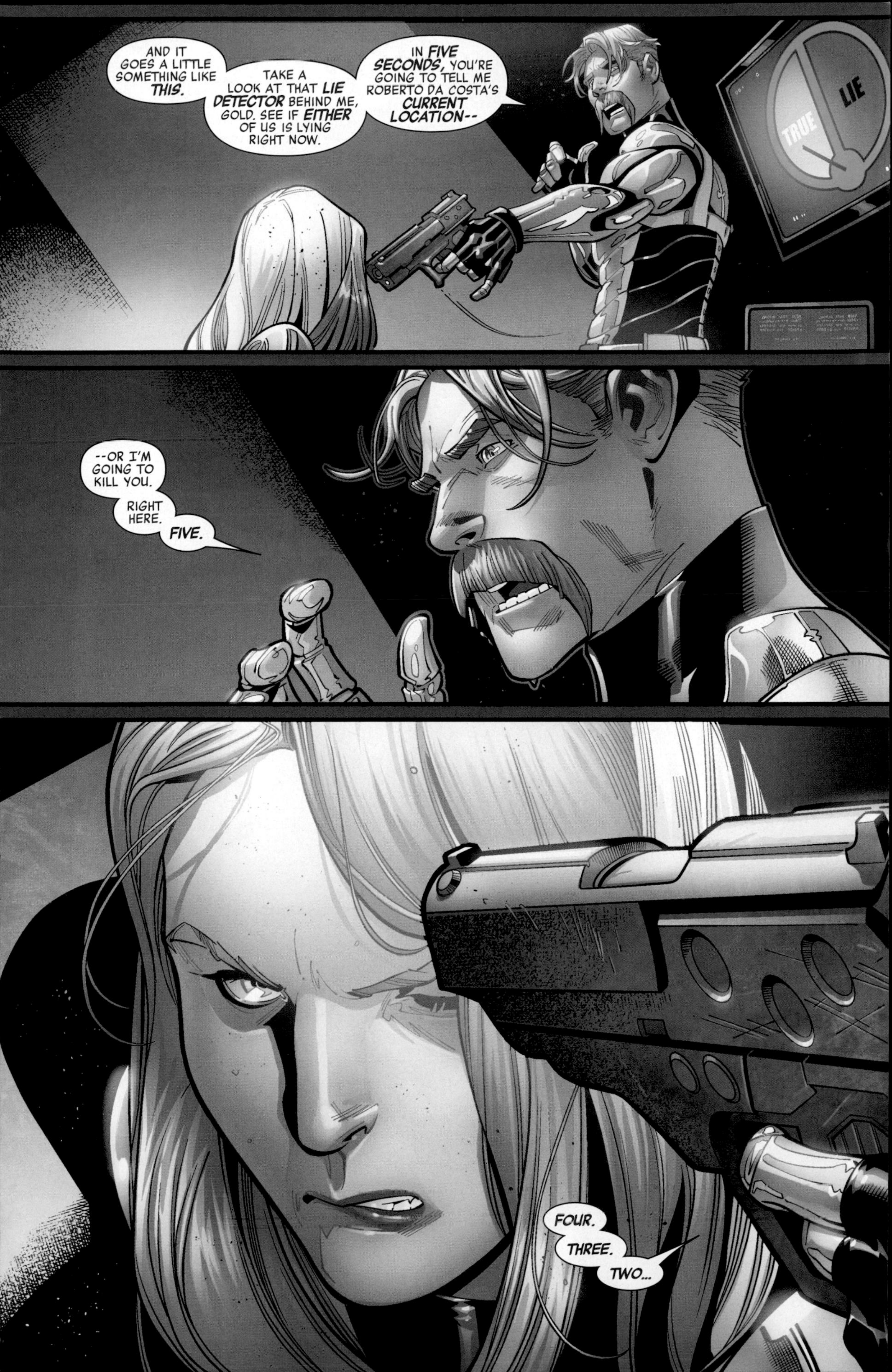
AND IT GOES A LITTLE SOMETHING LIKE THIS.
TAKE A LOOK AT THAT LIE DETECTOR BEHIND ME, GOLD. SEE IF EITHER OF US IS LYING RIGHT NOW.
IN FIVE SECONDS, YOU'RE GOING TO TELL ME ROBERTO DA COSTA'S CURRENT LOCATION--
TRUE
LIE
--OR I'M GOING TO KILL YOU.
RIGHT HERE. FIVE.
FOUR.
THREE.
TWO...

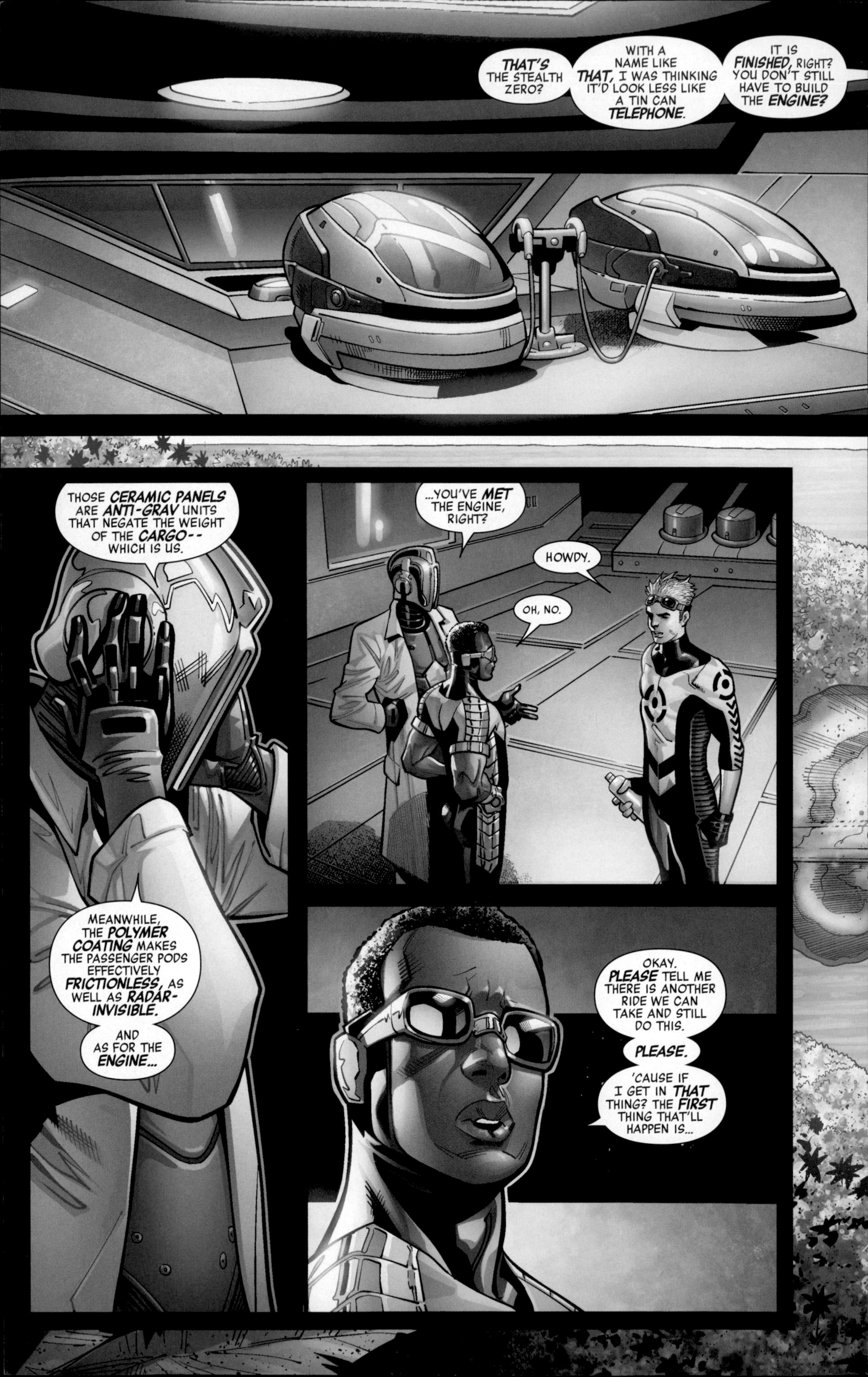
THAT'S THE STEALTH ZERO?
WITH A NAME LIKE THAT, I WAS THINKING IT'D LOOK LESS LIKE A TIN CAN TELEPHONE.
IT IS FINISHED, RIGHT? YOU DON'T STILL HAVE TO BUILD THE ENGINE?
THOSE CERAMIC PANELS ARE ANTI-GRAV UNITS THAT NEGATE THE WEIGHT OF THE CARGO-- WHICH IS US.
...YOU'VE MET THE ENGINE, RIGHT?
HOWDY.
OH, NO.
MEANWHILE, THE POLYMER COATING MAKES THE PASSENGER PODS EFFECTIVELY FRICTIONLESS, AS WELL AS RADAR-INVISIBLE.
AND AS FOR THE ENGINE...
OKAY. PLEASE TELL ME THERE IS ANOTHER RIDE WE CAN TAKE AND STILL DO THIS.
PLEASE.
'CAUSE IF I GET IN THAT THING? THE FIRST THING THAT'LL HAPPEN IS...

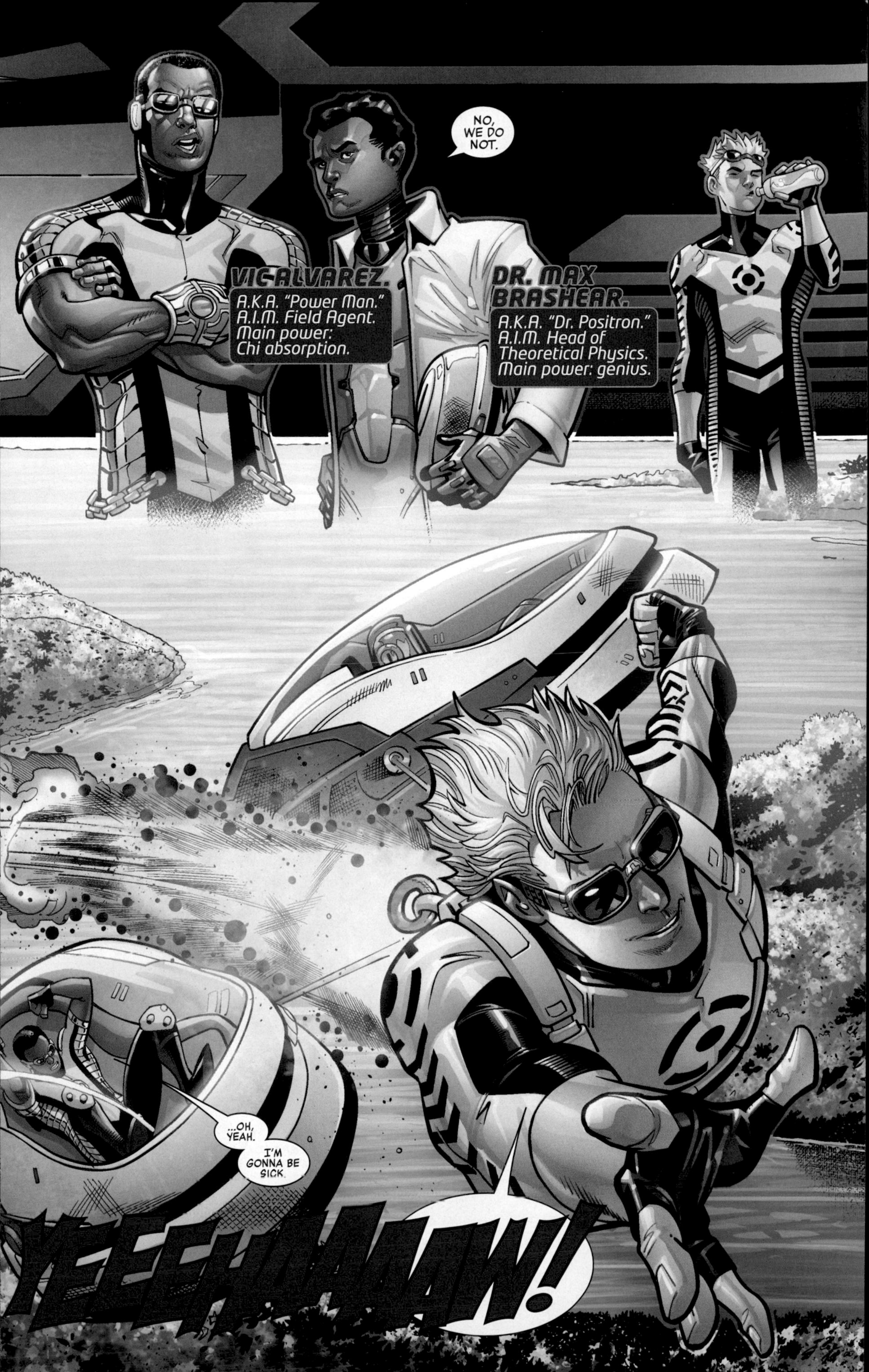

NO, WE DO NOT.
VIC ALVAREZ.
A.K.A. "Power Man." A.I.M. Field Agent. Main power: Chi absorption.
DR. MAX BRASHEAR.
A.K.A. "Dr. Positron." A.I.M. Head of Theoretical Physics. Main power: genius.
...OH, YEAH.
I'M GONNA BE SICK.
YEE-HAAAW!

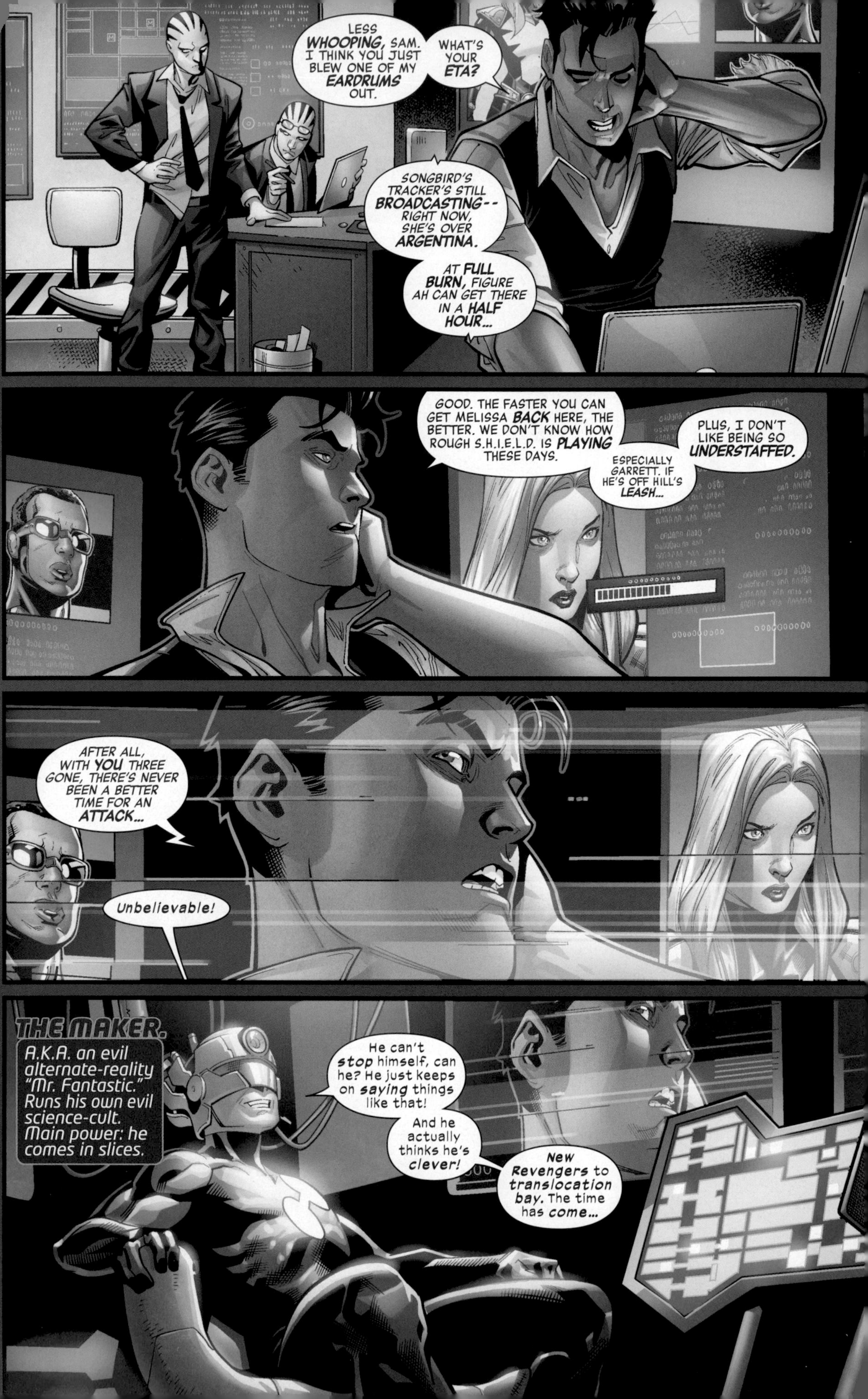
LESS WHOOPING, SAM. I THINK YOU JUST BLEW ONE OF MY EARDRUMS OUT.
WHAT'S YOUR ETA?
SONGBIRD'S TRACKER'S STILL BROADCASTING-- RIGHT NOW, SHE'S OVER ARGENTINA.
AT FULL BURN, FIGURE AH CAN GET THERE IN A HALF HOUR...
GOOD. THE FASTER YOU CAN GET MELISSA BACK HERE, THE BETTER. WE DON'T KNOW HOW ROUGH S.H.I.E.L.D. IS PLAYING THESE DAYS.
ESPECIALLY GARRETT. IF HE'S OFF HILL'S LEASH...
PLUS, I DON'T LIKE BEING SO UNDERSTAFFED.
AFTER ALL, WITH YOU THREE GONE, THERE'S NEVER BEEN A BETTER TIME FOR AN ATTACK...
Unbelievable!
THE MAKER.
A.K.A. an evil alternate-reality "Mr. Fantastic." Runs his own evil science-cult. Main power: he comes in slices.
He can't stop himself, can he? He just keeps on saying things like that!
And he actually thinks he's clever!
New Revengers to translocation bay. The time has come...

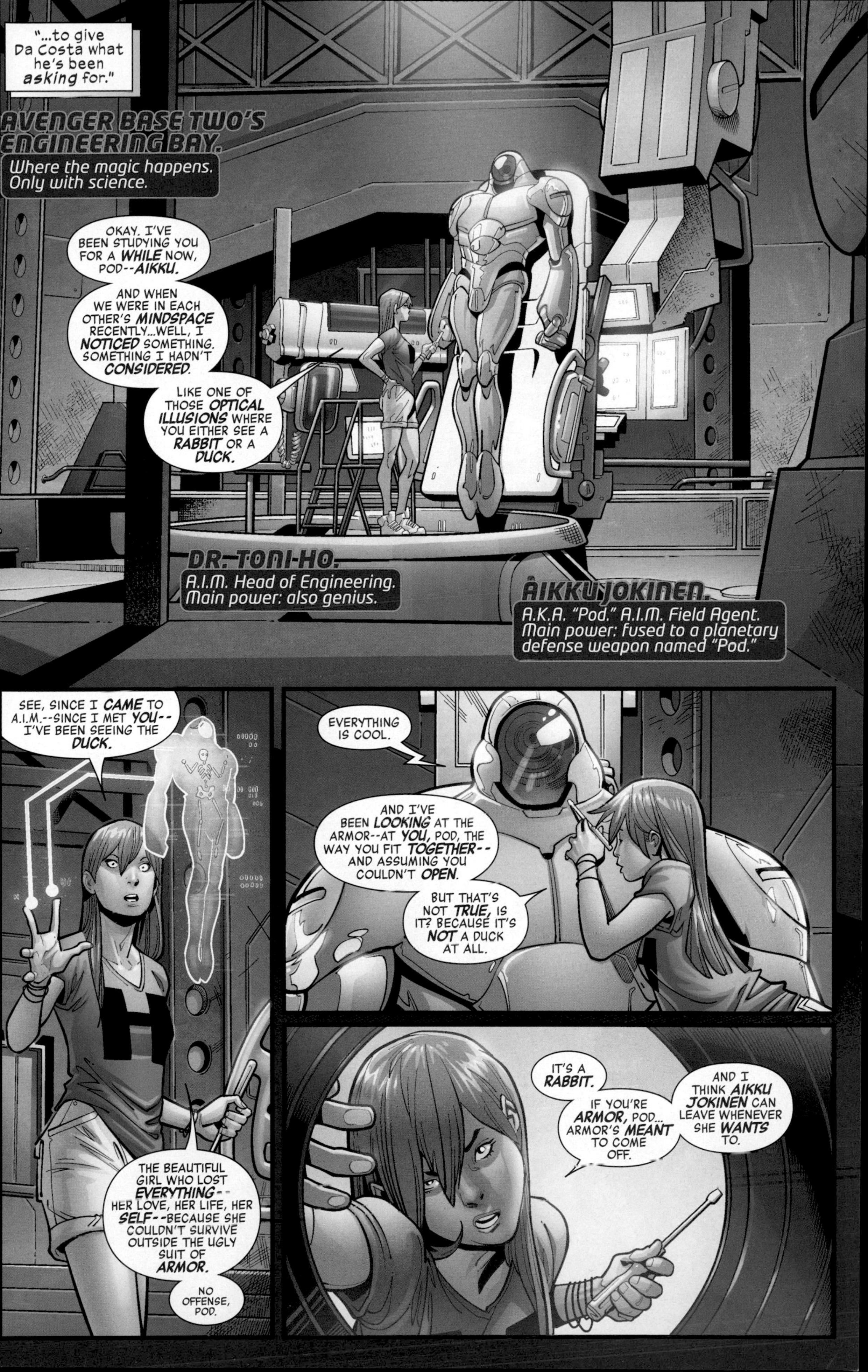
"...to give Da Costa what he's been asking for."
AVENGER BASE TWO'S ENGINEERING BAY.
Where the magic happens. Only with science.
OKAY. I'VE BEEN STUDYING YOU FOR A WHILE NOW, POD--AIKKU.
AND WHEN WE WERE IN EACH OTHER'S MINDSPACE RECENTLY...WELL, I NOTICED SOMETHING. SOMETHING I HADN'T CONSIDERED.
LIKE ONE OF THOSE OPTICAL ILLUSIONS WHERE YOU EITHER SEE A RABBIT OR A DUCK.
DR. TONI HO.
A.I.M. Head of Engineering. Main power: also genius.
AIKKU JOKINEN.
A.K.A. "Pod." A.I.M. Field Agent. Main power: fused to a planetary defense weapon named "Pod."
SEE, SINCE I CAME TO A.I.M.--SINCE I MET YOU-- I'VE BEEN SEEING THE DUCK.
THE BEAUTIFUL GIRL WHO LOST EVERYTHING-- HER LOVE, HER LIFE, HER SELF--BECAUSE SHE COULDN'T SURVIVE OUTSIDE THE UGLY SUIT OF ARMOR.
NO OFFENSE, POD.
EVERYTHING IS COOL.
AND I'VE BEEN LOOKING AT THE ARMOR--AT YOU, POD, THE WAY YOU FIT TOGETHER-- AND ASSUMING YOU COULDN'T OPEN.
BUT THAT'S NOT TRUE, IS IT? BECAUSE IT'S NOT A DUCK AT ALL.
IT'S A RABBIT.
IF YOU'RE ARMOR, POD... ARMOR'S MEANT TO COME OFF.
AND I THINK AIKKU JOKINEN CAN LEAVE WHENEVER SHE WANTS TO.

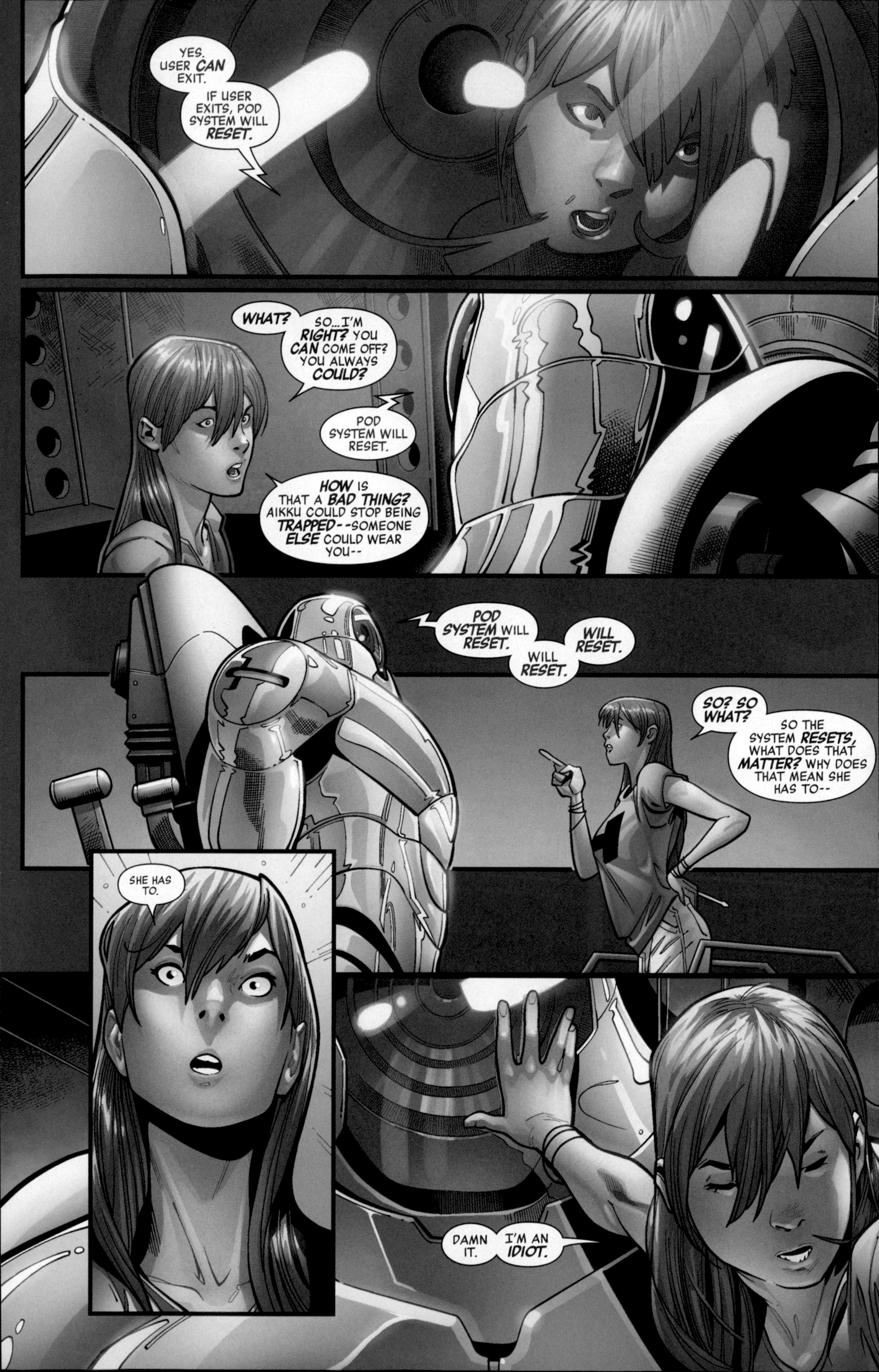
YES. USER CAN EXIT.
IF USER EXITS, POD SYSTEM WILL RESET.
WHAT?
SO...I'M RIGHT? YOU CAN COME OFF? YOU ALWAYS COULD?
POD SYSTEM WILL RESET.
HOW IS THAT A BAD THING? AIKKU COULD STOP BEING TRAPPED--SOMEONE ELSE COULD WEAR YOU--
POD SYSTEM WILL RESET.
WILL RESET.
WILL RESET.
SO? SO WHAT?
SO THE SYSTEM RESETS, WHAT DOES THAT MATTER? WHY DOES THAT MEAN SHE HAS TO--
SHE HAS TO.
DAMN IT.
I'M AN IDIOT.

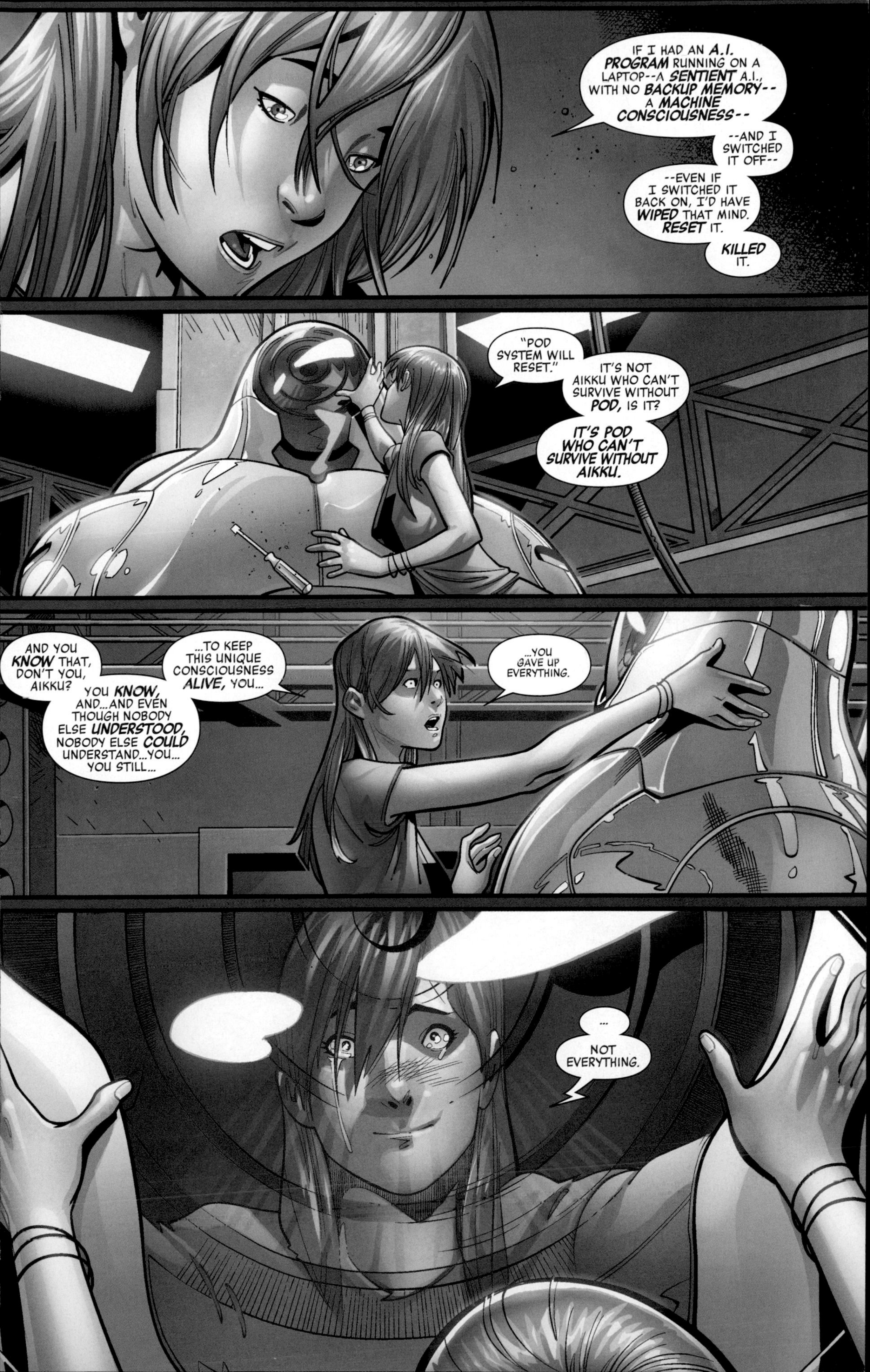
IF I HAD AN A.I. PROGRAM RUNNING ON A LAPTOP--A SENTIENT A.I., WITH NO BACKUP MEMORY--A MACHINE CONSCIOUSNESS--
--AND I SWITCHED IT OFF--
--EVEN IF I SWITCHED IT BACK ON, I'D HAVE WIPED THAT MIND. RESET IT.
KILLED IT.
"POD SYSTEM WILL RESET."
IT'S NOT AIKKU WHO CAN'T SURVIVE WITHOUT POD, IS IT?
IT'S POD WHO CAN'T SURVIVE WITHOUT AIKKU.
AND YOU KNOW THAT, DON'T YOU, AIKKU?
YOU KNOW, AND...AND EVEN THOUGH NOBODY ELSE UNDERSTOOD, NOBODY ELSE COULD UNDERSTAND...YOU... YOU STILL...
...TO KEEP THIS UNIQUE CONSCIOUSNESS ALIVE, YOU...
...YOU GAVE UP EVERYTHING.
...
NOT EVERYTHING.

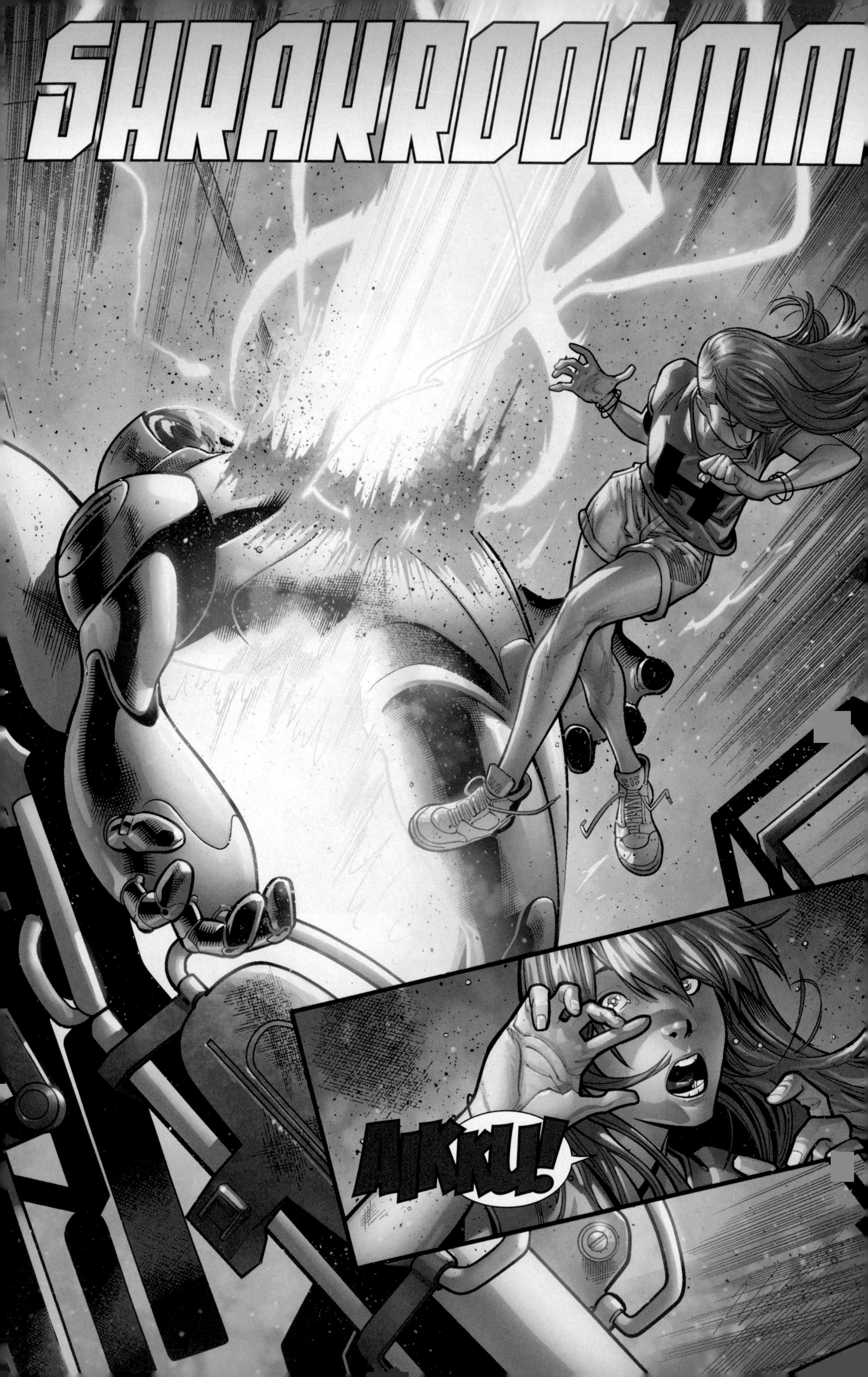
SHRAKROOOMM
AIKKU!

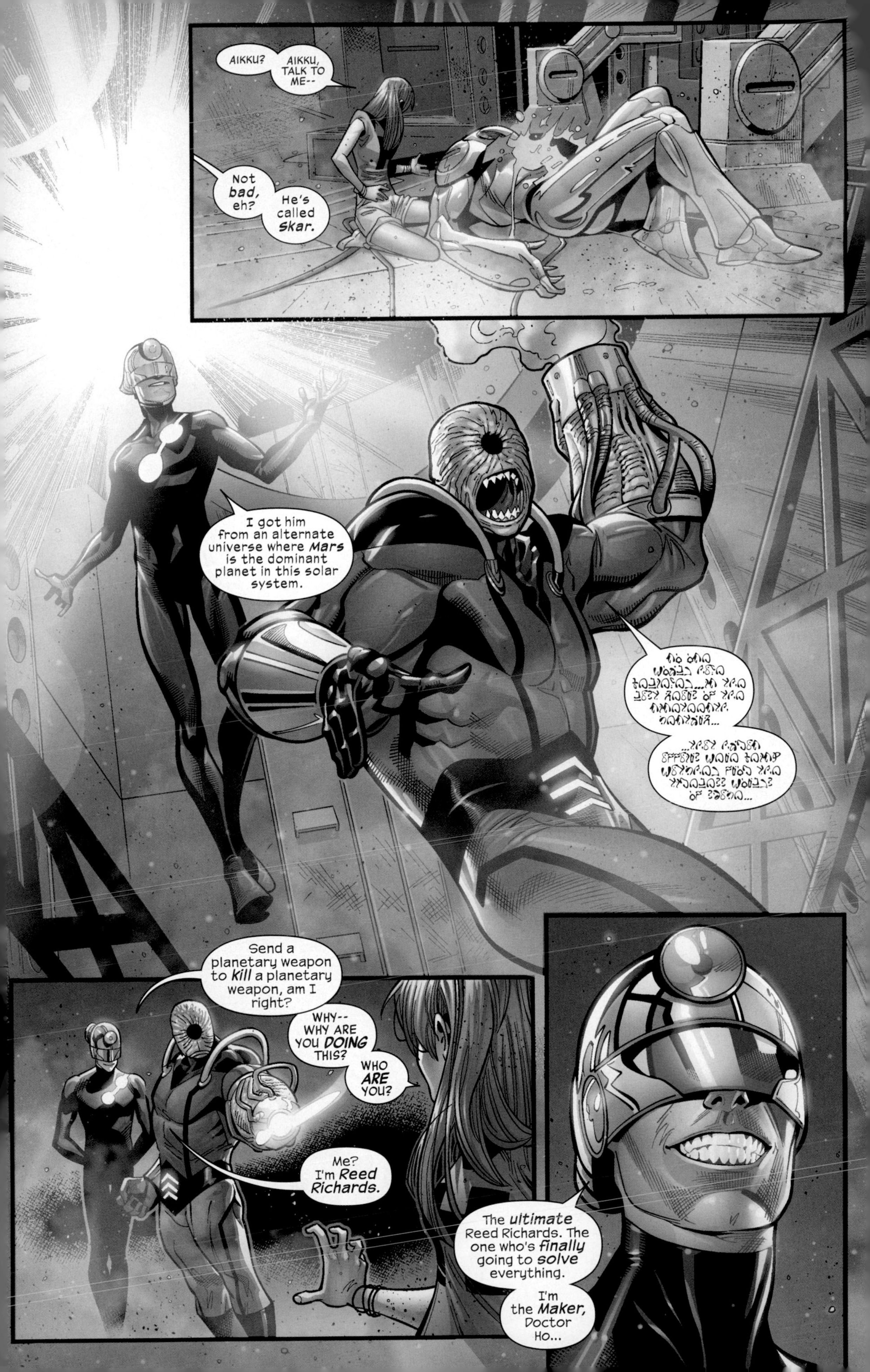

AIKKU?
AIKKU, TALK TO ME--
Not bad, eh?
He's called Skar.
I got him from an alternate universe where Mars is the dominant planet in this solar system.
Send a planetary weapon to kill a planetary weapon, am I right?
WHY-- WHY ARE YOU DOING THIS?
WHO ARE YOU?
Me? I'm Reed Richards.
The ultimate Reed Richards. The one who's finally going to solve everything.
I'm the Maker, Doctor Ho...

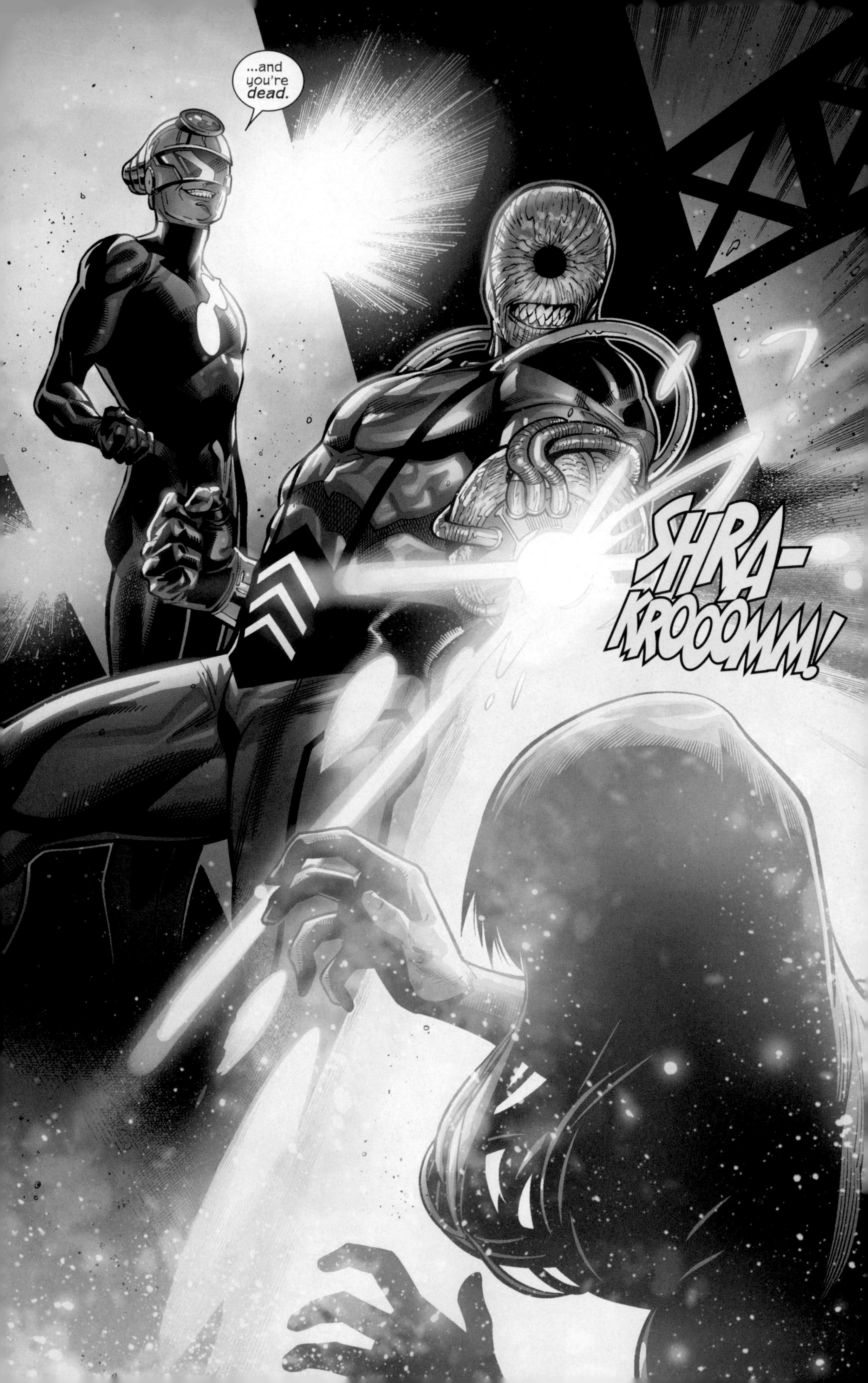
...and you're dead.
SHRA-KROOOMM!

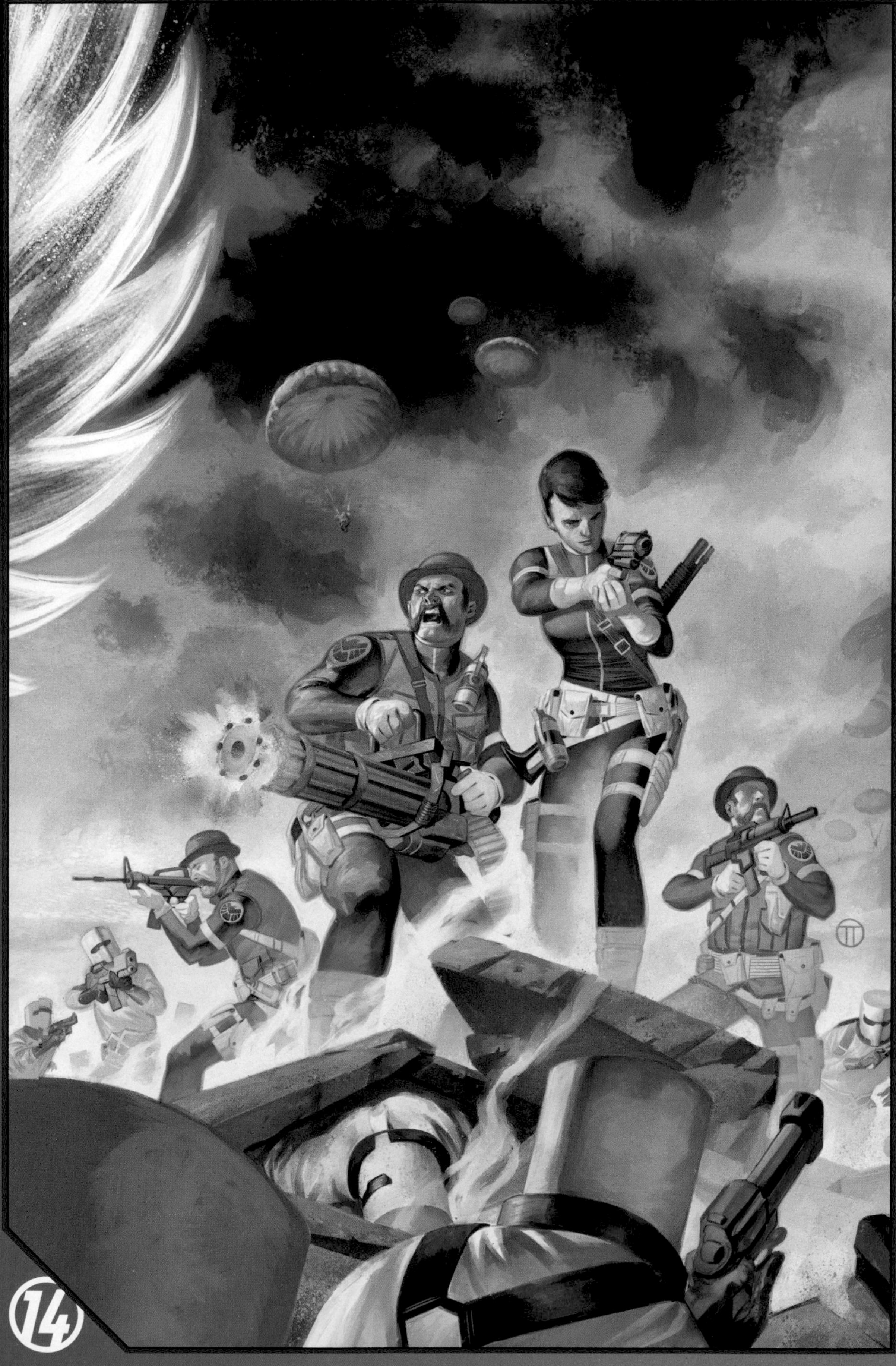
14

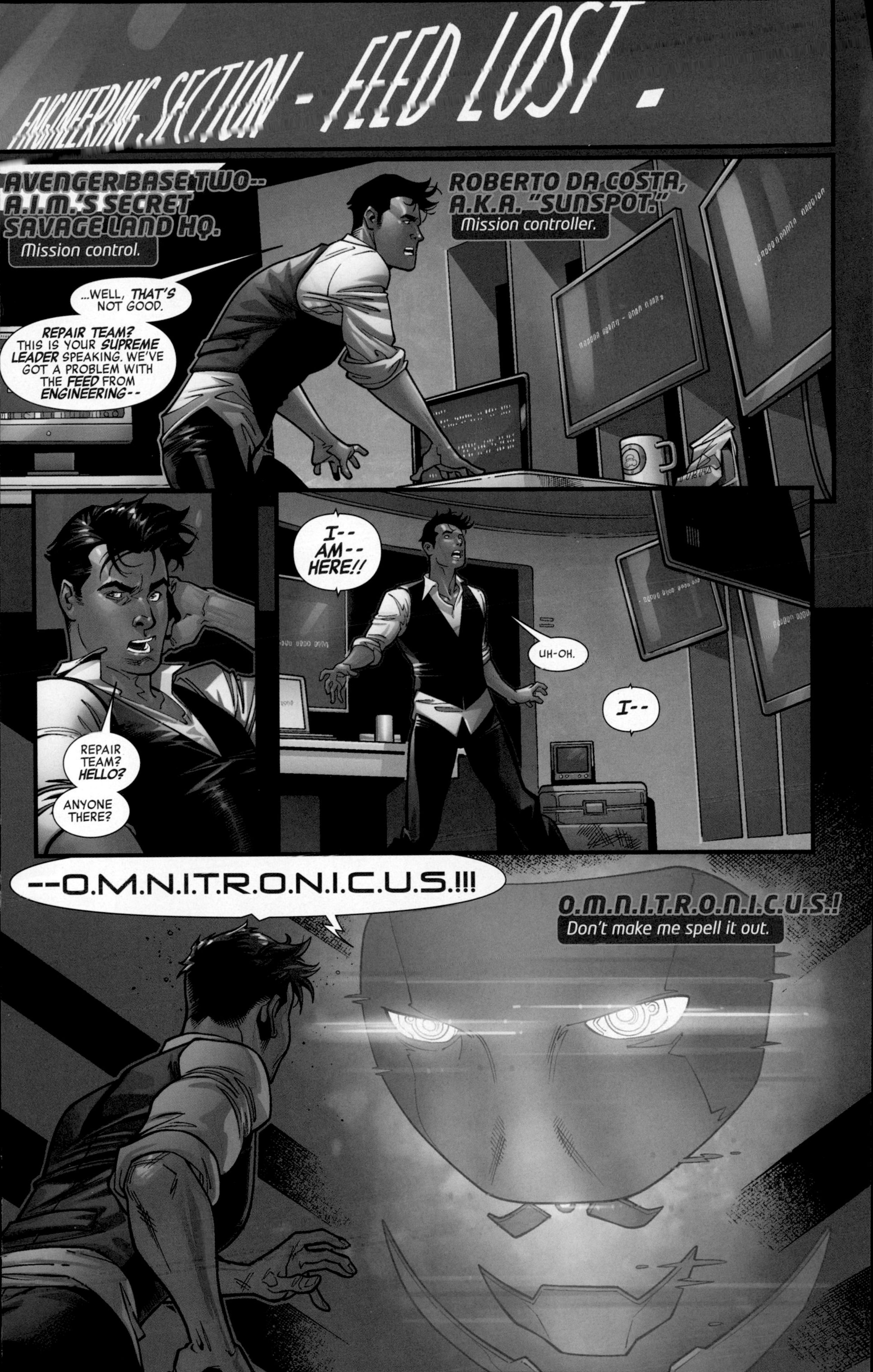
ENGINEERING SECTION - FEED LOST.
AVENGER BASE TWO-- A.I.M.'S SECRET SAVAGE LAND HQ.
Mission control.
ROBERTO DA COSTA, A.K.A. "SUNSPOT."
Mission controller.
...WELL, THAT'S NOT GOOD.
REPAIR TEAM? THIS IS YOUR SUPREME LEADER SPEAKING. WE'VE GOT A PROBLEM WITH THE FEED FROM ENGINEERING--
REPAIR TEAM? HELLO?
ANYONE THERE?
I-- AM-- HERE!!
UH-OH.
I--
--O.M.N.I.T.R.O.N.I.C.U.S.!!!
O.M.N.I.T.R.O.N.I.C.U.S.!
Don't make me spell it out.

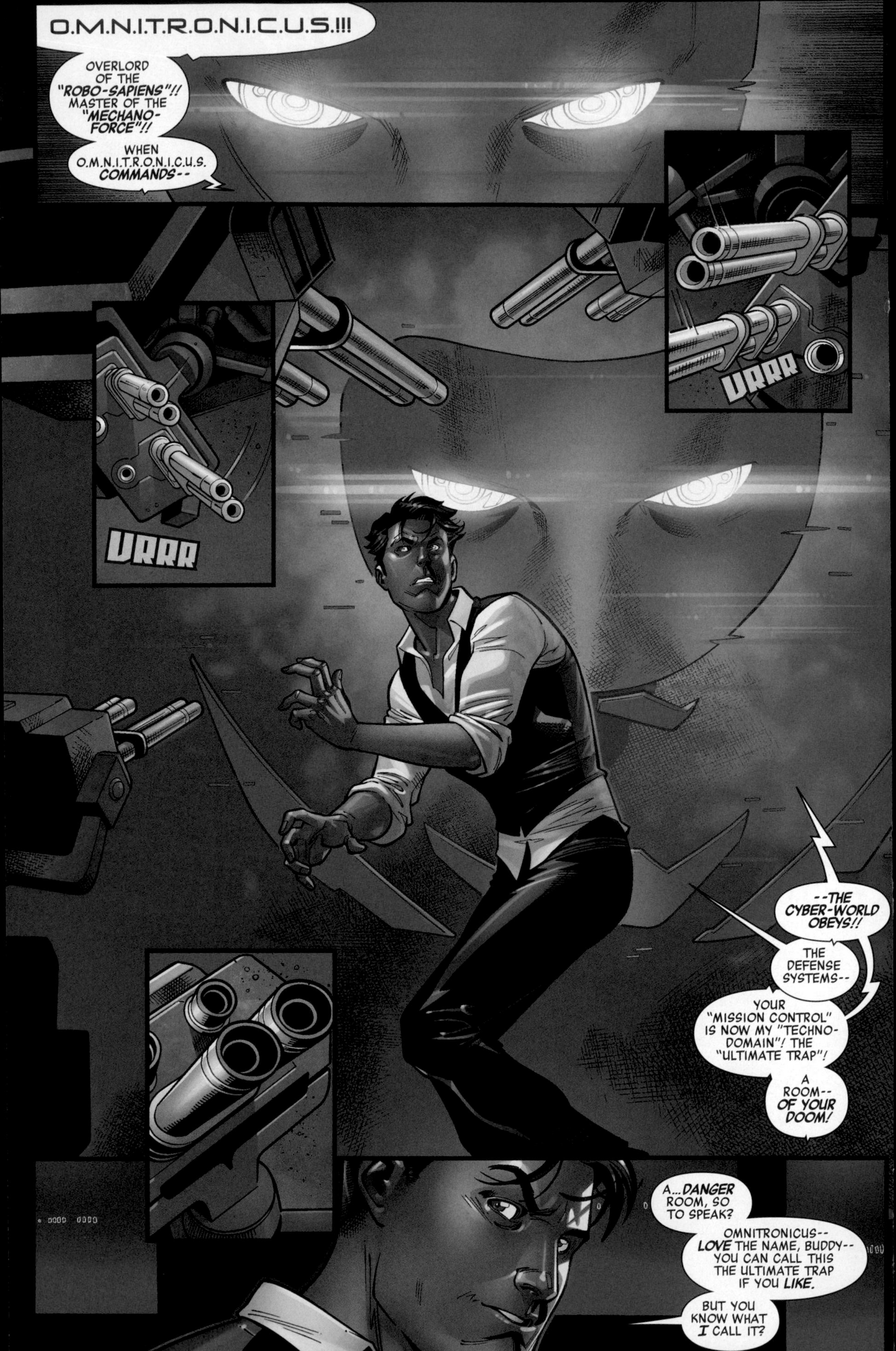
O.M.N.I.T.R.O.N.I.C.U.S.!!!
OVERLORD OF THE "ROBO-SAPIENS"!! MASTER OF THE "MECHANO-FORCE"!!
WHEN O.M.N.I.T.R.O.N.I.C.U.S. COMMANDS--
URRR
URRR
--THE CYBER-WORLD OBEYS!!
THE DEFENSE SYSTEMS--
YOUR "MISSION CONTROL" IS NOW MY "TECHNO-DOMAIN"! THE "ULTIMATE TRAP"!
A ROOM-- OF YOUR DOOM!
A...DANGER ROOM, SO TO SPEAK?
OMNITRONICUS-- LOVE THE NAME, BUDDY-- YOU CAN CALL THIS THE ULTIMATE TRAP IF YOU LIKE.
BUT YOU KNOW WHAT I CALL IT?

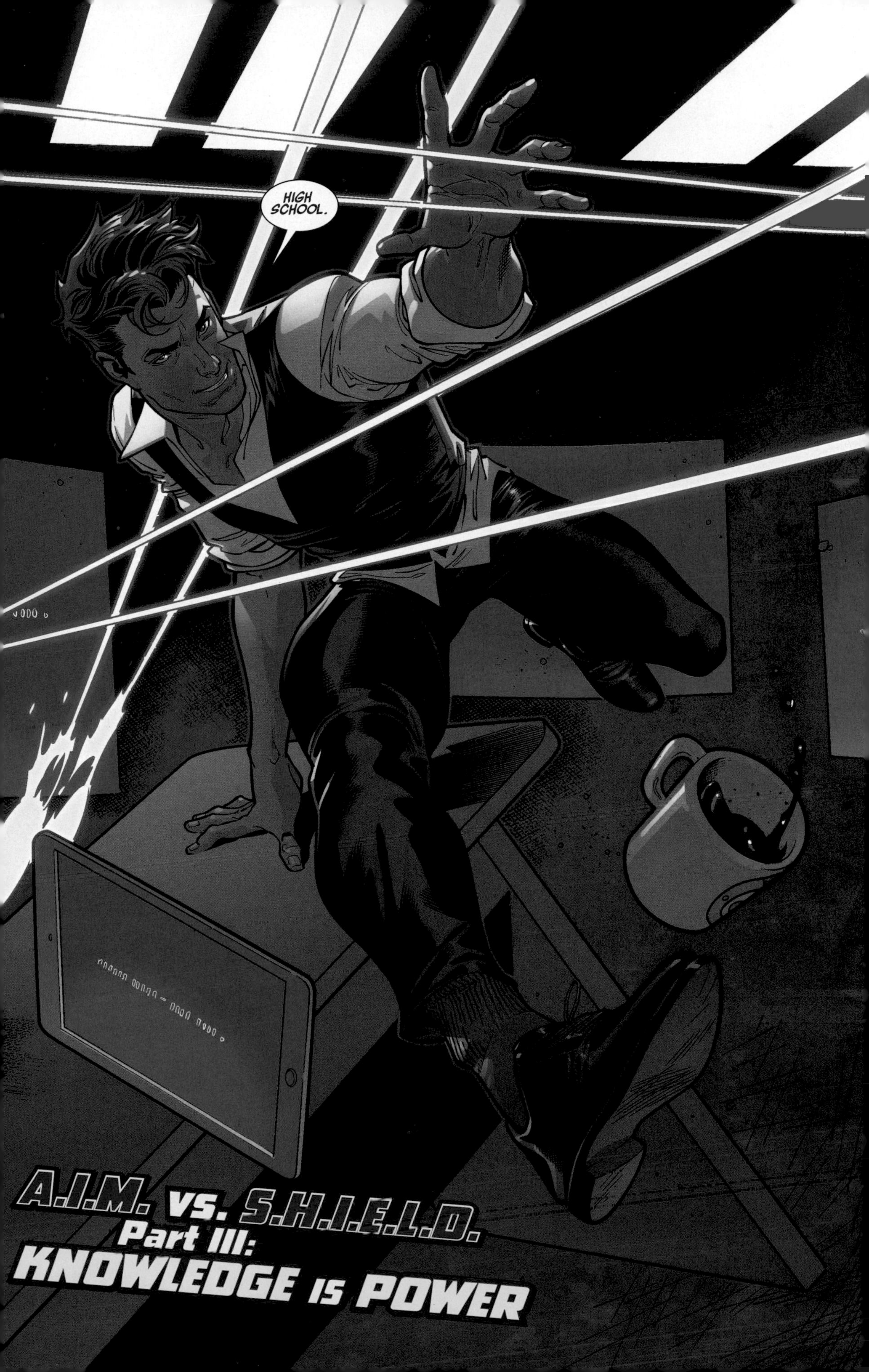
HIGH SCHOOL.
A.I.M. VS. S.H.I.E.L.D.
Part III:
KNOWLEDGE IS POWER

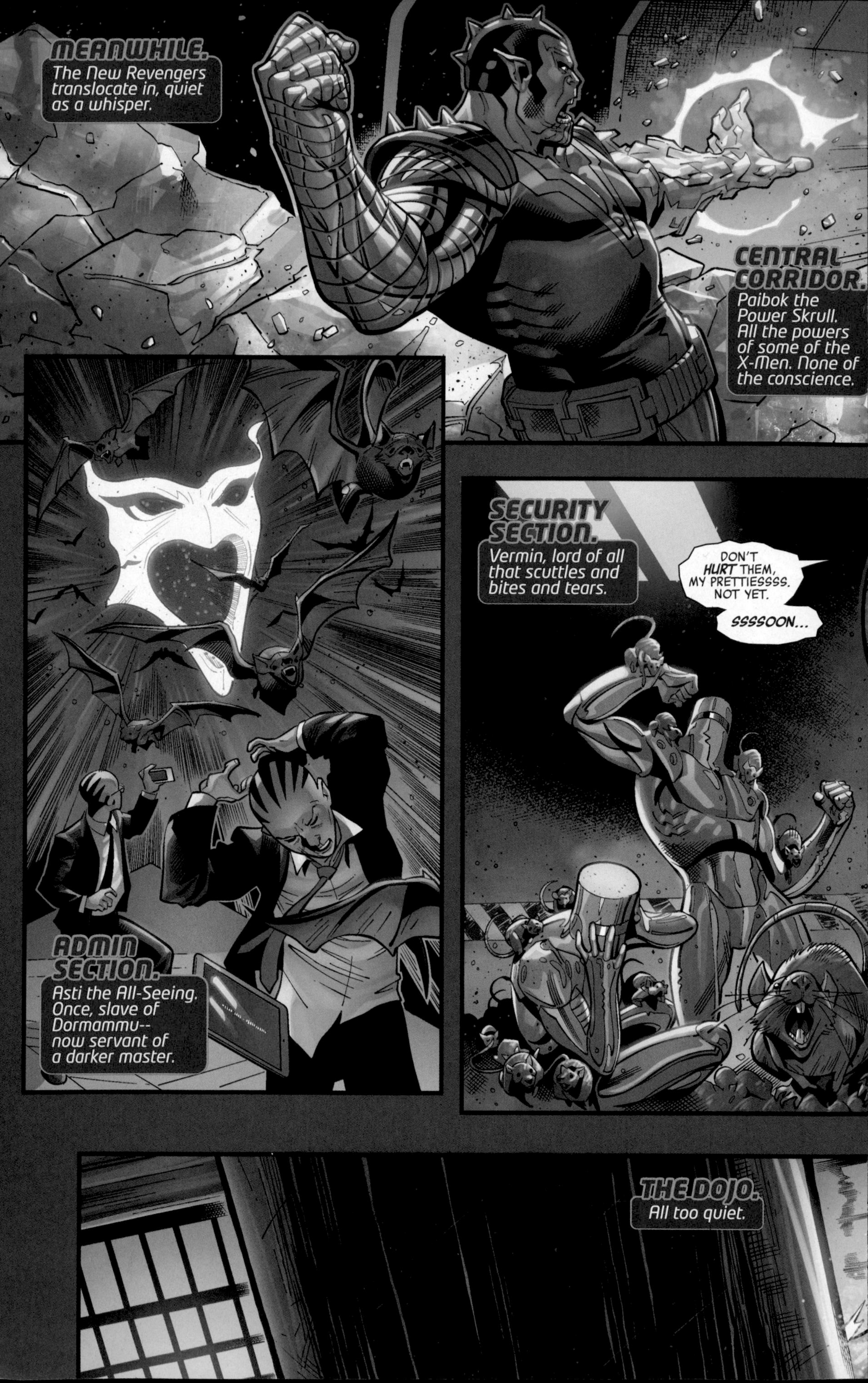
MEANWHILE.
The New Revengers translocate in, quiet as a whisper.
CENTRAL CORRIDOR.
Paibok the Power Skrull. All the powers of some of the X-Men. None of the conscience.
ADMIN SECTION.
Asti the All-Seeing. Once, slave of Dormammu-- now servant of a darker master.
SECURITY SECTION.
Vermin, lord of all that scuttles and bites and tears.
DON'T HURT THEM, MY PRETTIESSSS. NOT YET.
SSSSOON...
THE DOJO.
All too quiet.

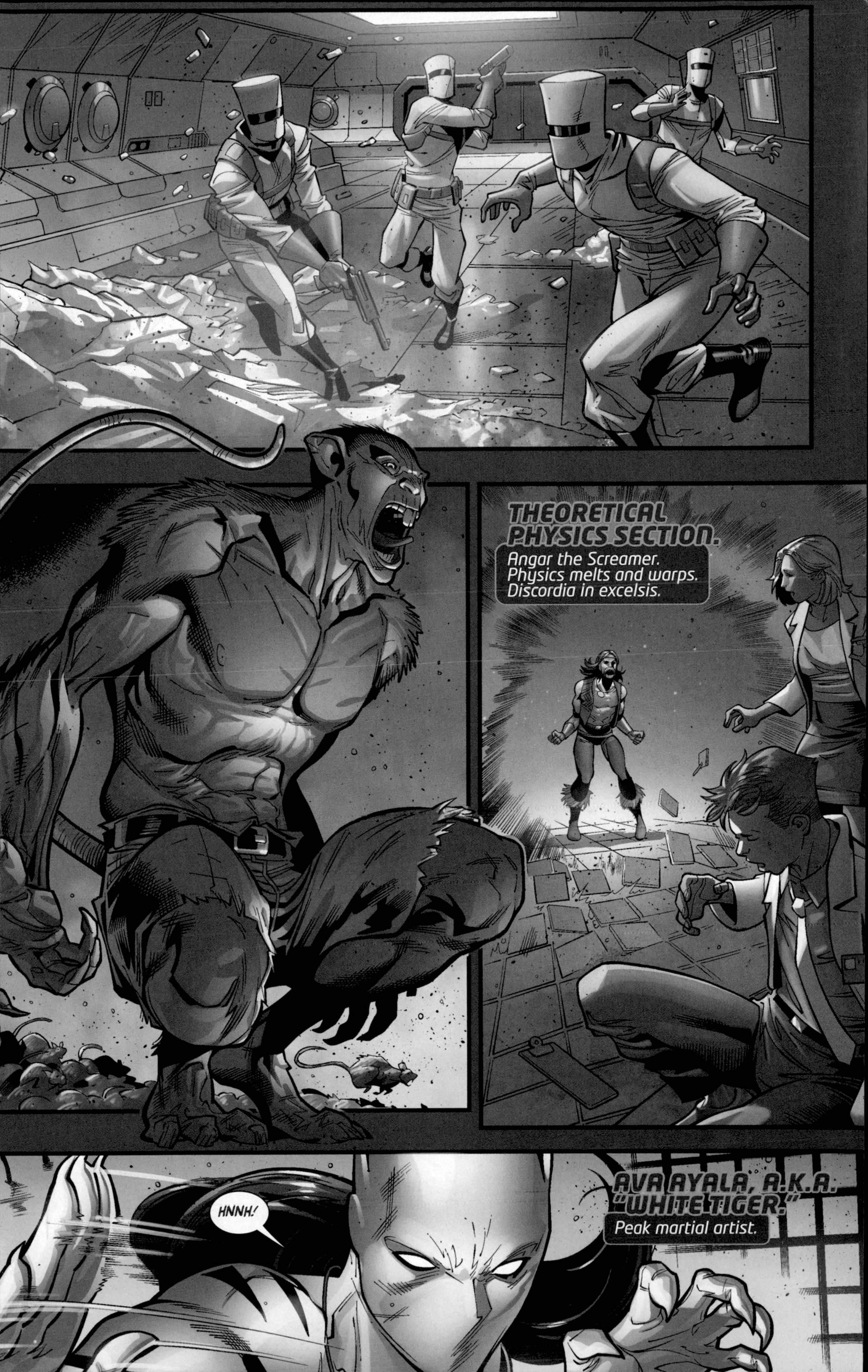
THEORETICAL PHYSICS SECTION.
Angar the Screamer.
Physics melts and warps.
Discordia in excelsis.
AVA AYALA, A.K.A. "WHITE TIGER."
Peak martial artist.
HNNH!

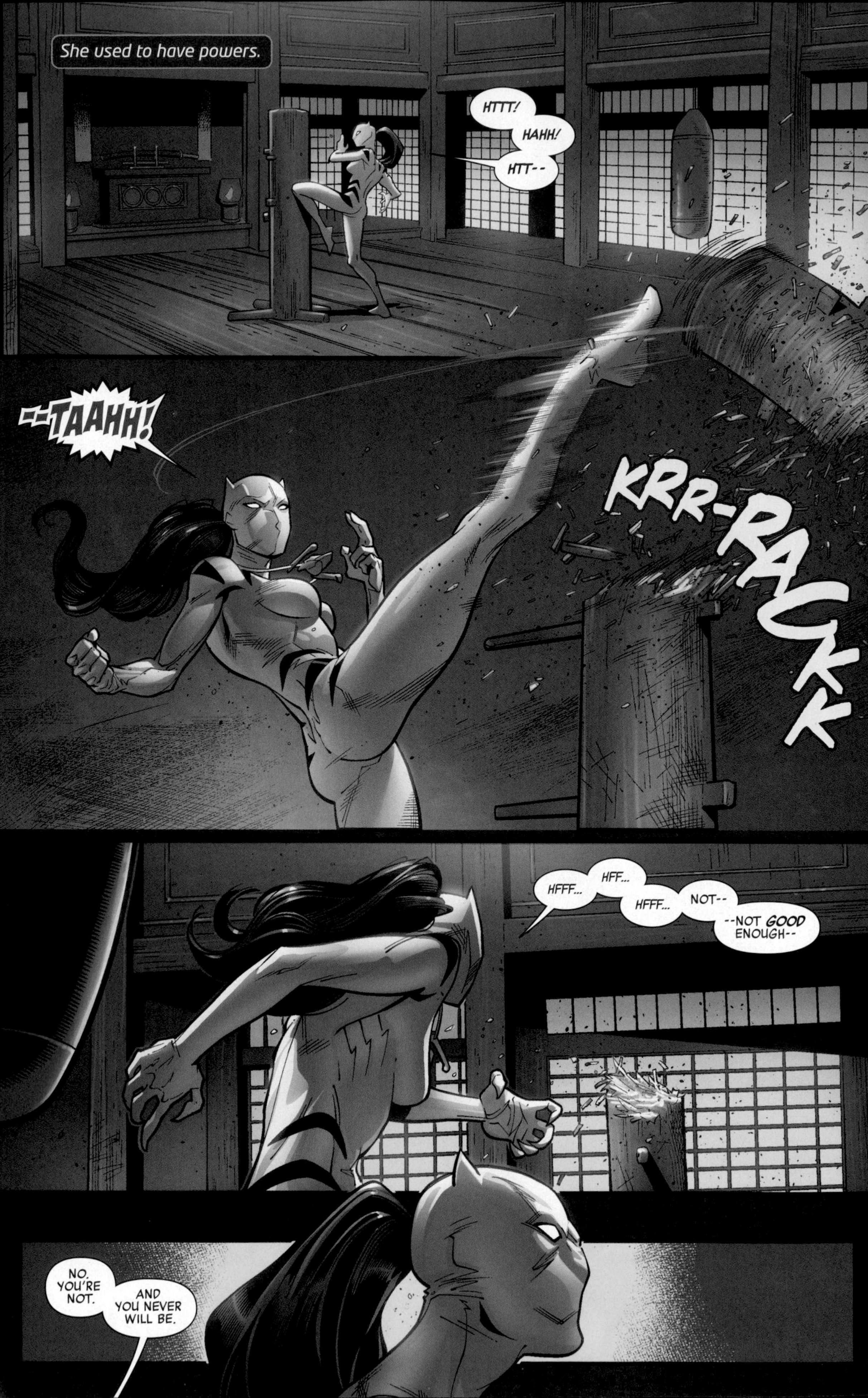
She used to have powers.
HTTT!
HAHH!
HTT--
--TAAHH!
KRR-RACKK
HFFF...
HFF...
HFFF...
NOT--
--NOT GOOD ENOUGH--
NO. YOU'RE NOT.
AND YOU NEVER WILL BE.

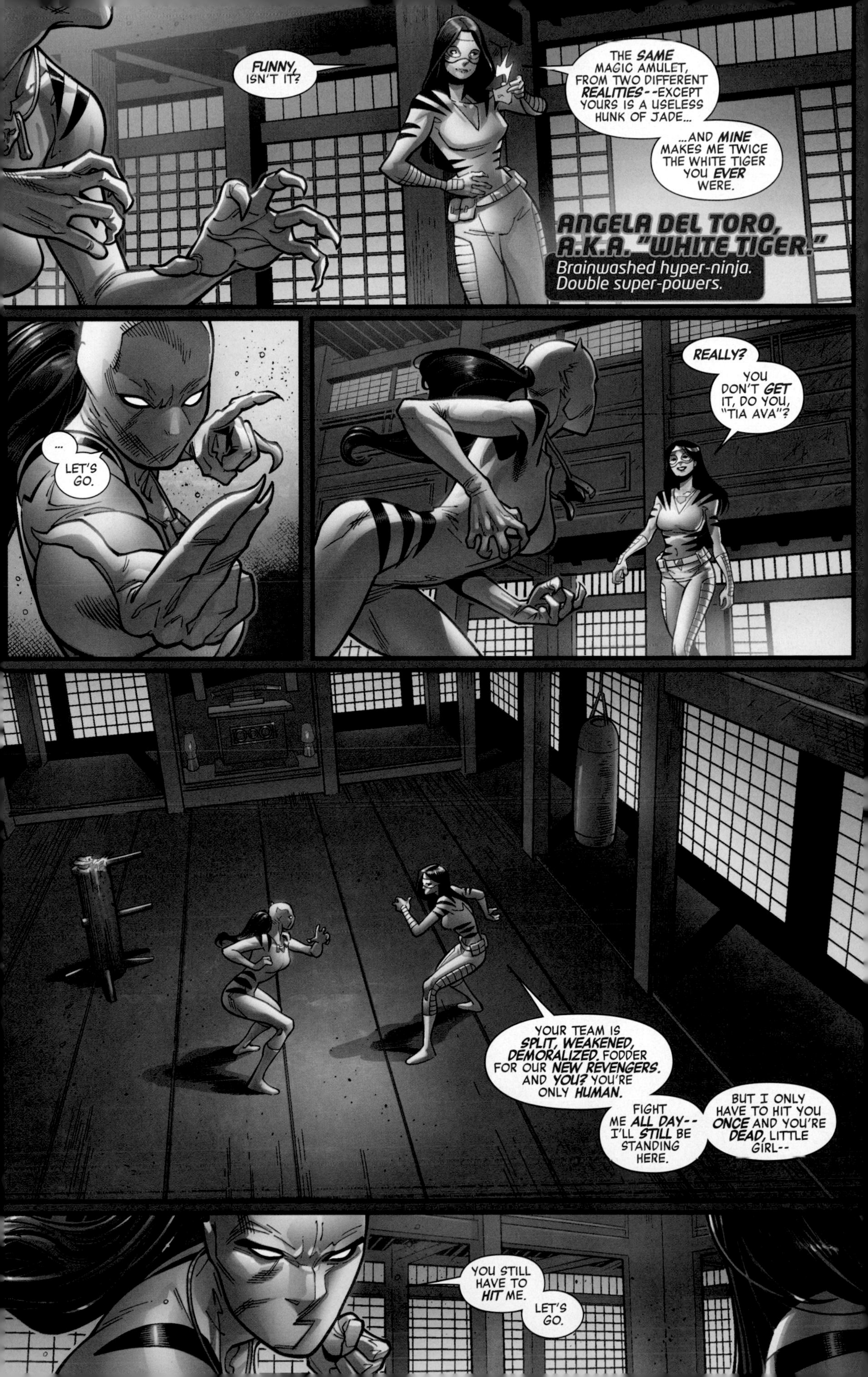
FUNNY, ISN'T IT?
THE SAME MAGIC AMULET, FROM TWO DIFFERENT REALITIES--EXCEPT YOURS IS A USELESS HUNK OF JADE...
...AND MINE MAKES ME TWICE THE WHITE TIGER YOU EVER WERE.
ANGELA DEL TORO, A.K.A. "WHITE TIGER."
Brainwashed hyper-ninja. Double super-powers.
... LET'S GO.
REALLY?
YOU DON'T GET IT, DO YOU, "TIA AVA"?
YOUR TEAM IS SPLIT, WEAKENED, DEMORALIZED. FODDER FOR OUR NEW REVENGERS. AND YOU? YOU'RE ONLY HUMAN.
FIGHT ME ALL DAY--I'LL STILL BE STANDING HERE.
BUT I ONLY HAVE TO HIT YOU ONCE AND YOU'RE DEAD, LITTLE GIRL--
YOU STILL HAVE TO HIT ME.
LET'S GO.

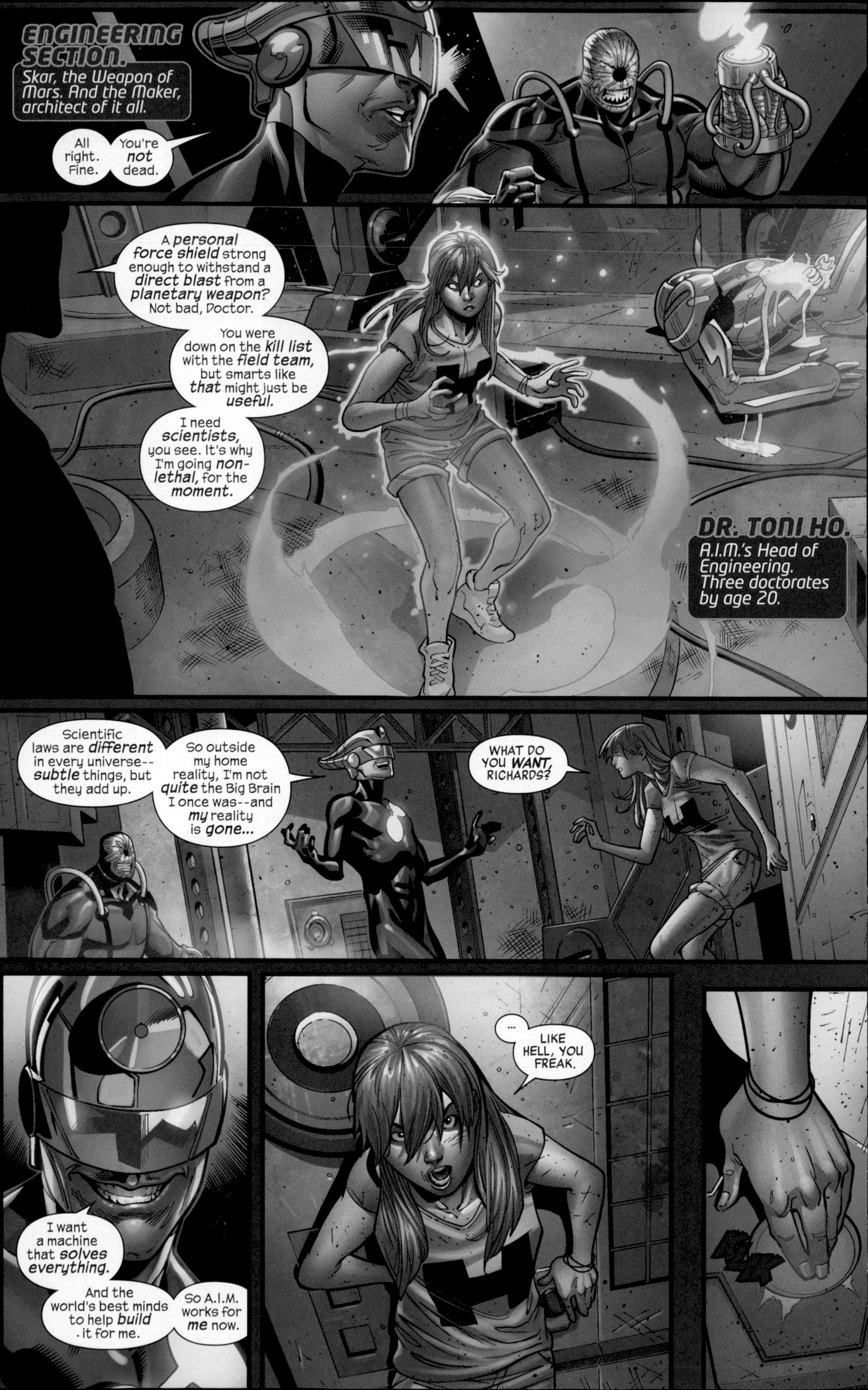
ENGINEERING SECTION.
Skar, the Weapon of Mars. And the Maker, architect of it all.
All right. Fine.
You're not dead.
A personal force shield strong enough to withstand a direct blast from a planetary weapon? Not bad, Doctor.
You were down on the kill list with the field team, but smarts like that might just be useful.
I need scientists, you see. It's why I'm going non-lethal, for the moment.
DR. TONI HO.
A.I.M.'s Head of Engineering. Three doctorates by age 20.
Scientific laws are different in every universe--subtle things, but they add up.
So outside my home reality, I'm not quite the Big Brain I once was--and my reality is gone...
WHAT DO YOU WANT, RICHARDS?
I want a machine that solves everything.
And the world's best minds to help build it for me.
So A.I.M. works for me now.
...
LIKE HELL, YOU FREAK.

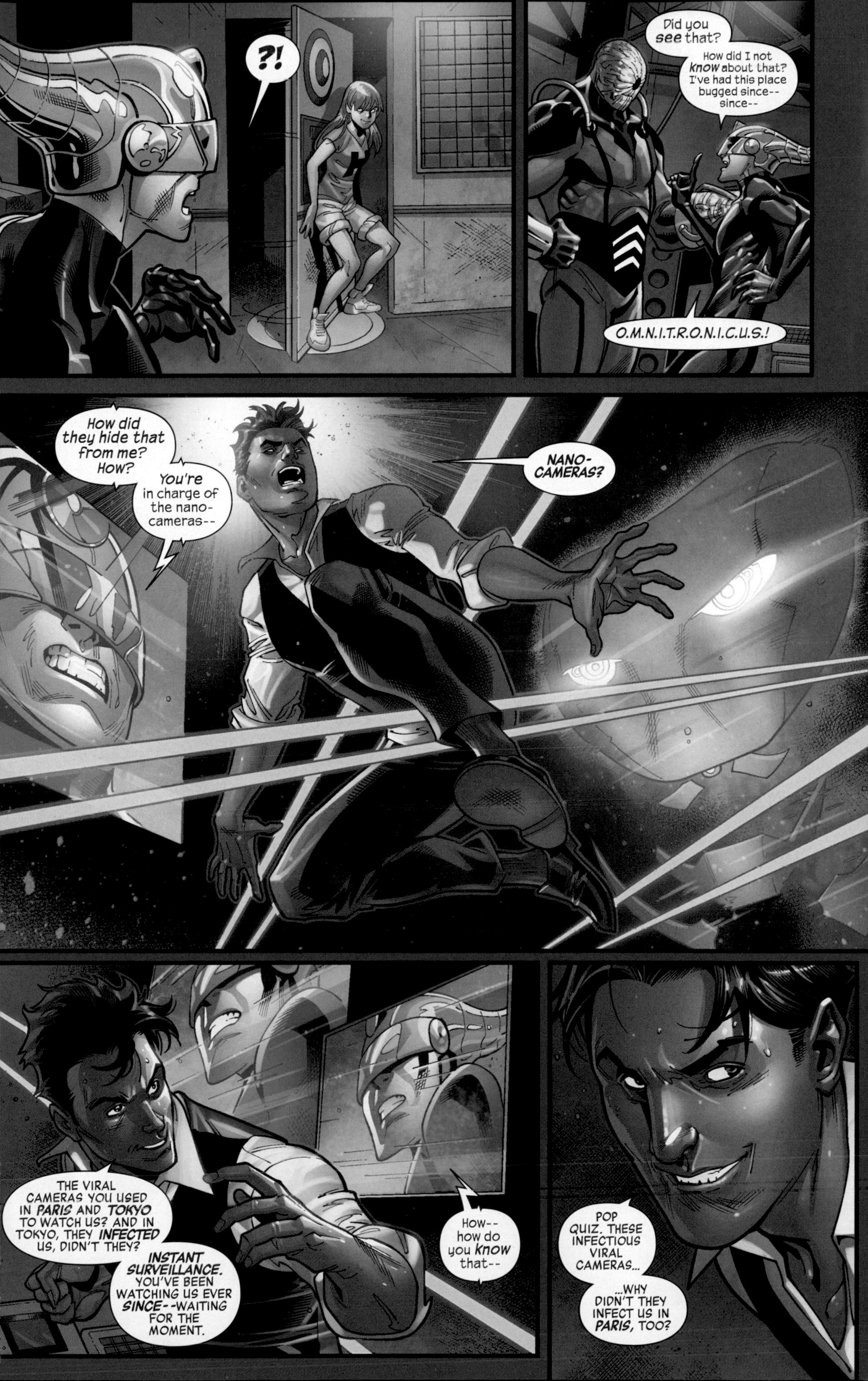
?!
Did you see that?
How did I not know about that? I've had this place bugged since-- since--
O.M.N.I.T.R.O.N.I.C.U.S.!
How did they hide that from me? How?
You're in charge of the nano-cameras--
NANO-CAMERAS?
THE VIRAL CAMERAS YOU USED IN PARIS AND TOKYO TO WATCH US? AND IN TOKYO, THEY INFECTED US, DIDN'T THEY?
INSTANT SURVEILLANCE. YOU'VE BEEN WATCHING US EVER SINCE--WAITING FOR THE MOMENT.
How-- how do you know that--
POP QUIZ. THESE INFECTIOUS VIRAL CAMERAS...
...WHY DIDN'T THEY INFECT US IN PARIS, TOO?

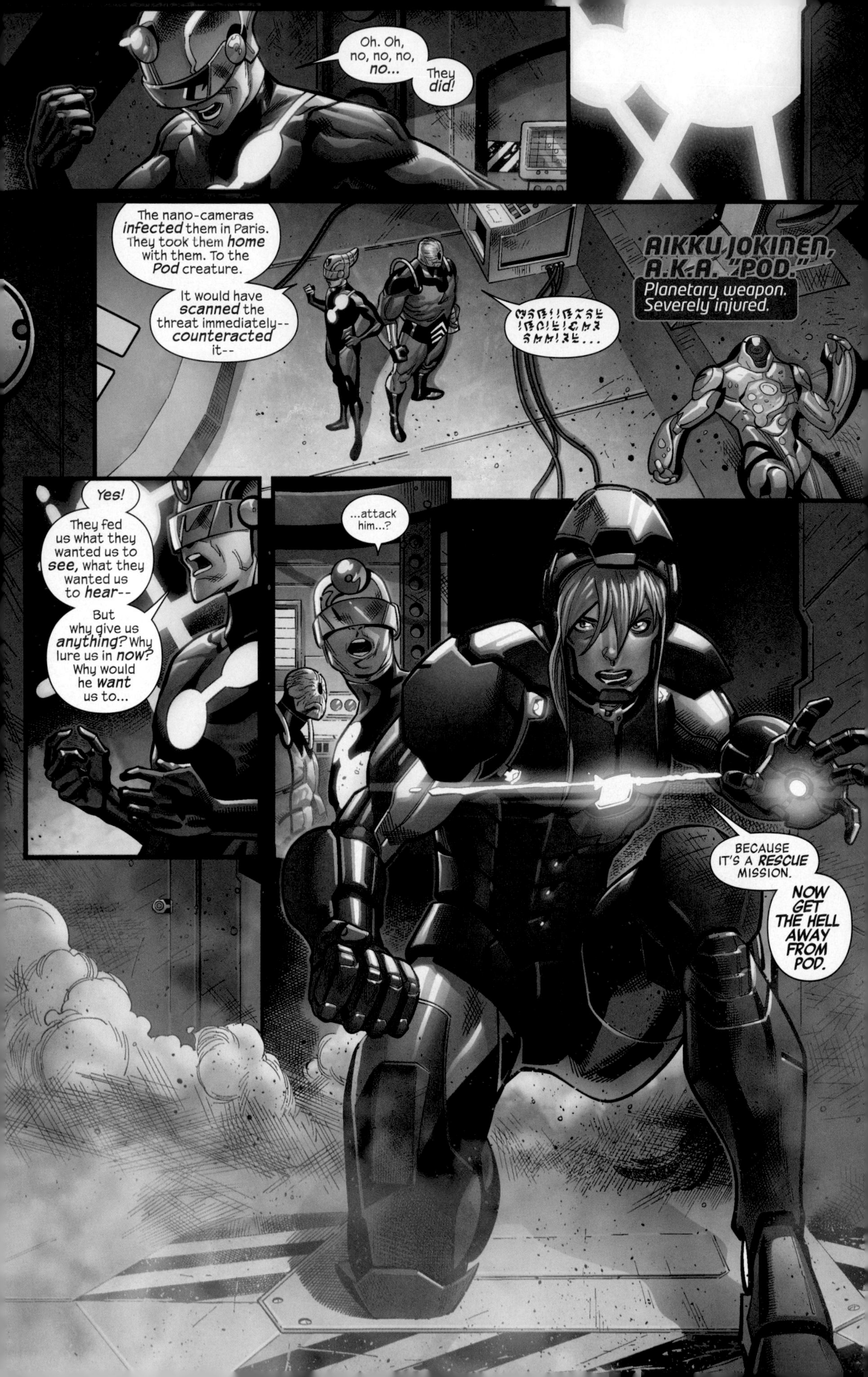
Oh. Oh, no, no, no, no...
They did!
The nano-cameras infected them in Paris. They took them home with them. To the Pod creature.
It would have scanned the threat immediately-- counteracted it--
AIKKU JOKINEN, A.K.A. "POD."
Planetary weapon. Severely injured.
Yes!
They fed us what they wanted us to see, what they wanted us to hear--
But why give us anything? Why lure us in now? Why would he want us to...
...attack him...?
BECAUSE IT'S A RESCUE MISSION.
NOW GET THE HELL AWAY FROM POD.

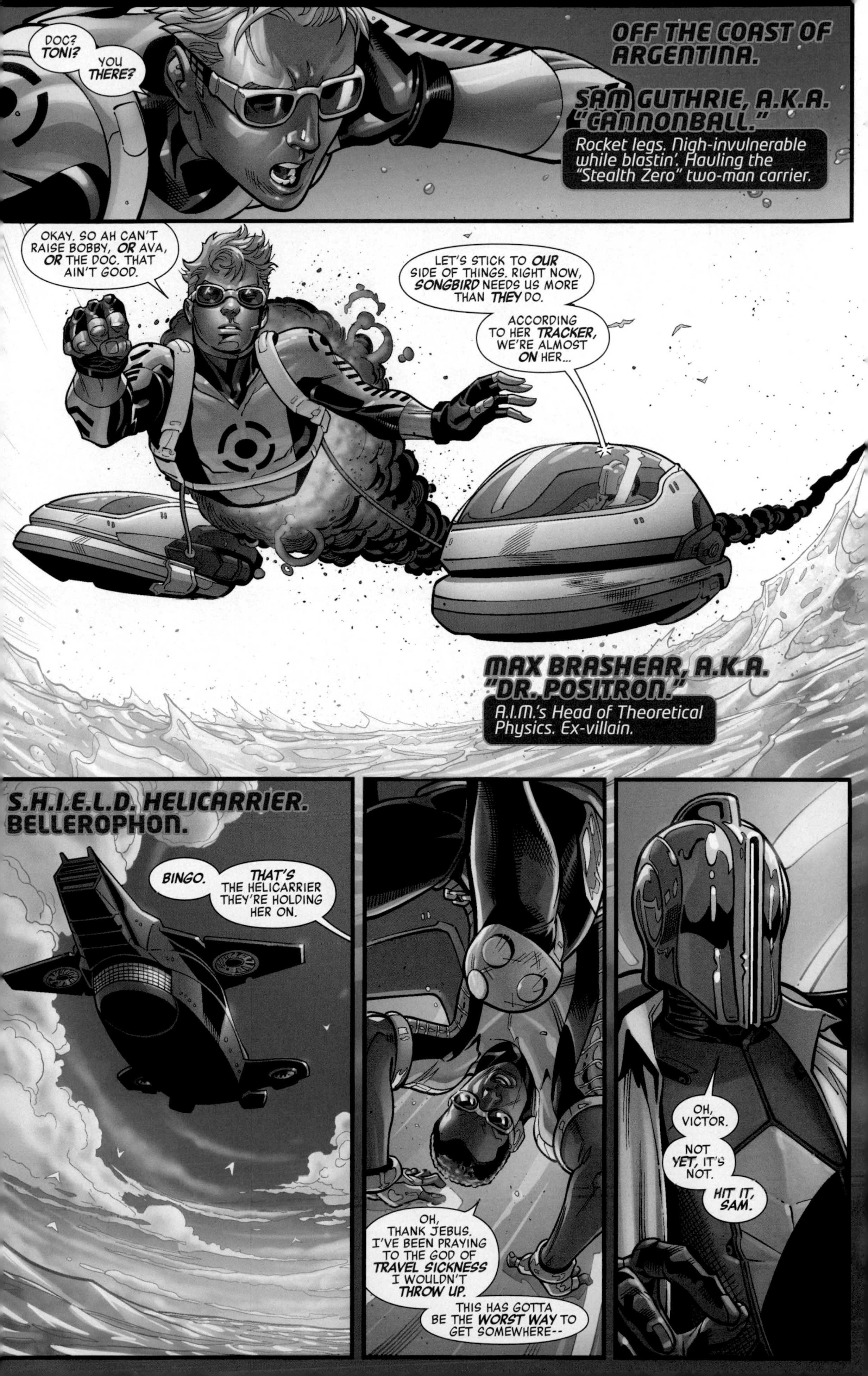

OFF THE COAST OF ARGENTINA.
DOC? TONI?
YOU THERE?
SAM GUTHRIE, A.K.A. "CANNONBALL."
Rocket legs. Nigh-invulnerable while blastin'. Hauling the "Stealth Zero" two-man carrier.
OKAY. SO AH CAN'T RAISE BOBBY, OR AVA, OR THE DOC. THAT AIN'T GOOD.
LET'S STICK TO OUR SIDE OF THINGS. RIGHT NOW, SONGBIRD NEEDS US MORE THAN THEY DO.
ACCORDING TO HER TRACKER, WE'RE ALMOST ON HER...
MAX BRASHEAR, A.K.A. "DR. POSITRON."
A.I.M.'s Head of Theoretical Physics. Ex-villain.
S.H.I.E.L.D. HELICARRIER. BELLEROPHON.
BINGO.
THAT'S THE HELICARRIER THEY'RE HOLDING HER ON.
OH, THANK JEBUS. I'VE BEEN PRAYING TO THE GOD OF TRAVEL SICKNESS I WOULDN'T THROW UP.
THIS HAS GOTTA BE THE WORST WAY TO GET SOMEWHERE--
OH, VICTOR.
NOT YET, IT'S NOT.
HIT IT, SAM.

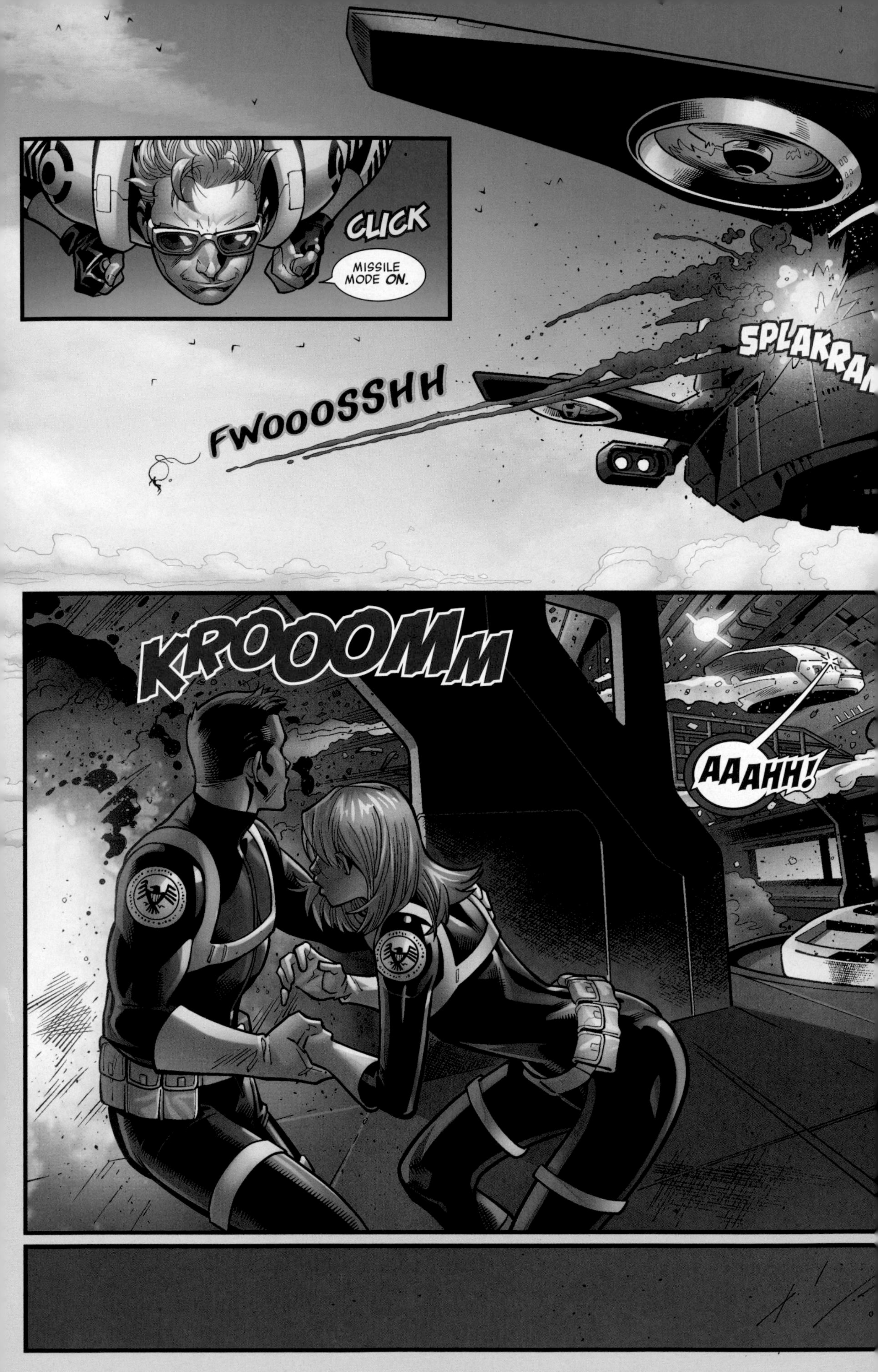
CLICK
MISSILE MODE ON.
FWOOOSSHH
SPLAKRAM
KROOOMM
AAAHH!

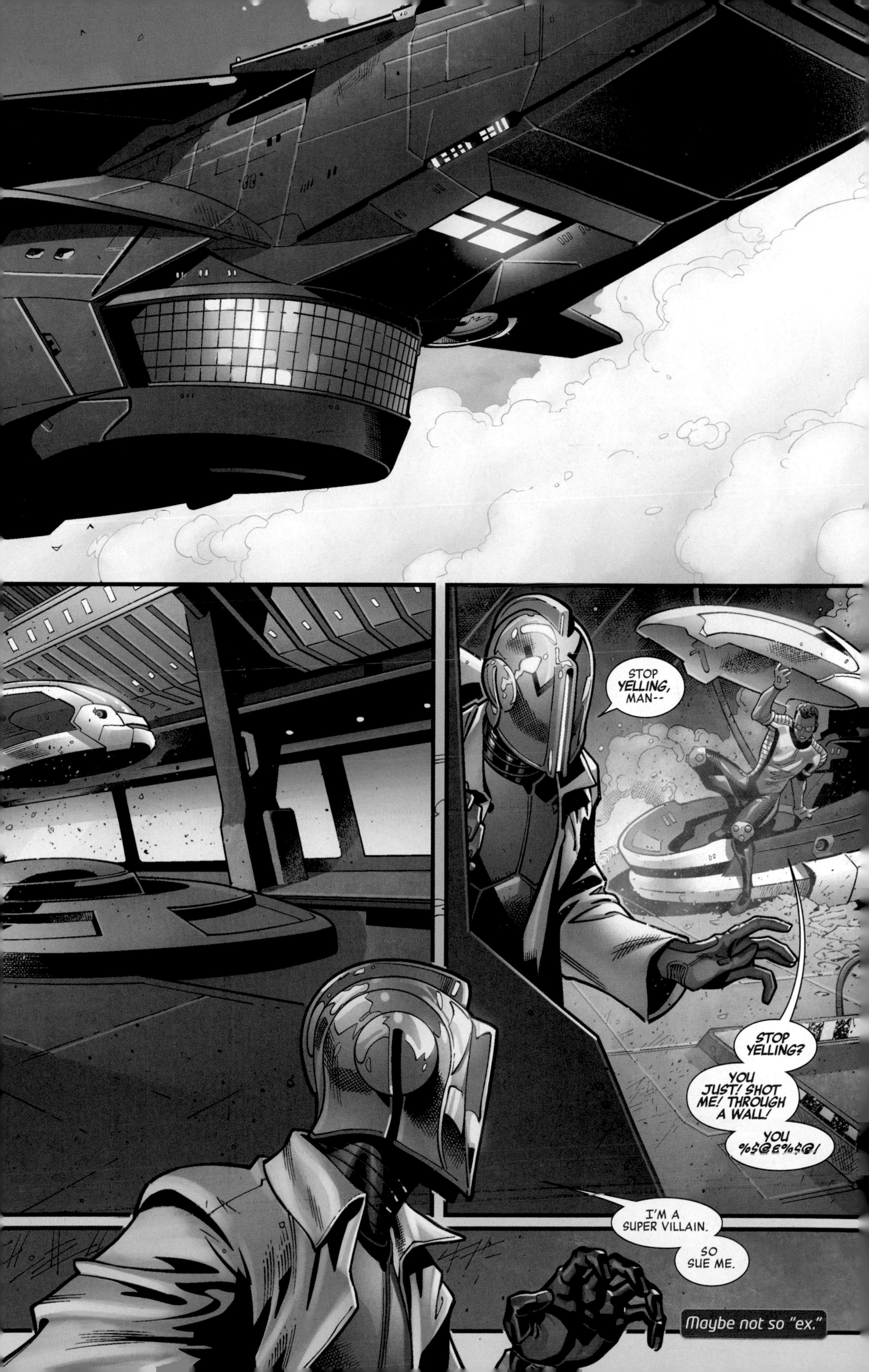

STOP YELLING, MAN--
STOP YELLING?
YOU JUST! SHOT ME! THROUGH A WALL!
YOU %$@&%$@!
I'M A SUPER VILLAIN.
SO SUE ME.
Maybe not so "ex."

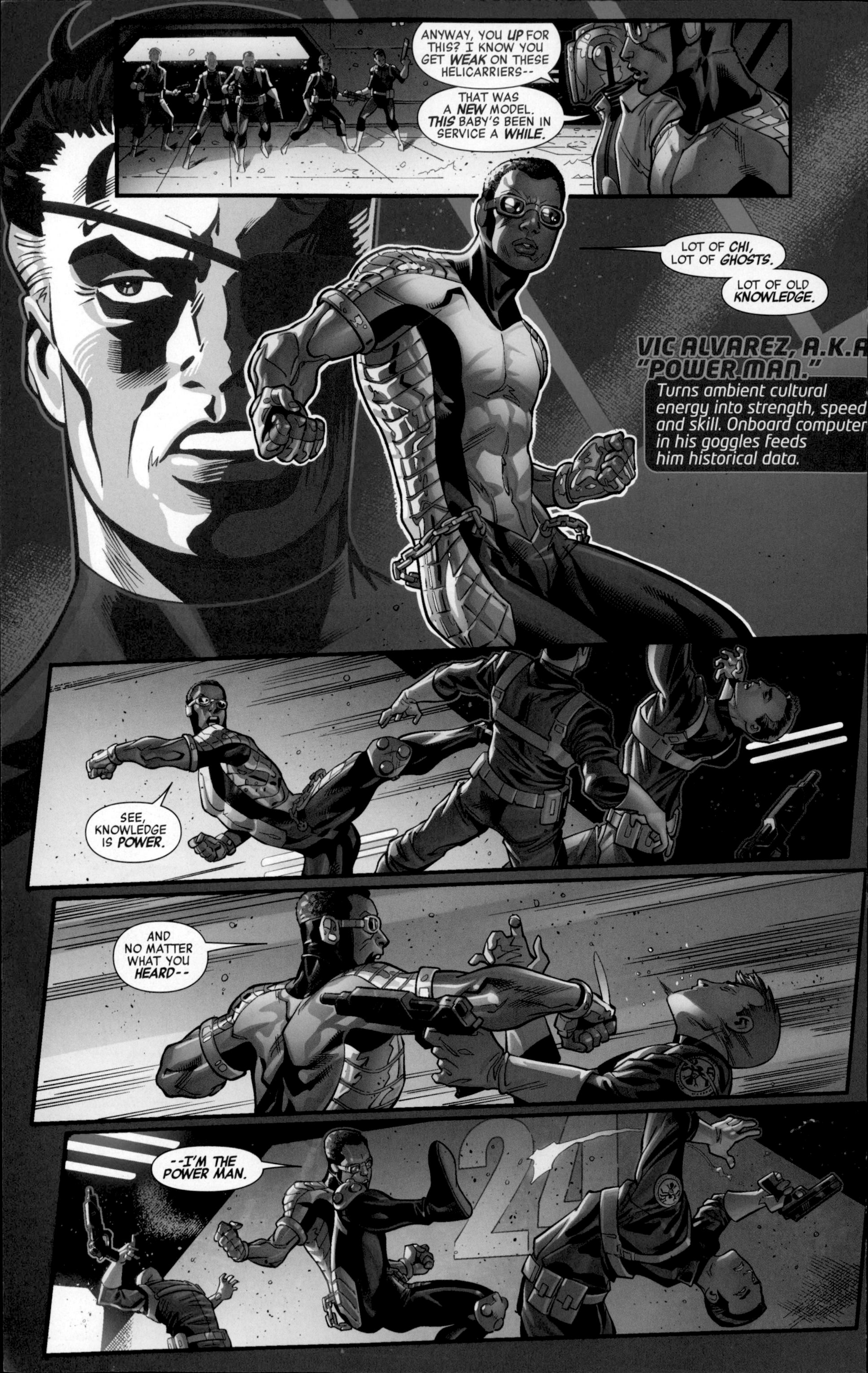
ANYWAY, YOU UP FOR THIS? I KNOW YOU GET WEAK ON THESE HELICARRIERS--
THAT WAS A NEW MODEL. THIS BABY'S BEEN IN SERVICE A WHILE.
LOT OF CHI, LOT OF GHOSTS.
LOT OF OLD KNOWLEDGE.
VIC ALVAREZ, A.K.A "POWER MAN."
Turns ambient cultural energy into strength, speed and skill. Onboard computer in his goggles feeds him historical data.
SEE, KNOWLEDGE IS POWER.
AND NO MATTER WHAT YOU HEARD--
--I'M THE POWER MAN.

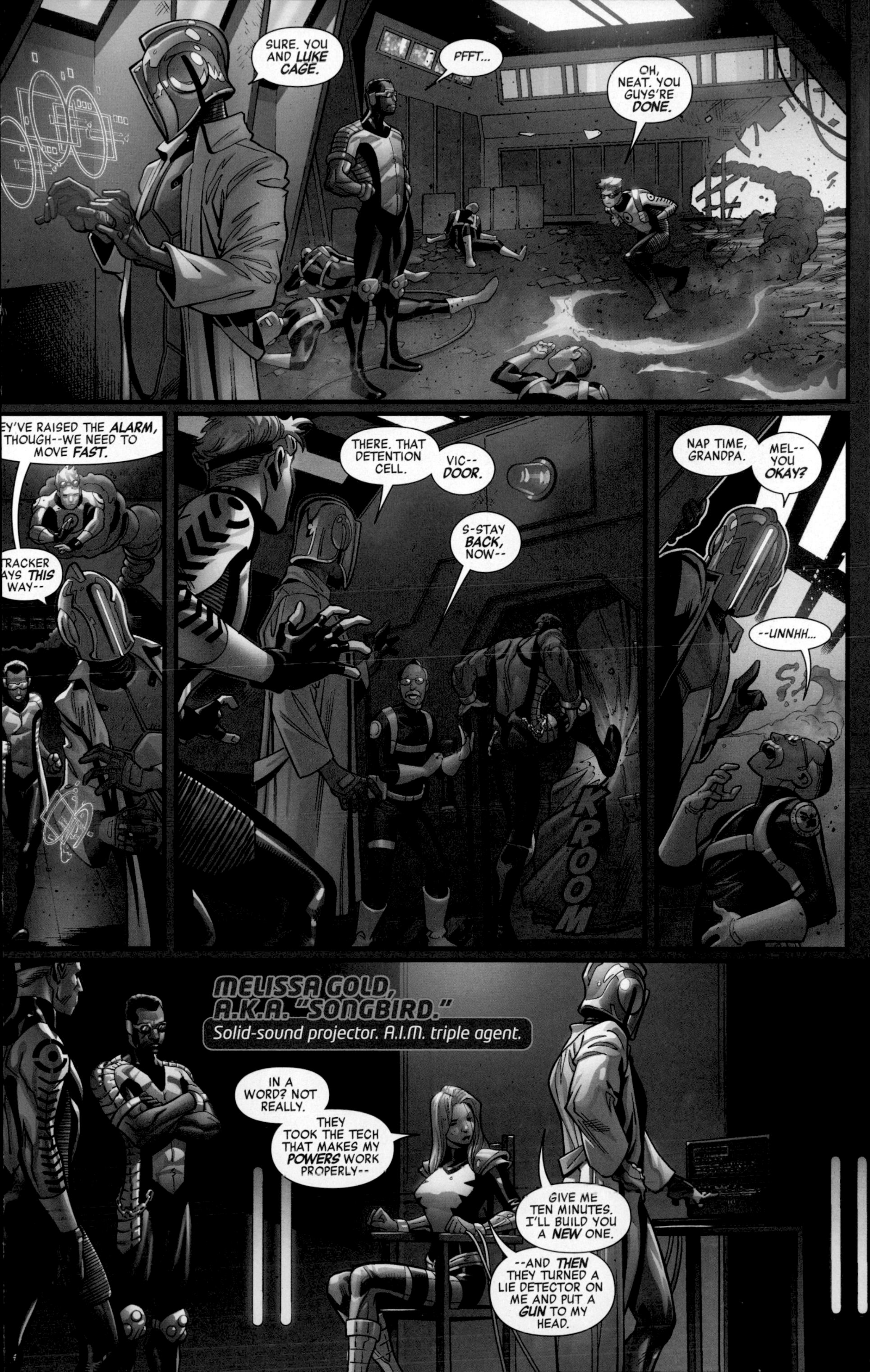
SURE. YOU AND LUKE CAGE.
PFFT...
OH, NEAT. YOU GUYS'RE DONE.
EY'VE RAISED THE ALARM, THOUGH--WE NEED TO MOVE FAST.
TRACKER AYS THIS WAY--
THERE. THAT DETENTION CELL.
VIC-- DOOR.
S-STAY BACK, NOW--
KROOM
NAP TIME, GRANDPA.
MEL-- YOU OKAY?
--UNNHH...
MELISSA GOLD, A.K.A. "SONGBIRD."
Solid-sound projector. A.I.M. triple agent.
IN A WORD? NOT REALLY.
THEY TOOK THE TECH THAT MAKES MY POWERS WORK PROPERLY--
GIVE ME TEN MINUTES. I'LL BUILD YOU A NEW ONE.
--AND THEN THEY TURNED A LIE DETECTOR ON ME AND PUT A GUN TO MY HEAD.

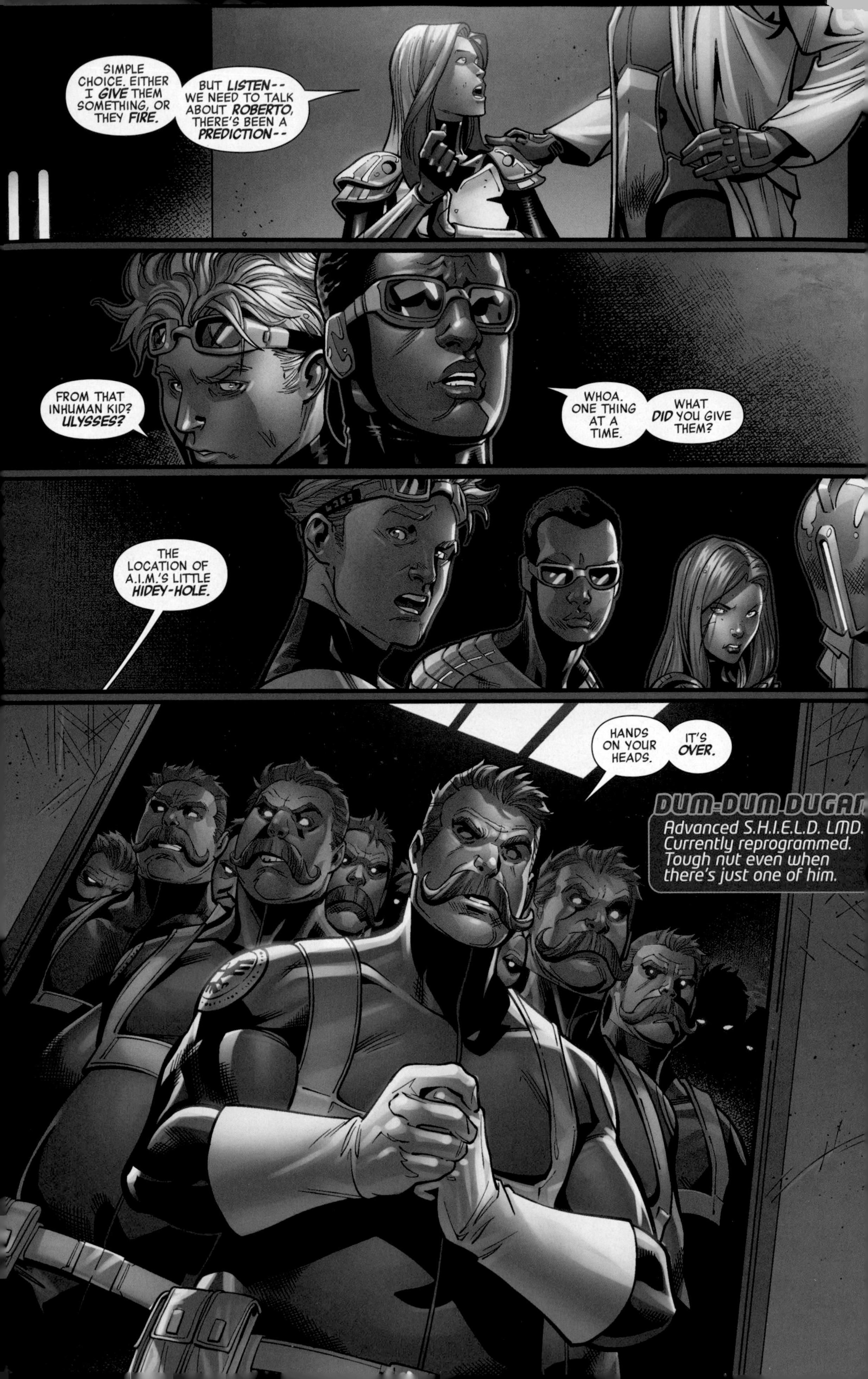
SIMPLE CHOICE. EITHER I GIVE THEM SOMETHING, OR THEY FIRE.
BUT LISTEN-- WE NEED TO TALK ABOUT ROBERTO, THERE'S BEEN A PREDICTION--
FROM THAT INHUMAN KID? ULYSSES?
WHOA. ONE THING AT A TIME.
WHAT DID YOU GIVE THEM?
THE LOCATION OF A.I.M.'S LITTLE HIDEY-HOLE.
HANDS ON YOUR HEADS.
IT'S OVER.
DUM-DUM DUGAN
Advanced S.H.I.E.L.D. LMD. Currently reprogrammed. Tough nut even when there's just one of him.

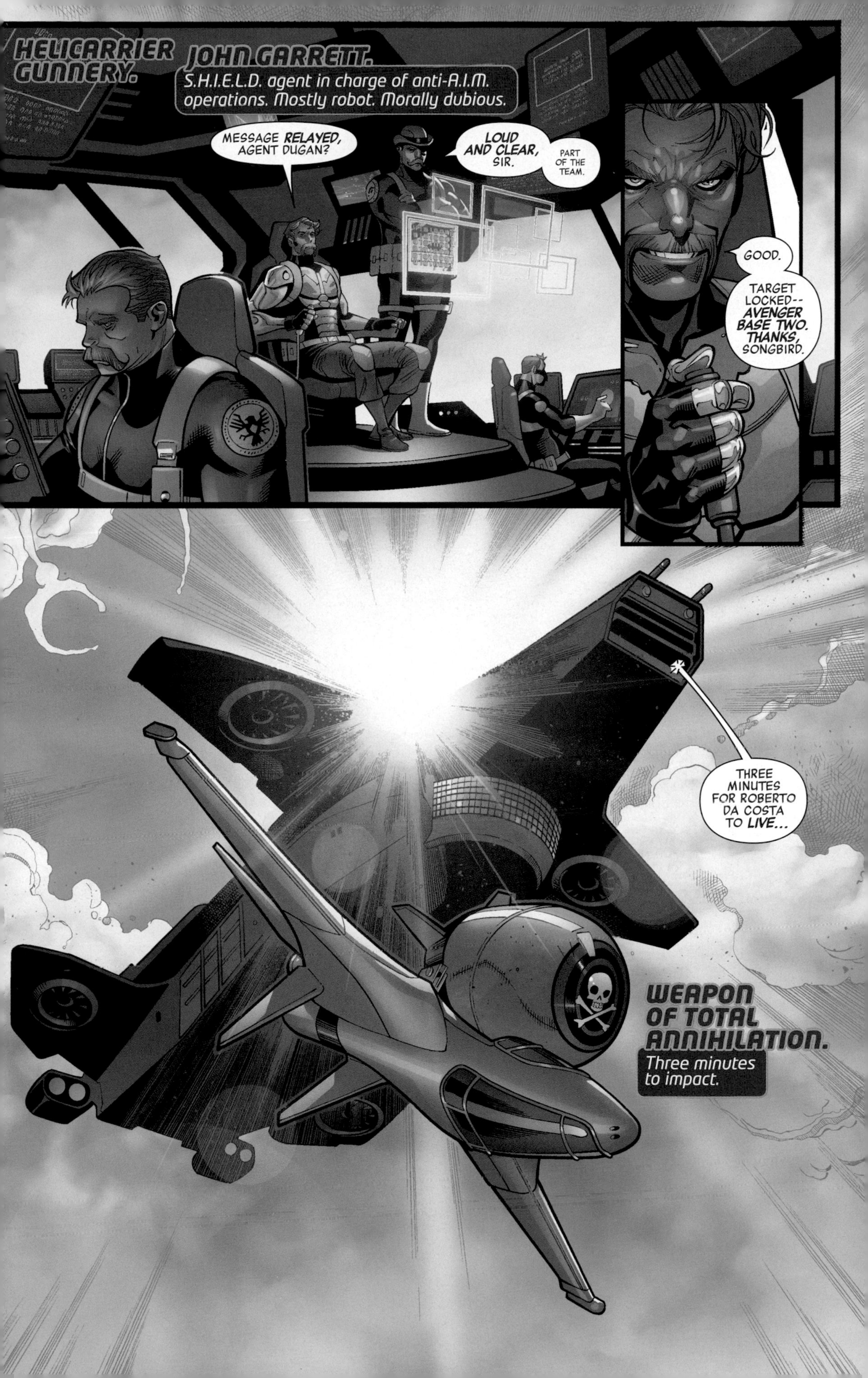
HELICARRIER GUNNERY.
JOHN GARRETT.
S.H.I.E.L.D. agent in charge of anti-A.I.M. operations. Mostly robot. Morally dubious.
MESSAGE RELAYED, AGENT DUGAN?
LOUD AND CLEAR, SIR.
PART OF THE TEAM.
GOOD.
TARGET LOCKED-- AVENGER BASE TWO. THANKS, SONGBIRD.
THREE MINUTES FOR ROBERTO DA COSTA TO LIVE...
WEAPON OF TOTAL ANNIHILATION.
Three minutes to impact.

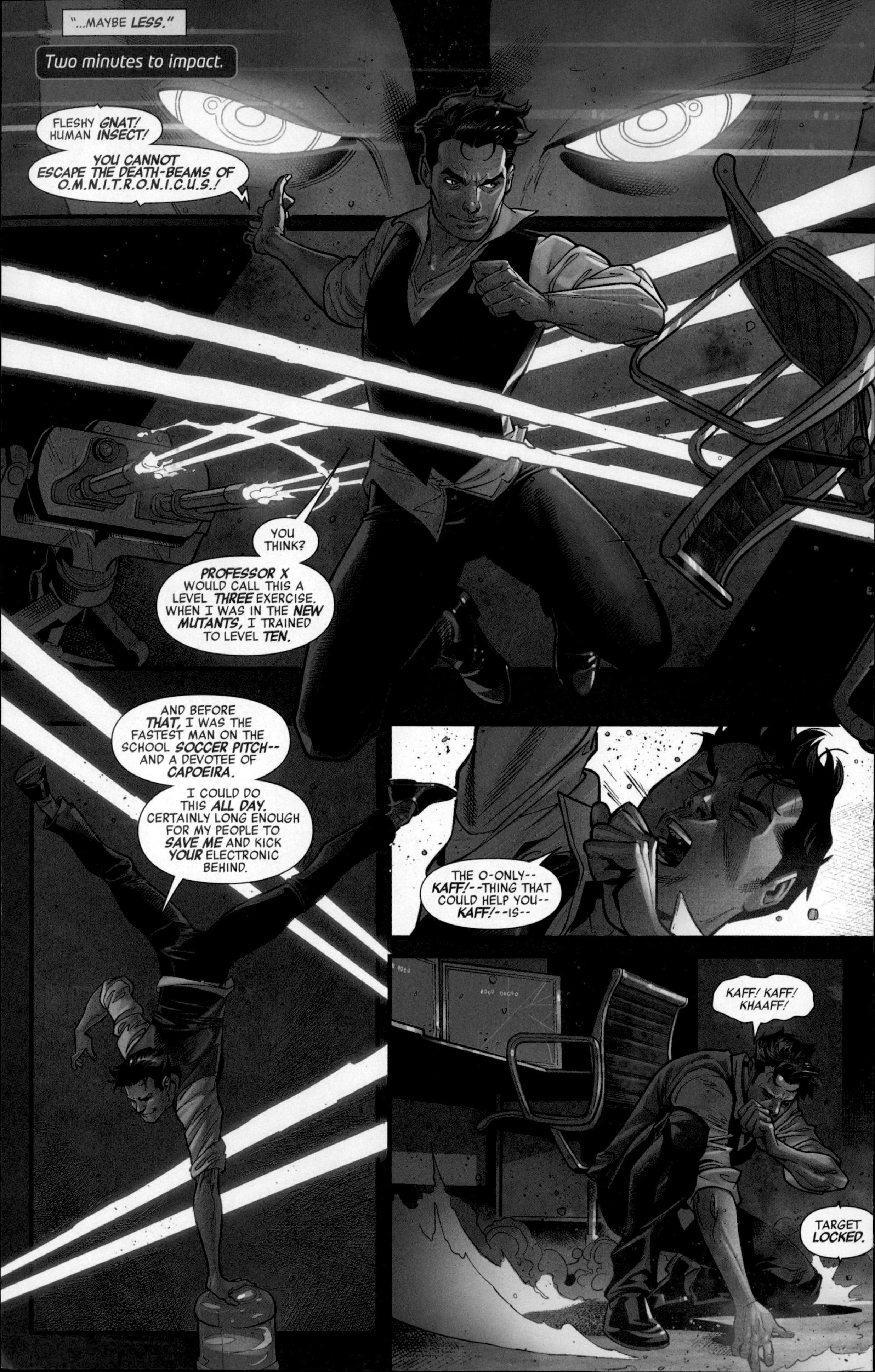
"...MAYBE LESS."
Two minutes to impact.
FLESHY GNAT! HUMAN INSECT!
YOU CANNOT ESCAPE THE DEATH-BEAMS OF O.M.N.I.T.R.O.N.I.C.U.S.!
YOU THINK?
PROFESSOR X WOULD CALL THIS A LEVEL THREE EXERCISE. WHEN I WAS IN THE NEW MUTANTS, I TRAINED TO LEVEL TEN.
AND BEFORE THAT, I WAS THE FASTEST MAN ON THE SCHOOL SOCCER PITCH-- AND A DEVOTEE OF CAPOEIRA.
I COULD DO THIS ALL DAY. CERTAINLY LONG ENOUGH FOR MY PEOPLE TO SAVE ME AND KICK YOUR ELECTRONIC BEHIND.
THE O-ONLY-- KAFF!--THING THAT COULD HELP YOU-- KAFF!--IS--
KAFF! KAFF! KHAAFF!
TARGET LOCKED.

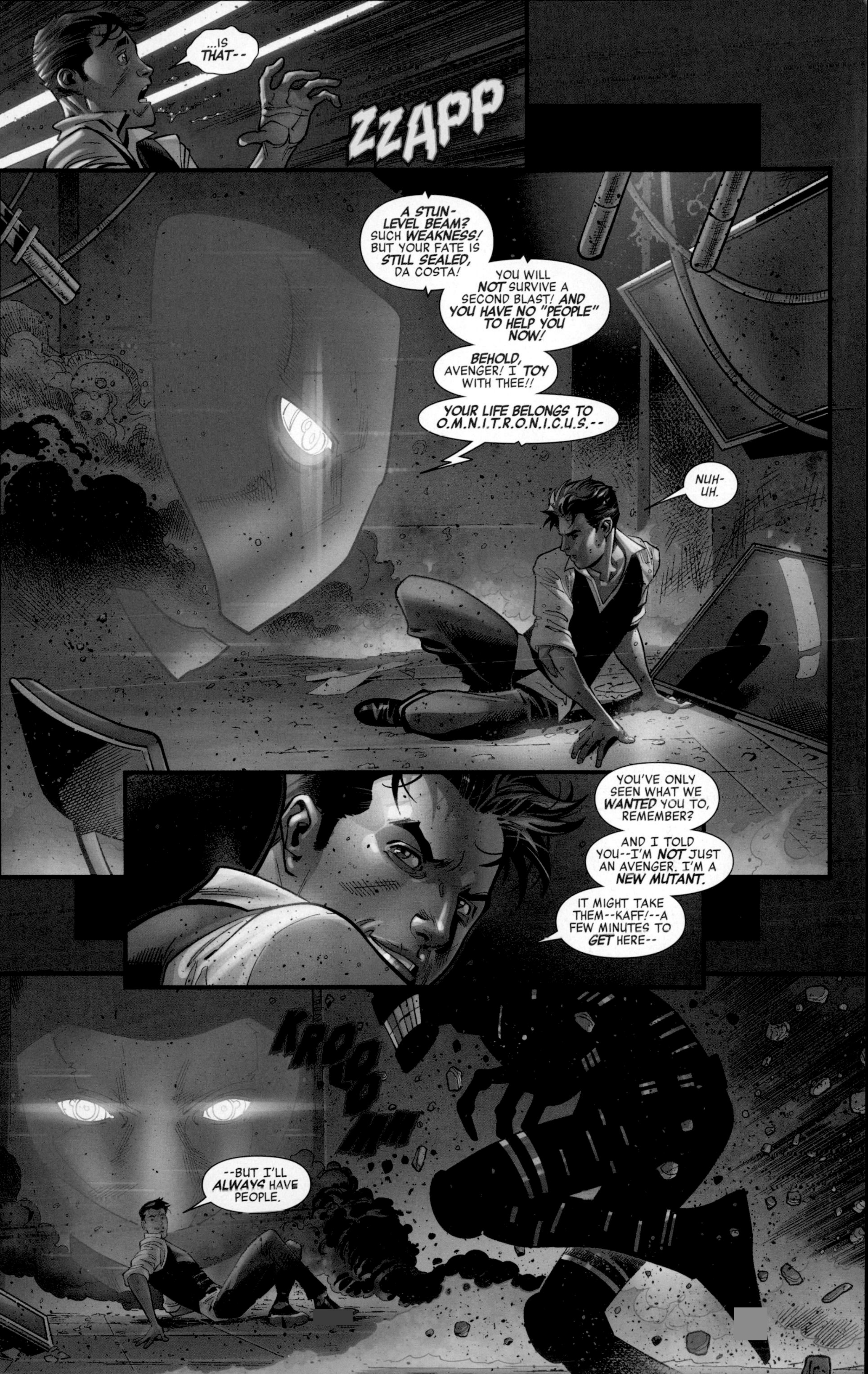

...IS THAT--
ZZAPP
A STUN-LEVEL BEAM? SUCH WEAKNESS! BUT YOUR FATE IS STILL SEALED, DA COSTA!
YOU WILL NOT SURVIVE A SECOND BLAST! AND YOU HAVE NO "PEOPLE" TO HELP YOU NOW!
BEHOLD, AVENGER! I TOY WITH THEE!!
YOUR LIFE BELONGS TO O.M.N.I.T.R.O.N.I.C.U.S.--
NUH-UH.
YOU'VE ONLY SEEN WHAT WE WANTED YOU TO, REMEMBER?
AND I TOLD YOU--I'M NOT JUST AN AVENGER. I'M A NEW MUTANT.
IT MIGHT TAKE THEM--KAFF!--A FEW MINUTES TO GET HERE--
KROOOMM
--BUT I'LL ALWAYS HAVE PEOPLE.

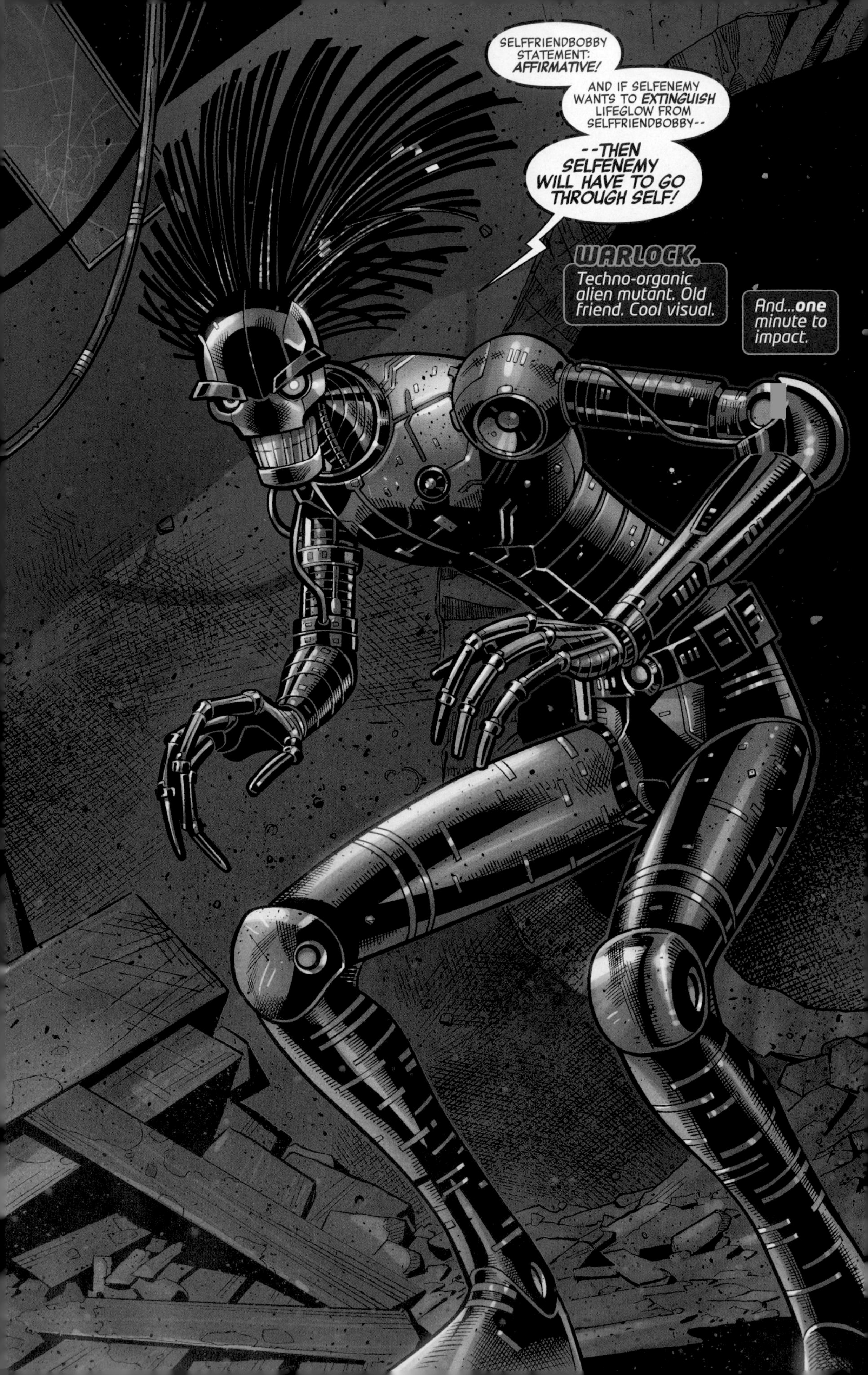
SELFFRIENDBOBBY STATEMENT: AFFIRMATIVE!
AND IF SELFENEMY WANTS TO EXTINGUISH LIFEGLOW FROM SELFFRIENDBOBBY--
--THEN SELFENEMY WILL HAVE TO GO THROUGH SELF!
WARLOCK.
Techno-organic alien mutant. Old friend. Cool visual.
And...one minute to impact.

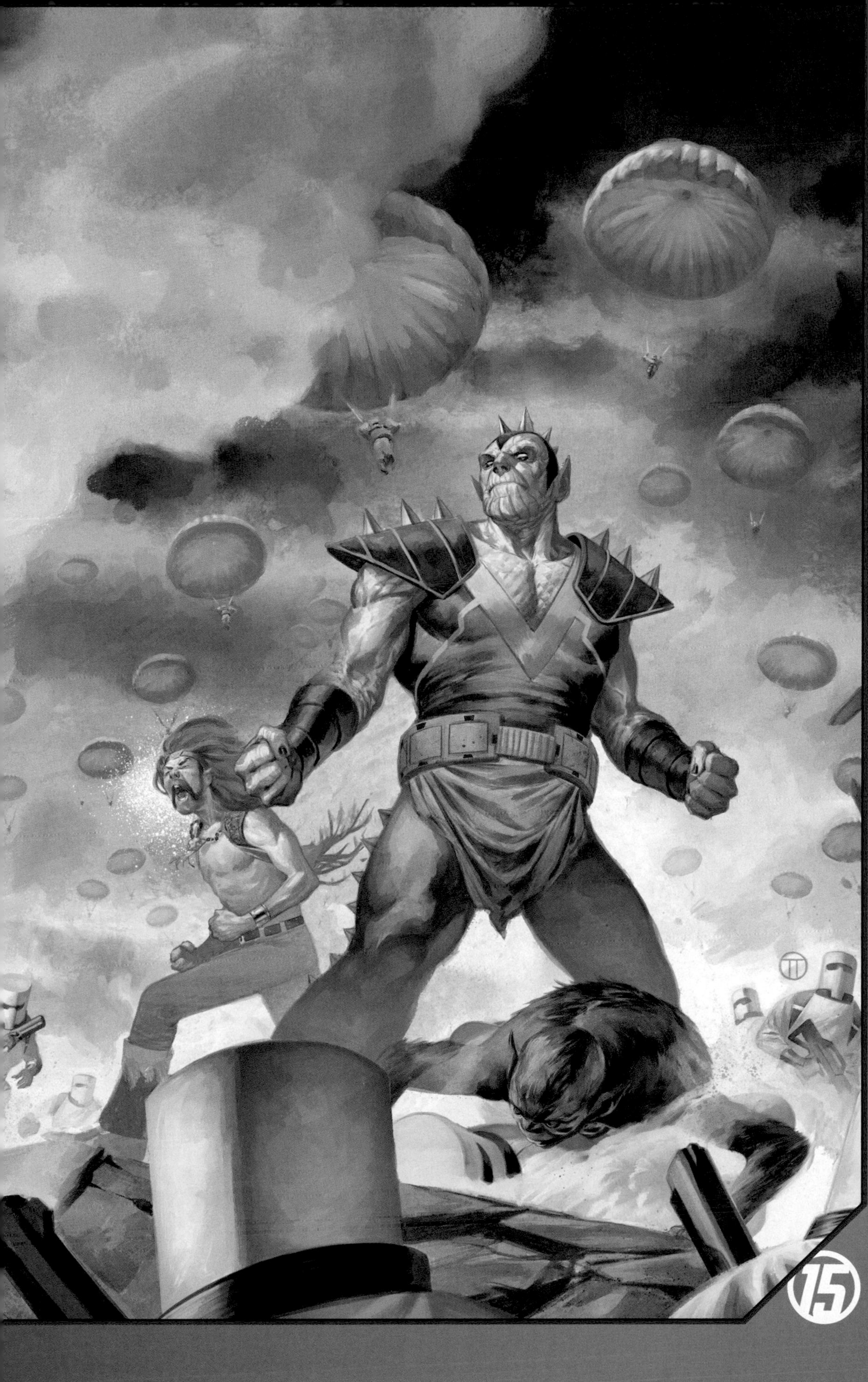
15

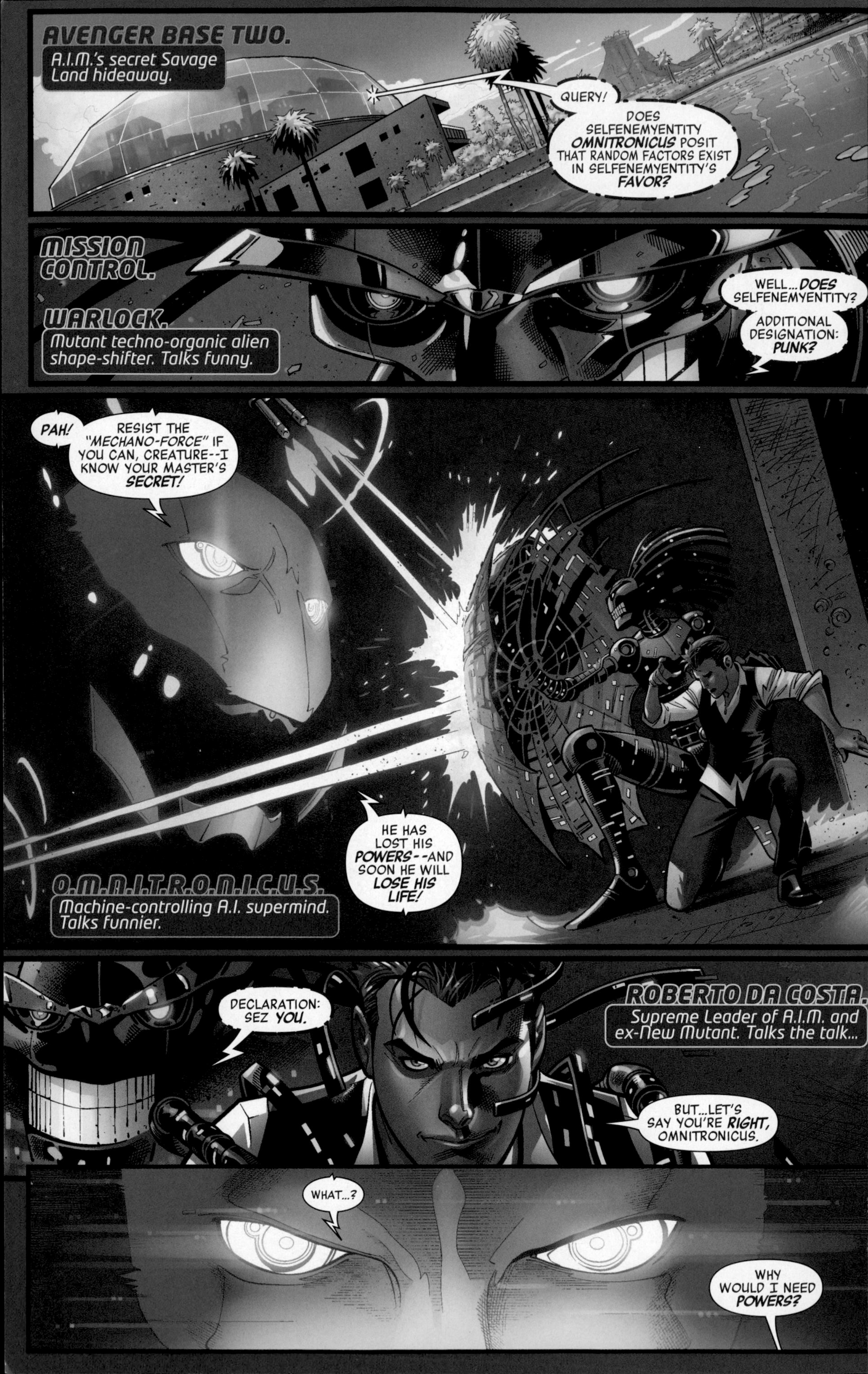

AVENGER BASE TWO.
A.I.M.'s secret Savage Land hideaway.
QUERY!
DOES SELFENEMYENTITY OMNITRONICUS POSIT THAT RANDOM FACTORS EXIST IN SELFENEMYENTITY'S FAVOR?
MISSION CONTROL.
WARLOCK.
Mutant techno-organic alien shape-shifter. Talks funny.
WELL...DOES SELFENEMYENTITY?
ADDITIONAL DESIGNATION: PUNK?
PAH!
RESIST THE "MECHANO-FORCE" IF YOU CAN, CREATURE--I KNOW YOUR MASTER'S SECRET!
HE HAS LOST HIS POWERS--AND SOON HE WILL LOSE HIS LIFE!
O.M.N.I.T.R.O.N.I.C.U.S.
Machine-controlling A.I. supermind. Talks funnier.
DECLARATION: SEZ YOU.
ROBERTO DA COSTA.
Supreme Leader of A.I.M. and ex-New Mutant. Talks the talk...
BUT...LET'S SAY YOU'RE RIGHT, OMNITRONICUS.
WHAT...?
WHY WOULD I NEED POWERS?

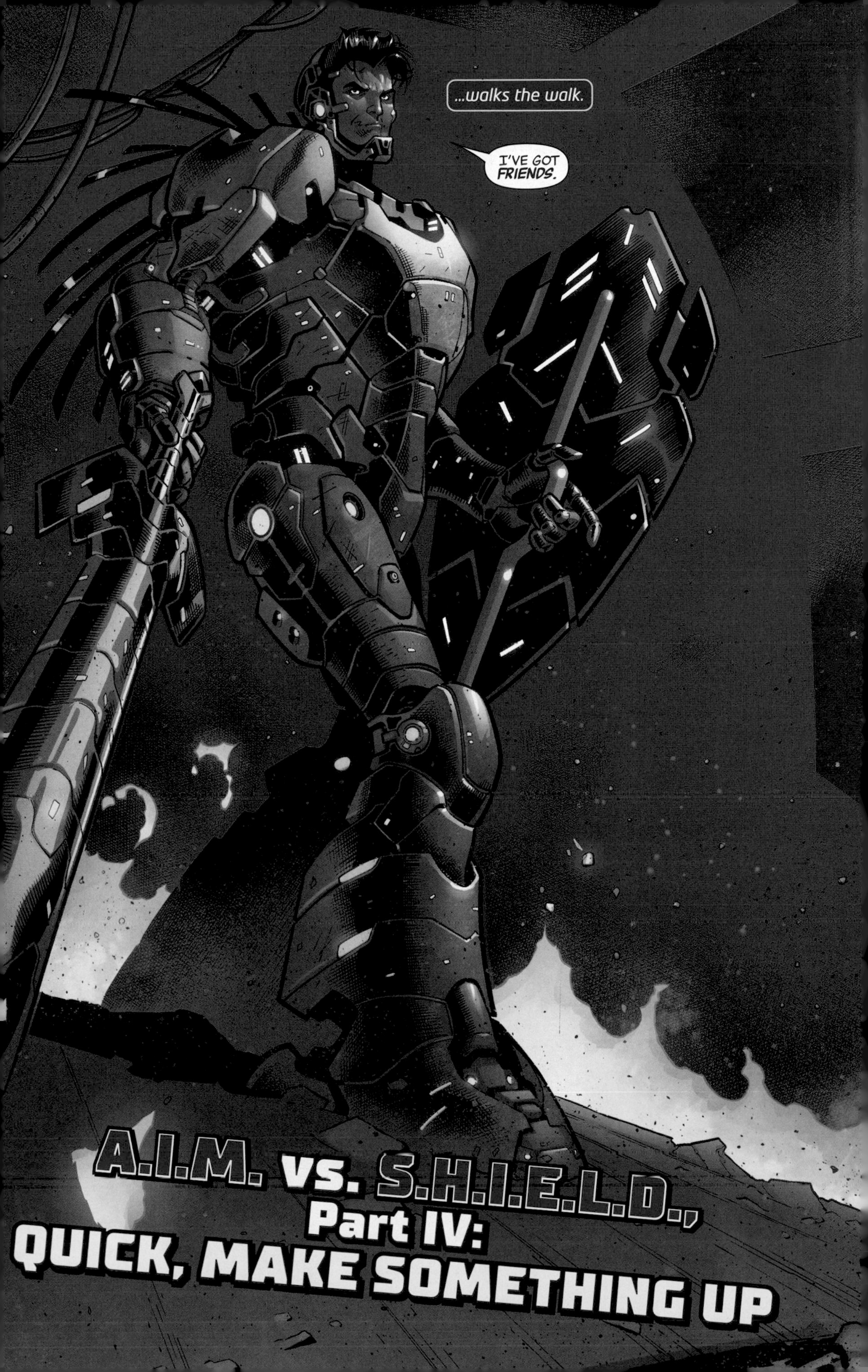
...walks the walk.
I'VE GOT FRIENDS.
A.I.M. vs. S.H.I.E.L.D., Part IV:
QUICK, MAKE SOMETHING UP

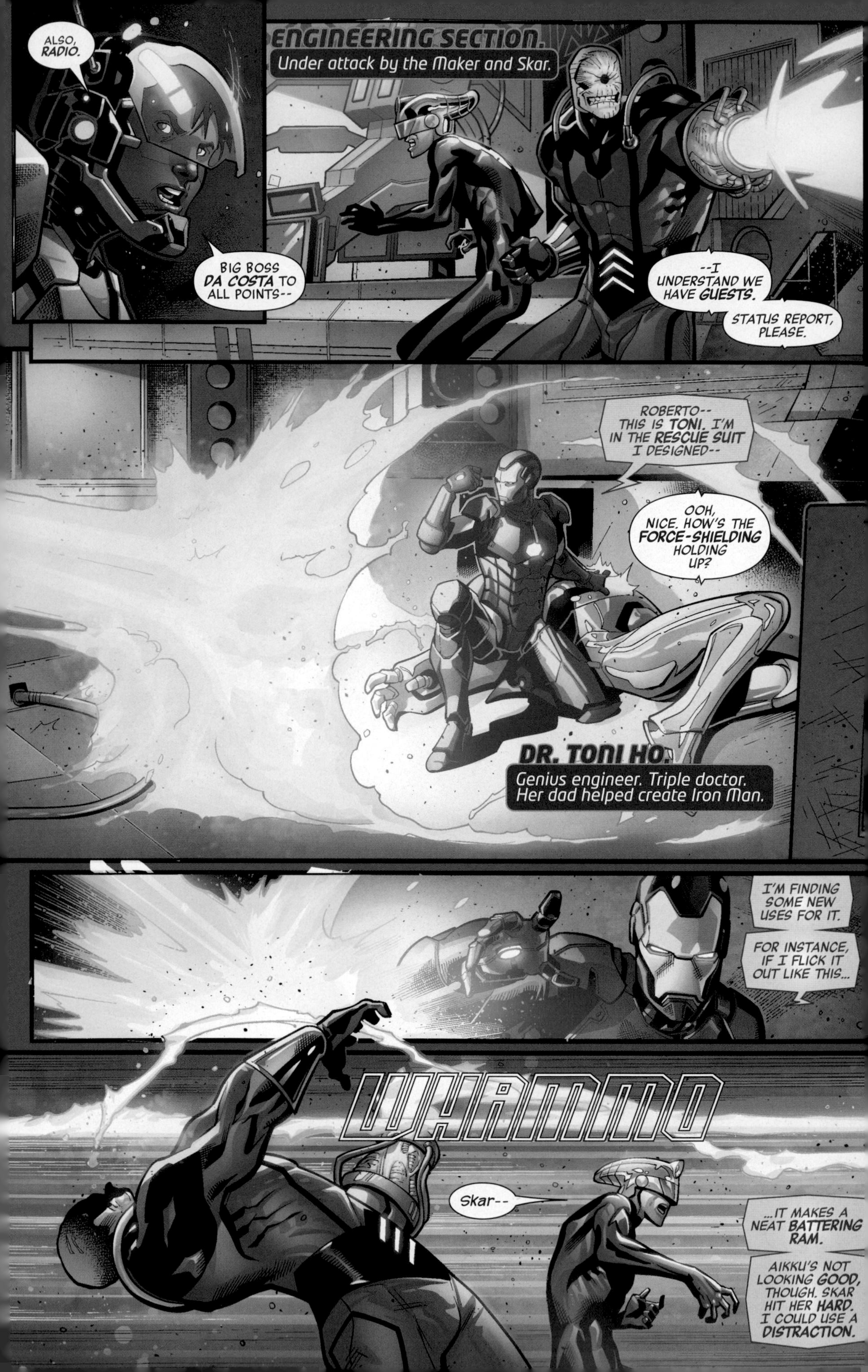
ALSO, RADIO.
ENGINEERING SECTION.
Under attack by the Maker and Skar.
BIG BOSS DA COSTA TO ALL POINTS--
--I UNDERSTAND WE HAVE GUESTS.
STATUS REPORT, PLEASE.
ROBERTO-- THIS IS TONI. I'M IN THE RESCUE SUIT I DESIGNED--
OOH, NICE. HOW'S THE FORCE-SHIELDING HOLDING UP?
DR. TONI HO.
Genius engineer. Triple doctor. Her dad helped create Iron Man.
I'M FINDING SOME NEW USES FOR IT.
FOR INSTANCE, IF I FLICK IT OUT LIKE THIS...
WHAMMO
Skar--
...IT MAKES A NEAT BATTERING RAM.
AIKKU'S NOT LOOKING GOOD, THOUGH. SKAR HIT HER HARD. I COULD USE A DISTRACTION.

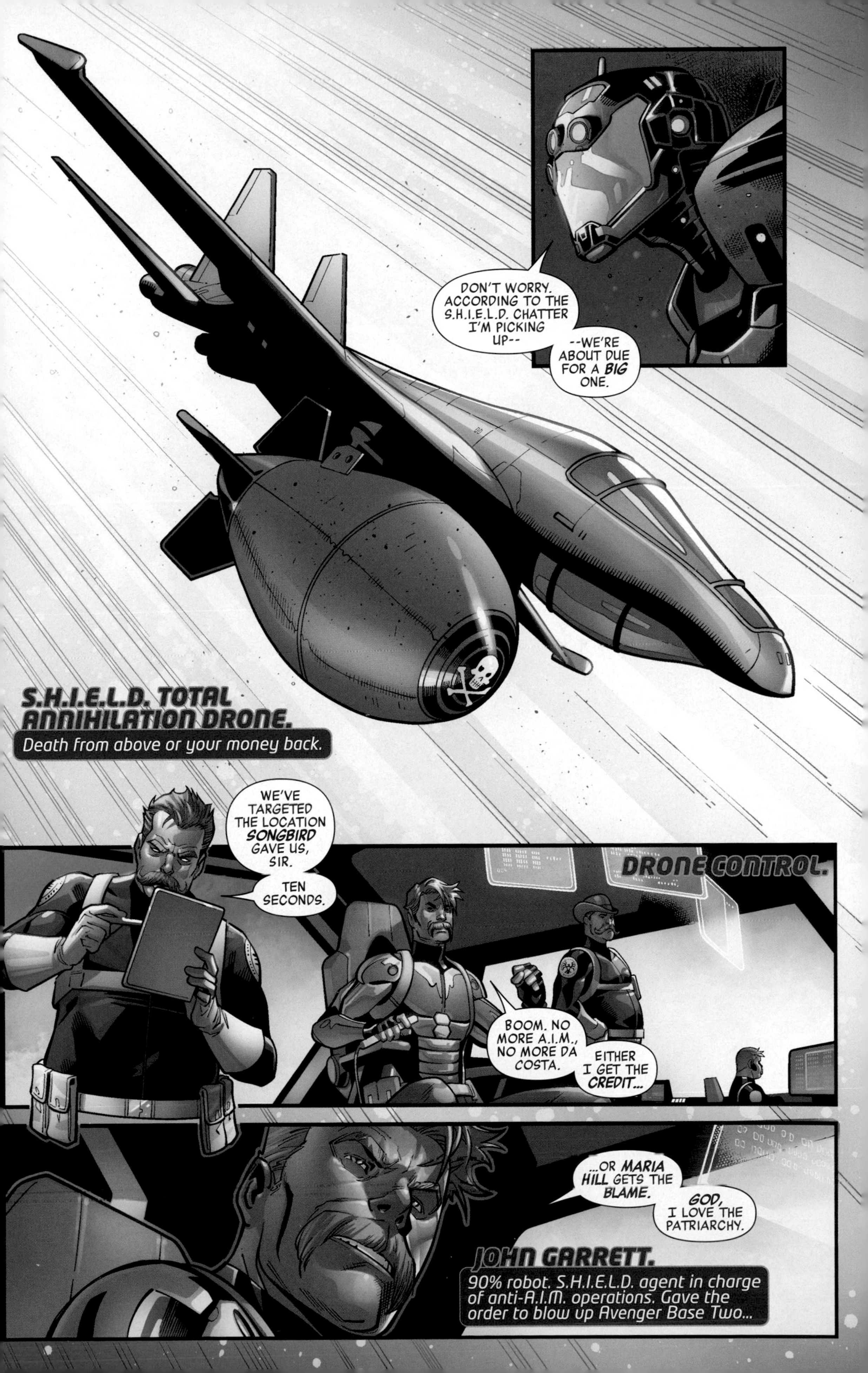
DON'T WORRY. ACCORDING TO THE S.H.I.E.L.D. CHATTER I'M PICKING UP--
--WE'RE ABOUT DUE FOR A BIG ONE.
S.H.I.E.L.D. TOTAL ANNIHILATION DRONE.
Death from above or your money back.
WE'VE TARGETED THE LOCATION SONGBIRD GAVE US, SIR.
TEN SECONDS.
DRONE CONTROL.
BOOM. NO MORE A.I.M., NO MORE DA COSTA.
EITHER I GET THE CREDIT...
...OR MARIA HILL GETS THE BLAME.
GOD, I LOVE THE PATRIARCHY.
JOHN GARRETT.
90% robot. S.H.I.E.L.D. agent in charge of anti-A.I.M. operations. Gave the order to blow up Avenger Base Two...

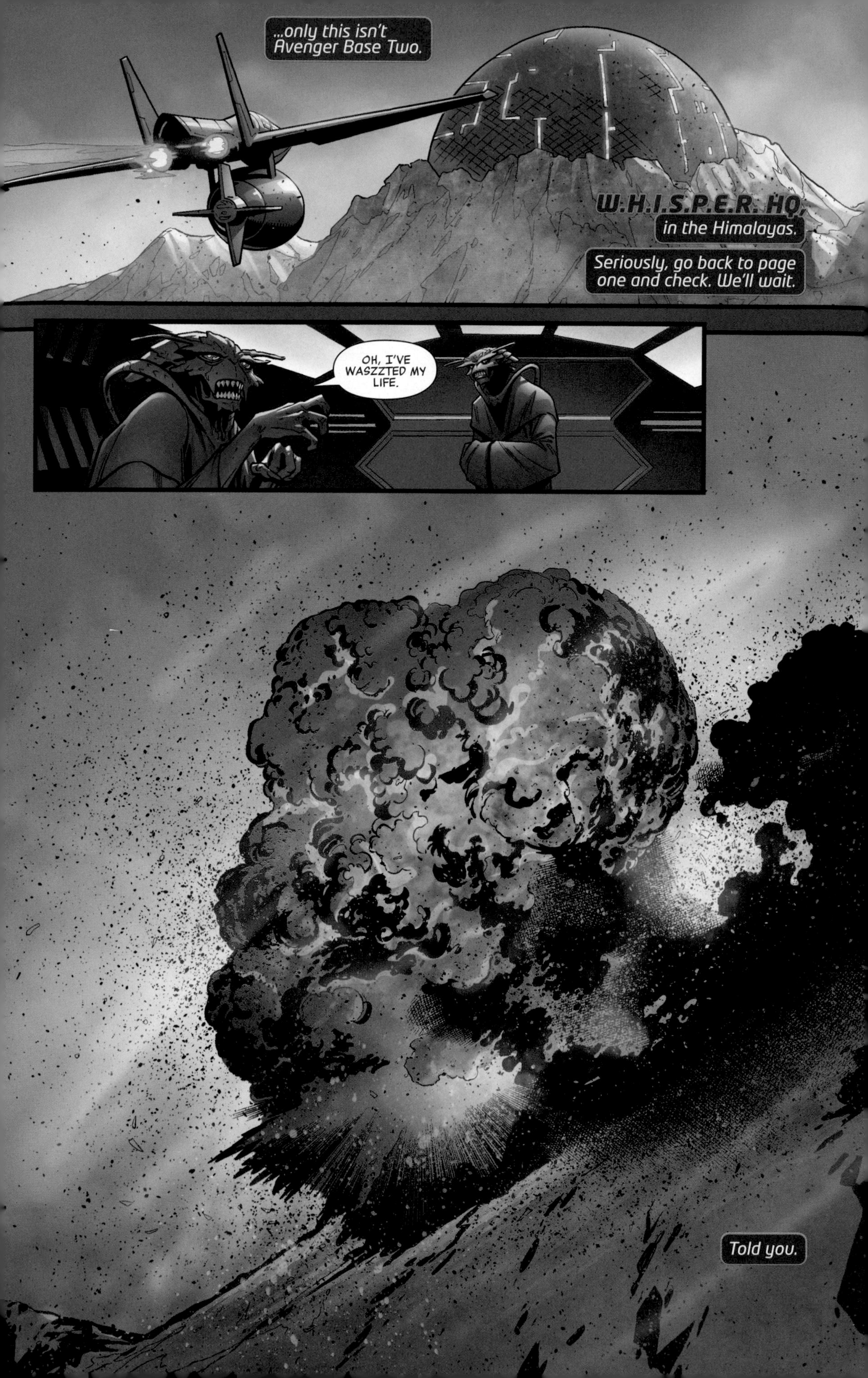
...only this isn't Avenger Base Two.
W.H.I.S.P.E.R. HQ,
in the Himalayas.
Seriously, go back to page one and check. We'll wait.
OH, I'VE WASZZTED MY LIFE.
Told you.

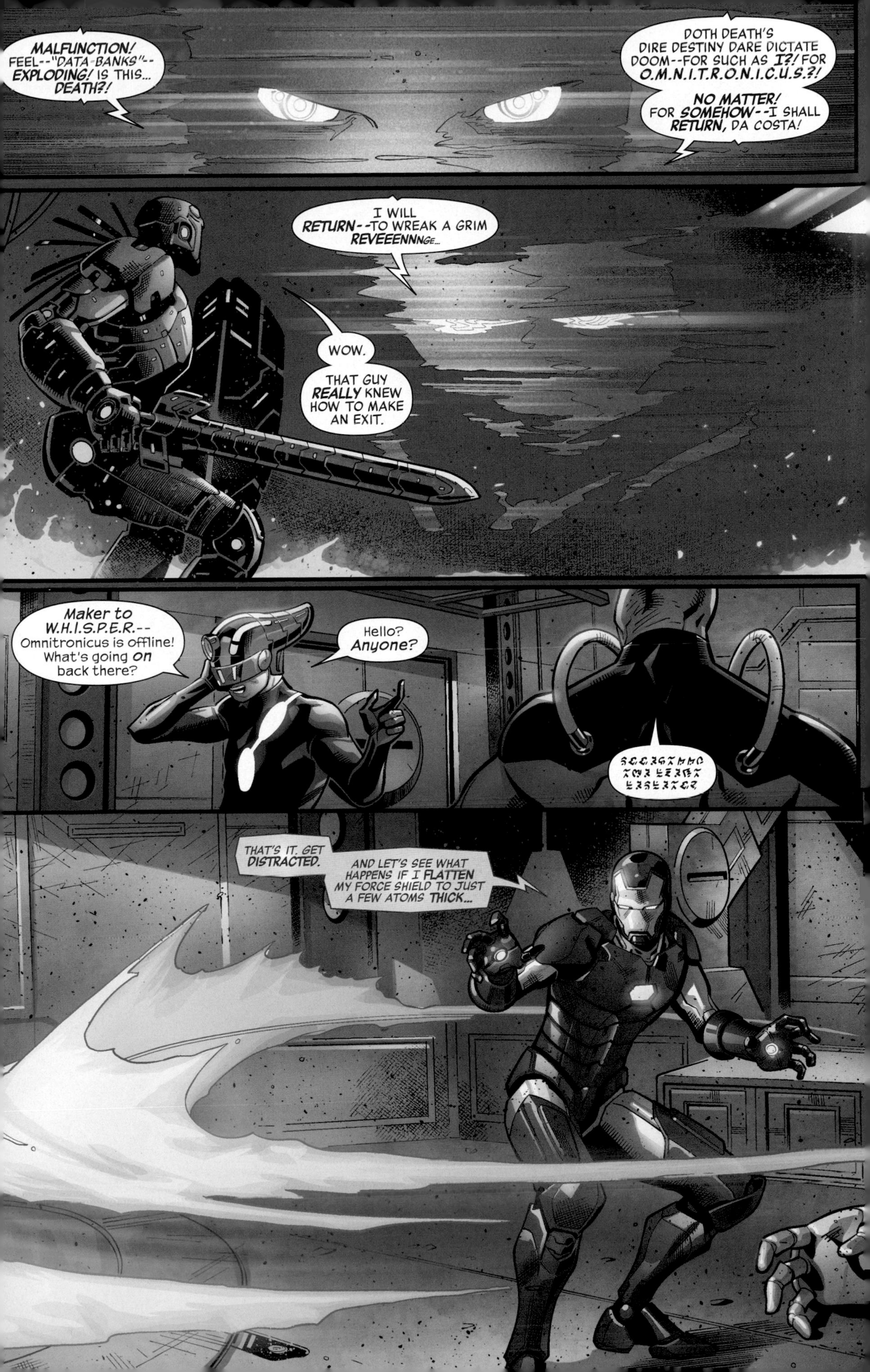
MALFUNCTION! FEEL--"DATA-BANKS"--EXPLODING! IS THIS... DEATH?!
DOTH DEATH'S DIRE DESTINY DARE DICTATE DOOM--FOR SUCH AS I?! FOR O.M.N.I.T.R.O.N.I.C.U.S.?!
NO MATTER! FOR SOMEHOW--I SHALL RETURN, DA COSTA!
I WILL RETURN--TO WREAK A GRIM REVEEEENNNGE...
WOW.
THAT GUY REALLY KNEW HOW TO MAKE AN EXIT.
Maker to W.H.I.S.P.E.R.--Omnitronicus is offline! What's going on back there?
Hello? Anyone?
THAT'S IT. GET DISTRACTED.
AND LET'S SEE WHAT HAPPENS IF I FLATTEN MY FORCE SHIELD TO JUST A FEW ATOMS THICK...

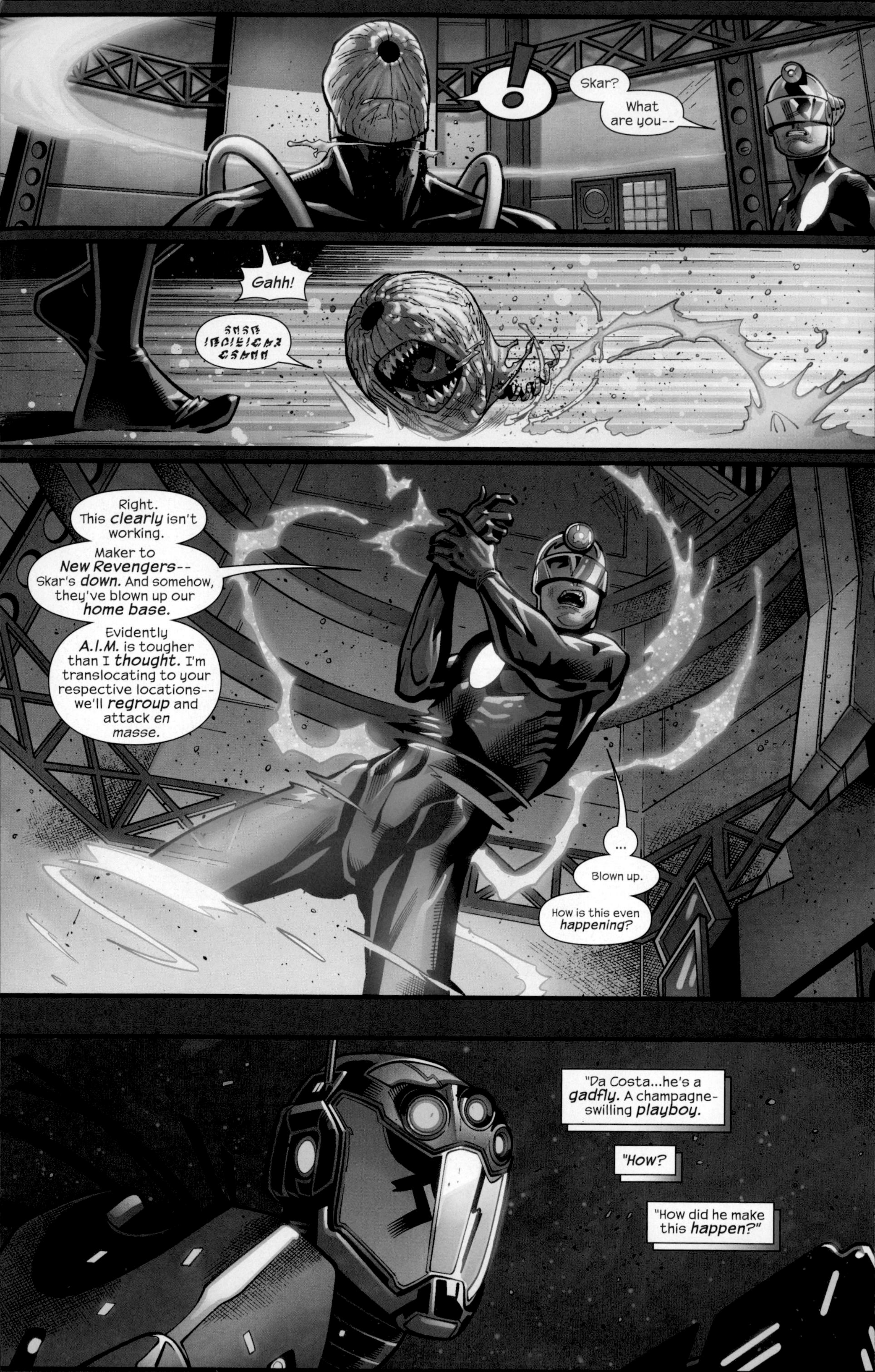
!
Skar?
What are you--
Gahh!
Right. This *clearly* isn't working.
Maker to *New Revengers*-- Skar's *down.* And somehow, they've blown up our *home base.*
Evidently *A.I.M.* is tougher than I *thought.* I'm translocating to your respective locations-- we'll *regroup* and attack *en masse.*
...
Blown up.
How is this even *happening?*
"Da Costa...he's a *gadfly.* A champagne-swilling *playboy.*
"How?
"How did he make this *happen?*"

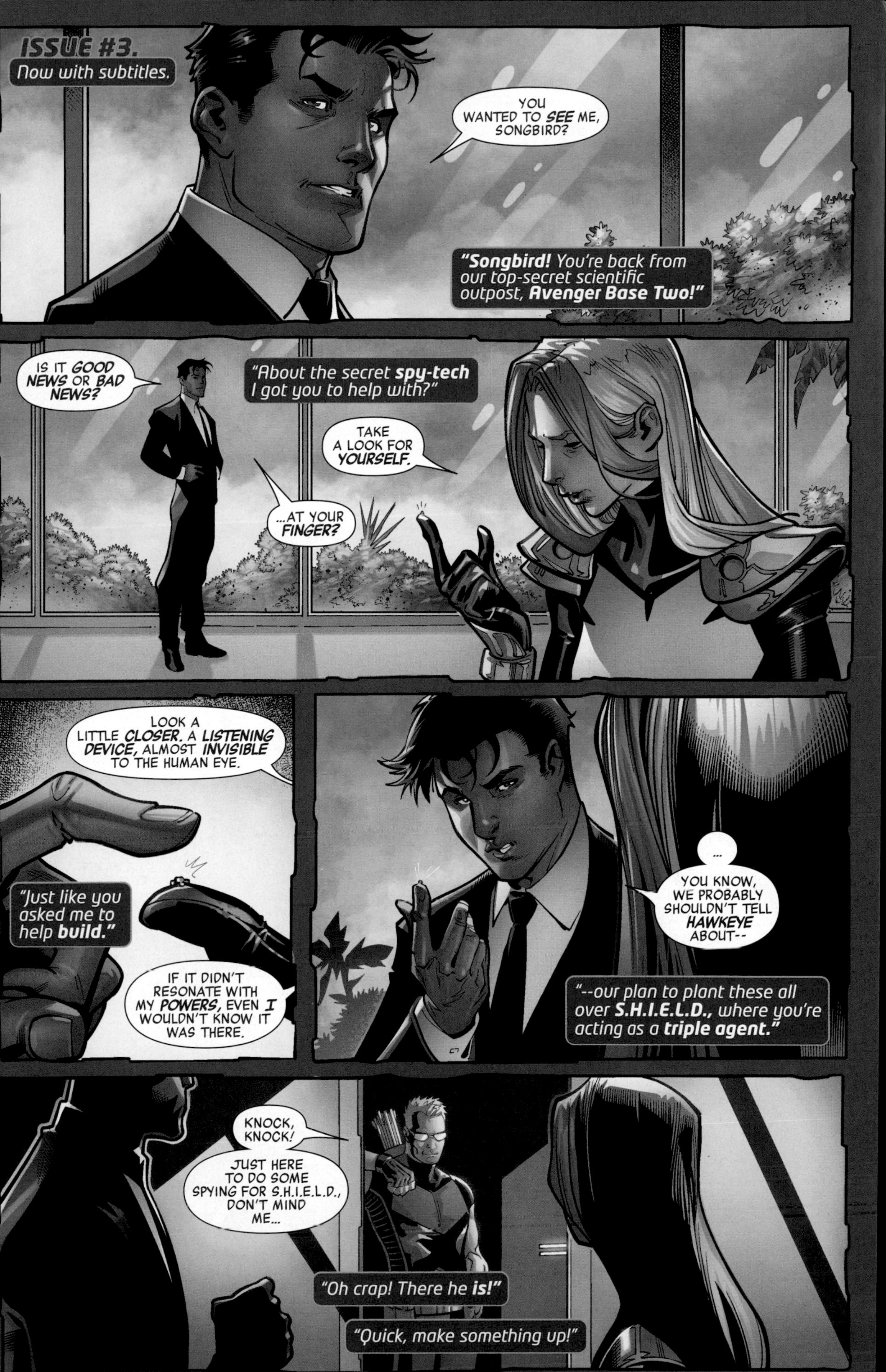
ISSUE #3.
Now with subtitles.
YOU WANTED TO SEE ME, SONGBIRD?
"Songbird! You're back from our top-secret scientific outpost, Avenger Base Two!"
IS IT GOOD NEWS OR BAD NEWS?
"About the secret spy-tech I got you to help with?"
TAKE A LOOK FOR YOURSELF.
...AT YOUR FINGER?
LOOK A LITTLE CLOSER. A LISTENING DEVICE, ALMOST INVISIBLE TO THE HUMAN EYE.
"Just like you asked me to help build."
IF IT DIDN'T RESONATE WITH MY POWERS, EVEN I WOULDN'T KNOW IT WAS THERE.
...
YOU KNOW, WE PROBABLY SHOULDN'T TELL HAWKEYE ABOUT--
"--our plan to plant these all over S.H.I.E.L.D., where you're acting as a triple agent."
KNOCK, KNOCK!
JUST HERE TO DO SOME SPYING FOR S.H.I.E.L.D., DON'T MIND ME...
"Oh crap! There he is!"
"Quick, make something up!"

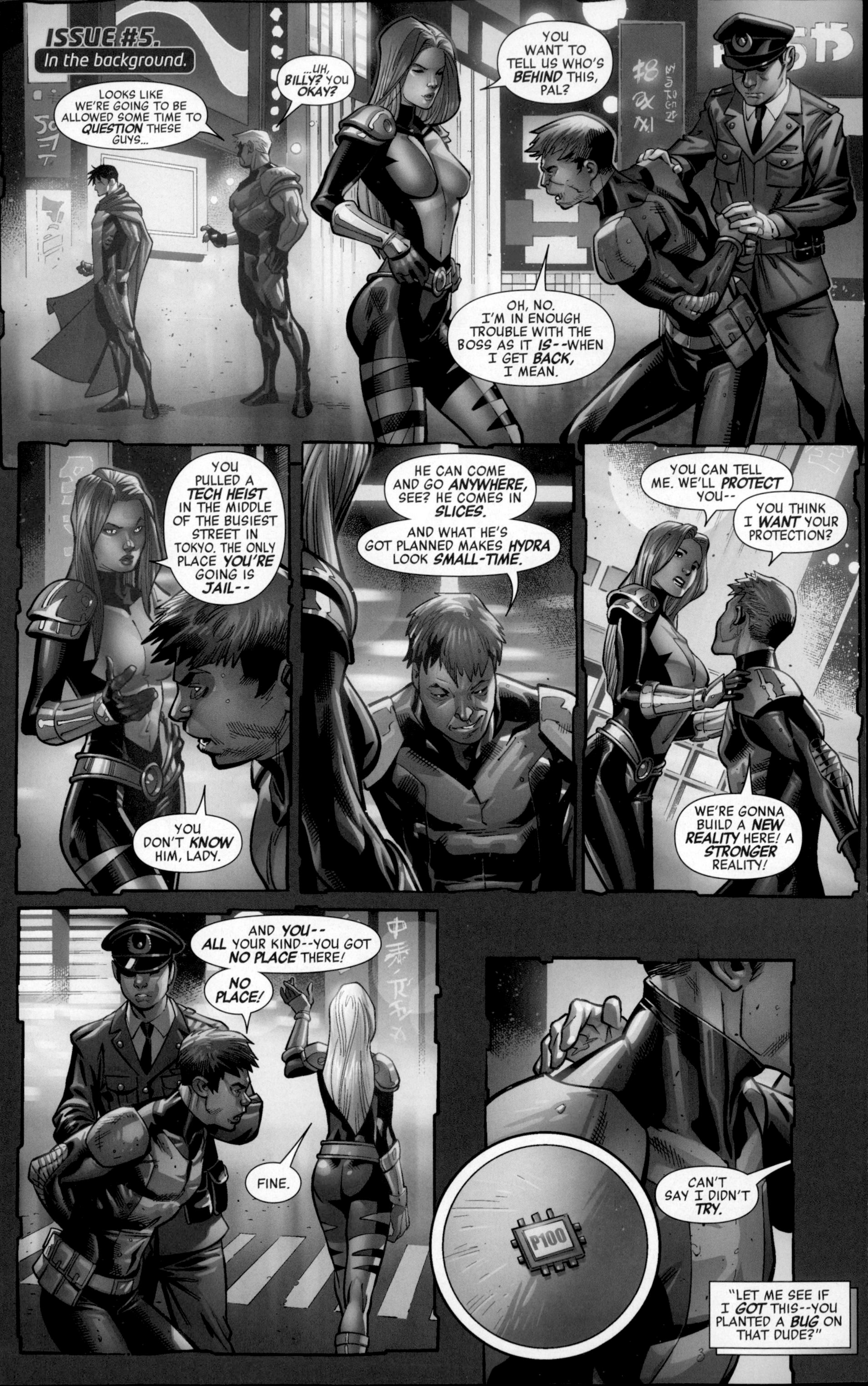
ISSUE #5.
In the background.
LOOKS LIKE WE'RE GOING TO BE ALLOWED SOME TIME TO QUESTION THESE GUYS...
...UH, BILLY? YOU OKAY?
YOU WANT TO TELL US WHO'S BEHIND THIS, PAL?
OH, NO. I'M IN ENOUGH TROUBLE WITH THE BOSS AS IT IS--WHEN I GET BACK, I MEAN.
YOU PULLED A TECH HEIST IN THE MIDDLE OF THE BUSIEST STREET IN TOKYO. THE ONLY PLACE YOU'RE GOING IS JAIL--
YOU DON'T KNOW HIM, LADY.
HE CAN COME AND GO ANYWHERE, SEE? HE COMES IN SLICES.
AND WHAT HE'S GOT PLANNED MAKES HYDRA LOOK SMALL-TIME.
YOU CAN TELL ME. WE'LL PROTECT YOU--
YOU THINK I WANT YOUR PROTECTION?
WE'RE GONNA BUILD A NEW REALITY HERE! A STRONGER REALITY!
AND YOU-- ALL YOUR KIND--YOU GOT NO PLACE THERE!
NO PLACE!
FINE.
P100
CAN'T SAY I DIDN'T TRY.
"LET ME SEE IF I GOT THIS--YOU PLANTED A BUG ON THAT DUDE?"

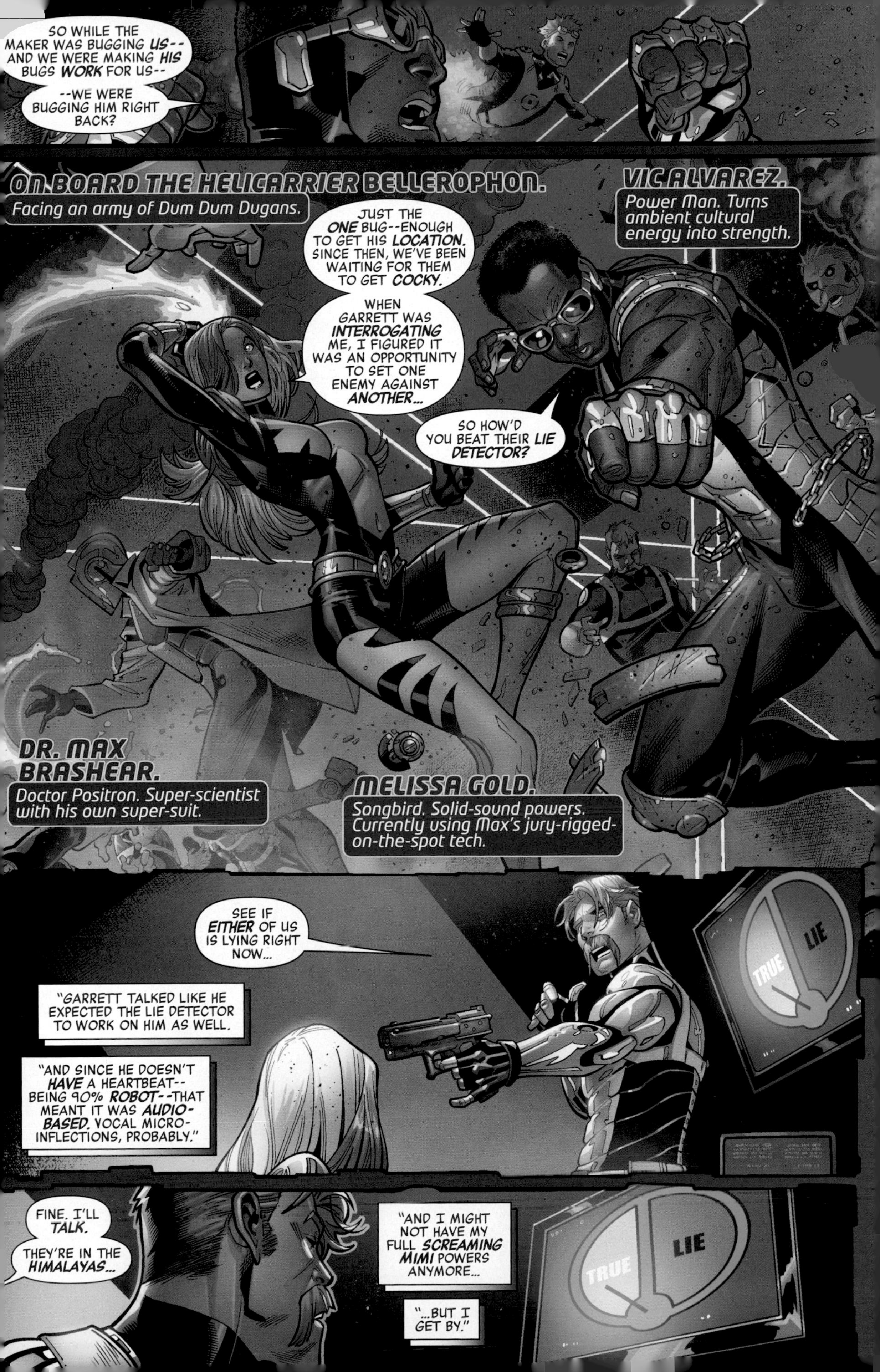
SO WHILE THE MAKER WAS BUGGING US--AND WE WERE MAKING HIS BUGS WORK FOR US--
--WE WERE BUGGING HIM RIGHT BACK?
ON BOARD THE HELICARRIER BELLEROPHON.
Facing an army of Dum Dum Dugans.
VIC ALVAREZ.
Power Man. Turns ambient cultural energy into strength.
JUST THE ONE BUG--ENOUGH TO GET HIS LOCATION. SINCE THEN, WE'VE BEEN WAITING FOR THEM TO GET COCKY.
WHEN GARRETT WAS INTERROGATING ME, I FIGURED IT WAS AN OPPORTUNITY TO SET ONE ENEMY AGAINST ANOTHER...
SO HOW'D YOU BEAT THEIR LIE DETECTOR?
DR. MAX BRASHEAR.
Doctor Positron. Super-scientist with his own super-suit.
MELISSA GOLD.
Songbird. Solid-sound powers. Currently using Max's jury-rigged-on-the-spot tech.
SEE IF EITHER OF US IS LYING RIGHT NOW...
"GARRETT TALKED LIKE HE EXPECTED THE LIE DETECTOR TO WORK ON HIM AS WELL.
"AND SINCE HE DOESN'T HAVE A HEARTBEAT--BEING 90% ROBOT--THAT MEANT IT WAS AUDIO-BASED. VOCAL MICRO-INFLECTIONS, PROBABLY."
TRUE
LIE
FINE. I'LL TALK.
THEY'RE IN THE HIMALAYAS...
"AND I MIGHT NOT HAVE MY FULL SCREAMING MIMI POWERS ANYMORE...
"...BUT I GET BY."
TRUE
LIE

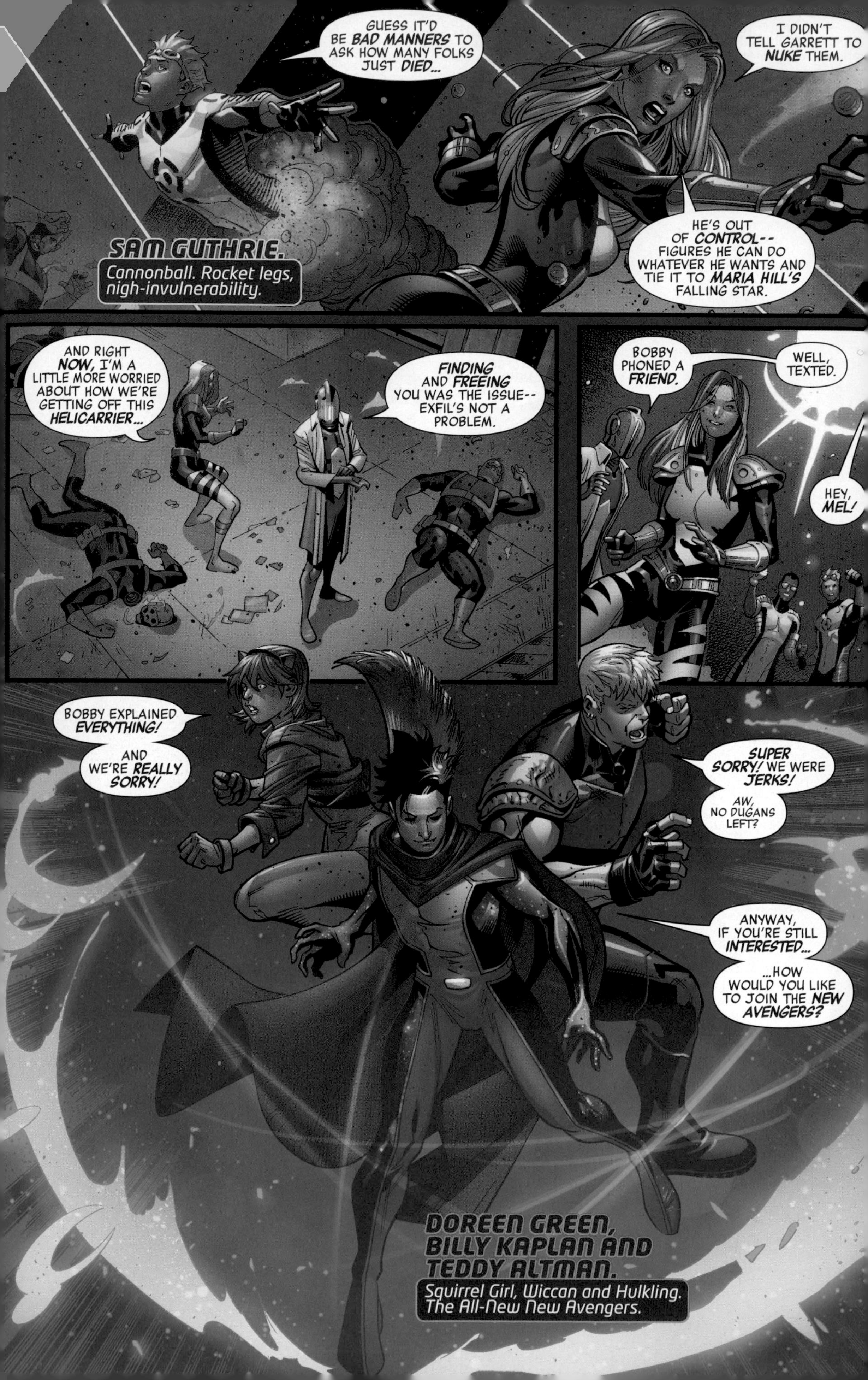
GUESS IT'D BE BAD MANNERS TO ASK HOW MANY FOLKS JUST DIED...
I DIDN'T TELL GARRETT TO NUKE THEM.
SAM GUTHRIE.
Cannonball. Rocket legs, nigh-invulnerability.
HE'S OUT OF CONTROL-- FIGURES HE CAN DO WHATEVER HE WANTS AND TIE IT TO MARIA HILL'S FALLING STAR.
AND RIGHT NOW, I'M A LITTLE MORE WORRIED ABOUT HOW WE'RE GETTING OFF THIS HELICARRIER...
FINDING AND FREEING YOU WAS THE ISSUE-- EXFIL'S NOT A PROBLEM.
BOBBY PHONED A FRIEND.
WELL, TEXTED.
HEY, MEL!
BOBBY EXPLAINED EVERYTHING!
AND WE'RE REALLY SORRY!
SUPER SORRY! WE WERE JERKS!
AW, NO DUGANS LEFT?
ANYWAY, IF YOU'RE STILL INTERESTED...
...HOW WOULD YOU LIKE TO JOIN THE NEW AVENGERS?
DOREEN GREEN, BILLY KAPLAN AND TEDDY ALTMAN.
Squirrel Girl, Wiccan and Hulkling. The All-New New Avengers.

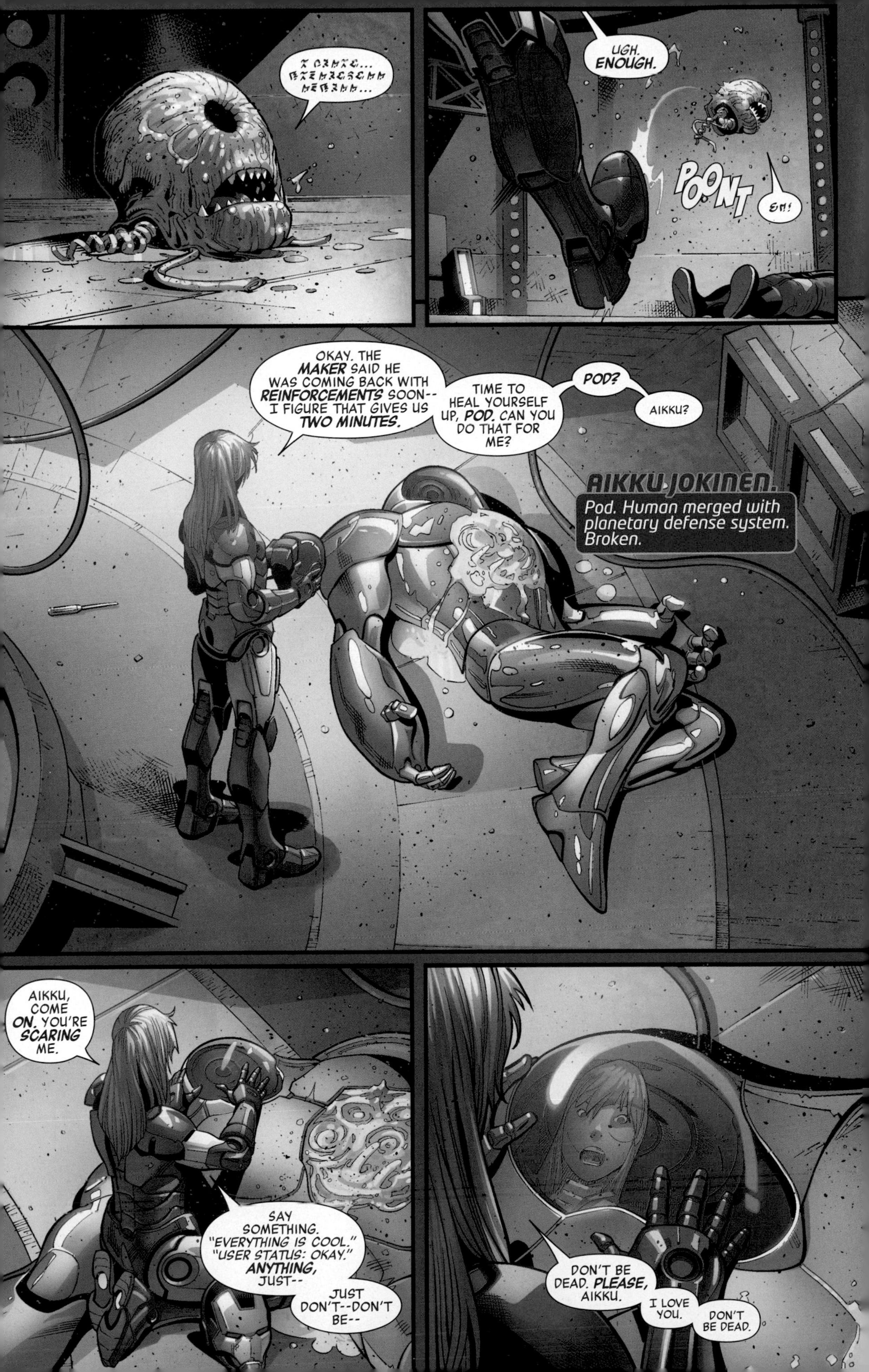

UGH. ENOUGH.
POONT
OKAY. THE MAKER SAID HE WAS COMING BACK WITH REINFORCEMENTS SOON-- I FIGURE THAT GIVES US TWO MINUTES.
TIME TO HEAL YOURSELF UP, POD. CAN YOU DO THAT FOR ME?
POD?
AIKKU?
AIKKU JOKINEN.
Pod. Human merged with planetary defense system. Broken.
AIKKU, COME ON. YOU'RE SCARING ME.
SAY SOMETHING. "EVERYTHING IS COOL." "USER STATUS: OKAY." ANYTHING, JUST--
JUST DON'T--DON'T BE--
DON'T BE DEAD. PLEASE, AIKKU.
I LOVE YOU.
DON'T BE DEAD.

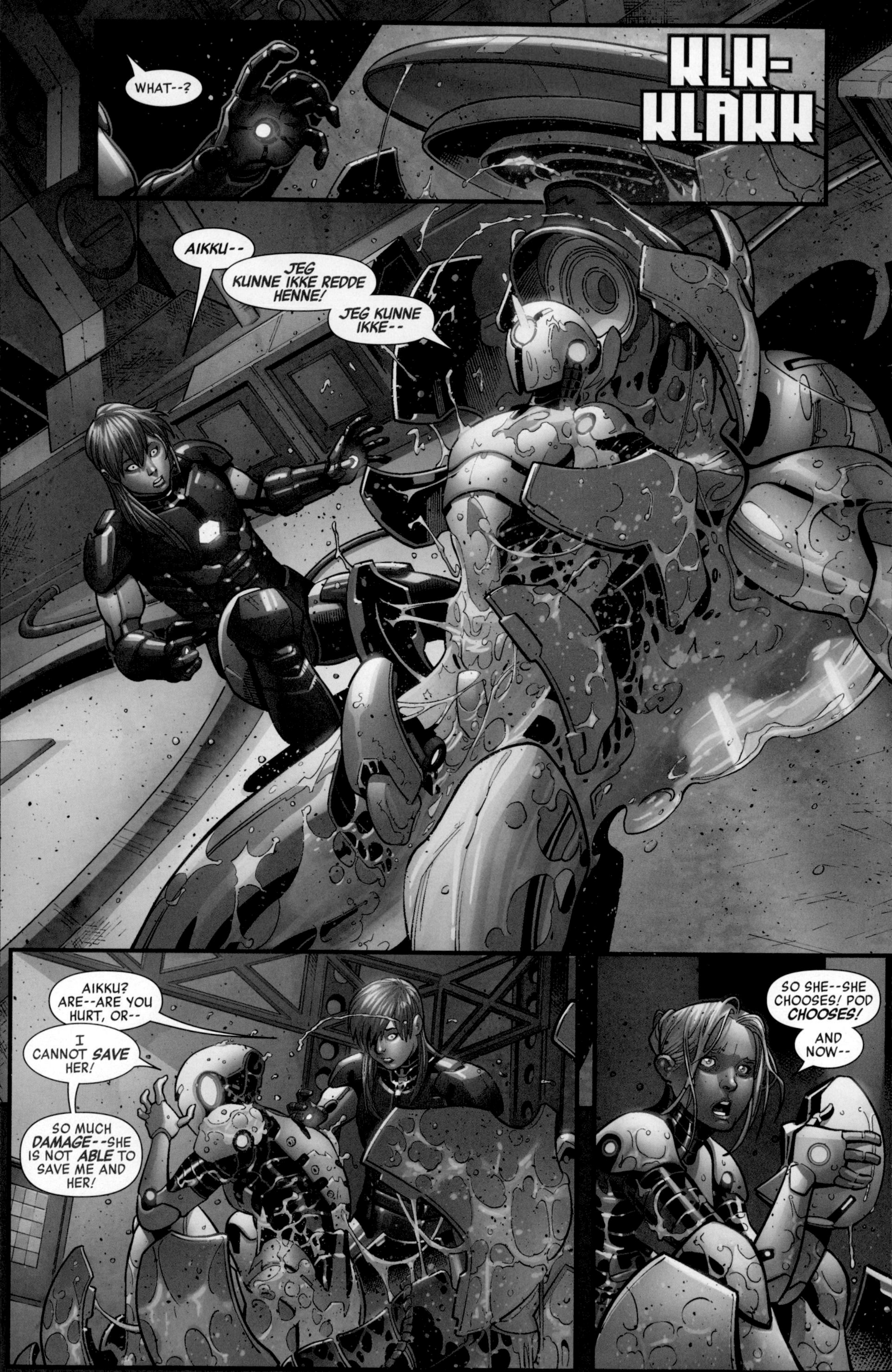
KLK-KLAKK
WHAT--?
AIKKU--
JEG KUNNE IKKE REDDE HENNE!
JEG KUNNE IKKE--
AIKKU? ARE--ARE YOU HURT, OR--
I CANNOT SAVE HER!
SO MUCH DAMAGE--SHE IS NOT ABLE TO SAVE ME AND HER!
SO SHE--SHE CHOOSES! POD CHOOSES!
AND NOW--

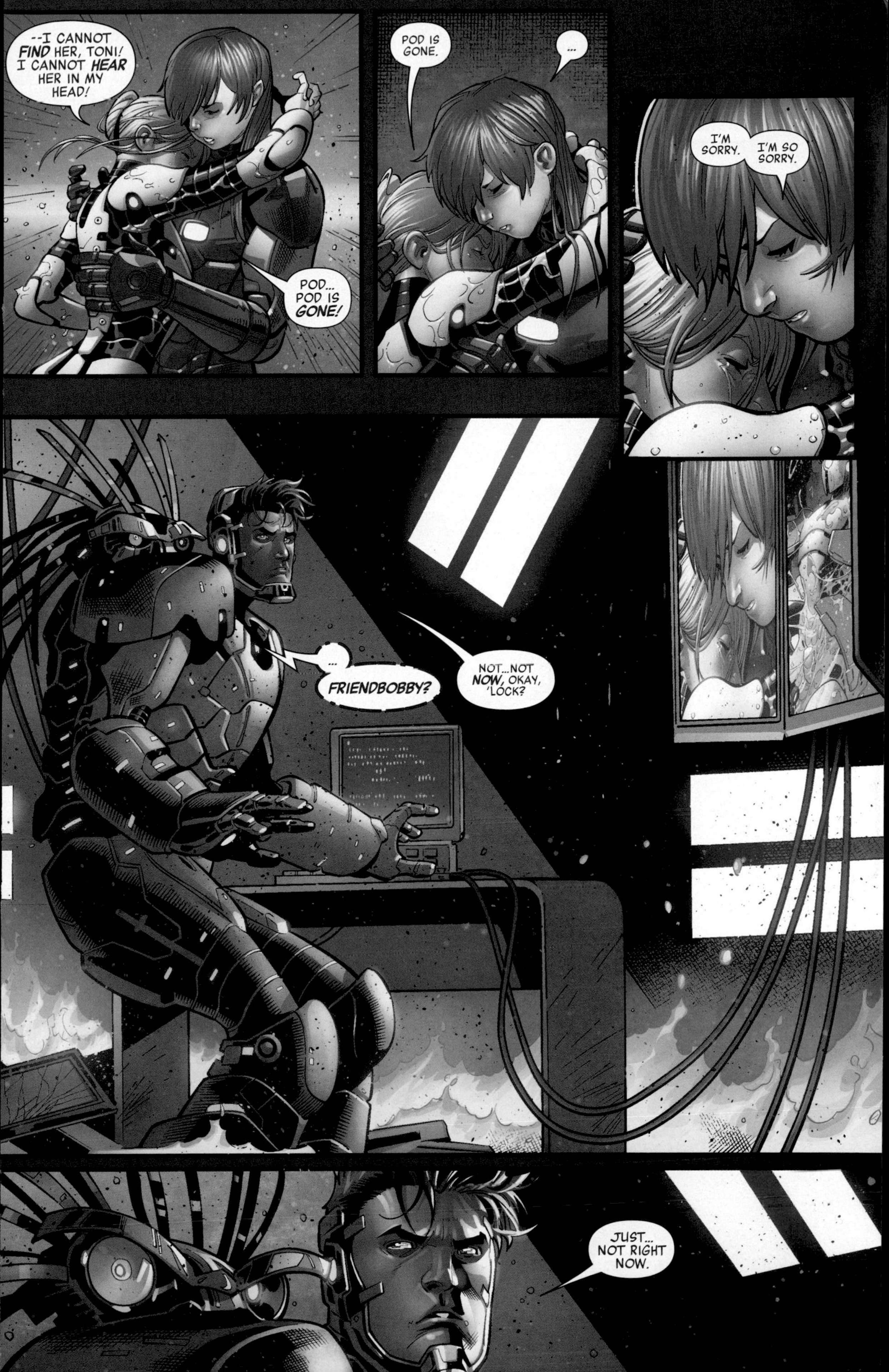
--I CANNOT FIND HER, TONI! I CANNOT HEAR HER IN MY HEAD!
POD... POD IS GONE!
POD IS GONE.
...
I'M SORRY.
I'M SO SORRY.
... FRIENDBOBBY?
NOT...NOT NOW, OKAY, 'LOCK?
JUST... NOT RIGHT NOW.

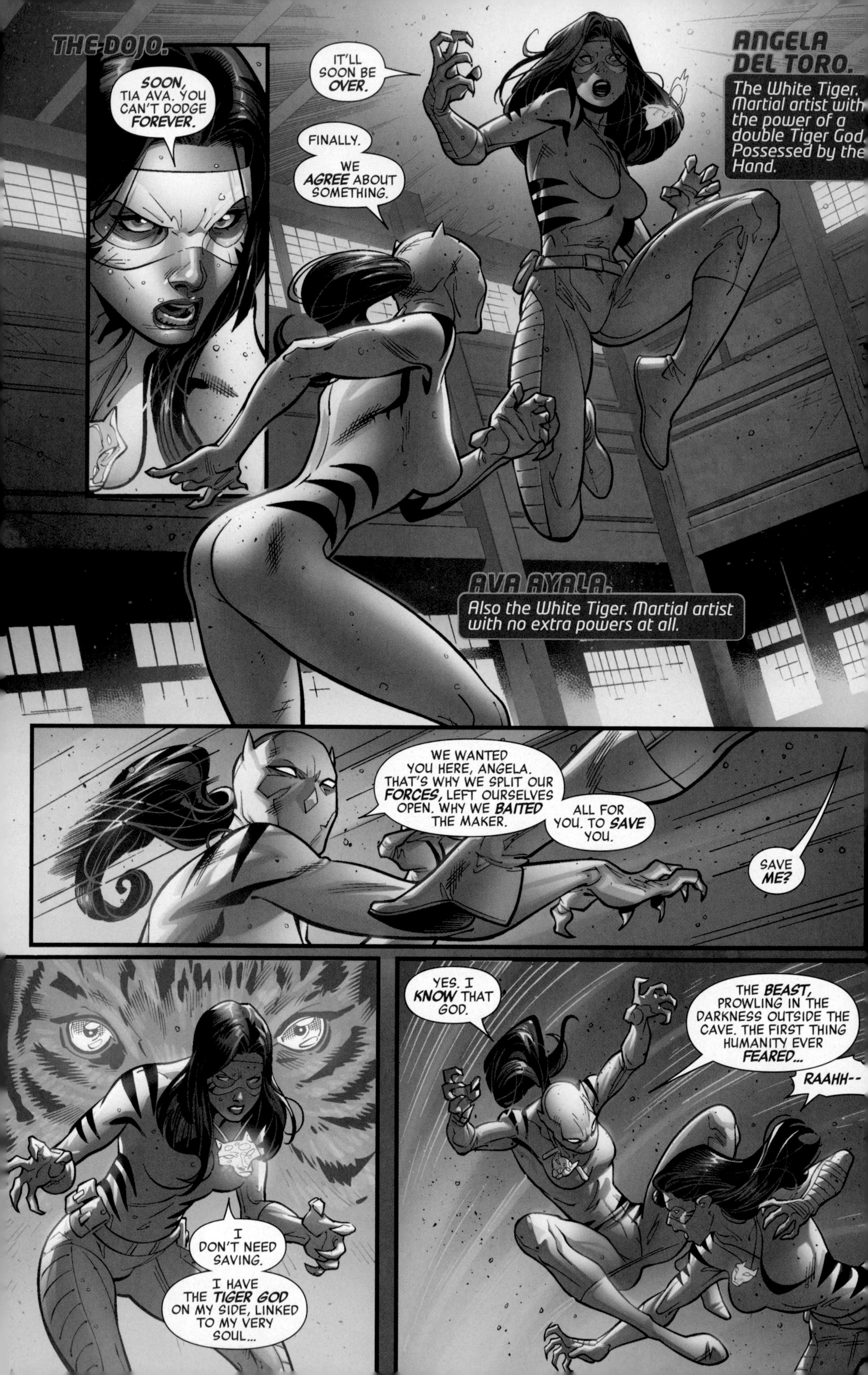

THE DOJO.
SOON, TIA AVA. YOU CAN'T DODGE FOREVER.
IT'LL SOON BE OVER.
FINALLY.
WE AGREE ABOUT SOMETHING.
ANGELA DEL TORO.
The White Tiger. Martial artist with the power of a double Tiger God. Possessed by the Hand.
AVA AYALA.
Also the White Tiger. Martial artist with no extra powers at all.
WE WANTED YOU HERE, ANGELA. THAT'S WHY WE SPLIT OUR FORCES, LEFT OURSELVES OPEN. WHY WE BAITED THE MAKER.
ALL FOR YOU. TO SAVE YOU.
SAVE ME?
I DON'T NEED SAVING.
I HAVE THE TIGER GOD ON MY SIDE, LINKED TO MY VERY SOUL...
YES. I KNOW THAT GOD.
THE BEAST, PROWLING IN THE DARKNESS OUTSIDE THE CAVE. THE FIRST THING HUMANITY EVER FEARED...
RAAHH--

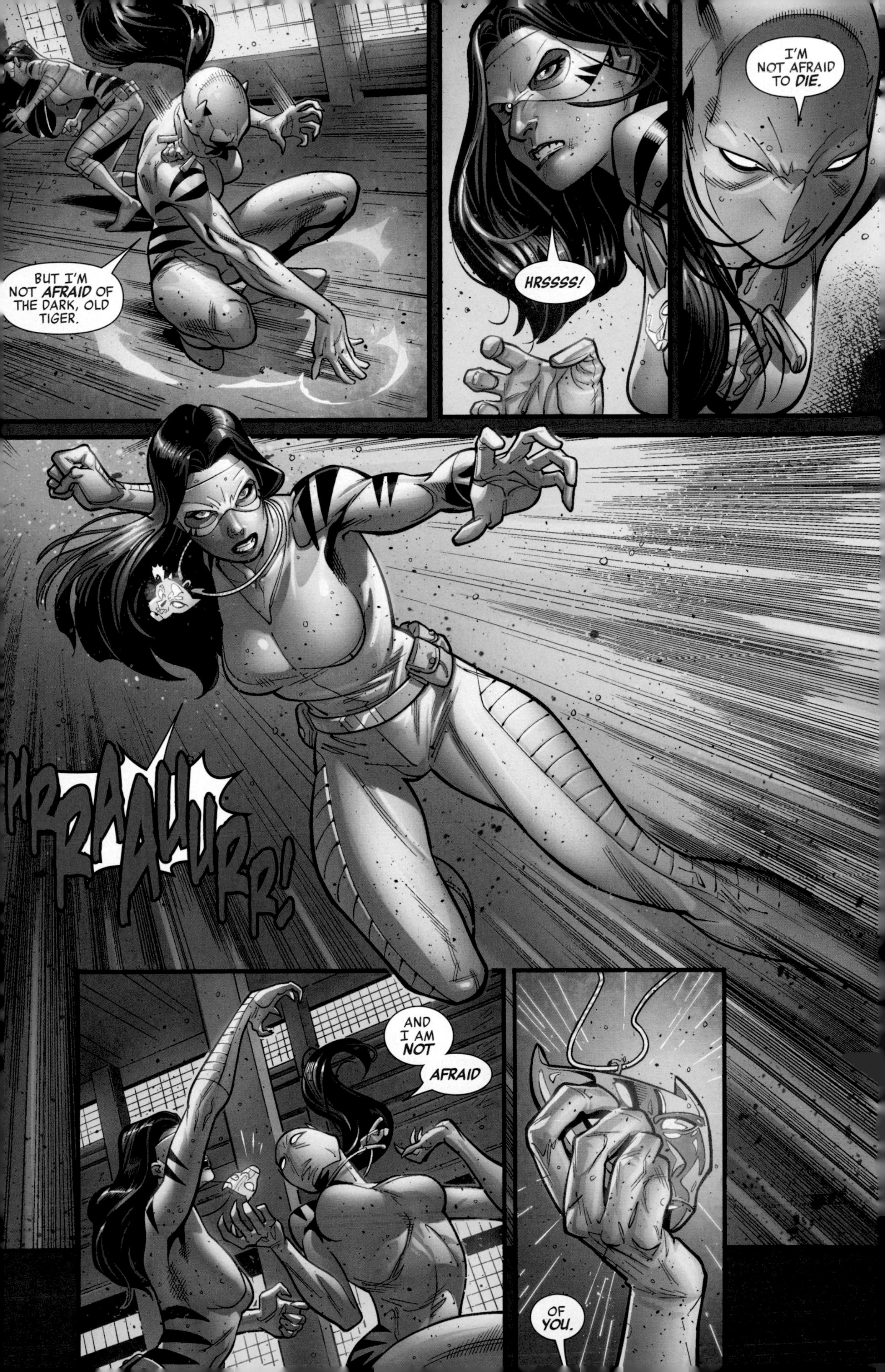
BUT I'M NOT AFRAID OF THE DARK, OLD TIGER.
HRSSSS!
I'M NOT AFRAID TO DIE.
HRRAAUURR!
AND I AM NOT
AFRAID
OF YOU.

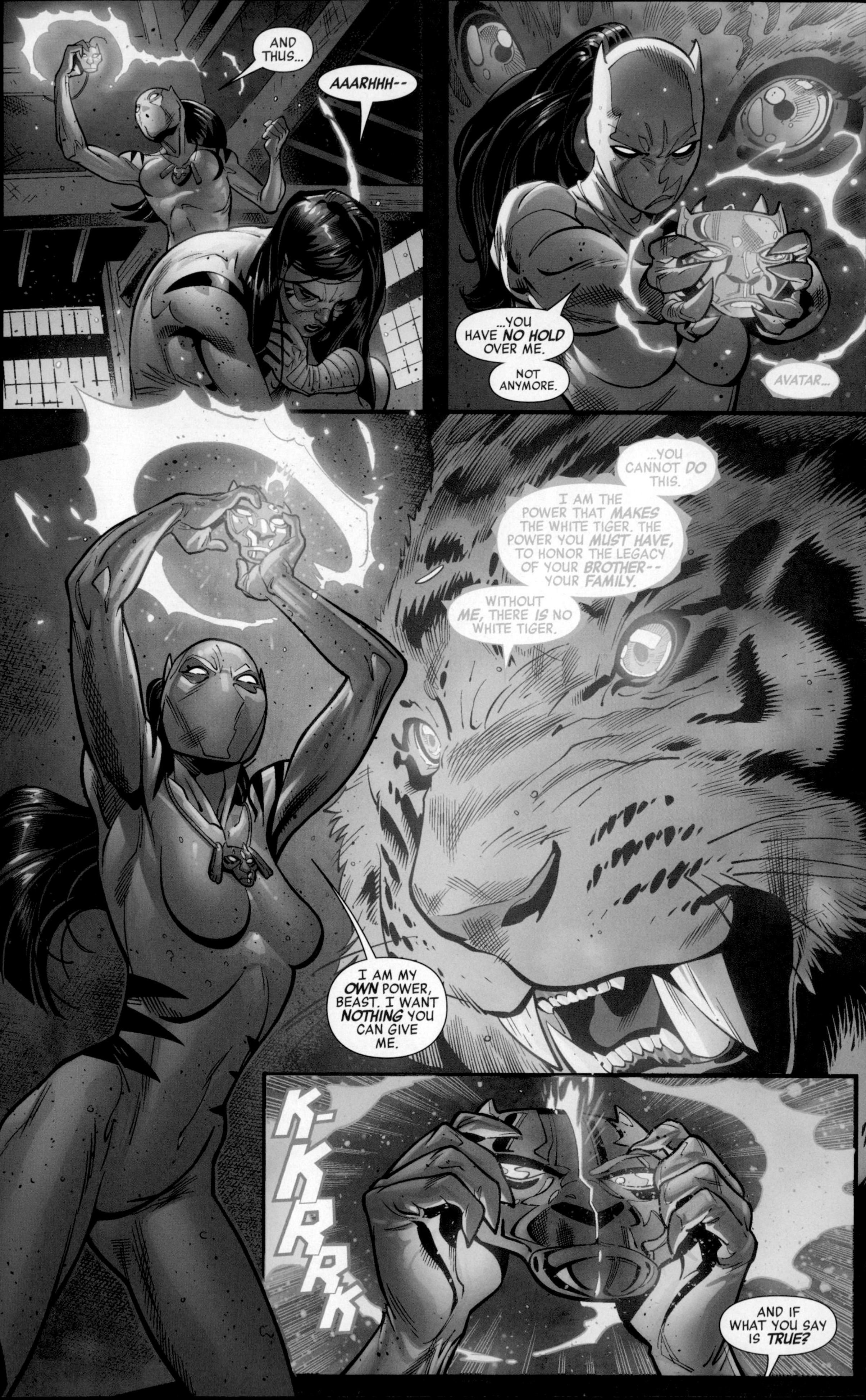
AND THUS...
AAARHHH--
...YOU HAVE NO HOLD OVER ME.
NOT ANYMORE.
AVATAR...
...YOU CANNOT DO THIS.
I AM THE POWER THAT MAKES THE WHITE TIGER. THE POWER YOU MUST HAVE, TO HONOR THE LEGACY OF YOUR BROTHER-- YOUR FAMILY.
WITHOUT ME, THERE IS NO WHITE TIGER.
I AM MY OWN POWER, BEAST. I WANT NOTHING YOU CAN GIVE ME.
K-KRRK
AND IF WHAT YOU SAY IS TRUE?

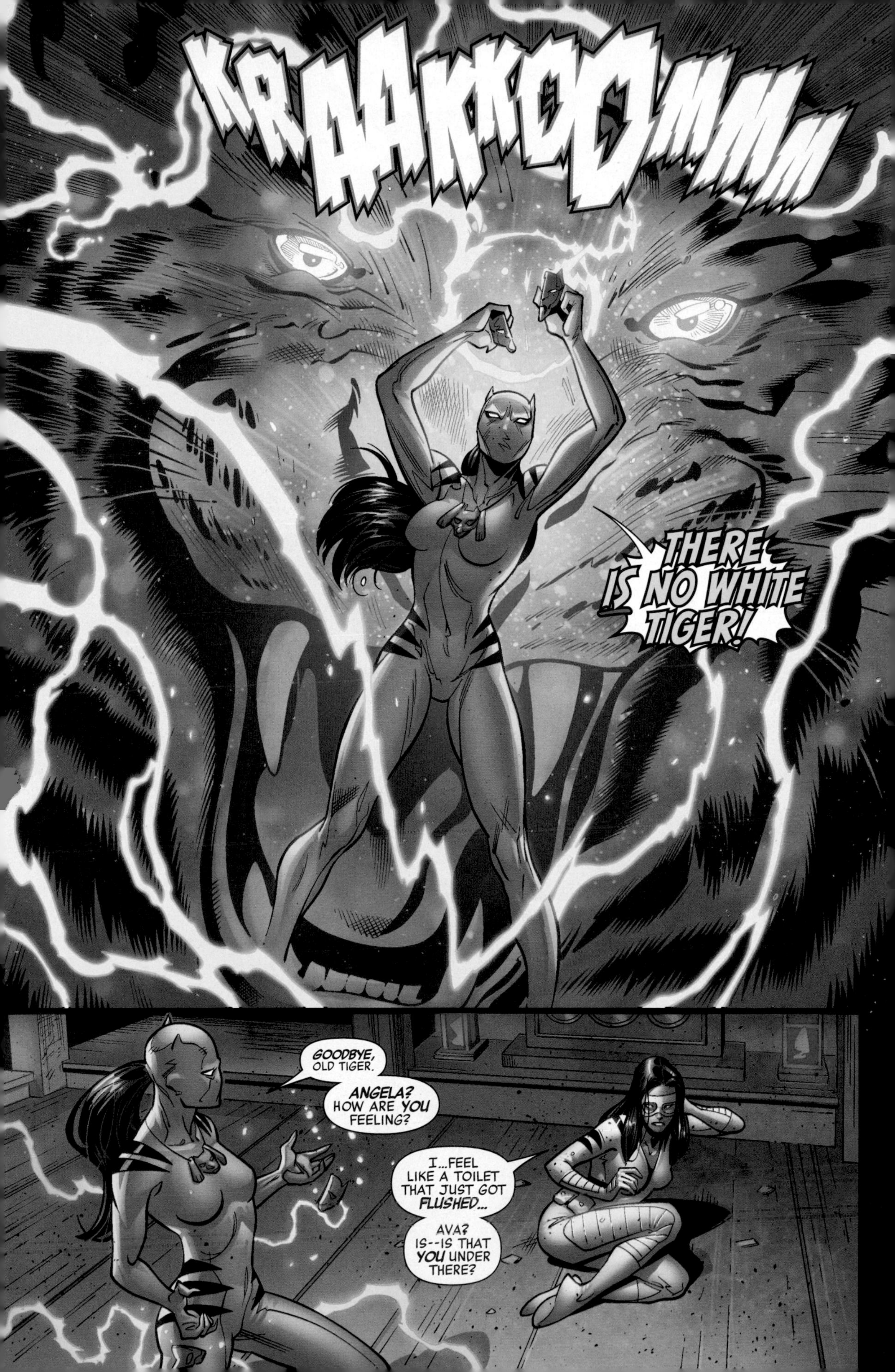
KRAAKKOOMMM
THERE IS NO WHITE TIGER!
GOODBYE, OLD TIGER.
ANGELA? HOW ARE YOU FEELING?
I...FEEL LIKE A TOILET THAT JUST GOT FLUSHED...
AVA? IS--IS THAT YOU UNDER THERE?

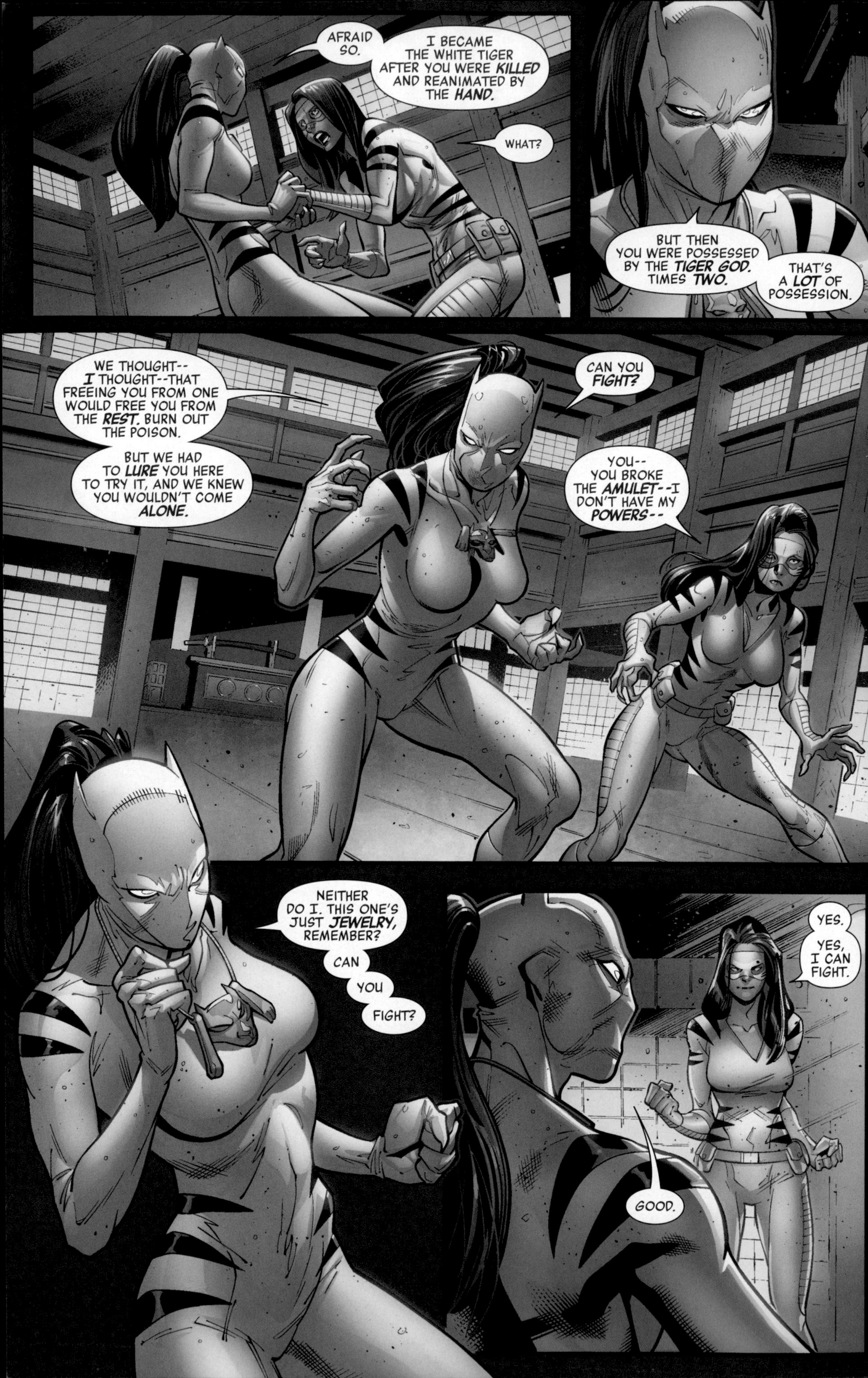
AFRAID SO.
I BECAME THE WHITE TIGER AFTER YOU WERE KILLED AND REANIMATED BY THE HAND.
WHAT?
BUT THEN YOU WERE POSSESSED BY THE TIGER GOD. TIMES TWO.
THAT'S A LOT OF POSSESSION.
WE THOUGHT-- I THOUGHT--THAT FREEING YOU FROM ONE WOULD FREE YOU FROM THE REST. BURN OUT THE POISON.
BUT WE HAD TO LURE YOU HERE TO TRY IT, AND WE KNEW YOU WOULDN'T COME ALONE.
CAN YOU FIGHT?
YOU-- YOU BROKE THE AMULET--I DON'T HAVE MY POWERS--
NEITHER DO I. THIS ONE'S JUST JEWELRY, REMEMBER?
CAN
YOU
FIGHT?
YES.
YES, I CAN FIGHT.
GOOD.

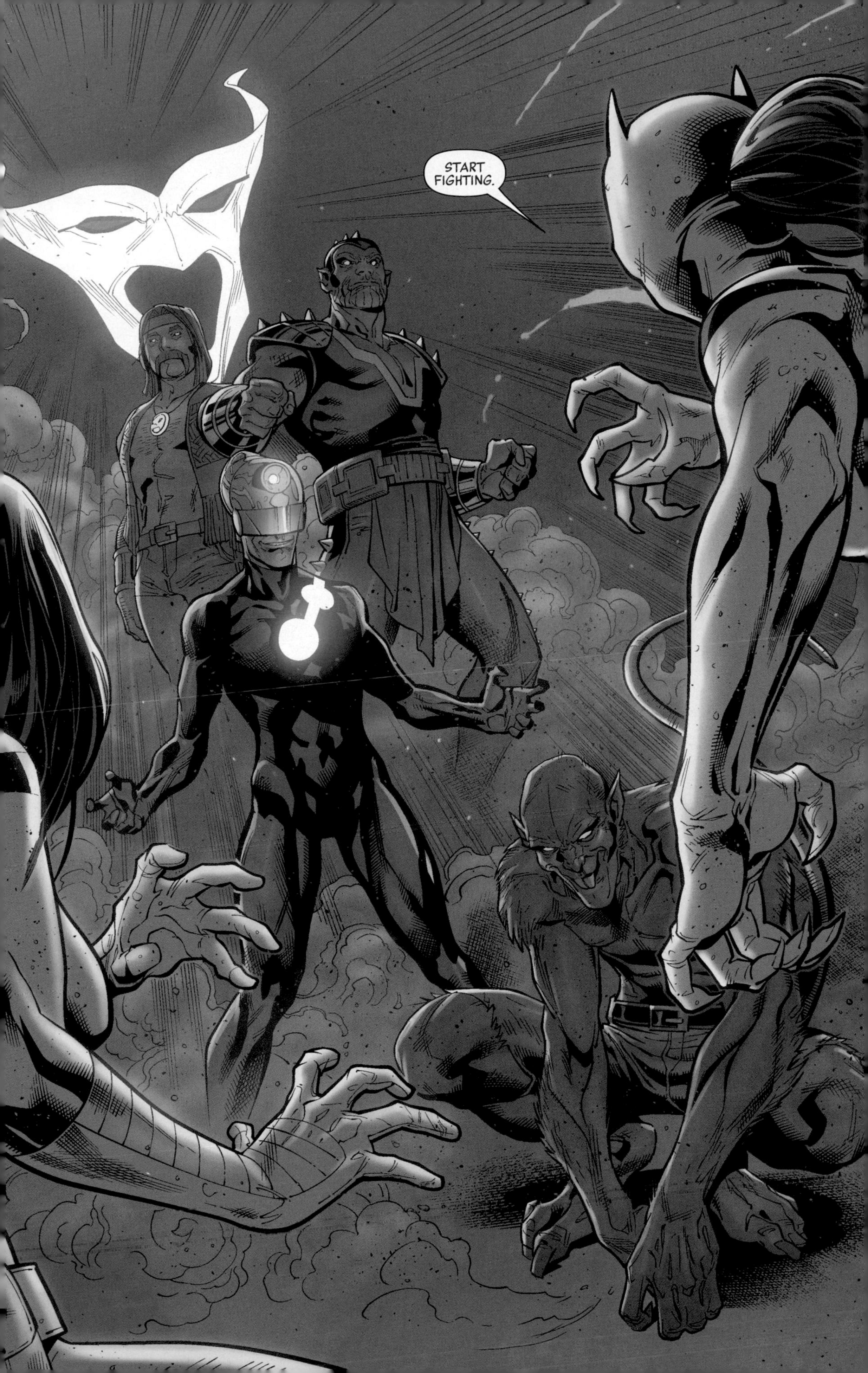
START FIGHTING.

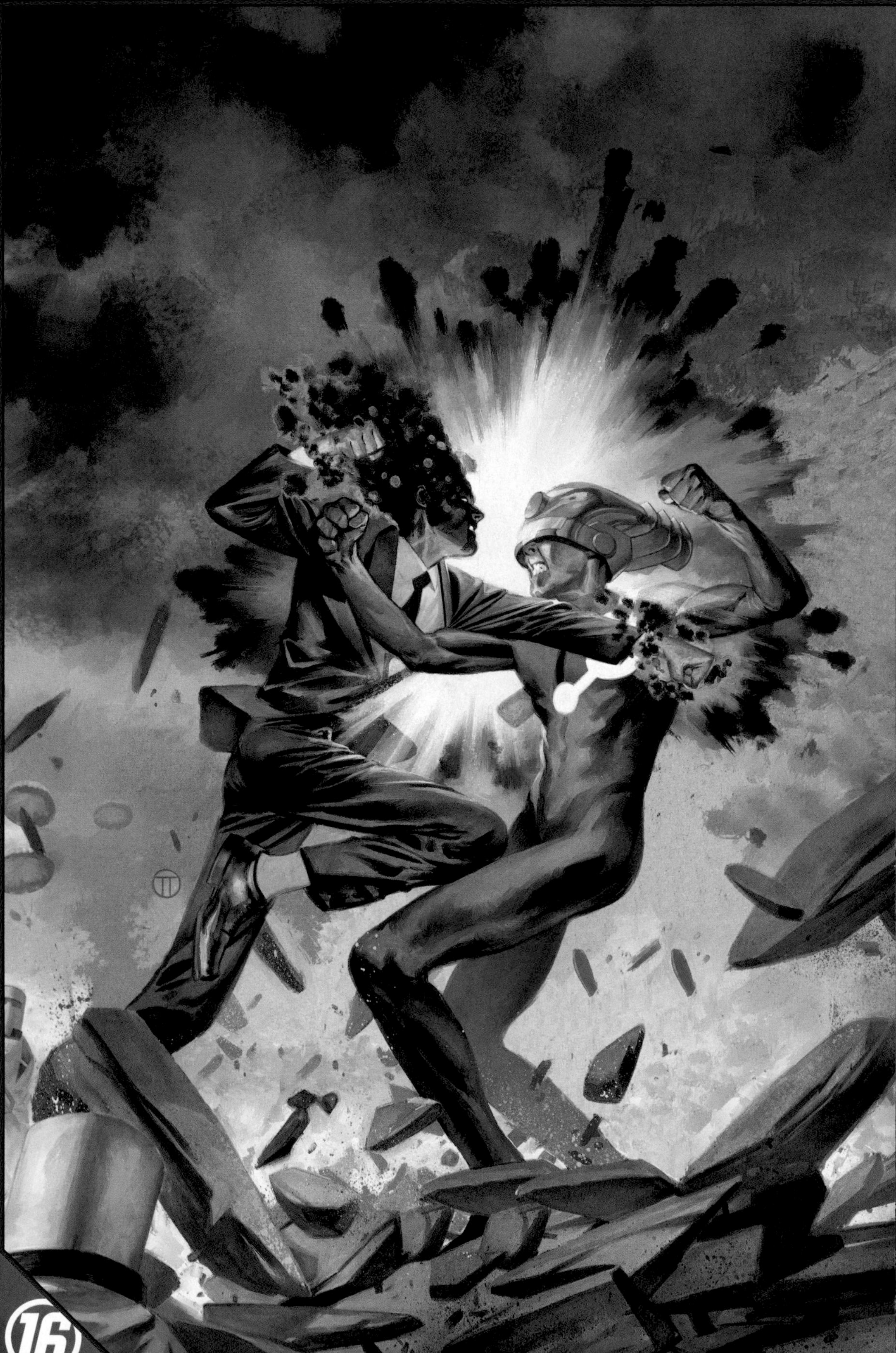
16

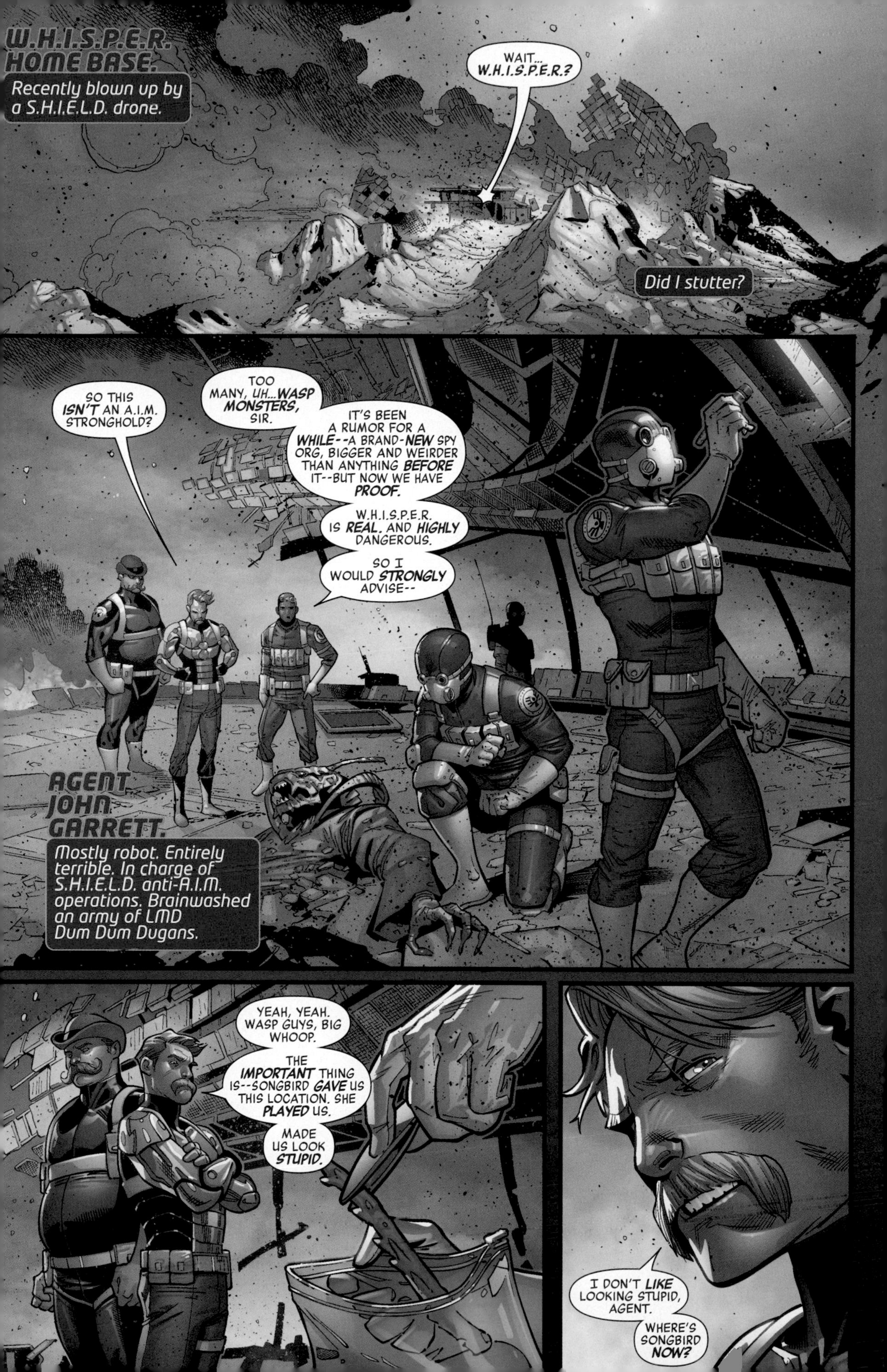
W.H.I.S.P.E.R. HOME BASE.
Recently blown up by a S.H.I.E.L.D. drone.
WAIT... W.H.I.S.P.E.R.?
Did I stutter?
SO THIS ISN'T AN A.I.M. STRONGHOLD?
TOO MANY, UH...WASP MONSTERS, SIR.
IT'S BEEN A RUMOR FOR A WHILE--A BRAND-NEW SPY ORG, BIGGER AND WEIRDER THAN ANYTHING BEFORE IT--BUT NOW WE HAVE PROOF.
W.H.I.S.P.E.R. IS REAL. AND HIGHLY DANGEROUS.
SO I WOULD STRONGLY ADVISE--
AGENT JOHN GARRETT.
Mostly robot. Entirely terrible. In charge of S.H.I.E.L.D. anti-A.I.M. operations. Brainwashed an army of LMD Dum Dum Dugans.
YEAH, YEAH. WASP GUYS, BIG WHOOP.
THE IMPORTANT THING IS--SONGBIRD GAVE US THIS LOCATION. SHE PLAYED US.
MADE US LOOK STUPID.
I DON'T LIKE LOOKING STUPID, AGENT.
WHERE'S SONGBIRD NOW?

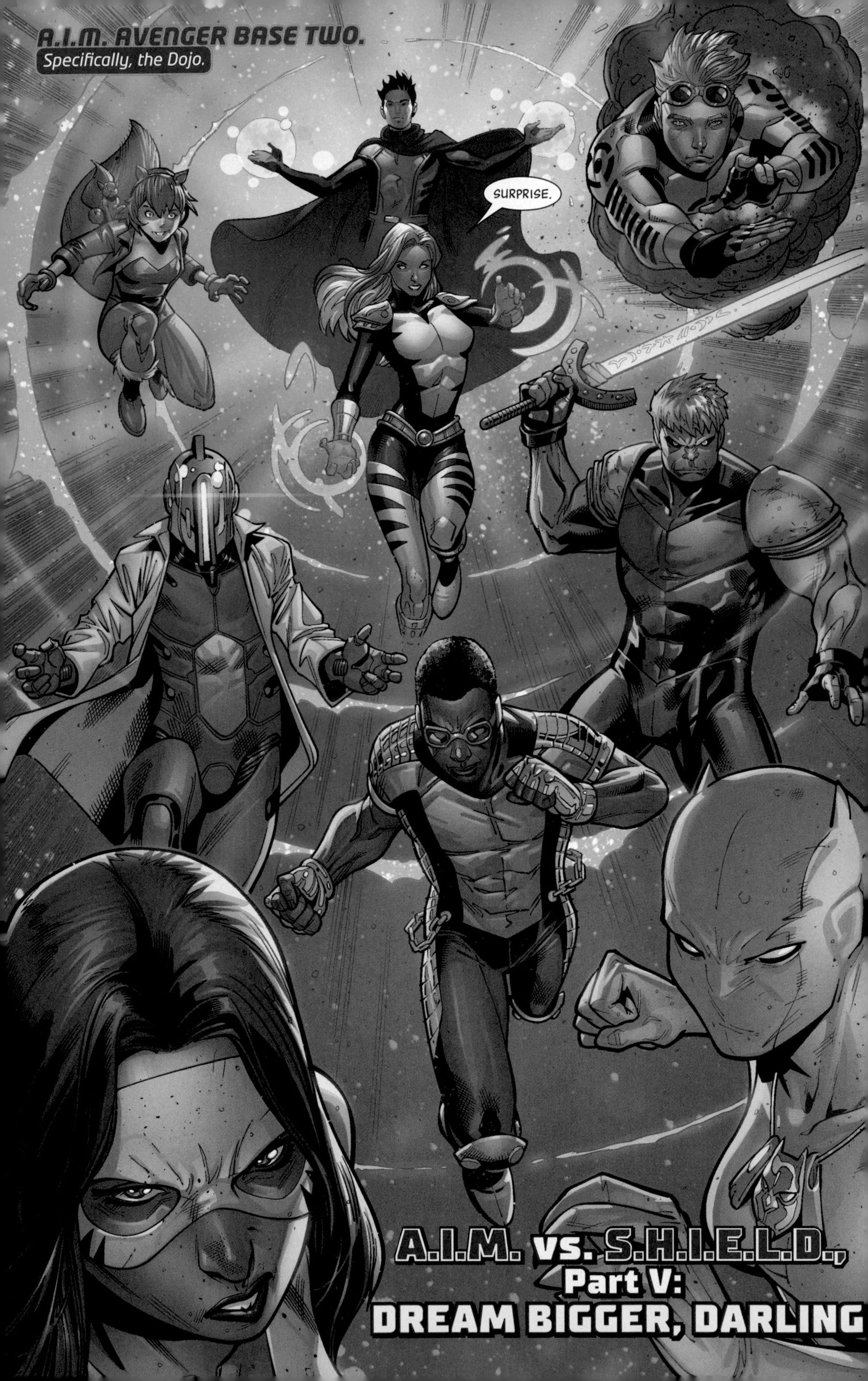
A.I.M. AVENGER BASE TWO.
Specifically, the Dojo.
SURPRISE.
A.I.M. vs. S.H.I.E.L.D.,
Part V:
DREAM BIGGER, DARLING

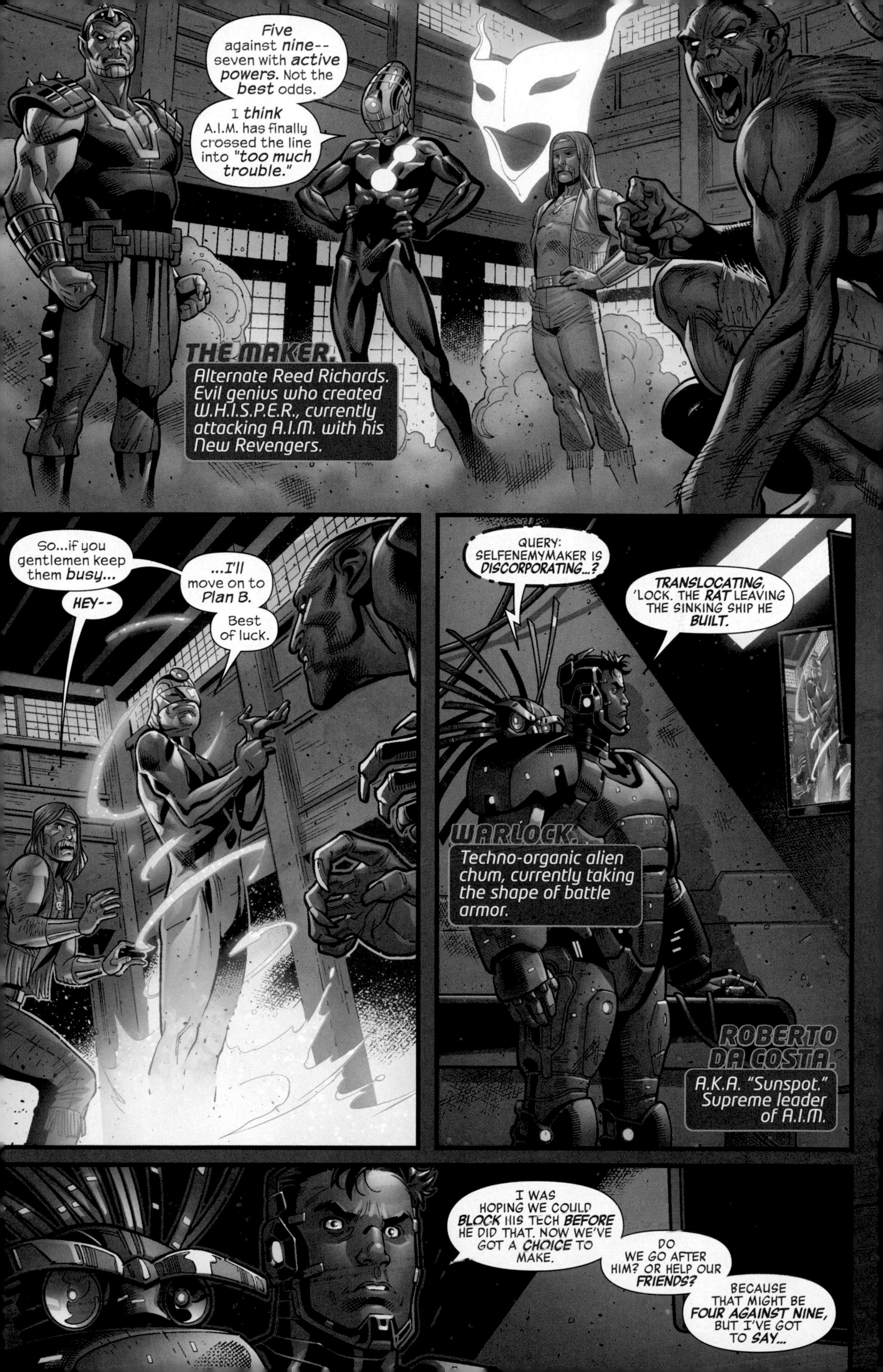
Five against nine-- seven with active powers. Not the best odds.
I think A.I.M. has finally crossed the line into "too much trouble."
THE MAKER.
Alternate Reed Richards. Evil genius who created W.H.I.S.P.E.R., currently attacking A.I.M. with his New Revengers.
So...if you gentlemen keep them busy...
...I'll move on to Plan B.
Best of luck.
HEY--
QUERY: SELFENEMYMAKER IS DISCORPORATING...?
TRANSLOCATING, 'LOCK. THE RAT LEAVING THE SINKING SHIP HE BUILT.
WARLOCK.
Techno-organic alien chum, currently taking the shape of battle armor.
ROBERTO DA COSTA.
A.K.A. "Sunspot." Supreme leader of A.I.M.
I WAS HOPING WE COULD BLOCK HIS TECH BEFORE HE DID THAT. NOW WE'VE GOT A CHOICE TO MAKE.
DO WE GO AFTER HIM? OR HELP OUR FRIENDS?
BECAUSE THAT MIGHT BE FOUR AGAINST NINE, BUT I'VE GOT TO SAY...

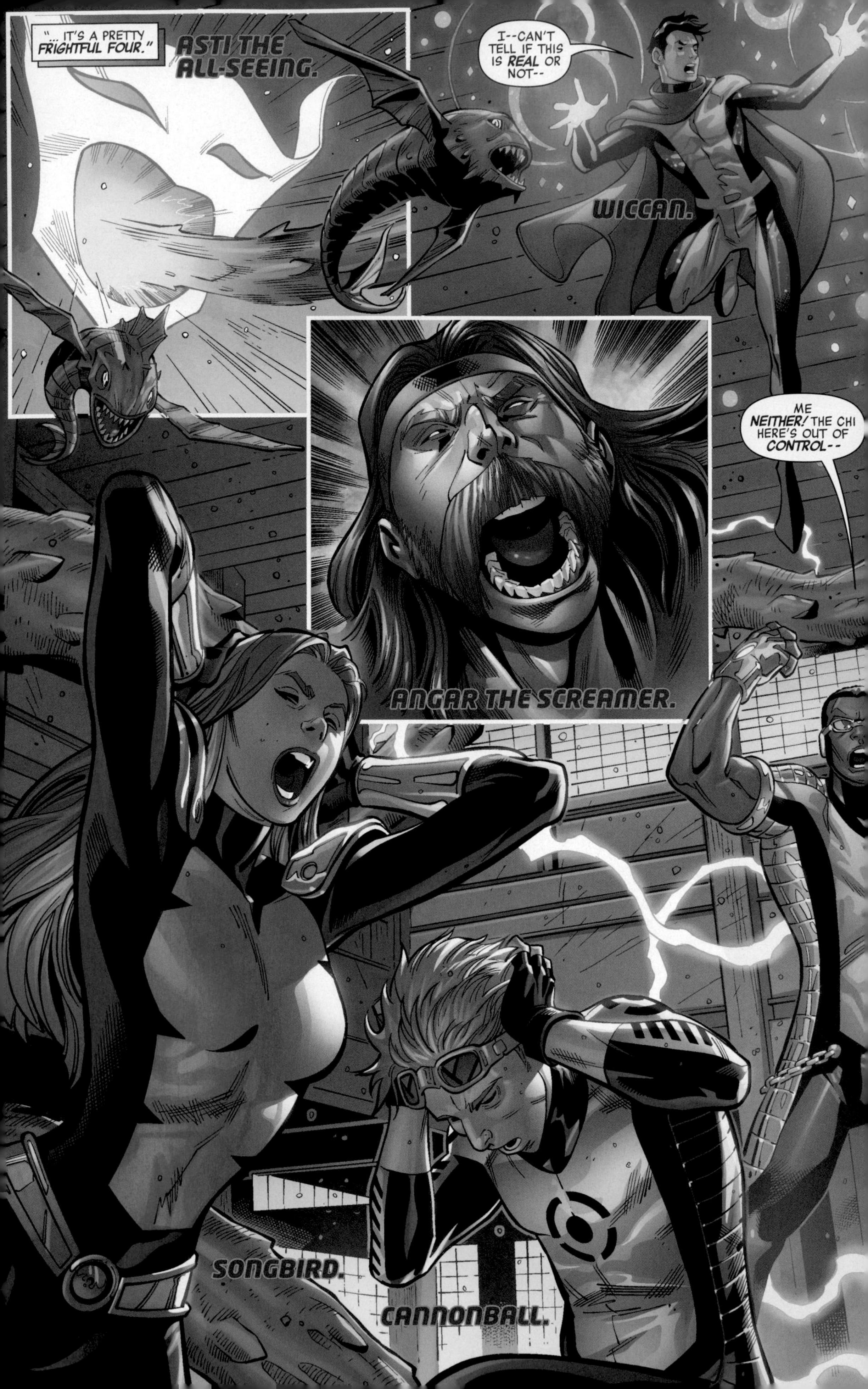
"... IT'S A PRETTY FRIGHTFUL FOUR."
ASTI THE ALL-SEEING.
I--CAN'T TELL IF THIS IS REAL OR NOT--
WICCAN.
ME NEITHER! THE CHI HERE'S OUT OF CONTROL--
ANGAR THE SCREAMER.
SONGBIRD.
CANNONBALL.

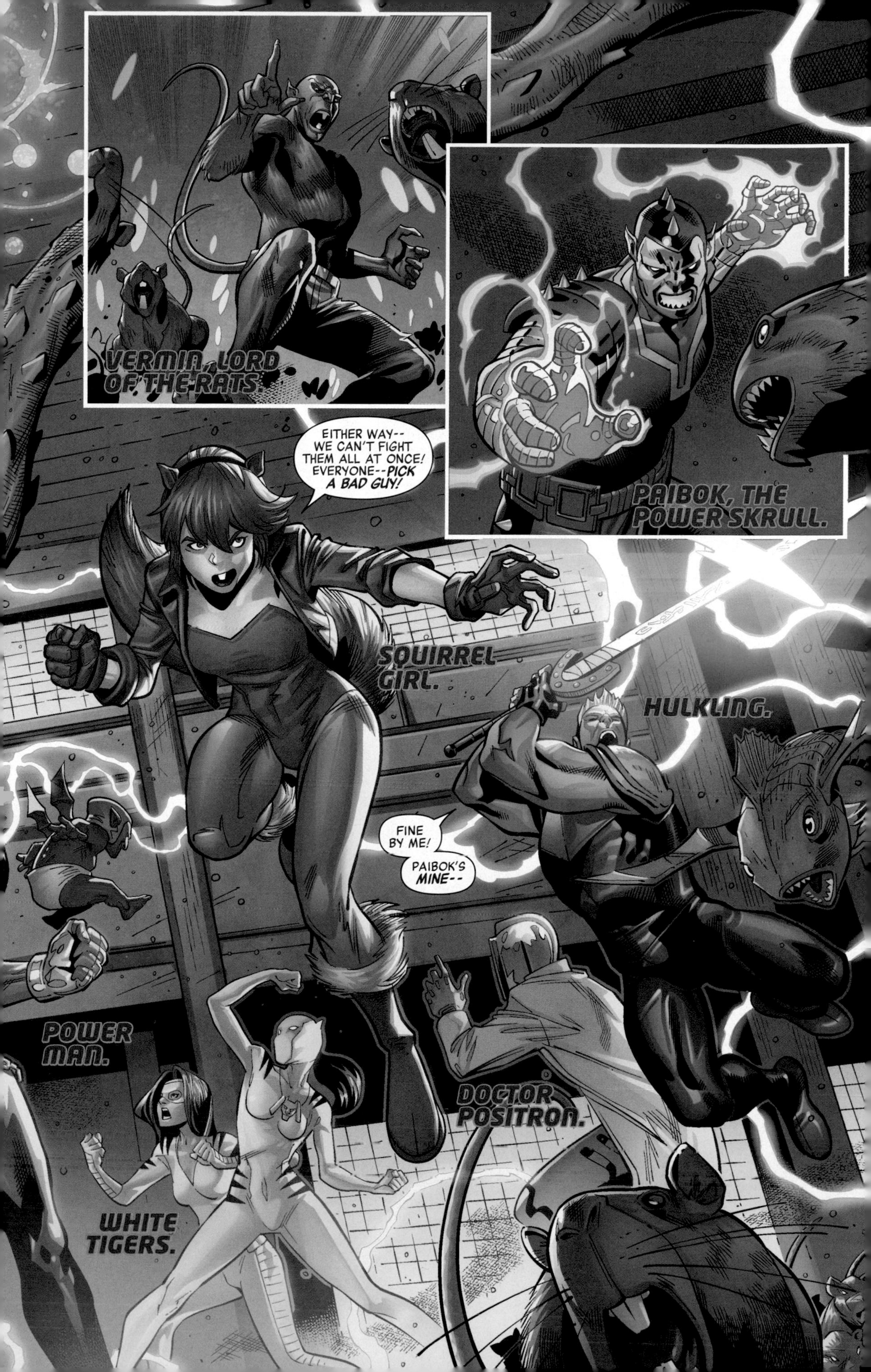
VERMIN, LORD OF THE RATS.
PAIBOK, THE POWER SKRULL.
EITHER WAY-- WE CAN'T FIGHT THEM ALL AT ONCE! EVERYONE--PICK A BAD GUY!
SQUIRREL GIRL.
HULKLING.
FINE BY ME!
PAIBOK'S MINE--
POWER MAN.
DOCTOR POSITRON.
WHITE TIGERS.

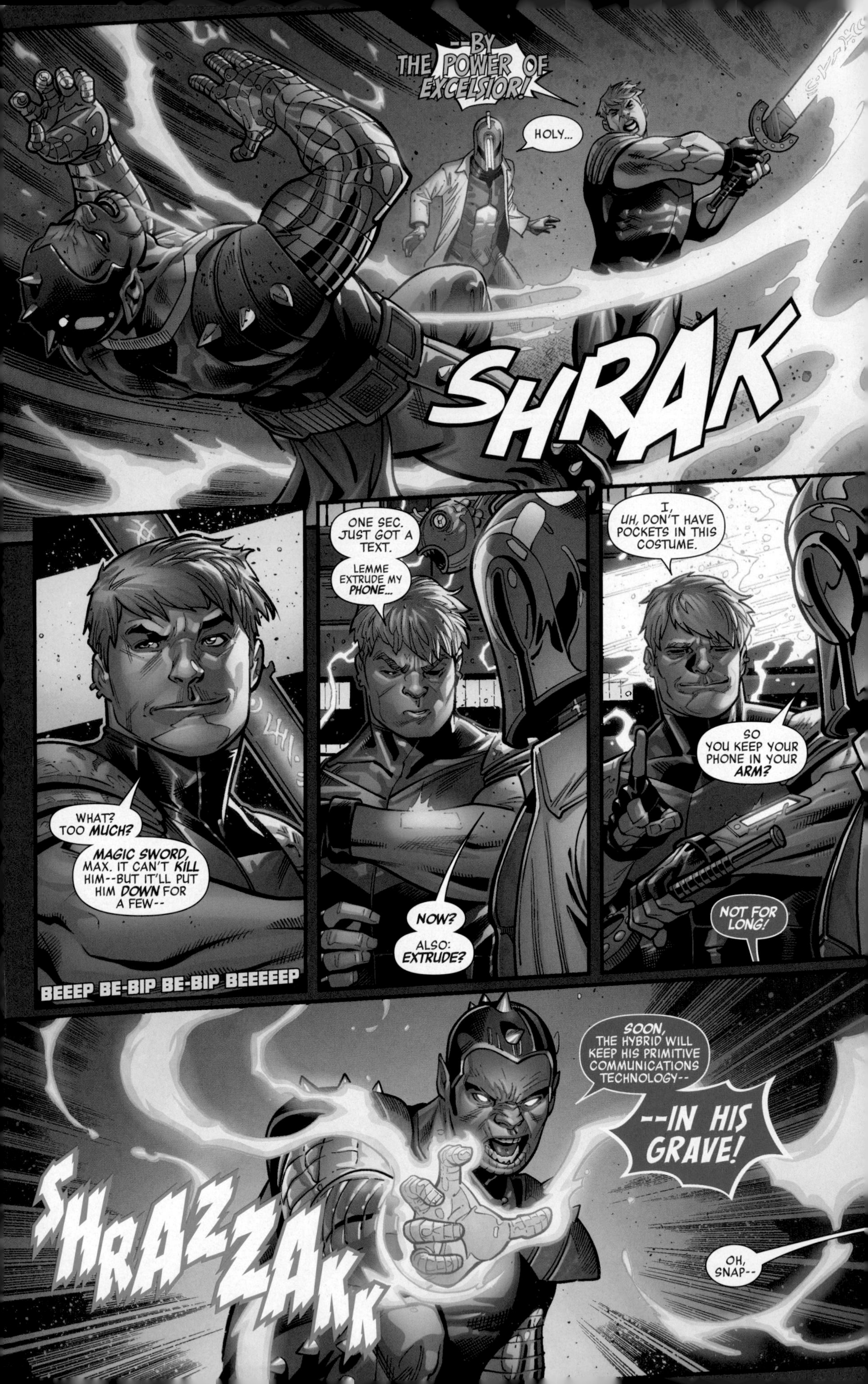
--BY THE POWER OF EXCELSIOR!
HOLY...
SHRAK
WHAT? TOO MUCH?
MAGIC SWORD, MAX. IT CAN'T KILL HIM--BUT IT'LL PUT HIM DOWN FOR A FEW--
BEEEP BE-BIP BE-BIP BEEEEEP
ONE SEC. JUST GOT A TEXT.
LEMME EXTRUDE MY PHONE...
NOW?
ALSO: EXTRUDE?
I, UH, DON'T HAVE POCKETS IN THIS COSTUME.
SO YOU KEEP YOUR PHONE IN YOUR ARM?
NOT FOR LONG!
SOON, THE HYBRID WILL KEEP HIS PRIMITIVE COMMUNICATIONS TECHNOLOGY--
--IN HIS GRAVE!
SHRAZZAKK
OH, SNAP--

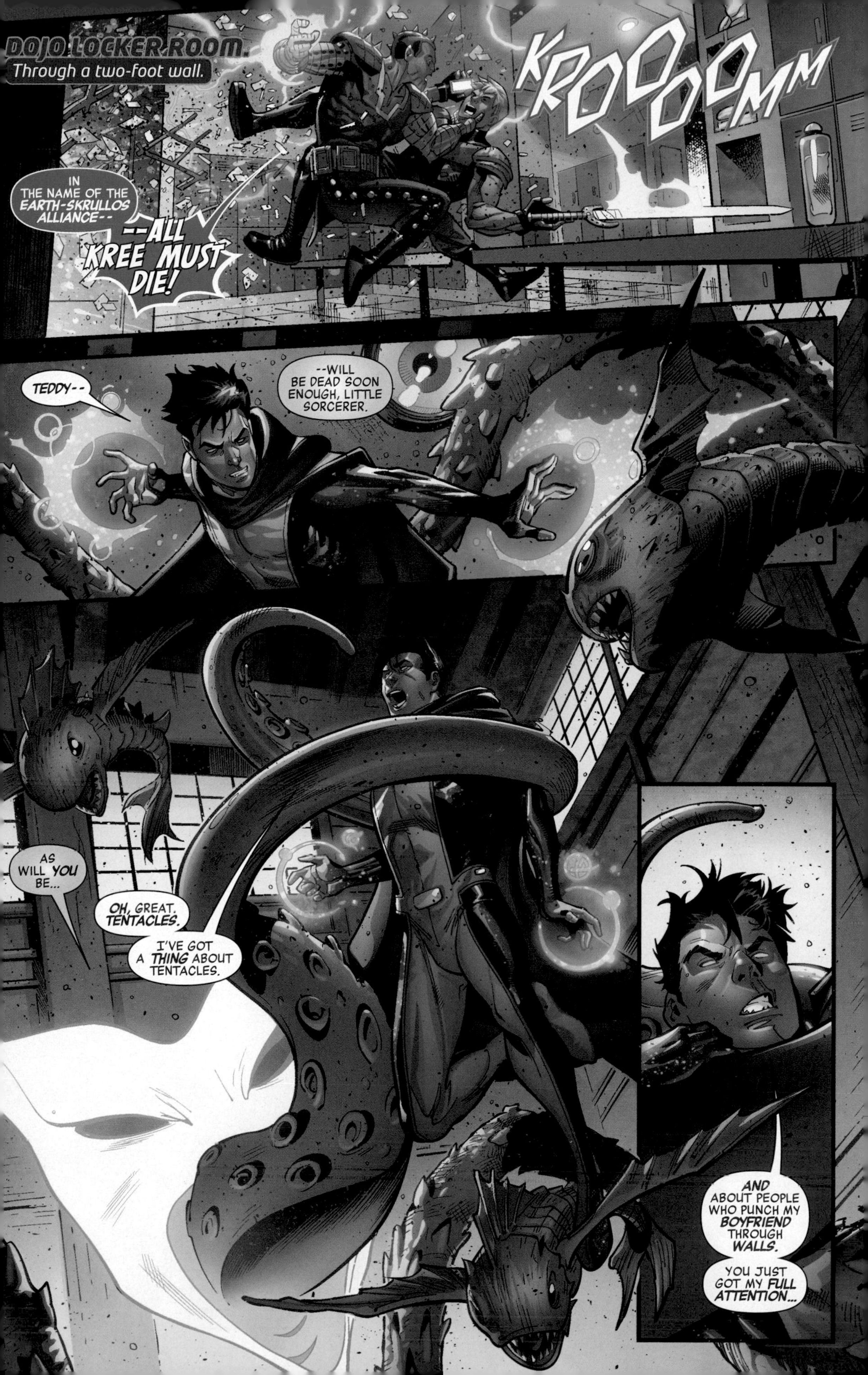
DOJO LOCKER ROOM.
Through a two-foot wall.
KROOOOMM
IN THE NAME OF THE EARTH-SKRULLOS ALLIANCE--
--ALL KREE MUST DIE!
TEDDY--
--WILL BE DEAD SOON ENOUGH, LITTLE SORCERER.
AS WILL YOU BE...
OH, GREAT. TENTACLES.
I'VE GOT A THING ABOUT TENTACLES.
AND ABOUT PEOPLE WHO PUNCH MY BOYFRIEND THROUGH WALLS.
YOU JUST GOT MY FULL ATTENTION...

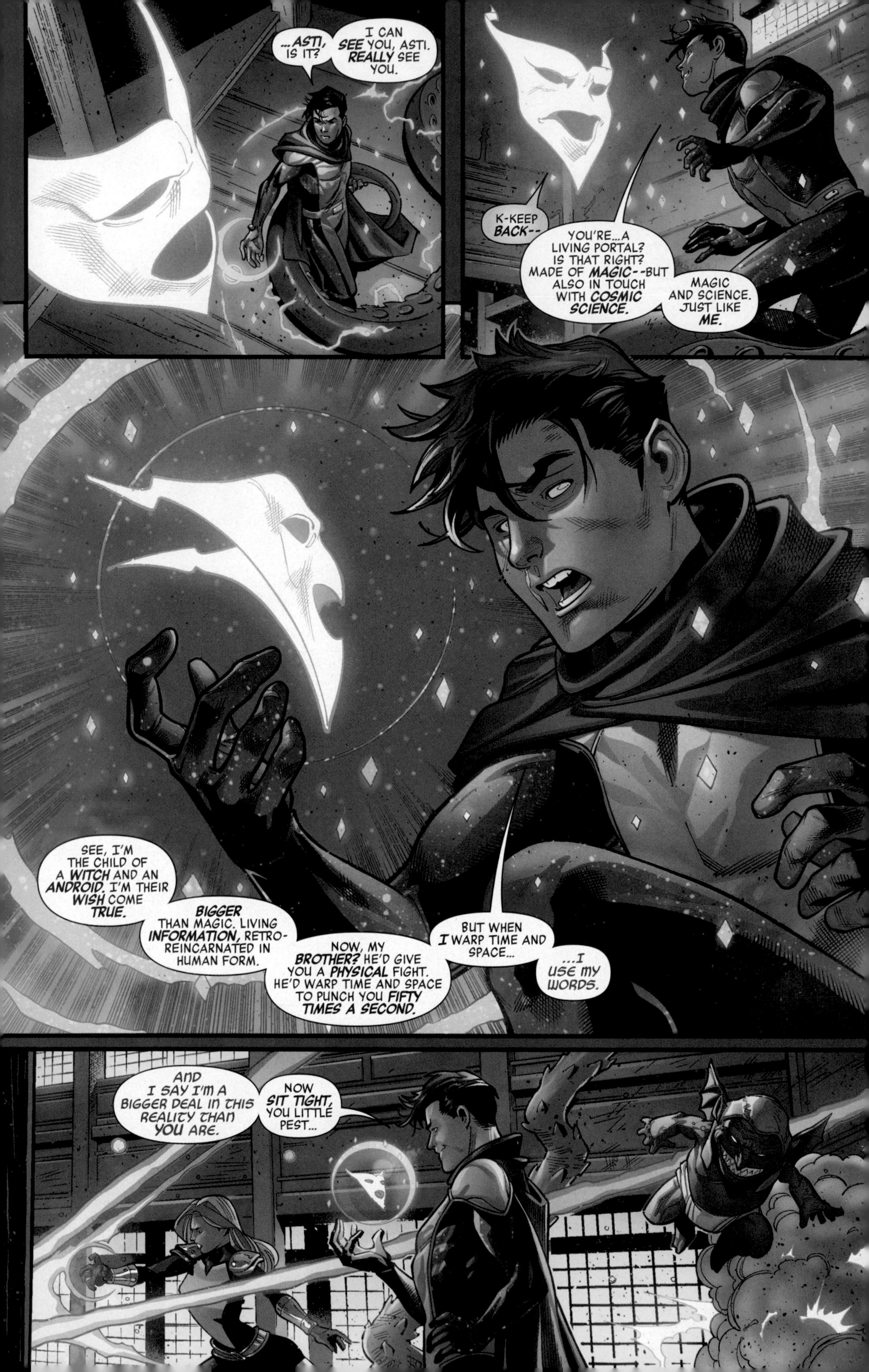
...ASTI, IS IT?
I CAN SEE YOU, ASTI. REALLY SEE YOU.
K-KEEP BACK--
YOU'RE...A LIVING PORTAL? IS THAT RIGHT? MADE OF MAGIC--BUT ALSO IN TOUCH WITH COSMIC SCIENCE.
MAGIC AND SCIENCE. JUST LIKE ME.
SEE, I'M THE CHILD OF A WITCH AND AN ANDROID. I'M THEIR WISH COME TRUE.
BIGGER THAN MAGIC. LIVING INFORMATION, RETRO-REINCARNATED IN HUMAN FORM.
NOW, MY BROTHER? HE'D GIVE YOU A PHYSICAL FIGHT. HE'D WARP TIME AND SPACE TO PUNCH YOU FIFTY TIMES A SECOND.
BUT WHEN I WARP TIME AND SPACE...
...I USE MY WORDS.
AND I SAY I'M A BIGGER DEAL IN THIS REALITY THAN YOU ARE.
NOW SIT TIGHT, YOU LITTLE PEST...

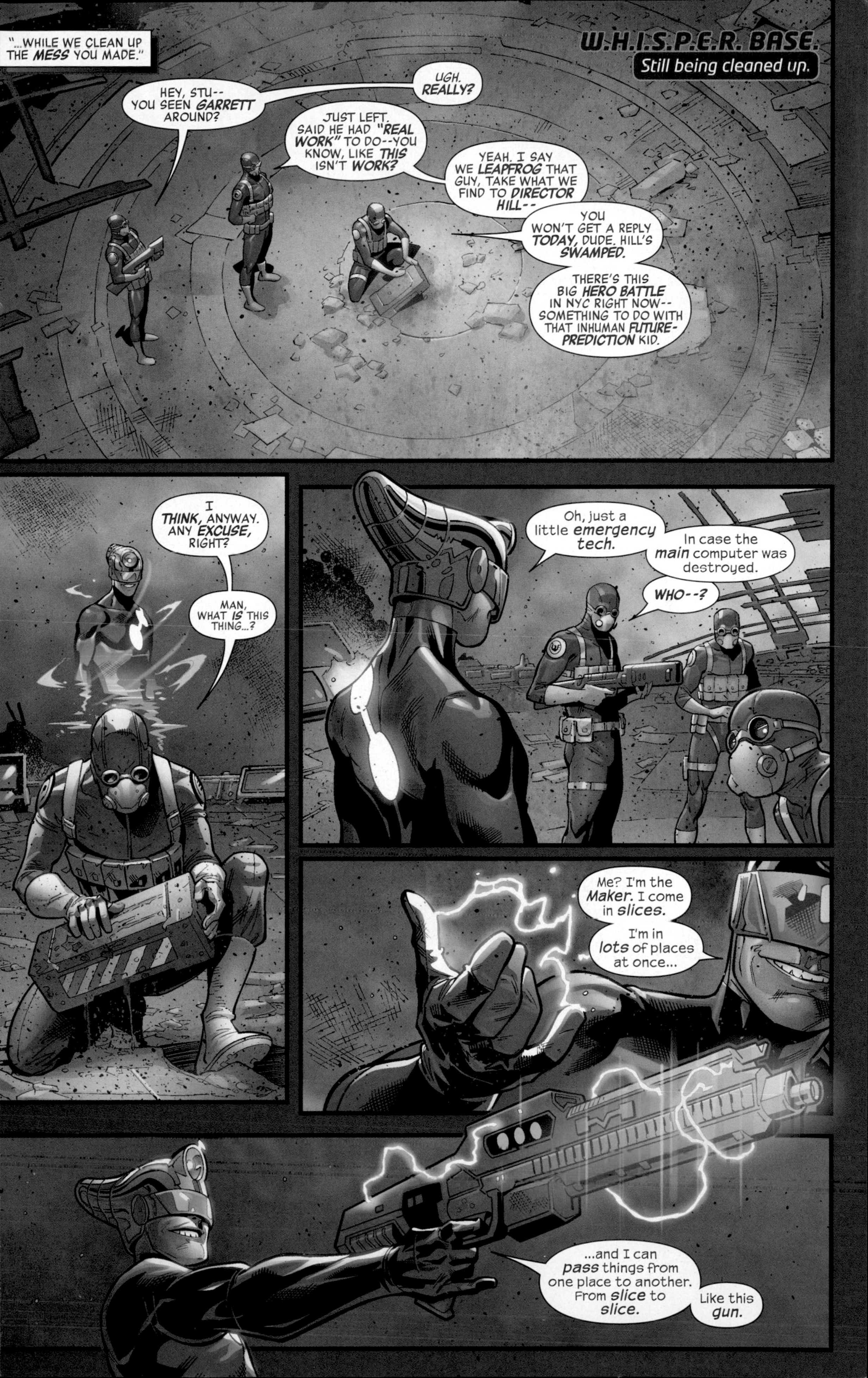
"...WHILE WE CLEAN UP THE MESS YOU MADE."
W.H.I.S.P.E.R. BASE.
Still being cleaned up.
HEY, STU-- YOU SEEN GARRETT AROUND?
UGH. REALLY?
JUST LEFT. SAID HE HAD "REAL WORK" TO DO--YOU KNOW, LIKE THIS ISN'T WORK?
YEAH. I SAY WE LEAPFROG THAT GUY, TAKE WHAT WE FIND TO DIRECTOR HILL--
YOU WON'T GET A REPLY TODAY, DUDE. HILL'S SWAMPED.
THERE'S THIS BIG HERO BATTLE IN NYC RIGHT NOW-- SOMETHING TO DO WITH THAT INHUMAN FUTURE-PREDICTION KID.
I THINK, ANYWAY. ANY EXCUSE, RIGHT?
MAN, WHAT IS THIS THING...?
Oh, just a little emergency tech.
In case the main computer was destroyed.
WHO--?
Me? I'm the Maker. I come in slices.
I'm in lots of places at once...
...and I can pass things from one place to another. From slice to slice.
Like this gun.

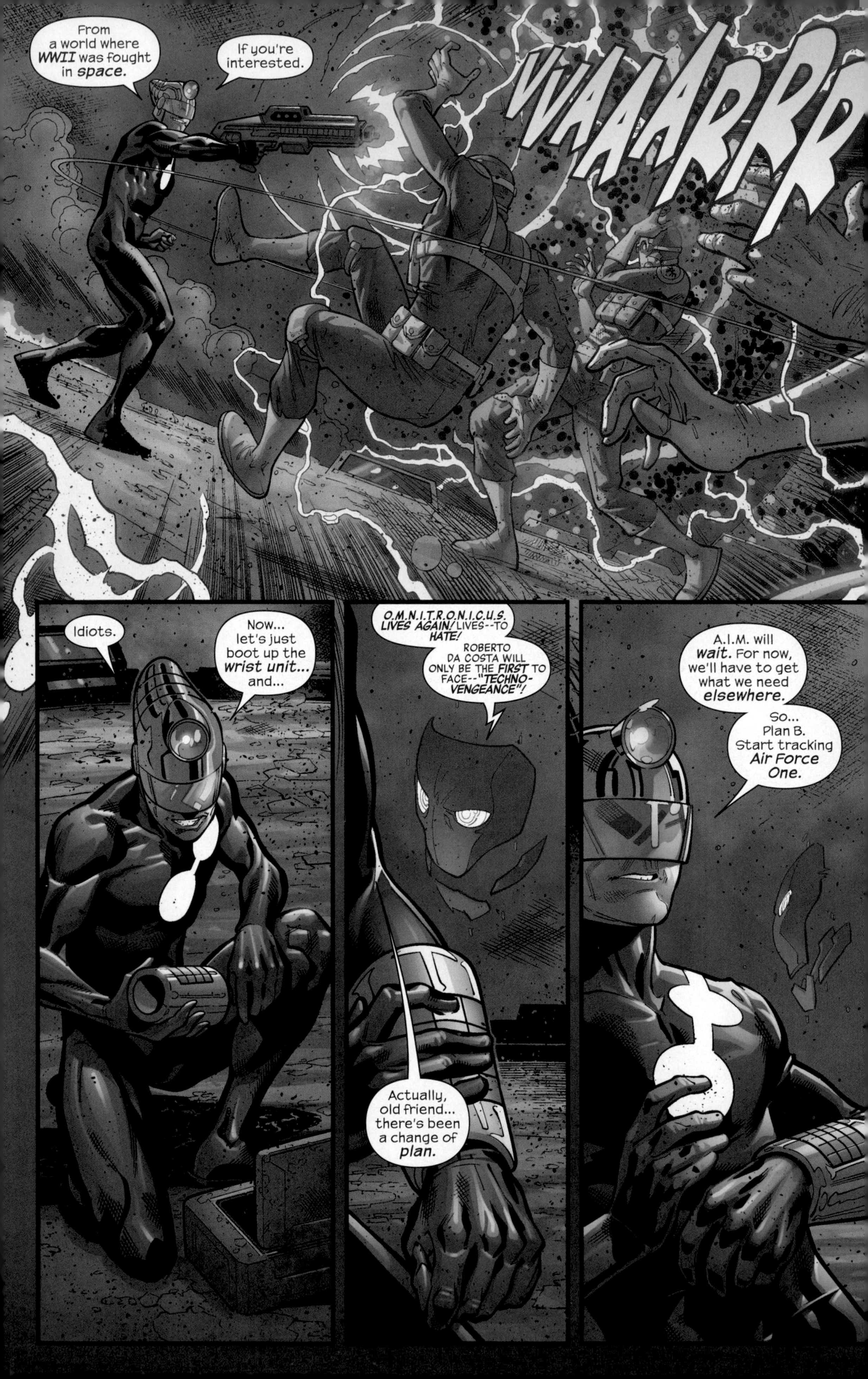
From a world where WWII was fought in space.
If you're interested.
VVAAAARRR
Idiots.
Now... let's just boot up the wrist unit... and...
O.M.N.I.T.R.O.N.I.C.U.S. LIVES AGAIN! LIVES--TO HATE!
ROBERTO DA COSTA WILL ONLY BE THE FIRST TO FACE--"TECHNO-VENGEANCE"!
Actually, old friend... there's been a change of plan.
A.I.M. will wait. For now, we'll have to get what we need elsewhere.
So... Plan B. Start tracking Air Force One.

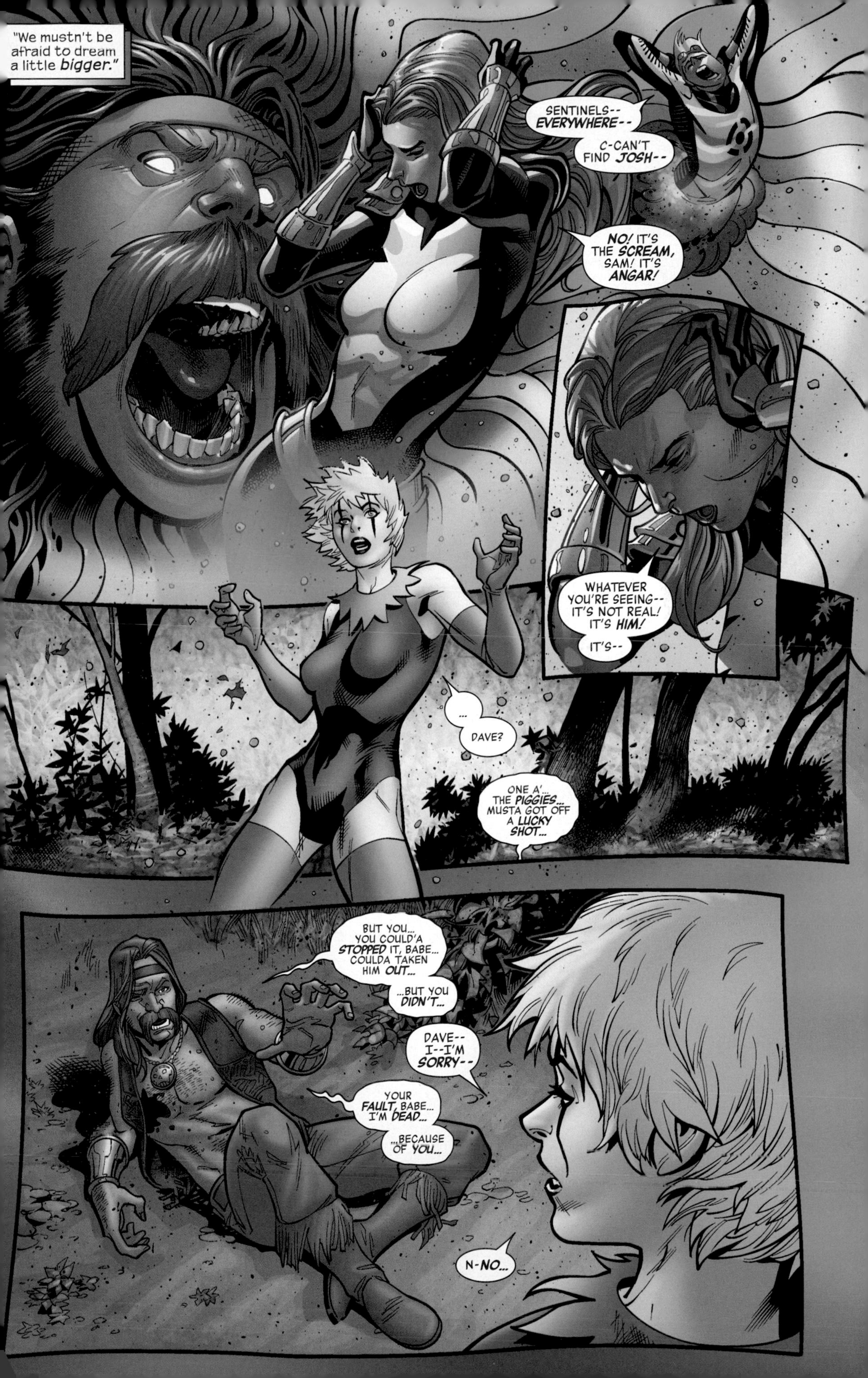
"We mustn't be afraid to dream a little *bigger.*"
SENTINELS-- *EVERYWHERE*--
C-CAN'T FIND *JOSH*--
NO! IT'S THE *SCREAM,* SAM! IT'S *ANGAR!*
WHATEVER YOU'RE SEEING-- IT'S NOT REAL! IT'S *HIM!*
IT'S--
...
DAVE?
ONE A'... THE *PIGGIES*... MUSTA GOT OFF A *LUCKY SHOT*...
BUT YOU... YOU COULD'A *STOPPED* IT, BABE... COULDA TAKEN HIM *OUT*...
...BUT YOU *DIDN'T*...
DAVE-- I--I'M *SORRY*--
YOUR *FAULT,* BABE... I'M *DEAD*...
...BECAUSE OF *YOU*...
N-*NO*...

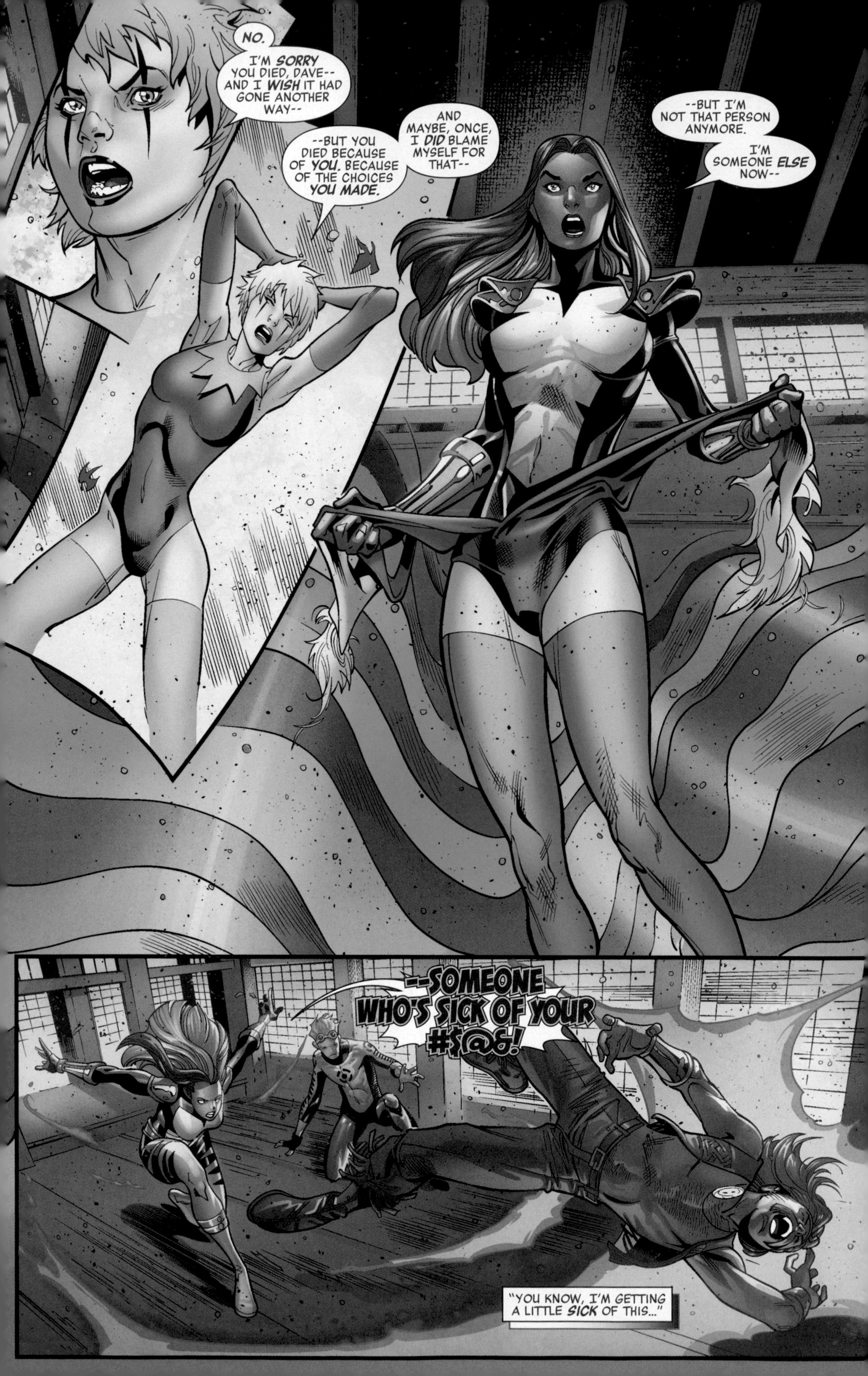
NO.
I'M SORRY YOU DIED, DAVE-- AND I WISH IT HAD GONE ANOTHER WAY--
--BUT YOU DIED BECAUSE OF YOU. BECAUSE OF THE CHOICES YOU MADE.
AND MAYBE, ONCE, I DID BLAME MYSELF FOR THAT--
--BUT I'M NOT THAT PERSON ANYMORE.
I'M SOMEONE ELSE NOW--
--SOMEONE WHO'S SICK OF YOUR #$@&!
"YOU KNOW, I'M GETTING A LITTLE SICK OF THIS..."

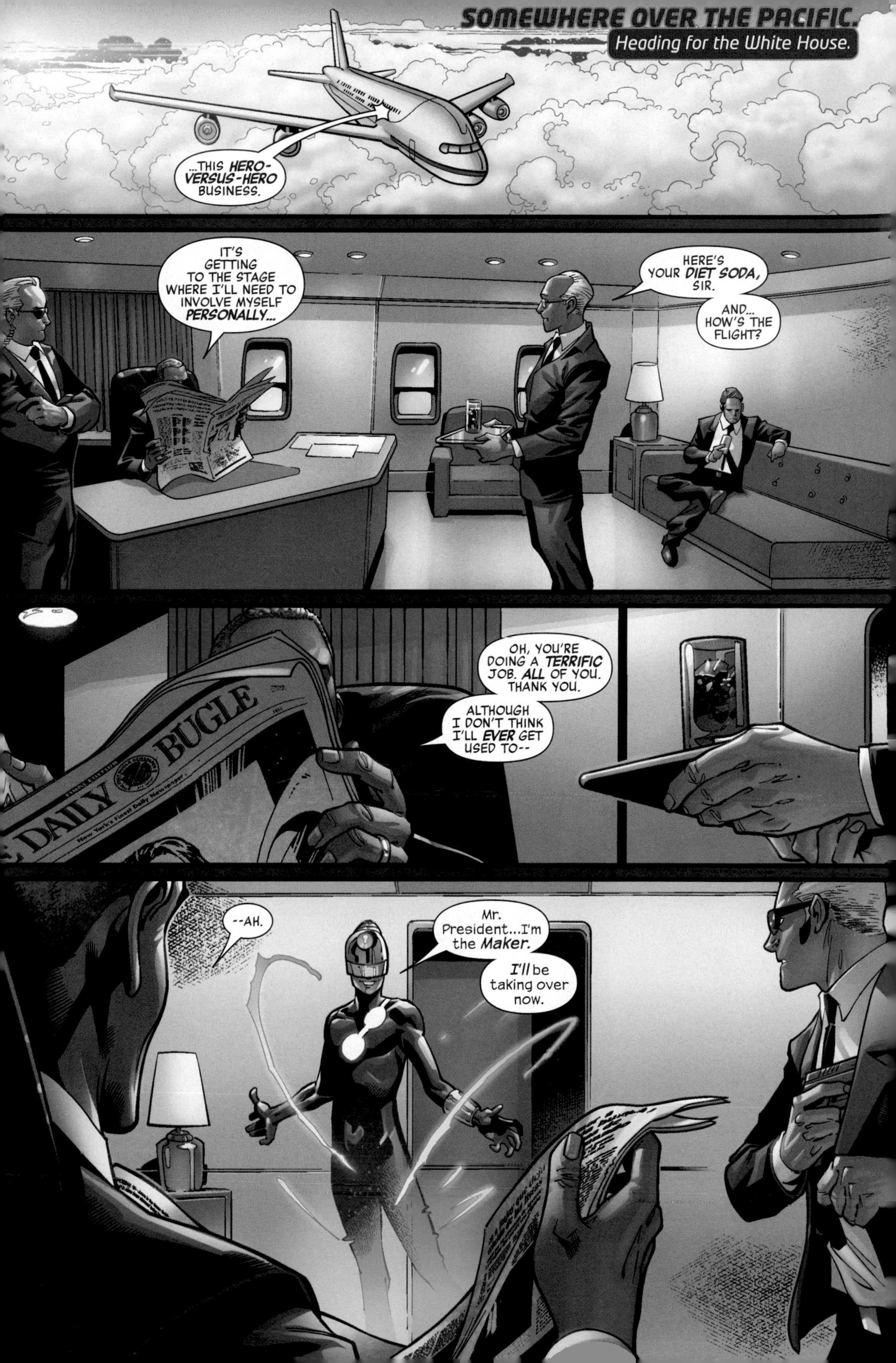
SOMEWHERE OVER THE PACIFIC.
Heading for the White House.
...THIS HERO-VERSUS-HERO BUSINESS.
IT'S GETTING TO THE STAGE WHERE I'LL NEED TO INVOLVE MYSELF PERSONALLY...
HERE'S YOUR DIET SODA, SIR.
AND... HOW'S THE FLIGHT?
DAILY BUGLE
New York's Finest Daily Newspaper
OH, YOU'RE DOING A TERRIFIC JOB. ALL OF YOU. THANK YOU.
ALTHOUGH I DON'T THINK I'LL EVER GET USED TO--
--AH.
Mr. President...I'm the Maker.
I'll be taking over now.

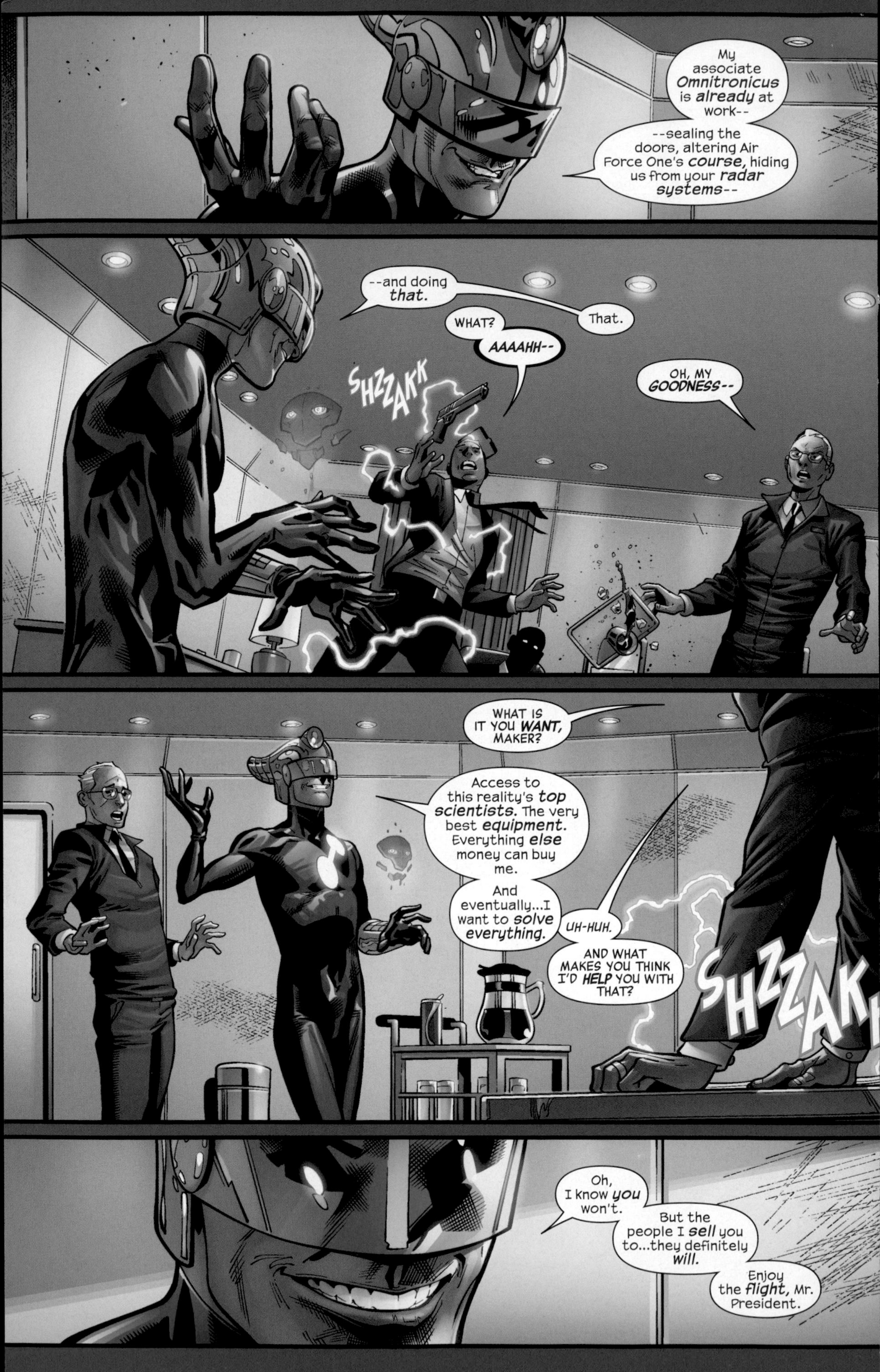

My associate Omnitronicus is already at work--
--sealing the doors, altering Air Force One's course, hiding us from your radar systems--
--and doing that.
That.
WHAT?
AAAAHH--
SHZZAKK
OH, MY GOODNESS--
WHAT IS IT YOU WANT, MAKER?
Access to this reality's top scientists. The very best equipment. Everything else money can buy me.
And eventually...I want to solve everything.
UH-HUH.
AND WHAT MAKES YOU THINK I'D HELP YOU WITH THAT?
SHZZAKK
Oh, I know you won't.
But the people I sell you to...they definitely will.
Enjoy the flight, Mr. President.

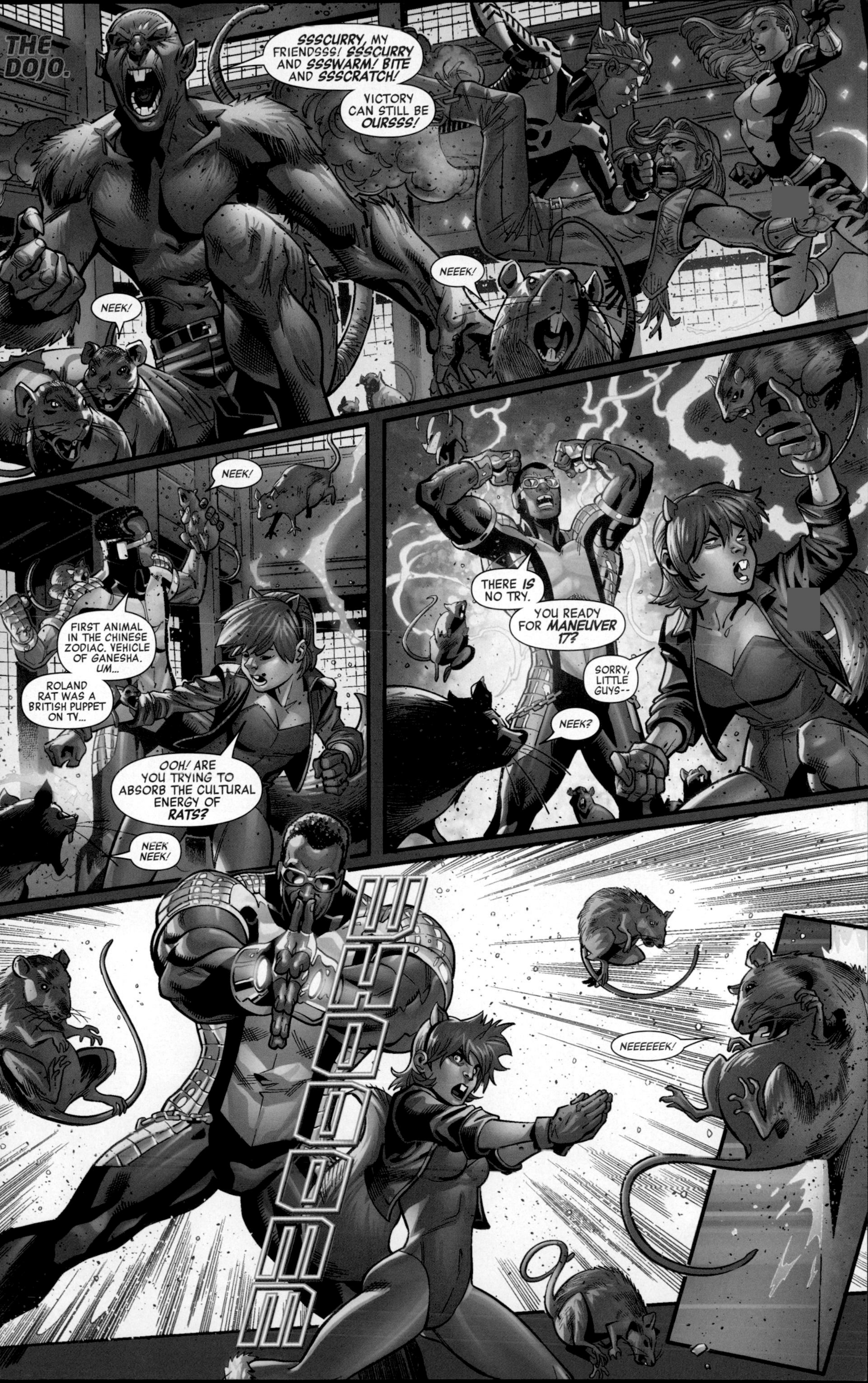
THE DOJO.
SSSCURRY, MY FRIENDSSS! SSSCURRY AND SSSWARM! BITE AND SSSCRATCH!
VICTORY CAN STILL BE OURSSS!
NEEEK!
NEEK!
NEEK!
FIRST ANIMAL IN THE CHINESE ZODIAC. VEHICLE OF GANESHA. UM...
ROLAND RAT WAS A BRITISH PUPPET ON TV...
OOH! ARE YOU TRYING TO ABSORB THE CULTURAL ENERGY OF RATS?
NEEK NEEK!
THERE IS NO TRY.
YOU READY FOR MANEUVER 17?
SORRY, LITTLE GUYS--
NEEK?
NEEEEEEK!

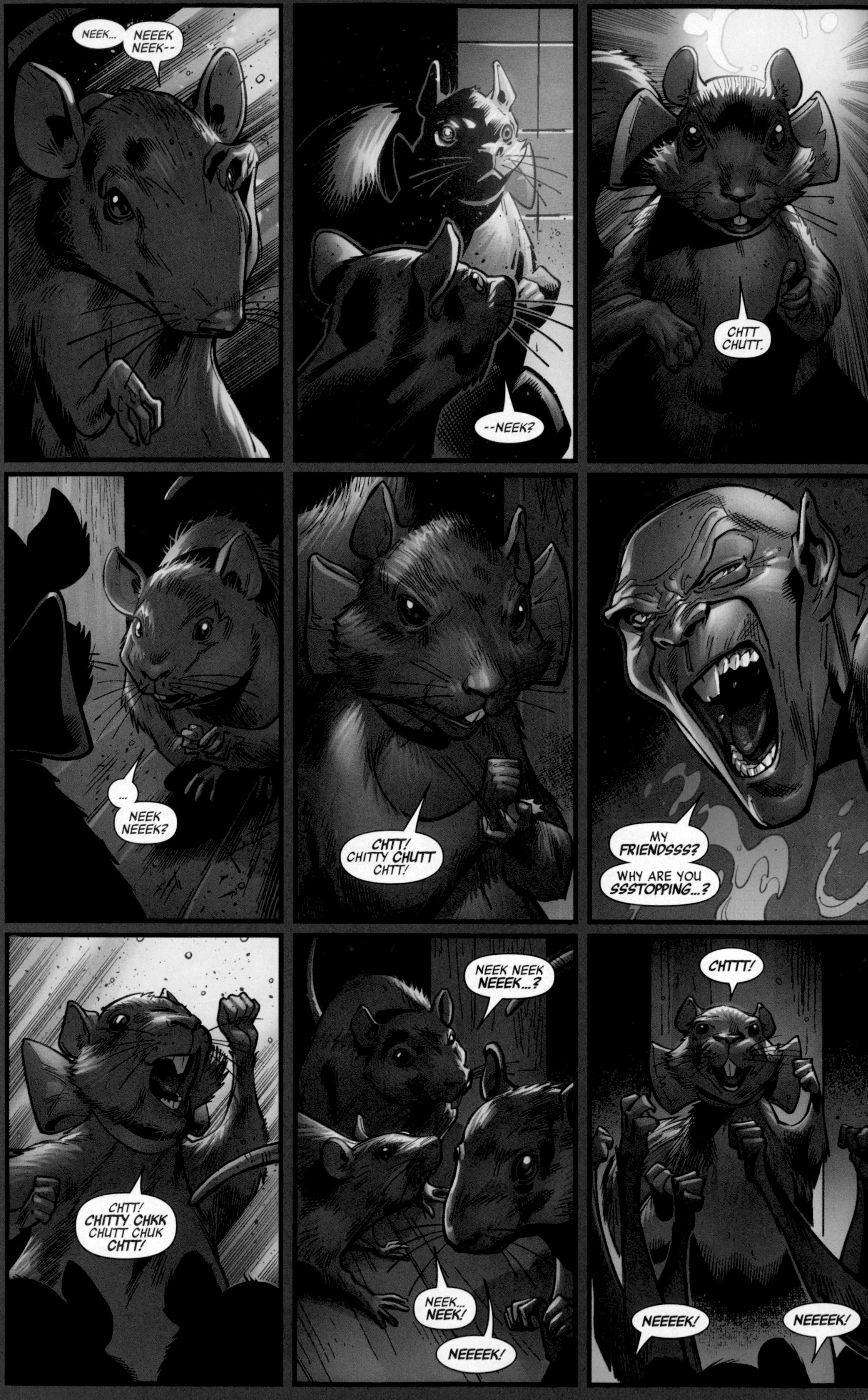
NEEK...
NEEEK NEEK--
--NEEK?
CHTT CHUTT.
... NEEK NEEEK?
CHTT! CHITTY CHUTT CHTT!
MY FRIENDSSS?
WHY ARE YOU SSSTOPPING...?
CHTT! CHITTY CHKK CHUTT CHUK CHTT!
NEEK NEEK NEEEK...?
NEEK... NEEK!
NEEEEK!
CHTTT!
NEEEEK!
NEEEEK!

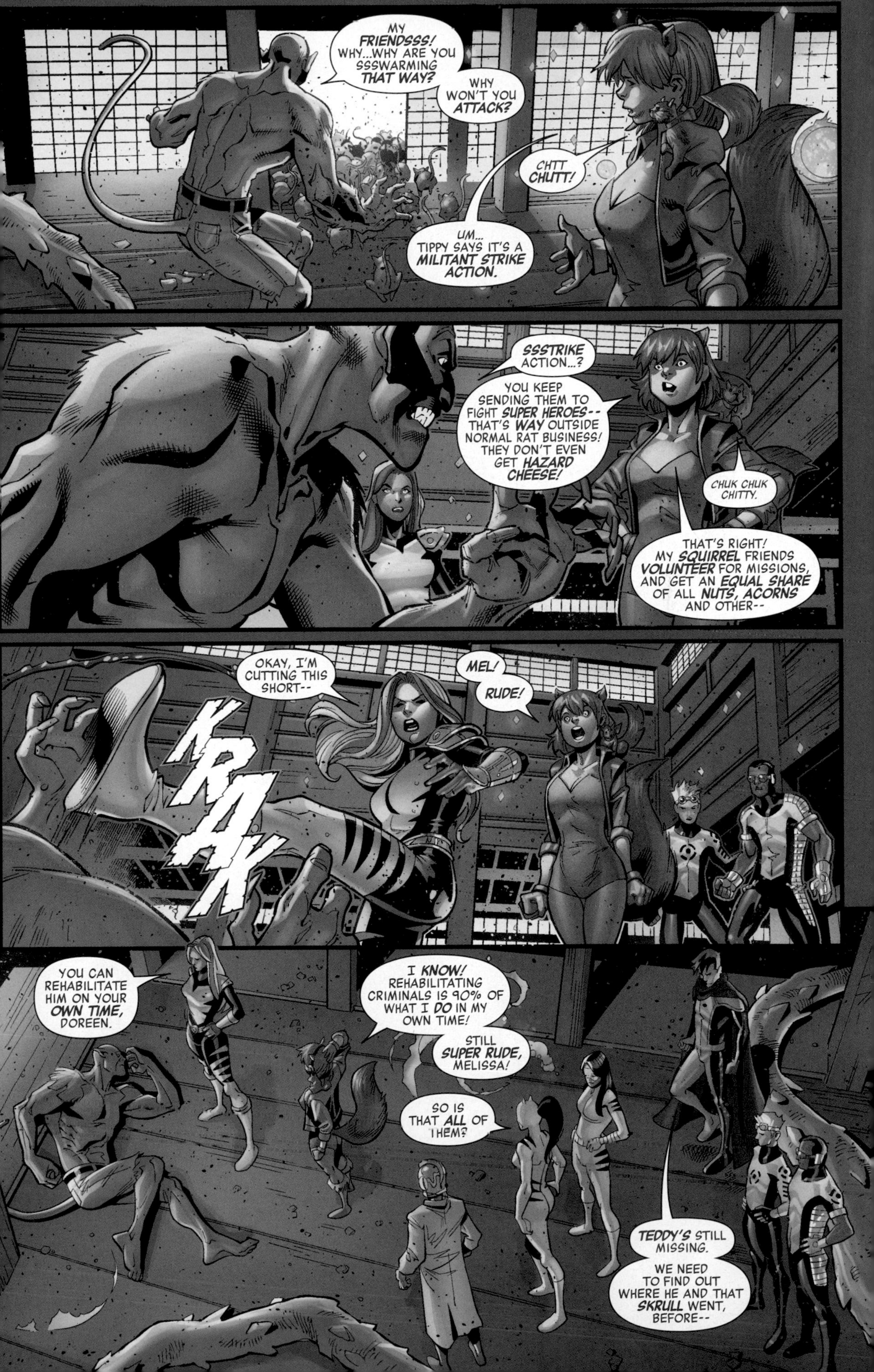
MY FRIENDSSS! WHY...WHY ARE YOU SSSWARMING THAT WAY?
WHY WON'T YOU ATTACK?
CHTT CHUTT!
UM... TIPPY SAYS IT'S A MILITANT STRIKE ACTION.
SSSTRIKE ACTION...?
YOU KEEP SENDING THEM TO FIGHT SUPER HEROES-- THAT'S WAY OUTSIDE NORMAL RAT BUSINESS! THEY DON'T EVEN GET HAZARD CHEESE!
CHUK CHUK CHITTY.
THAT'S RIGHT! MY SQUIRREL FRIENDS VOLUNTEER FOR MISSIONS, AND GET AN EQUAL SHARE OF ALL NUTS, ACORNS AND OTHER--
OKAY, I'M CUTTING THIS SHORT--
MEL!
RUDE!
KRAK
YOU CAN REHABILITATE HIM ON YOUR OWN TIME, DOREEN.
I KNOW! REHABILITATING CRIMINALS IS 90% OF WHAT I DO IN MY OWN TIME!
STILL SUPER RUDE, MELISSA!
SO IS THAT ALL OF THEM?
TEDDY'S STILL MISSING.
WE NEED TO FIND OUT WHERE HE AND THAT SKRULL WENT, BEFORE--

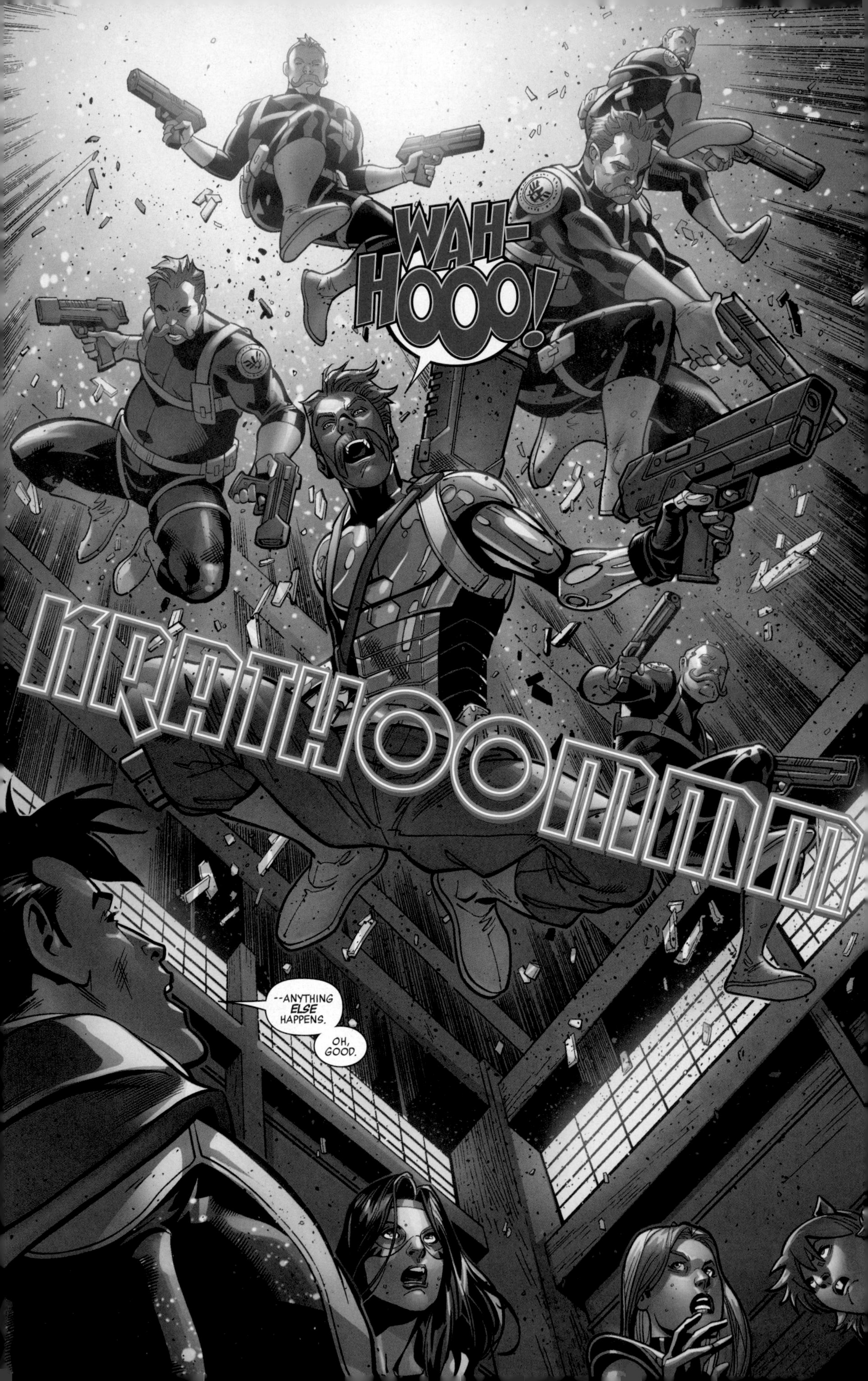
WAH-HOOO!
KRATHOOMMM
--ANYTHING ELSE HAPPENS.
OH, GOOD.

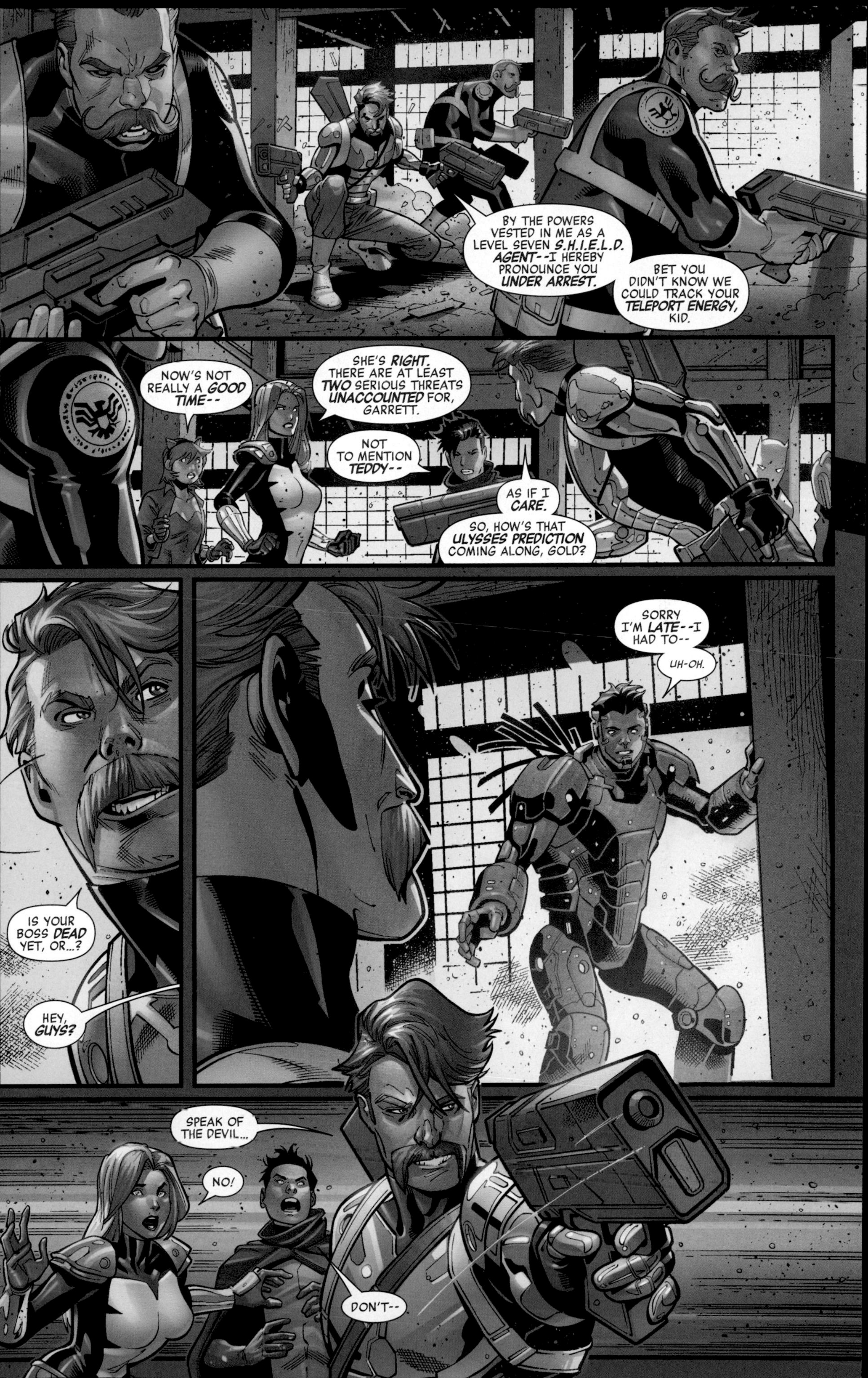
BY THE POWERS VESTED IN ME AS A LEVEL SEVEN S.H.I.E.L.D. AGENT--I HEREBY PRONOUNCE YOU UNDER ARREST.
BET YOU DIDN'T KNOW WE COULD TRACK YOUR TELEPORT ENERGY, KID.
NOW'S NOT REALLY A GOOD TIME--
SHE'S RIGHT. THERE ARE AT LEAST TWO SERIOUS THREATS UNACCOUNTED FOR, GARRETT.
NOT TO MENTION TEDDY--
AS IF I CARE.
SO, HOW'S THAT ULYSSES PREDICTION COMING ALONG, GOLD?
SORRY I'M LATE--I HAD TO--
UH-OH.
IS YOUR BOSS DEAD YET, OR...?
HEY, GUYS?
SPEAK OF THE DEVIL...
NO!
DON'T--

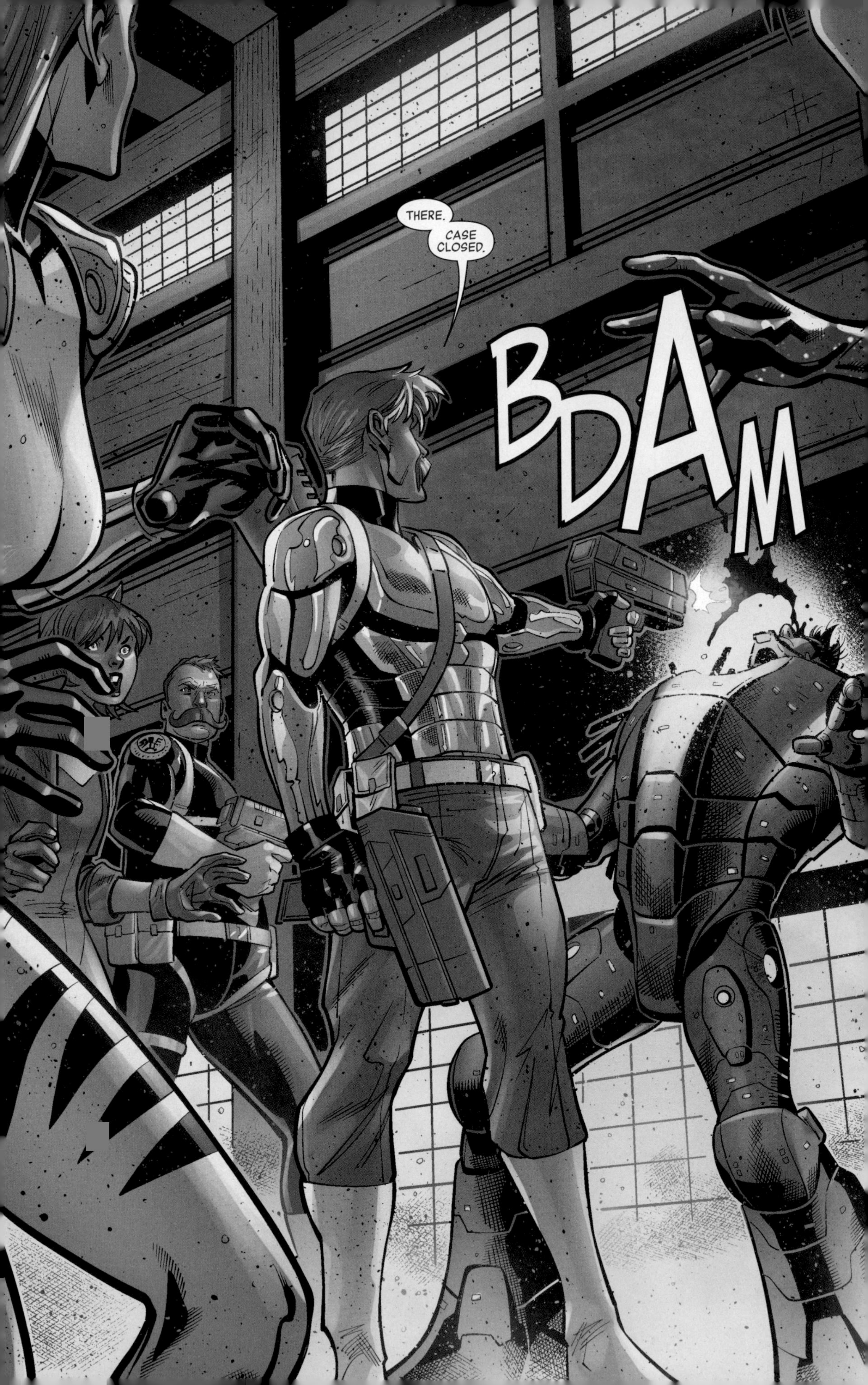
THERE.
CASE CLOSED.
BDAM

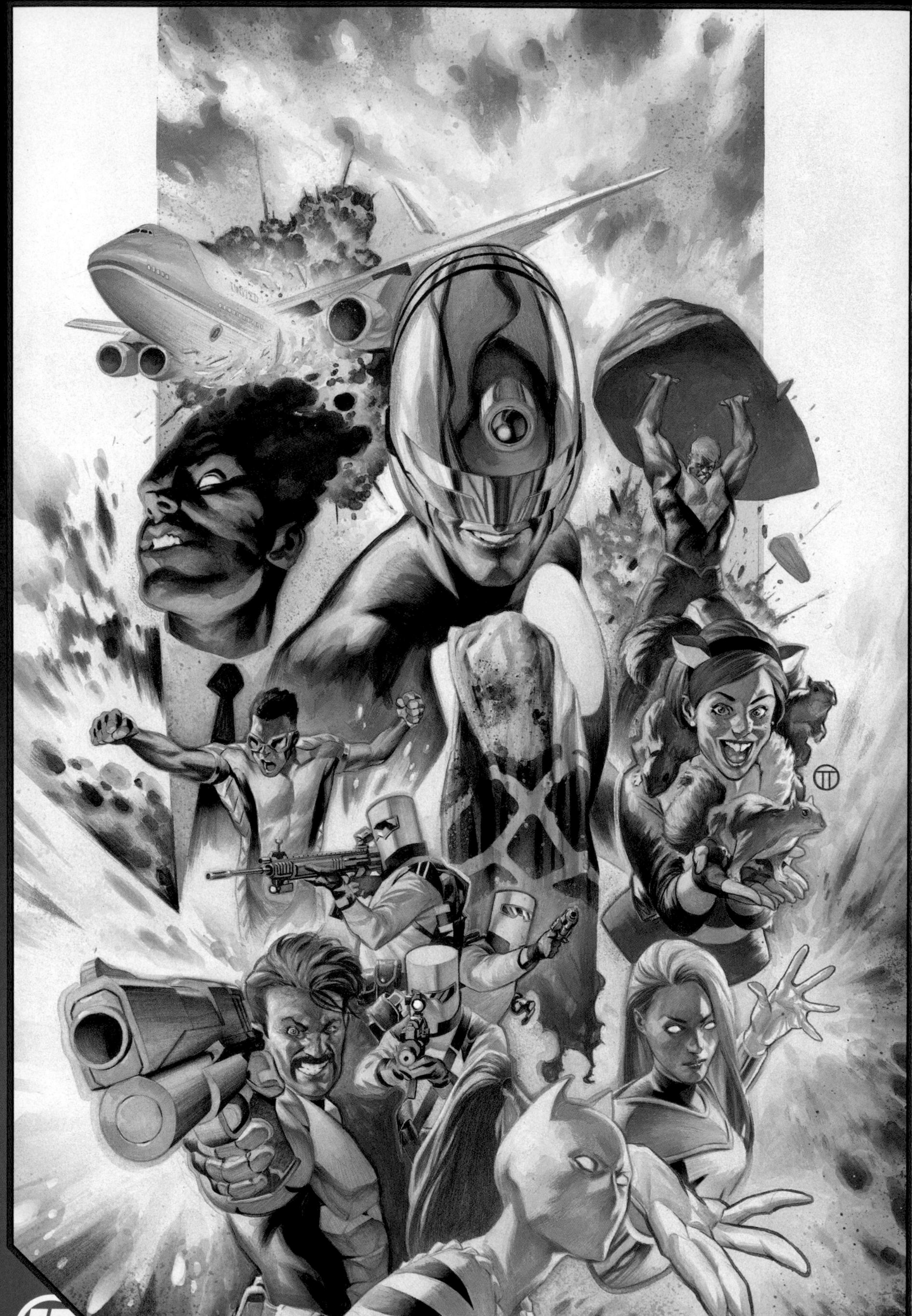
17

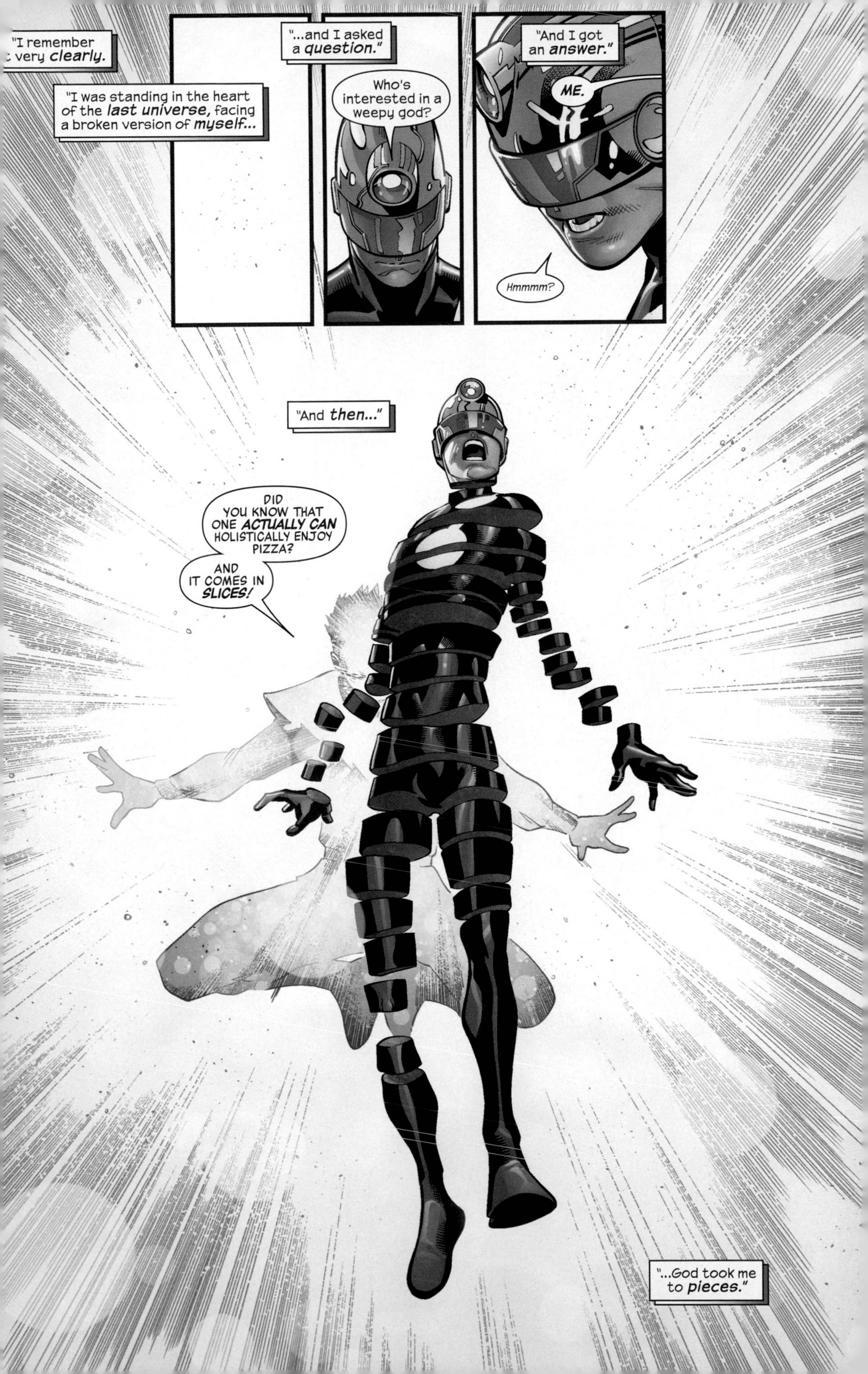
"I remember
t very clearly.
"I was standing in the heart of the last universe, facing a broken version of myself...
"...and I asked a question."
Who's interested in a weepy god?
"And I got an answer."
ME.
Hmmmm?
"And then..."
DID YOU KNOW THAT ONE ACTUALLY CAN HOLISTICALLY ENJOY PIZZA?
AND IT COMES IN SLICES!
"...God took me to pieces."

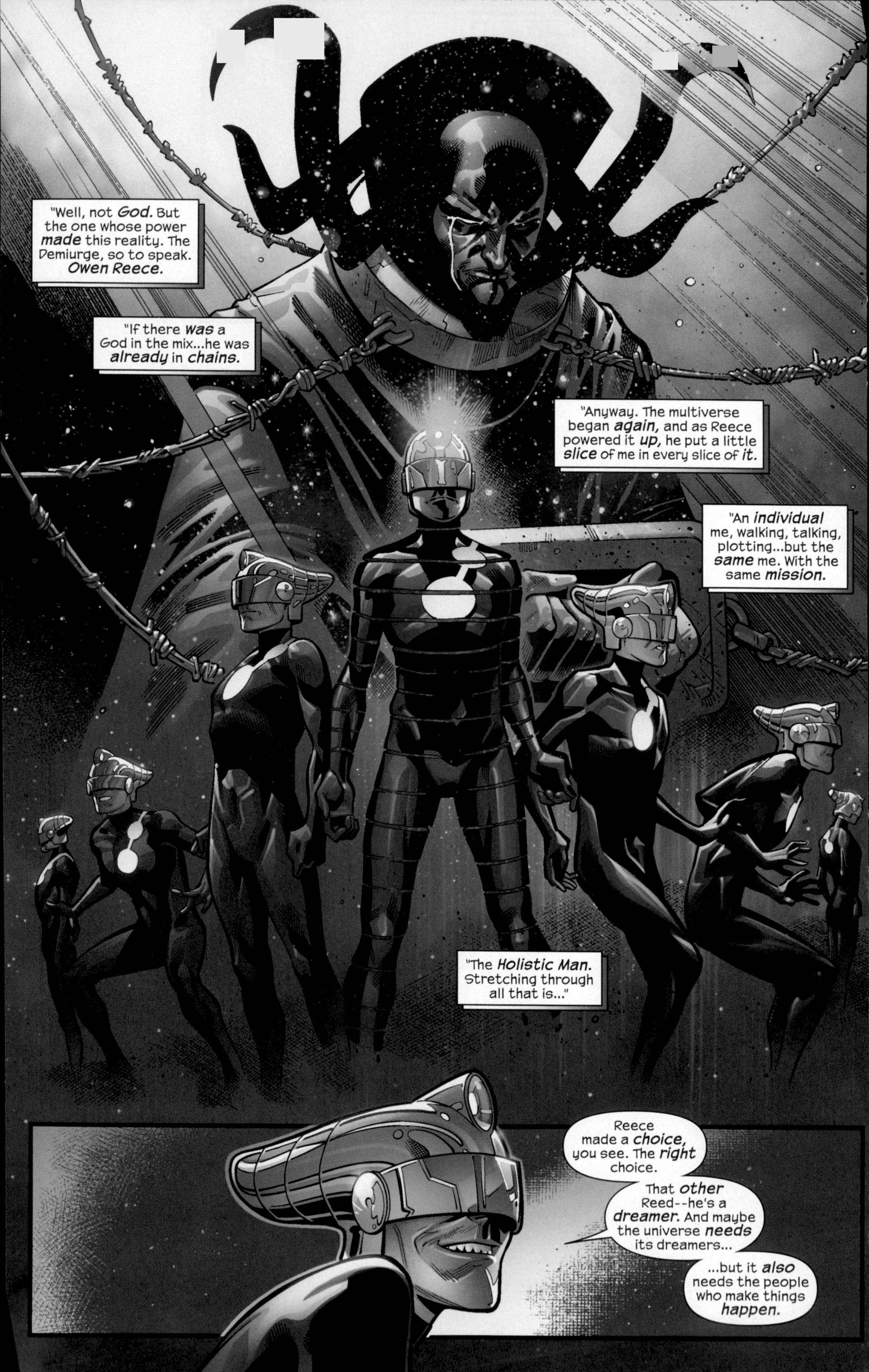
"Well, not God. But the one whose power made this reality. The Demiurge, so to speak. Owen Reece.
"If there was a God in the mix...he was already in chains.
"Anyway. The multiverse began again, and as Reece powered it up, he put a little slice of me in every slice of it.
"An individual me, walking, talking, plotting...but the same me. With the same mission.
"The Holistic Man. Stretching through all that is..."
Reece made a choice, you see. The right choice.
That other Reed--he's a dreamer. And maybe the universe needs its dreamers...
...but it also needs the people who make things happen.

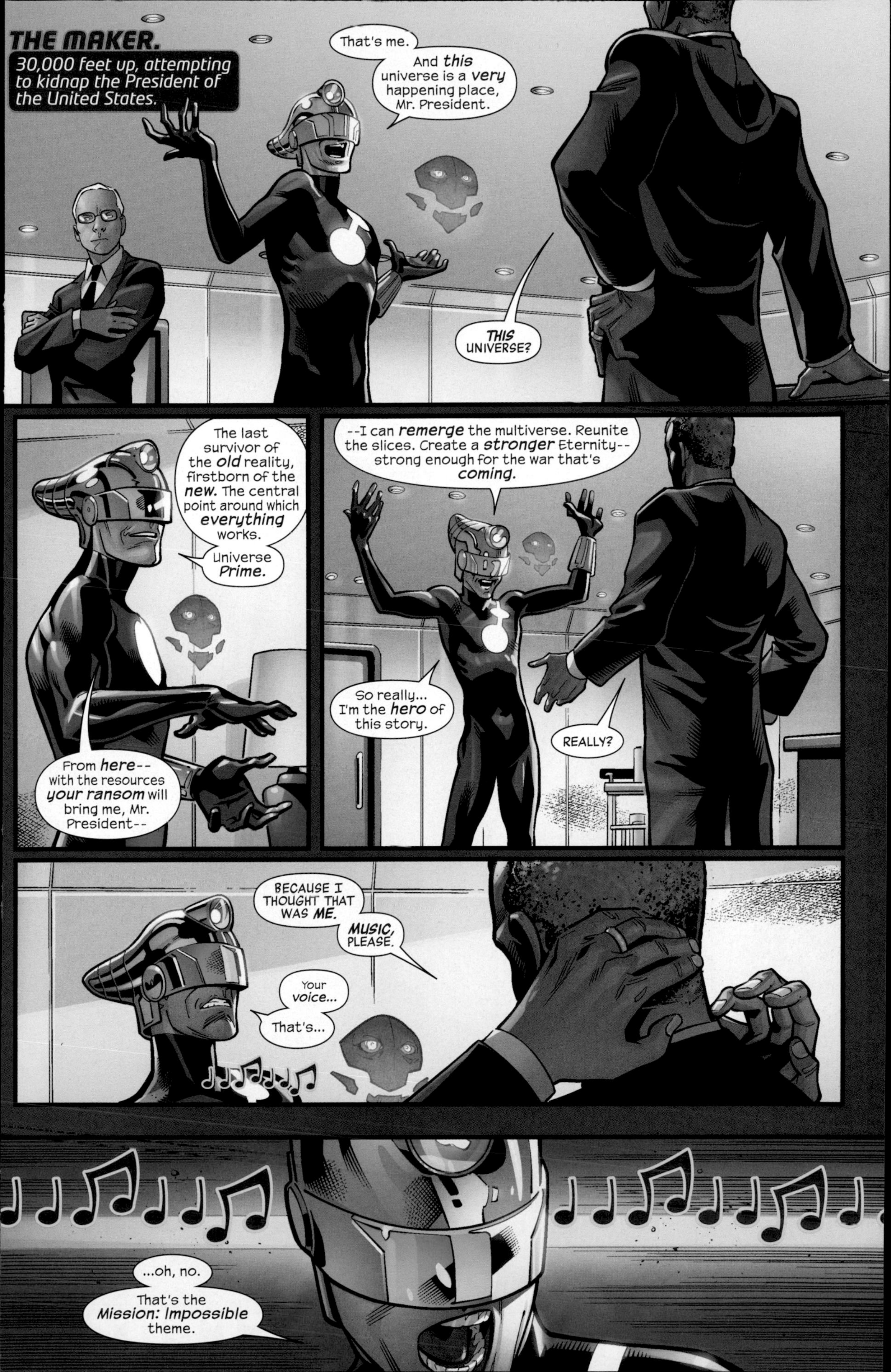
THE MAKER.
30,000 feet up, attempting to kidnap the President of the United States.
That's me.
And this universe is a very happening place, Mr. President.
THIS UNIVERSE?
The last survivor of the old reality, firstborn of the new. The central point around which everything works.
Universe Prime.
From here--with the resources your ransom will bring me, Mr. President--
--I can remerge the multiverse. Reunite the slices. Create a stronger Eternity--strong enough for the war that's coming.
So really... I'm the hero of this story.
REALLY?
BECAUSE I THOUGHT THAT WAS ME.
MUSIC, PLEASE.
Your voice...
That's...
...oh, no.
That's the Mission: Impossible theme.

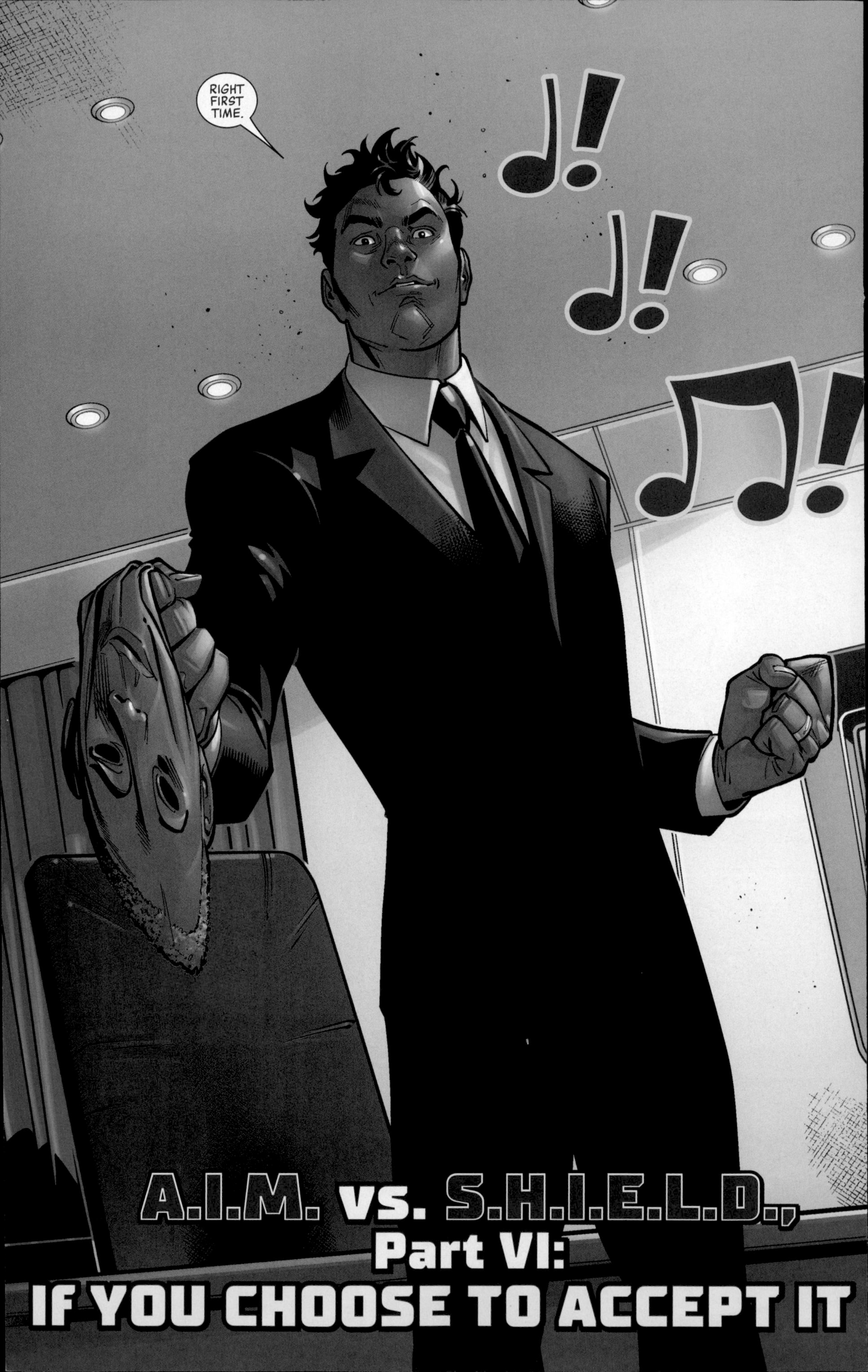
RIGHT FIRST TIME.
♩!
♩!
♫!
A.I.M. vs. S.H.I.E.L.D., Part VI:
IF YOU CHOOSE TO ACCEPT IT

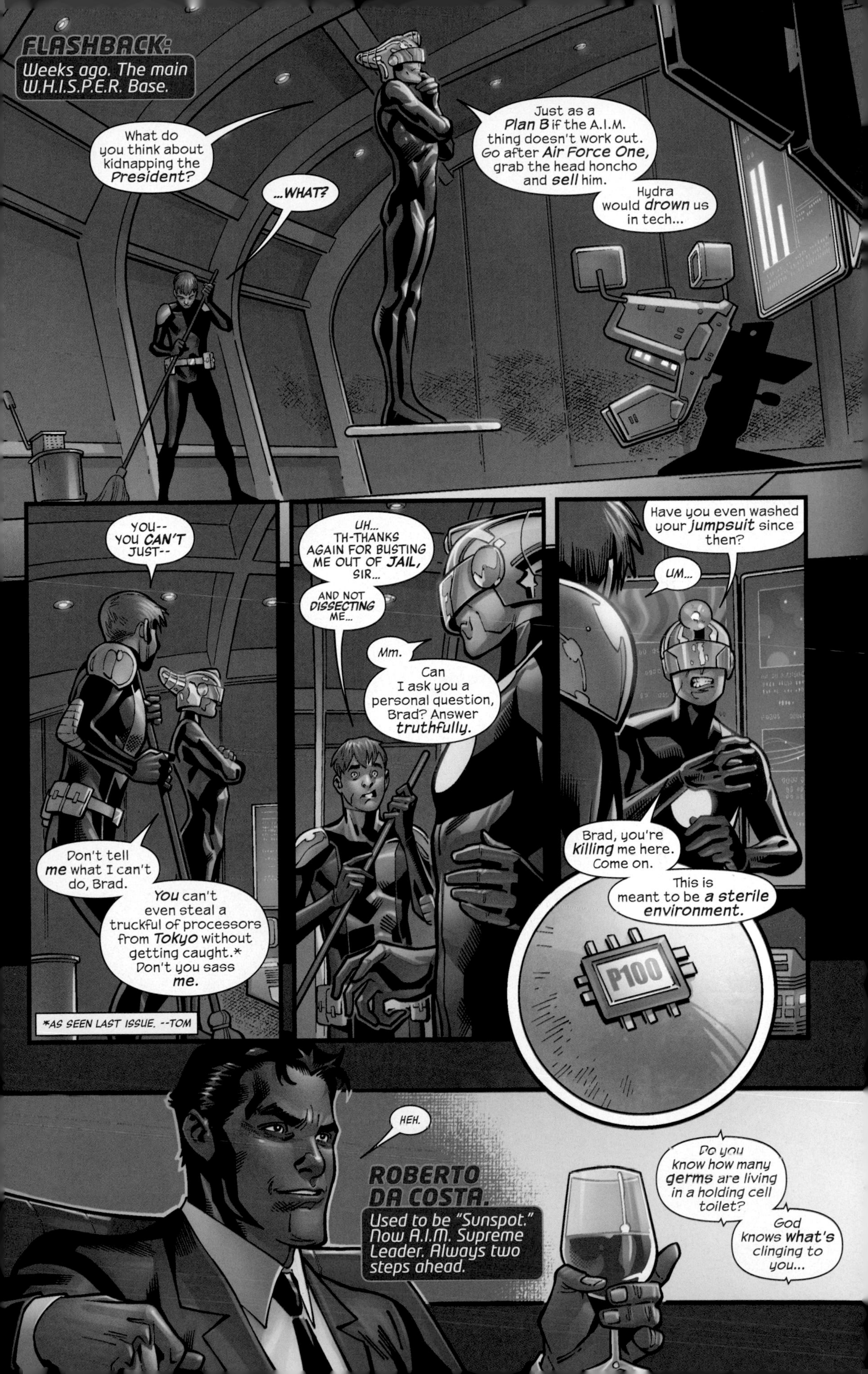
FLASHBACK:
Weeks ago. The main W.H.I.S.P.E.R. Base.
What do you think about kidnapping the President?
...WHAT?
Just as a Plan B if the A.I.M. thing doesn't work out. Go after Air Force One, grab the head honcho and sell him.
Hydra would drown us in tech...
YOU-- YOU CAN'T JUST--
Don't tell me what I can't do, Brad.
You can't even steal a truckful of processors from Tokyo without getting caught.* Don't you sass me.
*AS SEEN LAST ISSUE. --TOM
UH... TH-THANKS AGAIN FOR BUSTING ME OUT OF JAIL, SIR...
AND NOT DISSECTING ME...
Mm.
Can I ask you a personal question, Brad? Answer truthfully.
Have you even washed your jumpsuit since then?
UM...
Brad, you're killing me here. Come on.
This is meant to be a sterile environment.
P100
HEH.
ROBERTO DA COSTA.
Used to be "Sunspot." Now A.I.M. Supreme Leader. Always two steps ahead.
Do you know how many germs are living in a holding cell toilet?
God knows what's clinging to you...

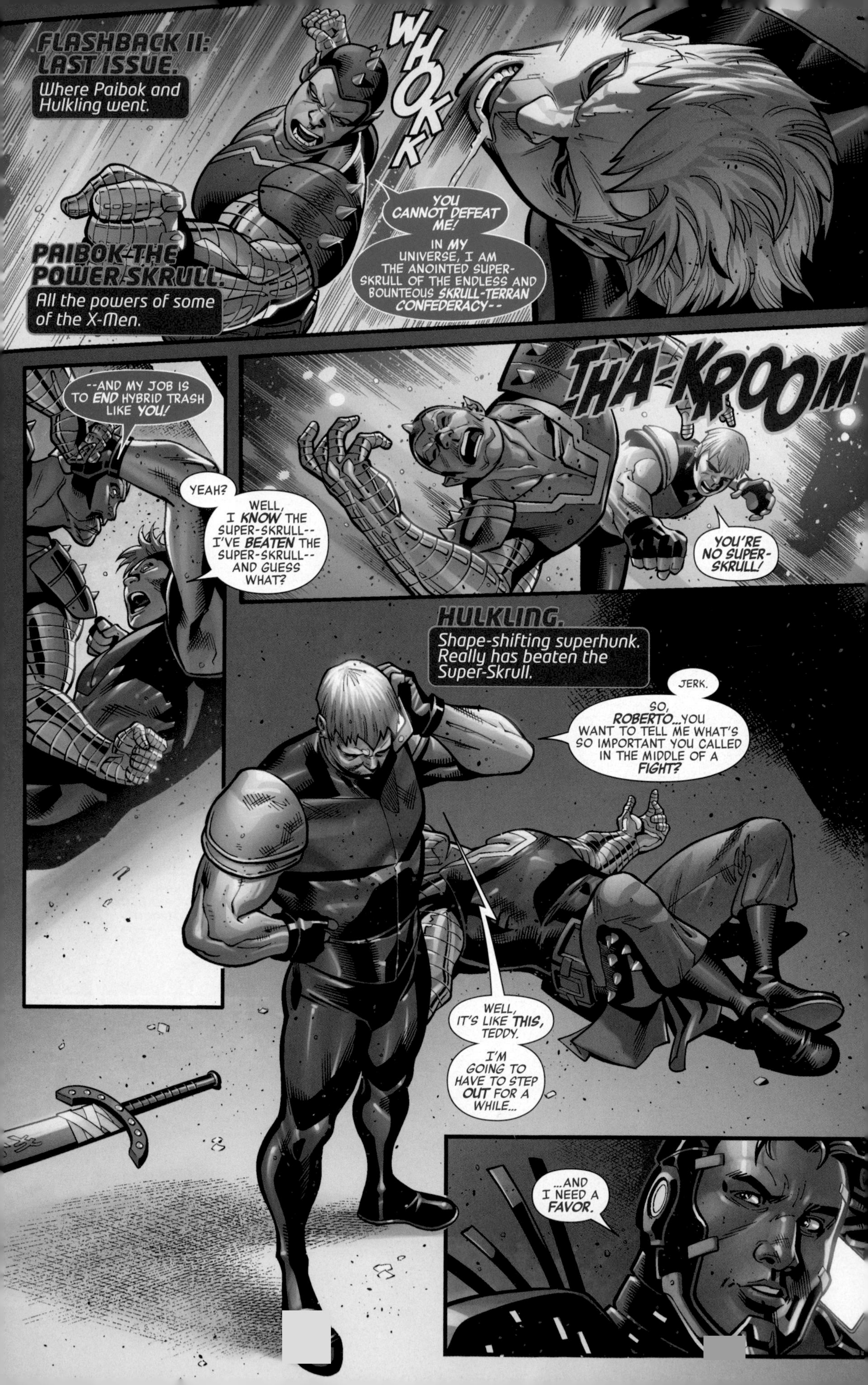
FLASHBACK II: LAST ISSUE.
Where Paibok and Hulkling went.
WHOKK
PAIBOK THE POWER SKRULL.
All the powers of some of the X-Men.
YOU CANNOT DEFEAT ME!
IN MY UNIVERSE, I AM THE ANOINTED SUPER-SKRULL OF THE ENDLESS AND BOUNTEOUS SKRULL-TERRAN CONFEDERACY--
--AND MY JOB IS TO END HYBRID TRASH LIKE YOU!
YEAH?
WELL, I KNOW THE SUPER-SKRULL-- I'VE BEATEN THE SUPER-SKRULL-- AND GUESS WHAT?
THA-KROOM
YOU'RE NO SUPER-SKRULL!
HULKLING.
Shape-shifting superhunk. Really has beaten the Super-Skrull.
JERK.
SO, ROBERTO...YOU WANT TO TELL ME WHAT'S SO IMPORTANT YOU CALLED IN THE MIDDLE OF A FIGHT?
WELL, IT'S LIKE THIS, TEDDY.
I'M GOING TO HAVE TO STEP OUT FOR A WHILE...
...AND I NEED A FAVOR.

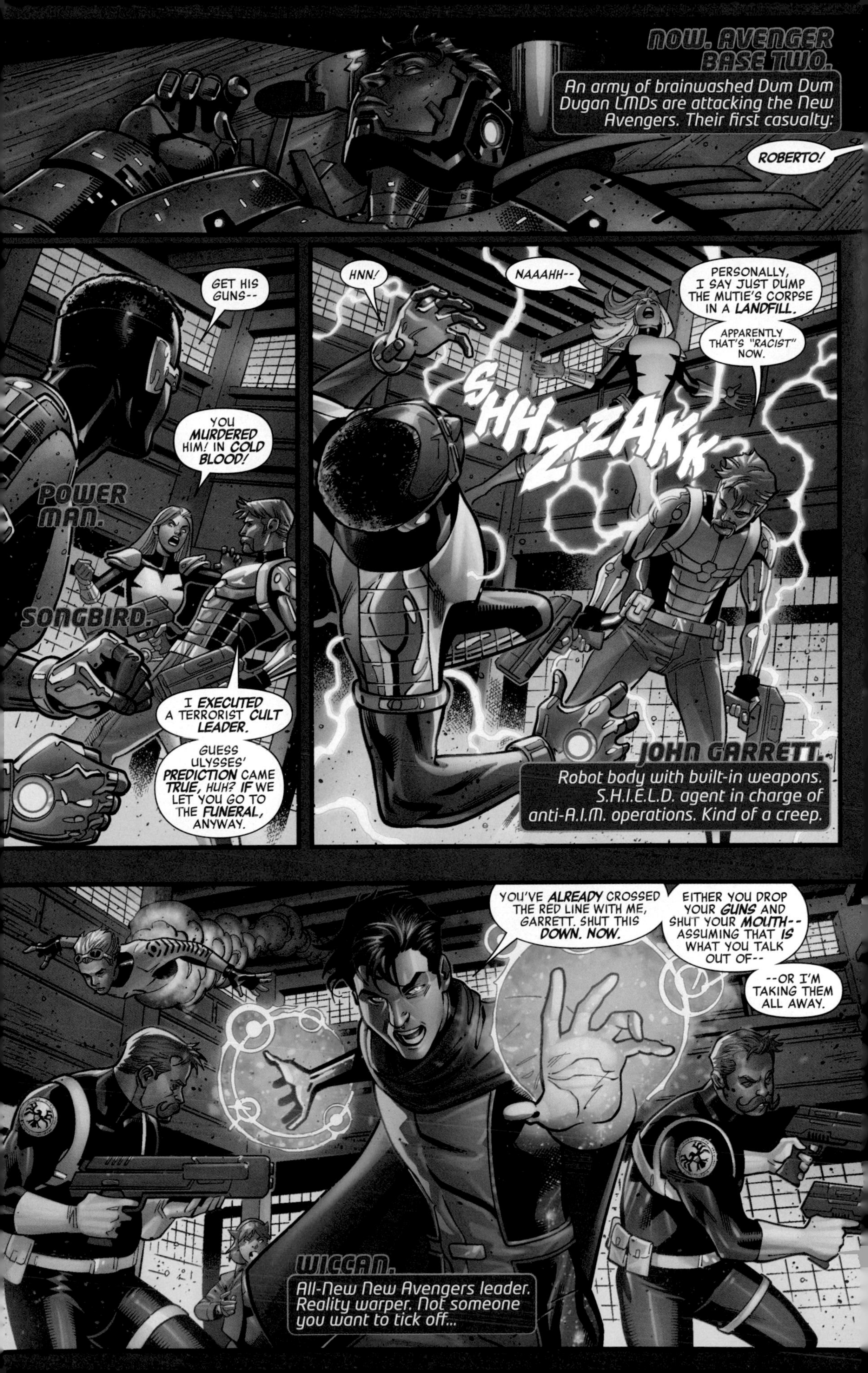

NOW. AVENGER BASE TWO.
An army of brainwashed Dum Dum Dugan LMDs are attacking the New Avengers. Their first casualty:
ROBERTO!
GET HIS GUNS--
YOU MURDERED HIM! IN COLD BLOOD!
POWER MAN.
SONGBIRD.
I EXECUTED A TERRORIST CULT LEADER.
GUESS ULYSSES' PREDICTION CAME TRUE, HUH? IF WE LET YOU GO TO THE FUNERAL, ANYWAY.
HNN!
NAAAHH--
PERSONALLY, I SAY JUST DUMP THE MUTIE'S CORPSE IN A LANDFILL.
APPARENTLY THAT'S "RACIST" NOW.
SHHZZZAKK
JOHN GARRETT.
Robot body with built-in weapons. S.H.I.E.L.D. agent in charge of anti-A.I.M. operations. Kind of a creep.
YOU'VE ALREADY CROSSED THE RED LINE WITH ME, GARRETT. SHUT THIS DOWN. NOW.
EITHER YOU DROP YOUR GUNS AND SHUT YOUR MOUTH-- ASSUMING THAT IS WHAT YOU TALK OUT OF--
--OR I'M TAKING THEM ALL AWAY.
WICCAN.
All-New New Avengers leader. Reality warper. Not someone you want to tick off...

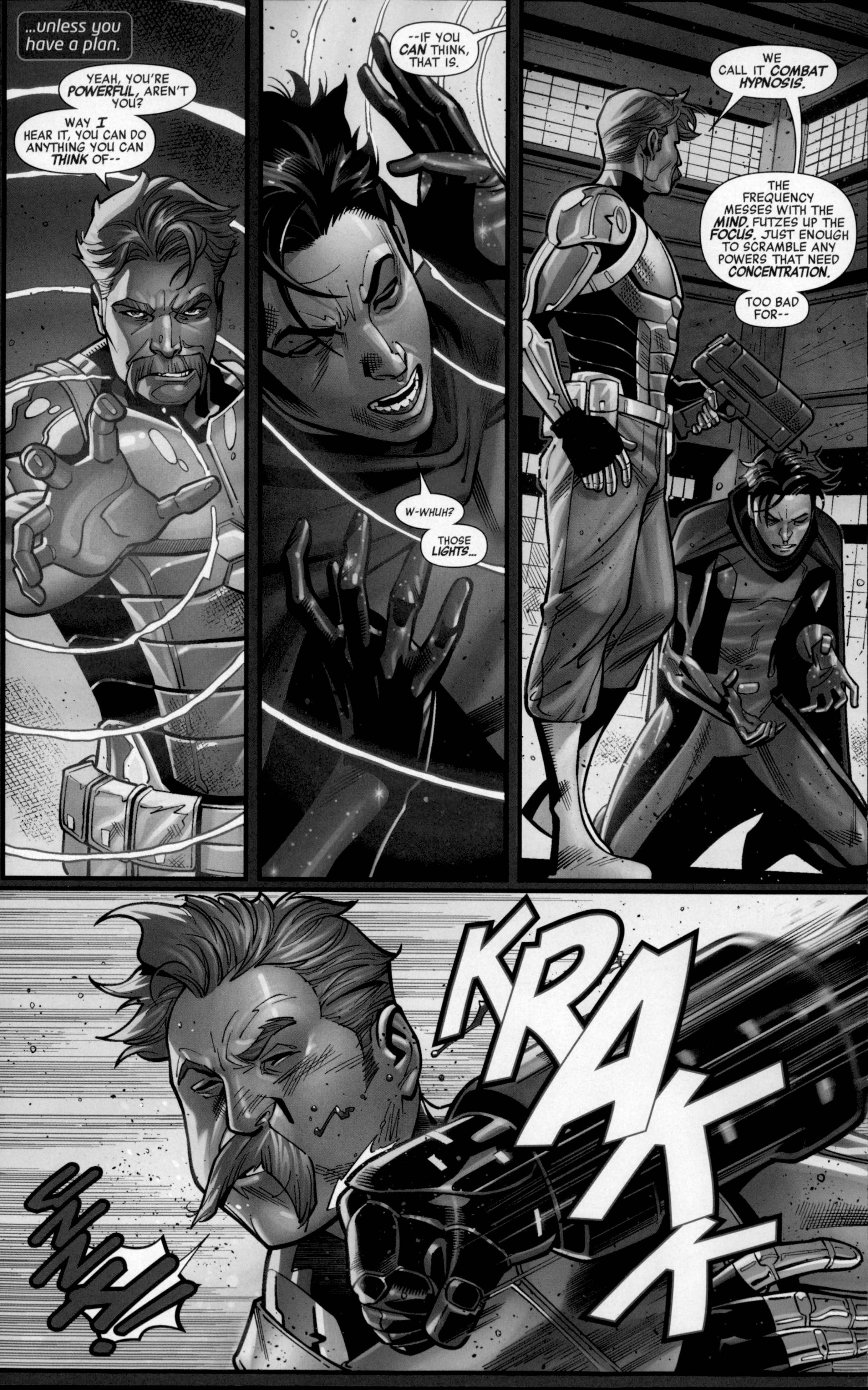

...unless you have a plan.
YEAH, YOU'RE POWERFUL, AREN'T YOU?
WAY I HEAR IT, YOU CAN DO ANYTHING YOU CAN THINK OF--
--IF YOU CAN THINK, THAT IS.
W-WHUH?
THOSE LIGHTS...
WE CALL IT COMBAT HYPNOSIS.
THE FREQUENCY MESSES WITH THE MIND, FUTZES UP THE FOCUS. JUST ENOUGH TO SCRAMBLE ANY POWERS THAT NEED CONCENTRATION.
TOO BAD FOR--
KRAKK
UNNH!

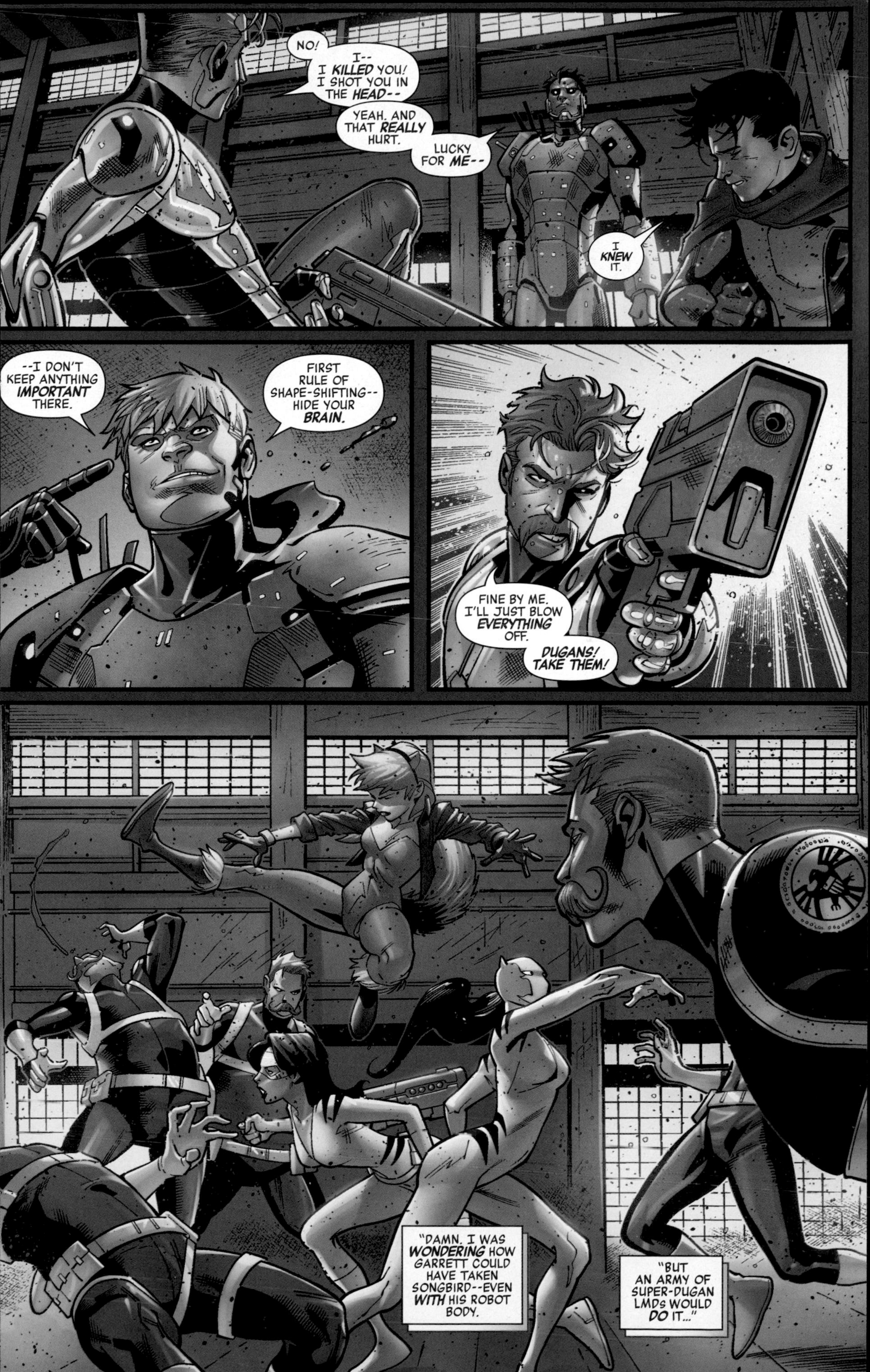
NO!
I-- I KILLED YOU! I SHOT YOU IN THE HEAD--
YEAH. AND THAT REALLY HURT.
LUCKY FOR ME--
I KNEW IT.
--I DON'T KEEP ANYTHING IMPORTANT THERE.
FIRST RULE OF SHAPE-SHIFTING--HIDE YOUR BRAIN.
FINE BY ME. I'LL JUST BLOW EVERYTHING OFF.
DUGANS! TAKE THEM!
"DAMN. I WAS WONDERING HOW GARRETT COULD HAVE TAKEN SONGBIRD--EVEN WITH HIS ROBOT BODY.
"BUT AN ARMY OF SUPER-DUGAN LMDs WOULD DO IT..."

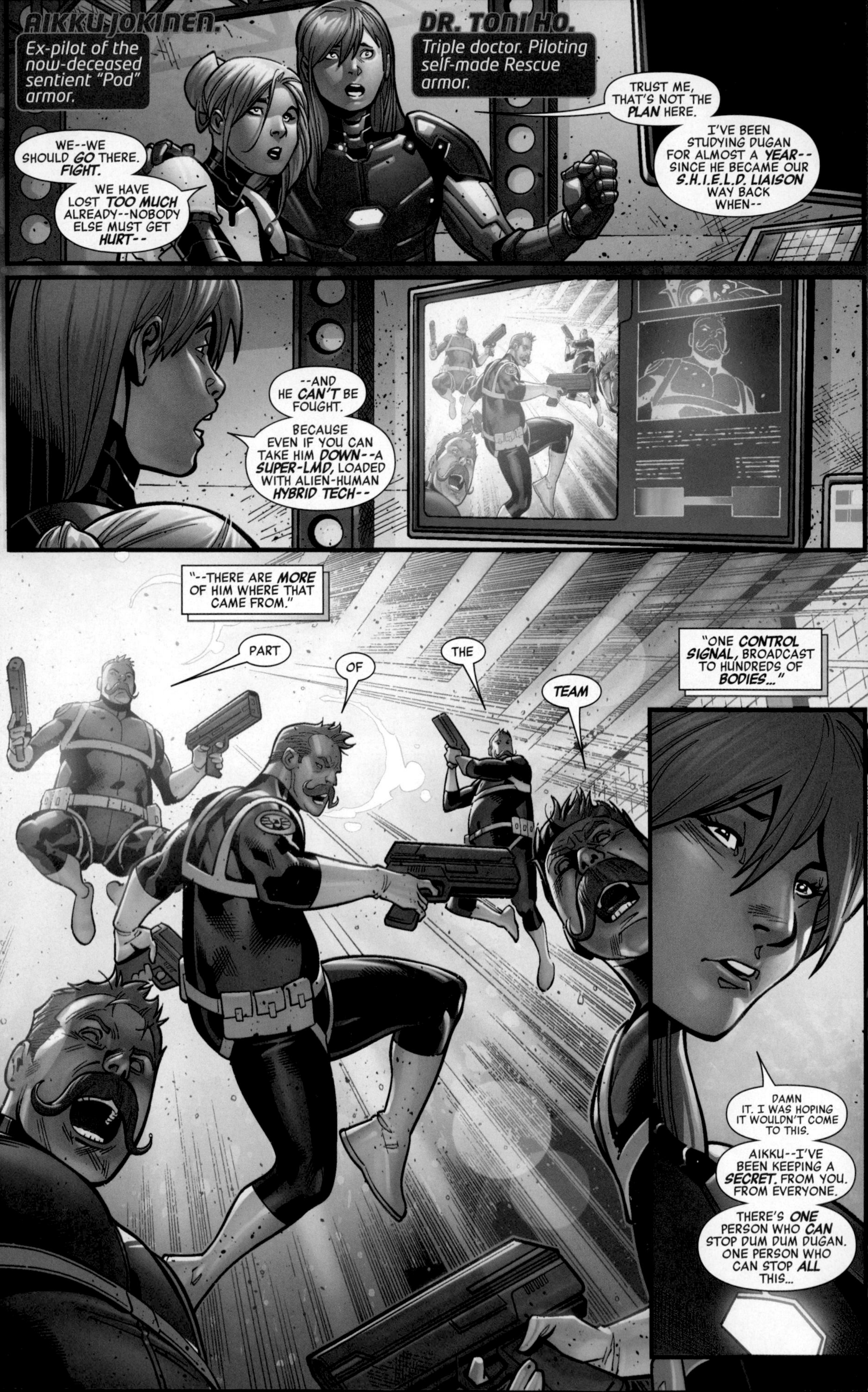
AIKKU JOKINEN.
Ex-pilot of the now-deceased sentient "Pod" armor.
DR. TONI HO.
Triple doctor. Piloting self-made Rescue armor.
WE--WE SHOULD GO THERE. FIGHT.
WE HAVE LOST TOO MUCH ALREADY--NOBODY ELSE MUST GET HURT--
TRUST ME, THAT'S NOT THE PLAN HERE.
I'VE BEEN STUDYING DUGAN FOR ALMOST A YEAR--SINCE HE BECAME OUR S.H.I.E.L.D. LIAISON WAY BACK WHEN--
--AND HE CAN'T BE FOUGHT.
BECAUSE EVEN IF YOU CAN TAKE HIM DOWN--A SUPER-LMD, LOADED WITH ALIEN-HUMAN HYBRID TECH--
"--THERE ARE MORE OF HIM WHERE THAT CAME FROM."
PART
OF
THE
TEAM
"ONE CONTROL SIGNAL, BROADCAST TO HUNDREDS OF BODIES..."
DAMN IT. I WAS HOPING IT WOULDN'T COME TO THIS.
AIKKU--I'VE BEEN KEEPING A SECRET. FROM YOU. FROM EVERYONE.
THERE'S ONE PERSON WHO CAN STOP DUM DUM DUGAN. ONE PERSON WHO CAN STOP ALL THIS...

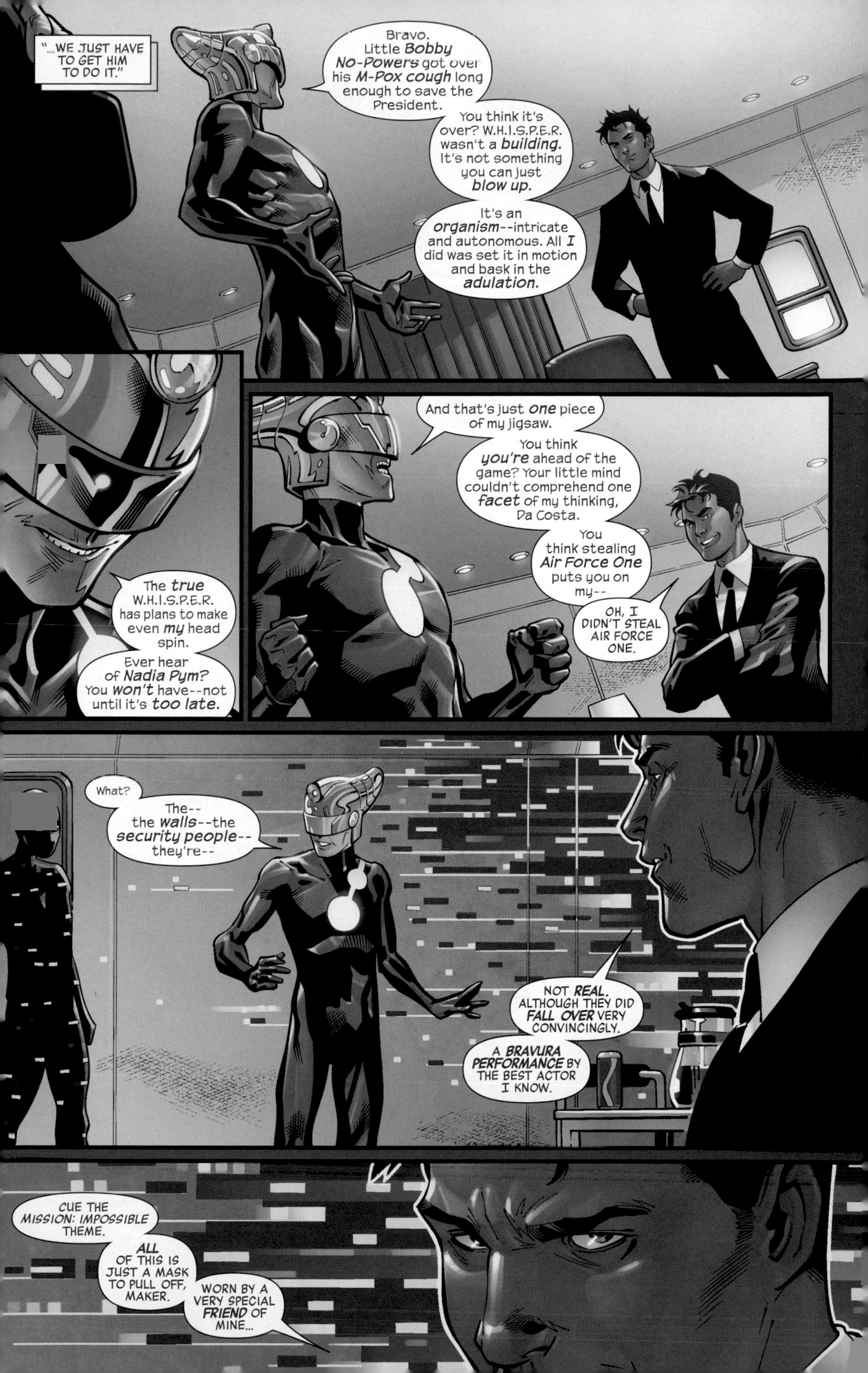
"...WE JUST HAVE TO GET HIM TO DO IT."
Bravo. Little Bobby No-Powers got over his M-Pox cough long enough to save the President.
You think it's over? W.H.I.S.P.E.R. wasn't a building. It's not something you can just blow up.
It's an organism--intricate and autonomous. All I did was set it in motion and bask in the adulation.
The true W.H.I.S.P.E.R. has plans to make even my head spin.
Ever hear of Nadia Pym? You won't have--not until it's too late.
And that's just one piece of my jigsaw.
You think you're ahead of the game? Your little mind couldn't comprehend one facet of my thinking, Da Costa.
You think stealing Air Force One puts you on my--
OH, I DIDN'T STEAL AIR FORCE ONE.
What?
The-- the walls--the security people-- they're--
NOT REAL. ALTHOUGH THEY DID FALL OVER VERY CONVINCINGLY.
A BRAVURA PERFORMANCE BY THE BEST ACTOR I KNOW.
CUE THE MISSION: IMPOSSIBLE THEME.
ALL OF THIS IS JUST A MASK TO PULL OFF, MAKER.
WORN BY A VERY SPECIAL FRIEND OF MINE...

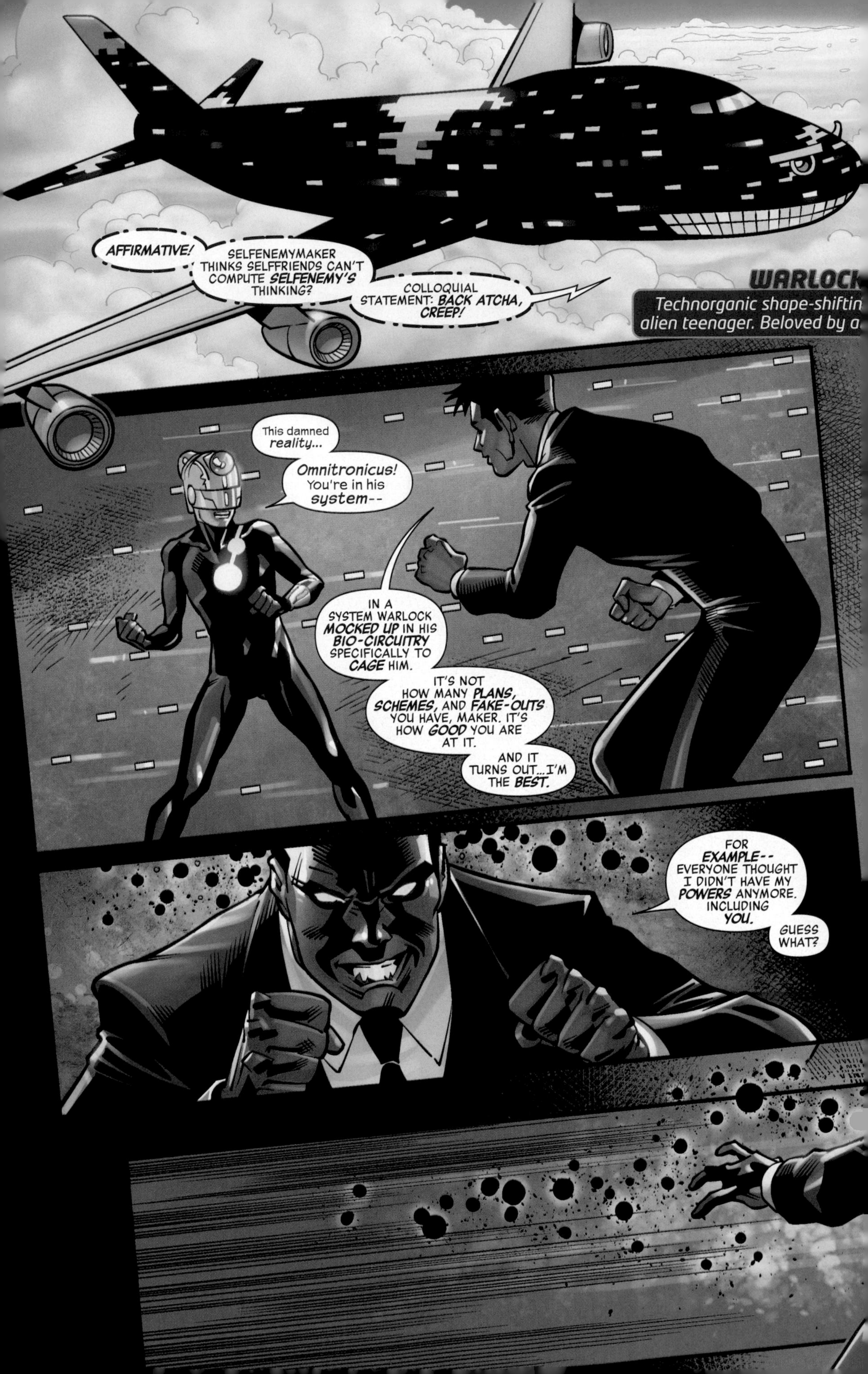
AFFIRMATIVE!
SELFENEMYMAKER THINKS SELFFRIENDS CAN'T COMPUTE SELFENEMY'S THINKING?
COLLOQUIAL STATEMENT: BACK ATCHA, CREEP!
WARLOCK
Technorganic shape-shiftin alien teenager. Beloved by a
This damned reality...
Omnitronicus! You're in his system--
IN A SYSTEM WARLOCK MOCKED UP IN HIS BIO-CIRCUITRY SPECIFICALLY TO CAGE HIM.
IT'S NOT HOW MANY PLANS, SCHEMES, AND FAKE-OUTS YOU HAVE, MAKER. IT'S HOW GOOD YOU ARE AT IT.
AND IT TURNS OUT...I'M THE BEST.
FOR EXAMPLE--EVERYONE THOUGHT I DIDN'T HAVE MY POWERS ANYMORE. INCLUDING YOU.
GUESS WHAT?

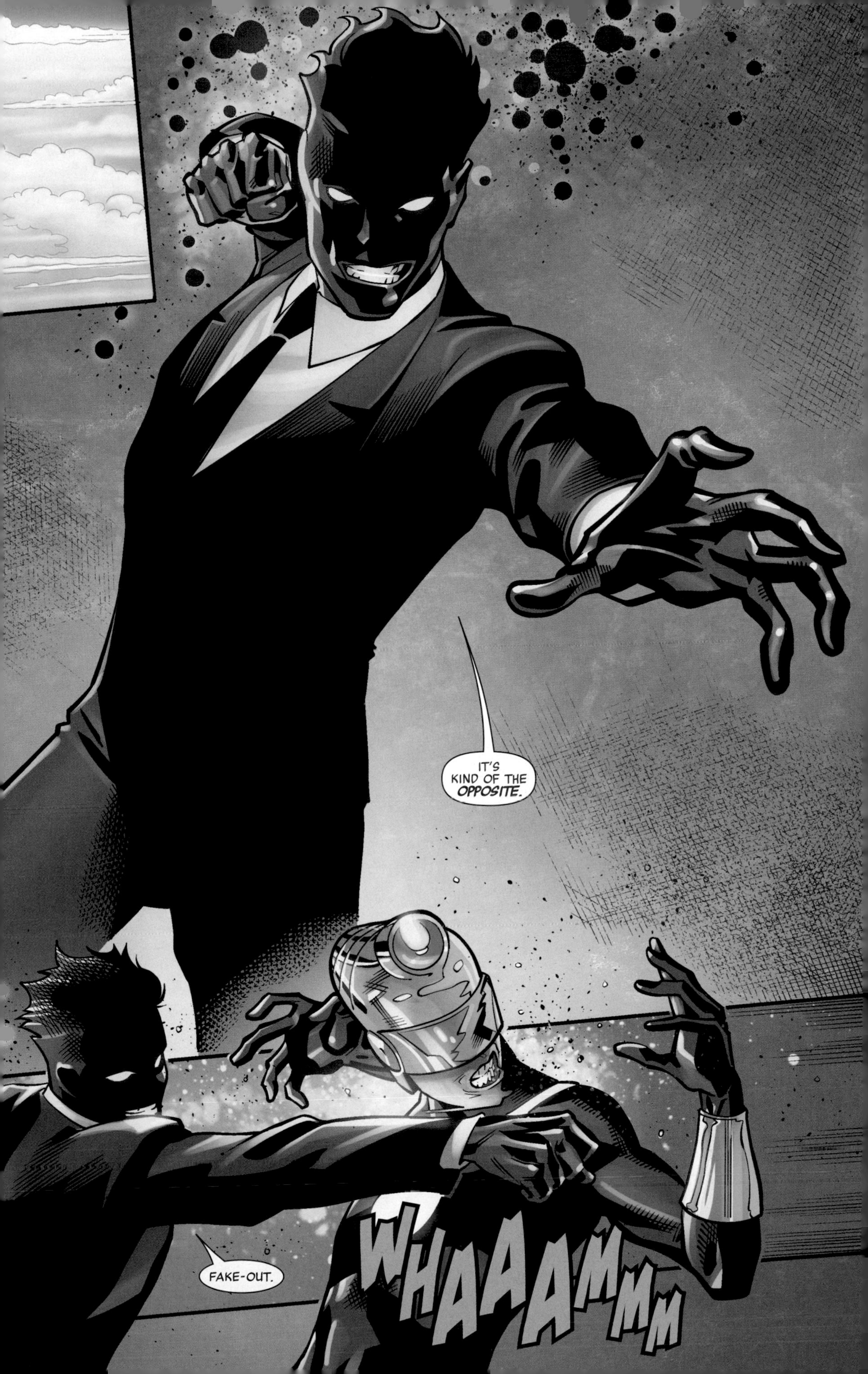
IT'S KIND OF THE *OPPOSITE*.
FAKE-OUT.
WHAAAMMM

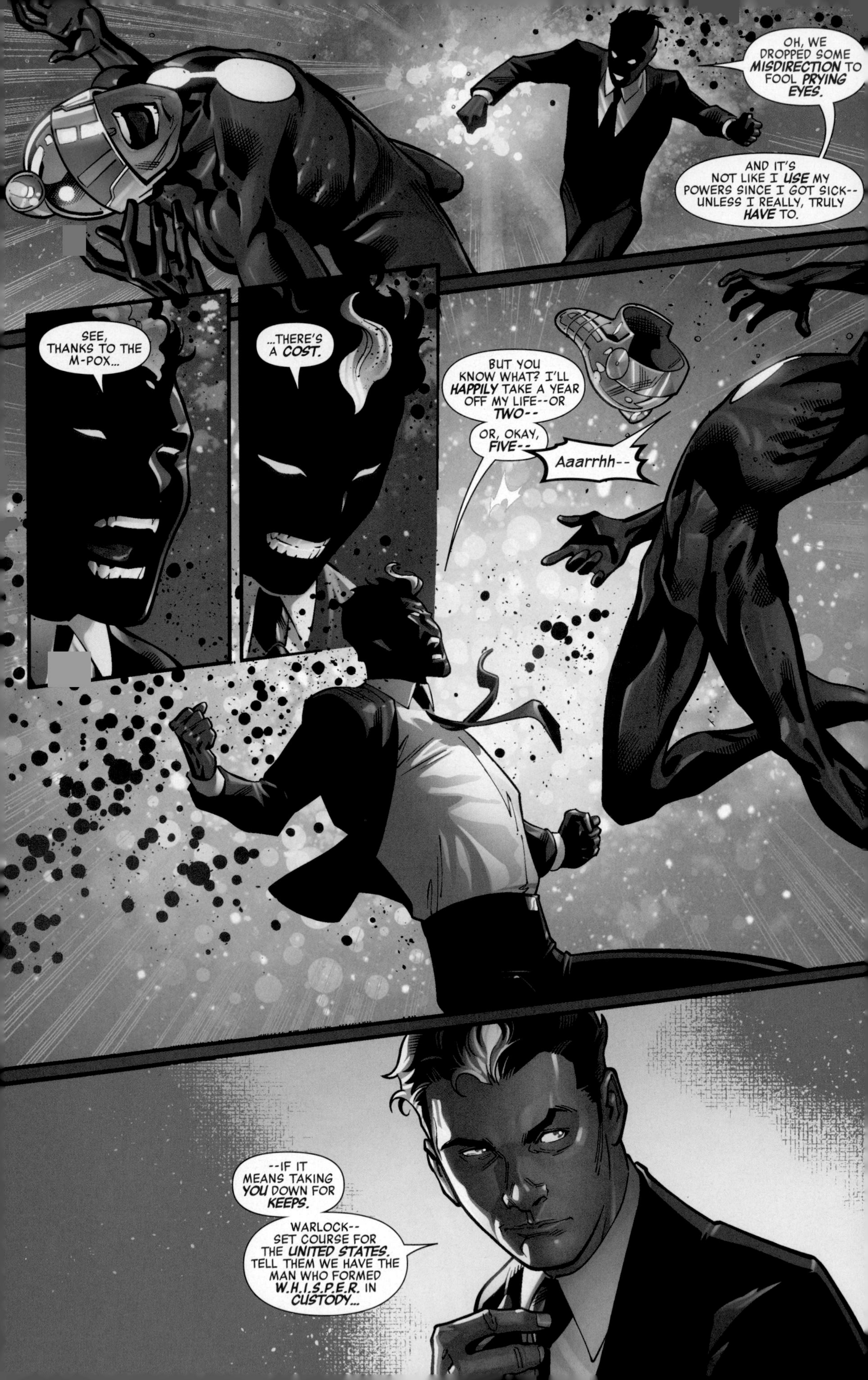

OH, WE DROPPED SOME MISDIRECTION TO FOOL PRYING EYES.
AND IT'S NOT LIKE I USE MY POWERS SINCE I GOT SICK--UNLESS I REALLY, TRULY HAVE TO.
SEE, THANKS TO THE M-POX...
...THERE'S A COST.
BUT YOU KNOW WHAT? I'LL HAPPILY TAKE A YEAR OFF MY LIFE--OR TWO--
OR, OKAY, FIVE--
Aaarrhh--
--IF IT MEANS TAKING YOU DOWN FOR KEEPS.
WARLOCK--SET COURSE FOR THE UNITED STATES. TELL THEM WE HAVE THE MAN WHO FORMED W.H.I.S.P.E.R. IN CUSTODY...

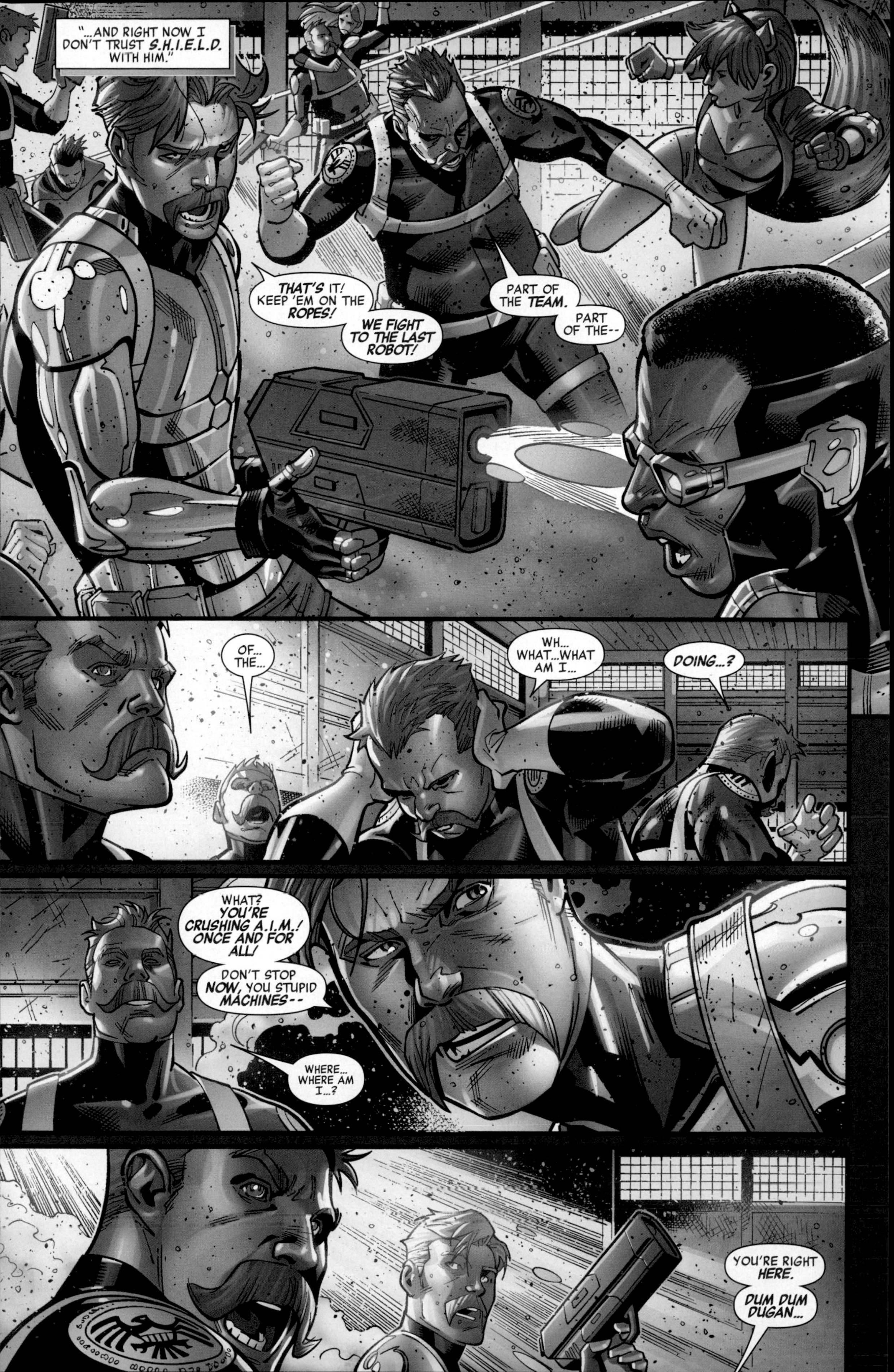

"...AND RIGHT NOW I DON'T TRUST S.H.I.E.L.D. WITH HIM."
THAT'S IT! KEEP 'EM ON THE ROPES!
WE FIGHT TO THE LAST ROBOT!
PART OF THE TEAM.
PART OF THE--
OF... THE...
WH... WHAT...WHAT AM I...
DOING...?
WHAT? YOU'RE CRUSHING A.I.M.! ONCE AND FOR ALL!
DON'T STOP NOW, YOU STUPID MACHINES--
WHERE... WHERE AM I...?
YOU'RE RIGHT HERE.
DUM DUM DUGAN...

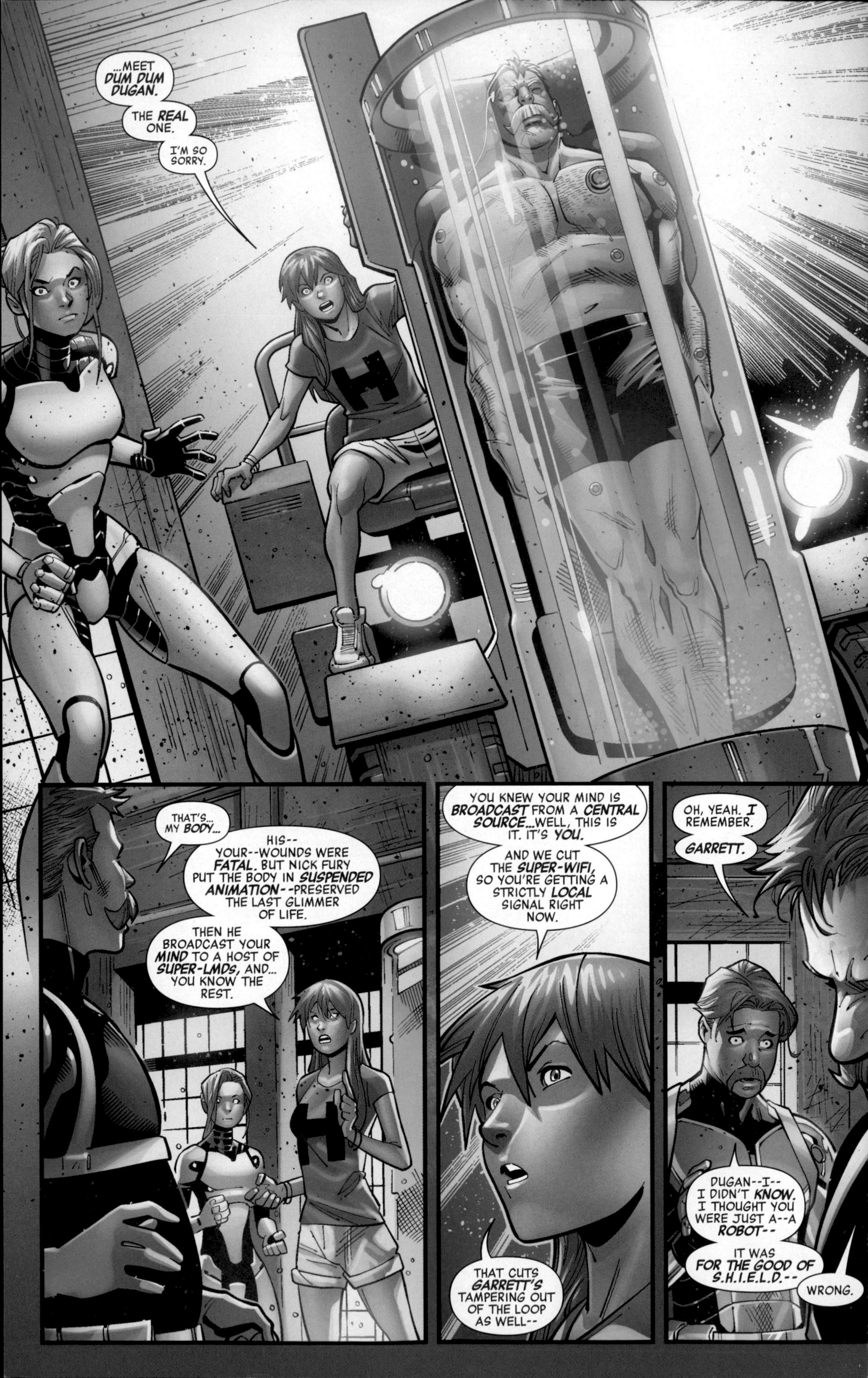

...MEET DUM DUM DUGAN.
THE REAL ONE.
I'M SO SORRY.
THAT'S... MY BODY...
HIS-- YOUR--WOUNDS WERE FATAL. BUT NICK FURY PUT THE BODY IN SUSPENDED ANIMATION--PRESERVED THE LAST GLIMMER OF LIFE.
THEN HE BROADCAST YOUR MIND TO A HOST OF SUPER-LMDS, AND... YOU KNOW THE REST.
YOU KNEW YOUR MIND IS BROADCAST FROM A CENTRAL SOURCE...WELL, THIS IS IT. IT'S YOU.
AND WE CUT THE SUPER-WIFI, SO YOU'RE GETTING A STRICTLY LOCAL SIGNAL RIGHT NOW.
THAT CUTS GARRETT'S TAMPERING OUT OF THE LOOP AS WELL--
OH, YEAH. I REMEMBER.
GARRETT.
DUGAN--I--I DIDN'T KNOW. I THOUGHT YOU WERE JUST A--A ROBOT--
IT WAS FOR THE GOOD OF S.H.I.E.L.D.--
WRONG.

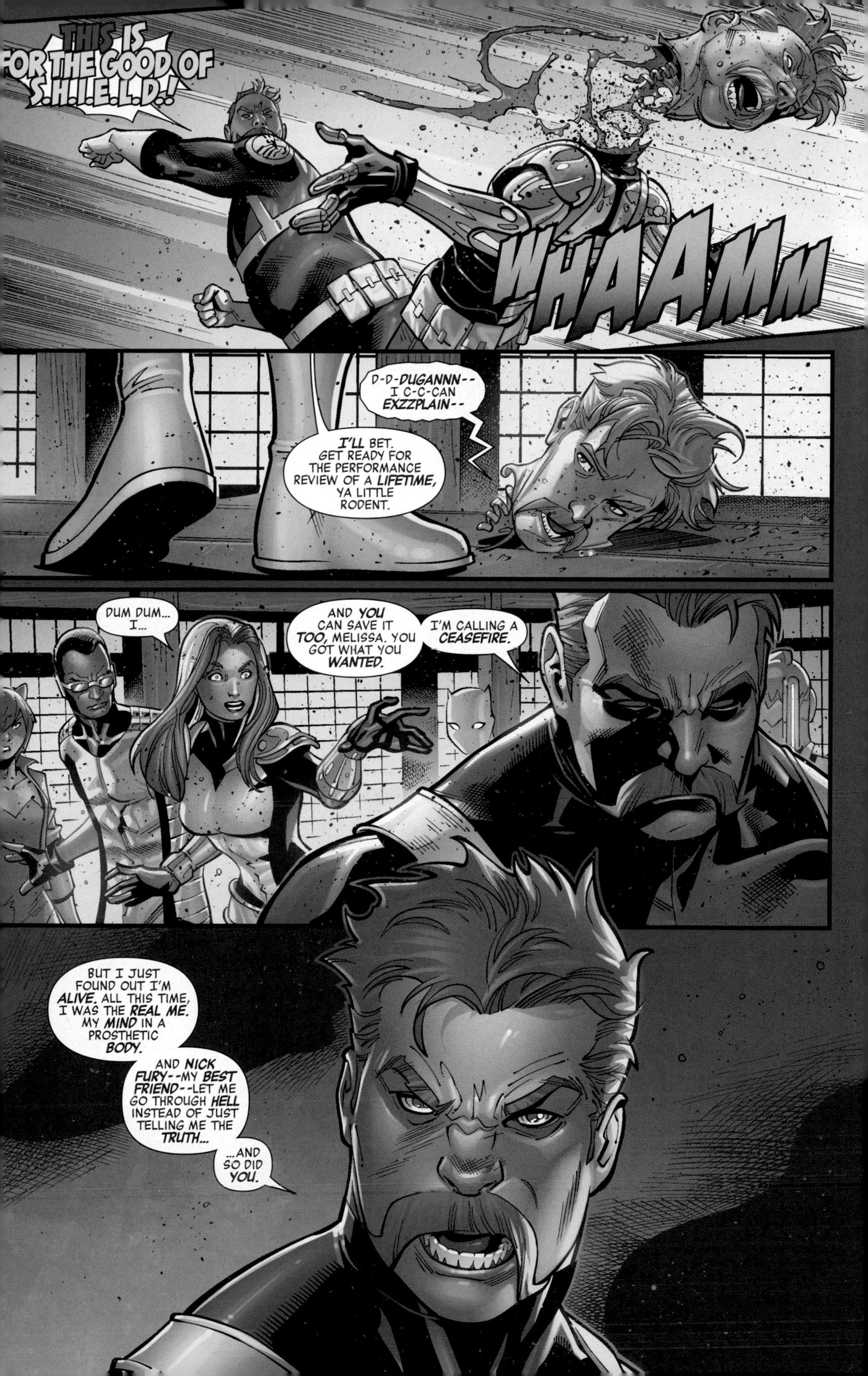
THIS IS FOR THE GOOD OF S.H.I.E.L.D.!
WHAAMM
D-D-DUGANNN-- I C-C-CAN EXZZPLAIN--
I'LL BET. GET READY FOR THE PERFORMANCE REVIEW OF A LIFETIME, YA LITTLE RODENT.
DUM DUM... I...
AND YOU CAN SAVE IT TOO, MELISSA. YOU GOT WHAT YOU WANTED.
I'M CALLING A CEASEFIRE.
BUT I JUST FOUND OUT I'M ALIVE. ALL THIS TIME, I WAS THE REAL ME. MY MIND IN A PROSTHETIC BODY.
AND NICK FURY--MY BEST FRIEND--LET ME GO THROUGH HELL INSTEAD OF JUST TELLING ME THE TRUTH...
...AND SO DID YOU.

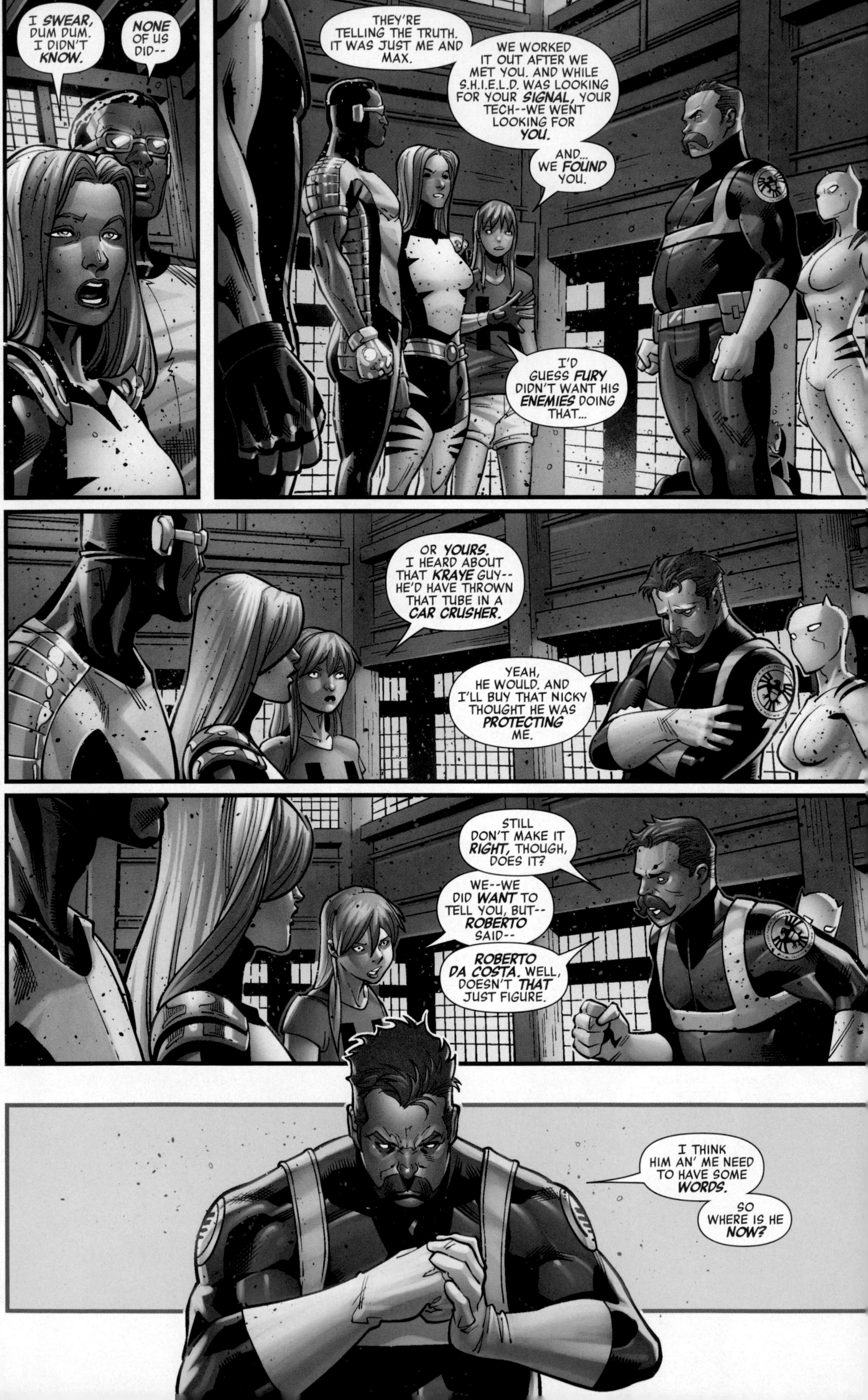
I SWEAR, DUM DUM. I DIDN'T KNOW.
NONE OF US DID--
THEY'RE TELLING THE TRUTH. IT WAS JUST ME AND MAX.
WE WORKED IT OUT AFTER WE MET YOU. AND WHILE S.H.I.E.L.D. WAS LOOKING FOR YOUR SIGNAL, YOUR TECH--WE WENT LOOKING FOR YOU.
AND... WE FOUND YOU.
I'D GUESS FURY DIDN'T WANT HIS ENEMIES DOING THAT...
OR YOURS. I HEARD ABOUT THAT KRAYE GUY--HE'D HAVE THROWN THAT TUBE IN A CAR CRUSHER.
YEAH, HE WOULD. AND I'LL BUY THAT NICKY THOUGHT HE WAS PROTECTING ME.
STILL DON'T MAKE IT RIGHT, THOUGH, DOES IT?
WE--WE DID WANT TO TELL YOU, BUT--ROBERTO SAID--
ROBERTO DA COSTA. WELL, DOESN'T THAT JUST FIGURE.
I THINK HIM AN' ME NEED TO HAVE SOME WORDS.
SO WHERE IS HE NOW?

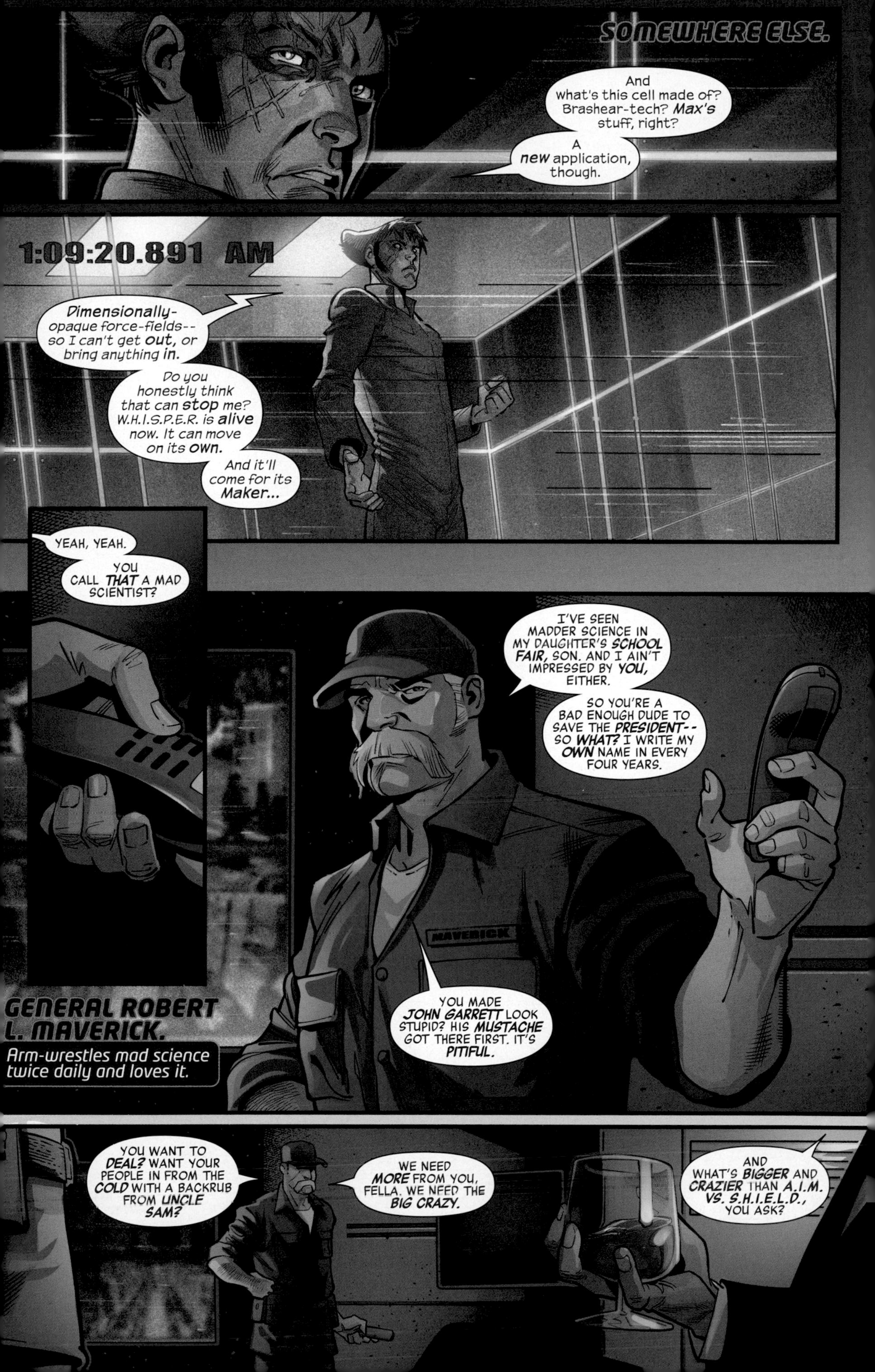
SOMEWHERE ELSE.
And what's this cell made of? Brashear-tech? Max's stuff, right?
A new application, though.
1:09:20.891 AM
Dimensionally-opaque force-fields--so I can't get out, or bring anything in.
Do you honestly think that can stop me? W.H.I.S.P.E.R. is alive now. It can move on its own.
And it'll come for its Maker...
YEAH, YEAH.
YOU CALL THAT A MAD SCIENTIST?
I'VE SEEN MADDER SCIENCE IN MY DAUGHTER'S SCHOOL FAIR, SON. AND I AIN'T IMPRESSED BY YOU, EITHER.
SO YOU'RE A BAD ENOUGH DUDE TO SAVE THE PRESIDENT--SO WHAT? I WRITE MY OWN NAME IN EVERY FOUR YEARS.
MAVERICK
GENERAL ROBERT L. MAVERICK.
Arm-wrestles mad science twice daily and loves it.
YOU MADE JOHN GARRETT LOOK STUPID? HIS MUSTACHE GOT THERE FIRST. IT'S PITIFUL.
YOU WANT TO DEAL? WANT YOUR PEOPLE IN FROM THE COLD WITH A BACKRUB FROM UNCLE SAM?
WE NEED MORE FROM YOU, FELLA. WE NEED THE BIG CRAZY.
AND WHAT'S BIGGER AND CRAZIER THAN A.I.M. VS. S.H.I.E.L.D., YOU ASK?

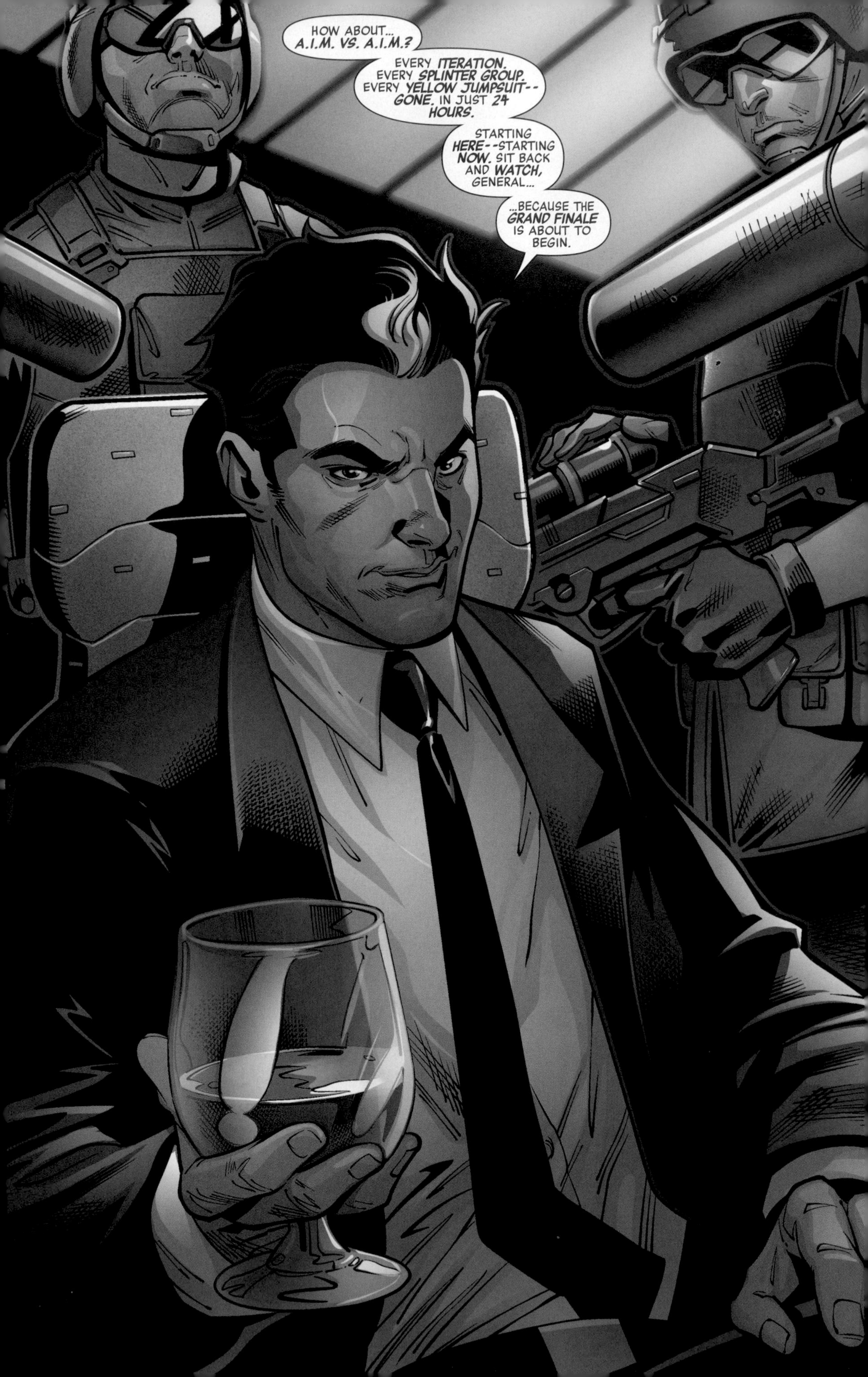
HOW ABOUT... A.I.M. VS. A.I.M.?
EVERY ITERATION. EVERY SPLINTER GROUP. EVERY YELLOW JUMPSUIT-- GONE. IN JUST 24 HOURS.
STARTING HERE--STARTING NOW. SIT BACK AND WATCH, GENERAL...
...BECAUSE THE GRAND FINALE IS ABOUT TO BEGIN.

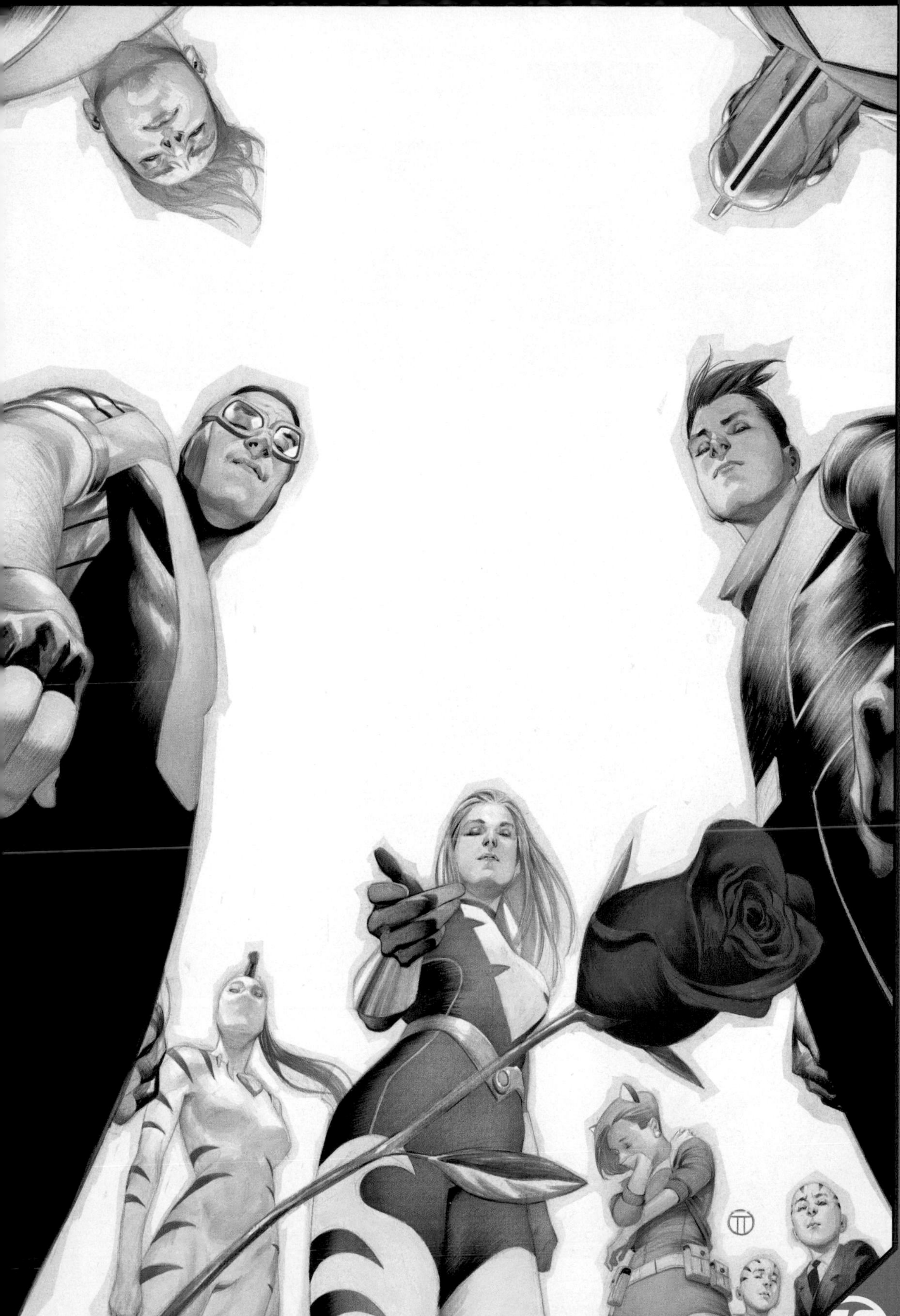
18

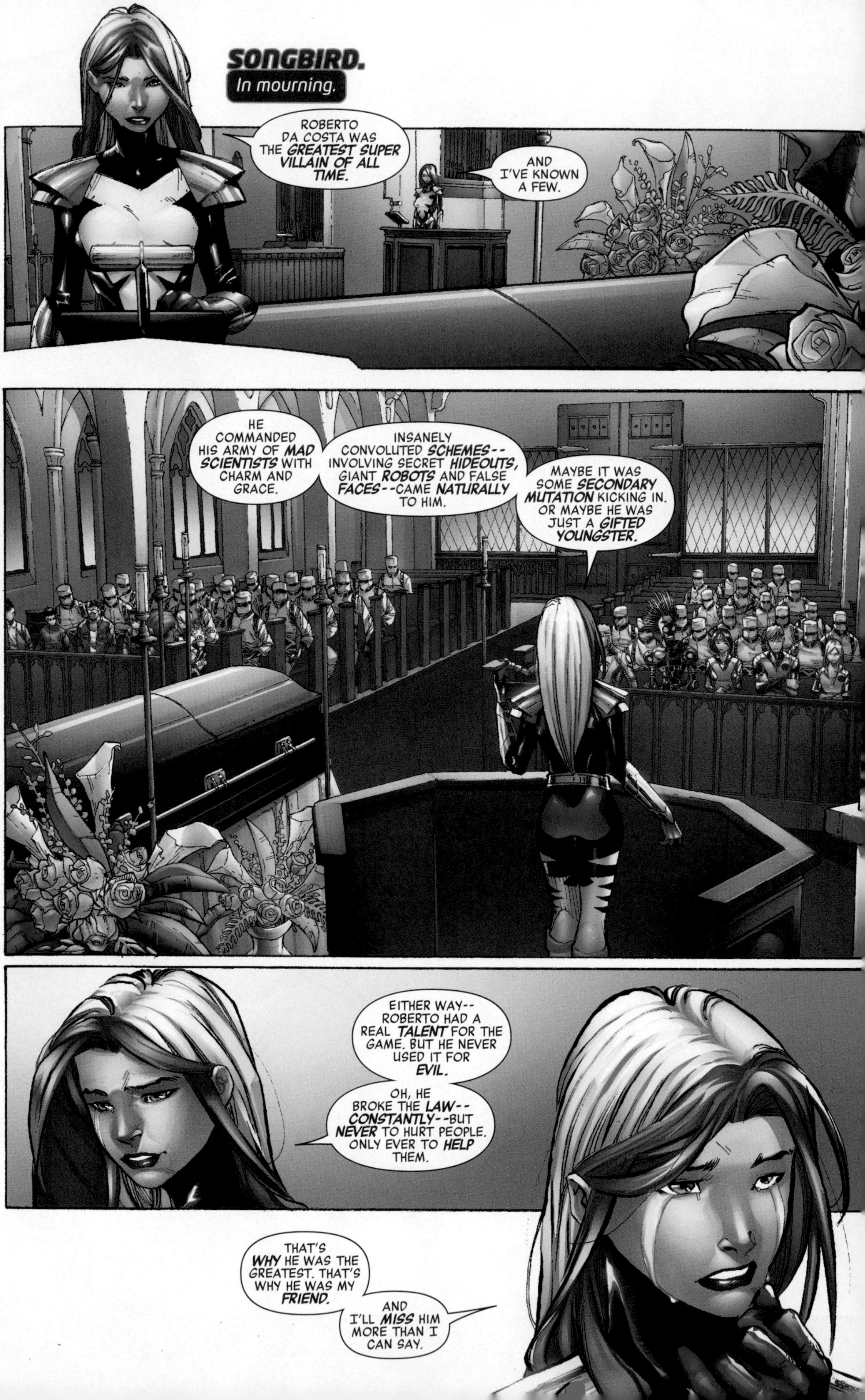
SONGBIRD.
In mourning.
ROBERTO DA COSTA WAS THE GREATEST SUPER VILLAIN OF ALL TIME.
AND I'VE KNOWN A FEW.
HE COMMANDED HIS ARMY OF MAD SCIENTISTS WITH CHARM AND GRACE.
INSANELY CONVOLUTED SCHEMES--INVOLVING SECRET HIDEOUTS, GIANT ROBOTS AND FALSE FACES--CAME NATURALLY TO HIM.
MAYBE IT WAS SOME SECONDARY MUTATION KICKING IN. OR MAYBE HE WAS JUST A GIFTED YOUNGSTER.
EITHER WAY--ROBERTO HAD A REAL TALENT FOR THE GAME. BUT HE NEVER USED IT FOR EVIL.
OH, HE BROKE THE LAW--CONSTANTLY--BUT NEVER TO HURT PEOPLE. ONLY EVER TO HELP THEM.
THAT'S WHY HE WAS THE GREATEST. THAT'S WHY HE WAS MY FRIEND.
AND I'LL MISS HIM MORE THAN I CAN SAY.

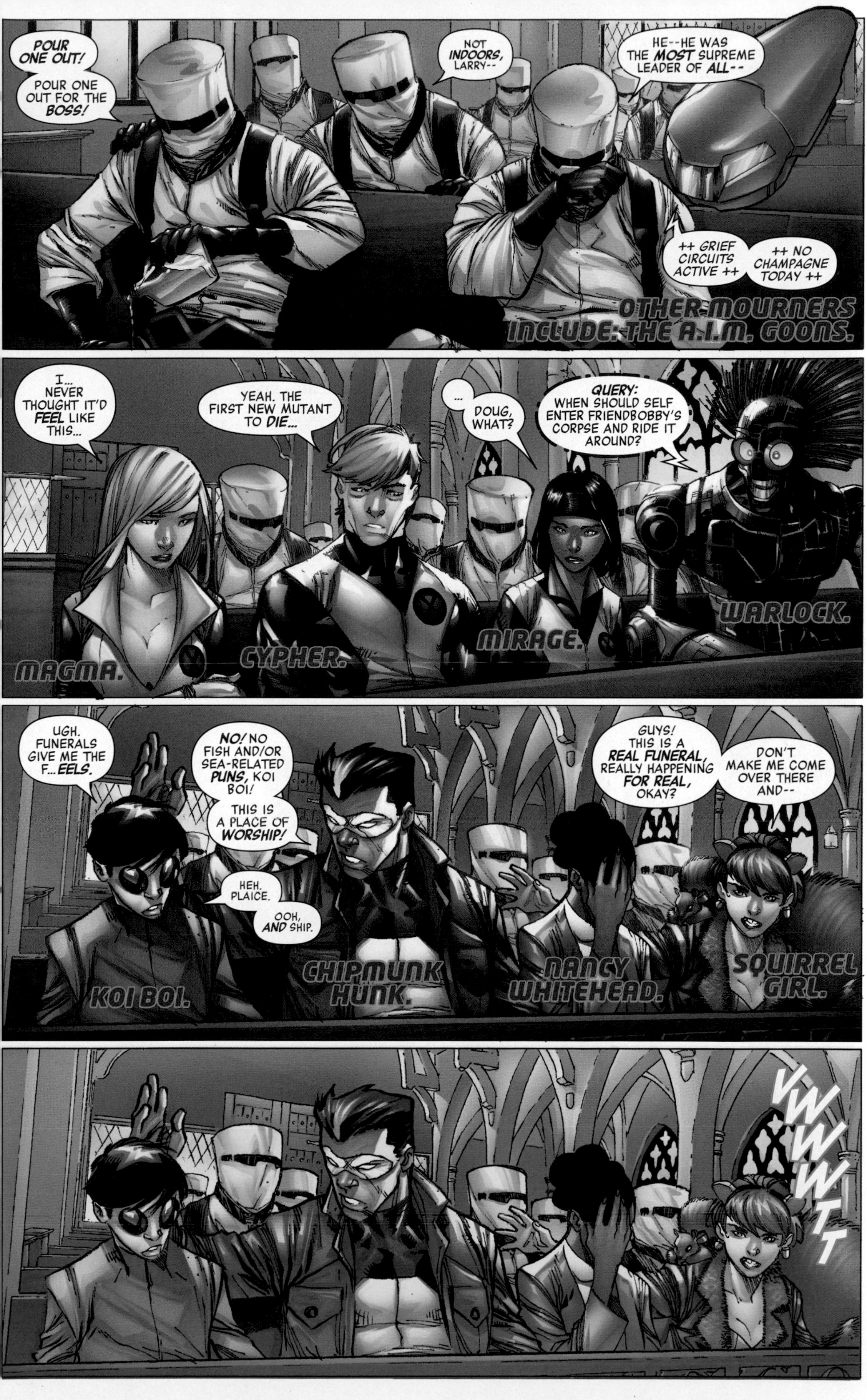
POUR ONE OUT!
POUR ONE OUT FOR THE BOSS!
NOT INDOORS, LARRY--
HE--HE WAS THE MOST SUPREME LEADER OF ALL--
++ GRIEF CIRCUITS ACTIVE ++
++ NO CHAMPAGNE TODAY ++
OTHER MOURNERS INCLUDE: THE A.I.M. GOONS.
I... NEVER THOUGHT IT'D FEEL LIKE THIS...
YEAH. THE FIRST NEW MUTANT TO DIE...
...
DOUG, WHAT?
QUERY: WHEN SHOULD SELF ENTER FRIENDBOBBY'S CORPSE AND RIDE IT AROUND?
MAGMA.
CYPHER.
MIRAGE.
WARLOCK.
UGH. FUNERALS GIVE ME THE F...EELS.
NO! NO FISH AND/OR SEA-RELATED PUNS, KOI BOI!
THIS IS A PLACE OF WORSHIP!
HEH. PLAICE.
OOH, AND SHIP.
GUYS! THIS IS A REAL FUNERAL, REALLY HAPPENING FOR REAL, OKAY?
DON'T MAKE ME COME OVER THERE AND--
KOI BOI.
CHIPMUNK HUNK.
NANCY WHITEHEAD.
SQUIRREL GIRL.
VWWWTT

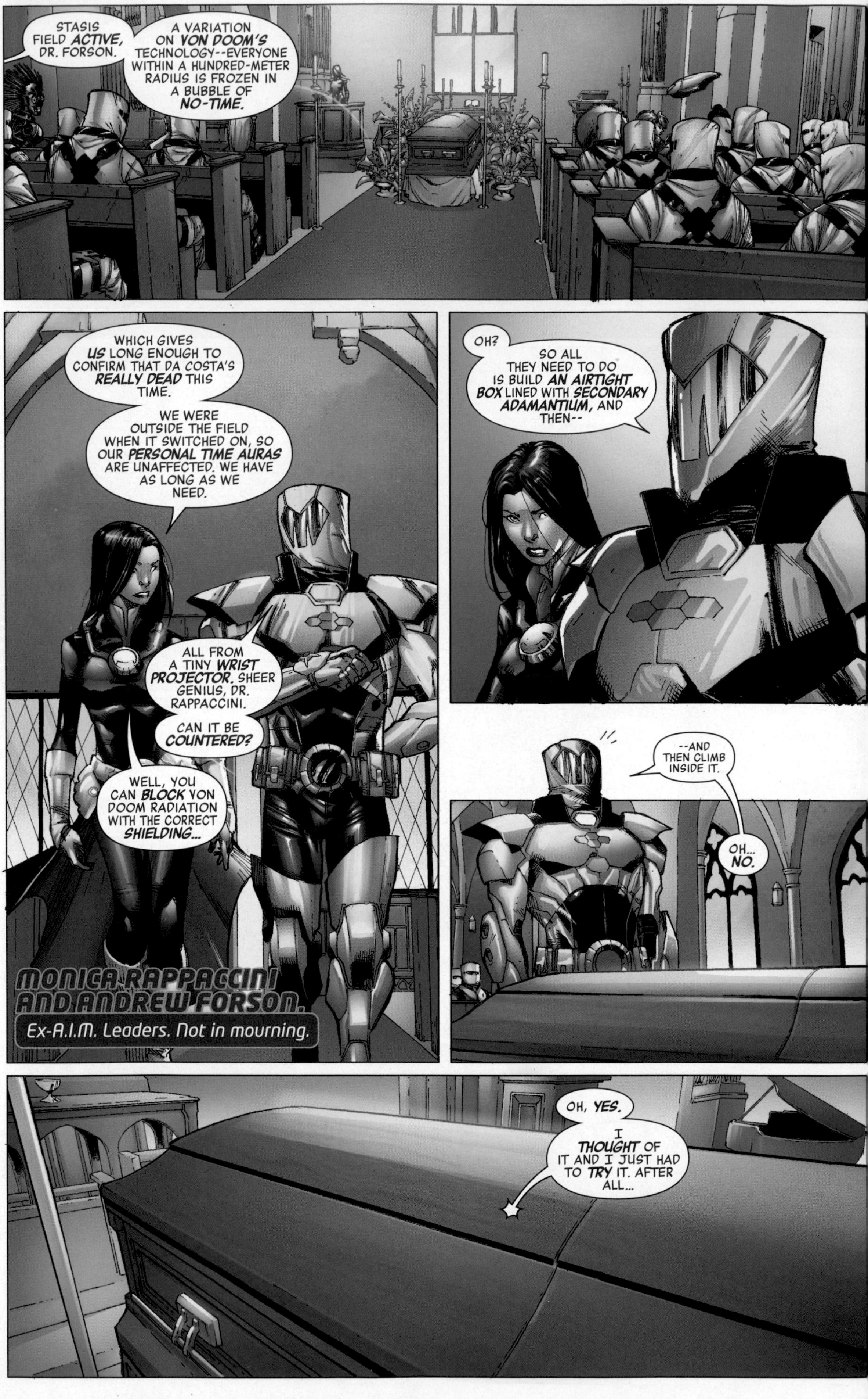
STASIS FIELD ACTIVE, DR. FORSON.
A VARIATION ON VON DOOM'S TECHNOLOGY--EVERYONE WITHIN A HUNDRED-METER RADIUS IS FROZEN IN A BUBBLE OF NO-TIME.
WHICH GIVES US LONG ENOUGH TO CONFIRM THAT DA COSTA'S REALLY DEAD THIS TIME.
WE WERE OUTSIDE THE FIELD WHEN IT SWITCHED ON, SO OUR PERSONAL TIME AURAS ARE UNAFFECTED. WE HAVE AS LONG AS WE NEED.
ALL FROM A TINY WRIST PROJECTOR. SHEER GENIUS, DR. RAPPACCINI.
CAN IT BE COUNTERED?
WELL, YOU CAN BLOCK VON DOOM RADIATION WITH THE CORRECT SHIELDING...
MONICA RAPPACCINI AND ANDREW FORSON.
Ex-A.I.M. Leaders. Not in mourning.
OH?
SO ALL THEY NEED TO DO IS BUILD AN AIRTIGHT BOX LINED WITH SECONDARY ADAMANTIUM, AND THEN--
--AND THEN CLIMB INSIDE IT.
OH... NO.
OH, YES.
I THOUGHT OF IT AND I JUST HAD TO TRY IT. AFTER ALL...

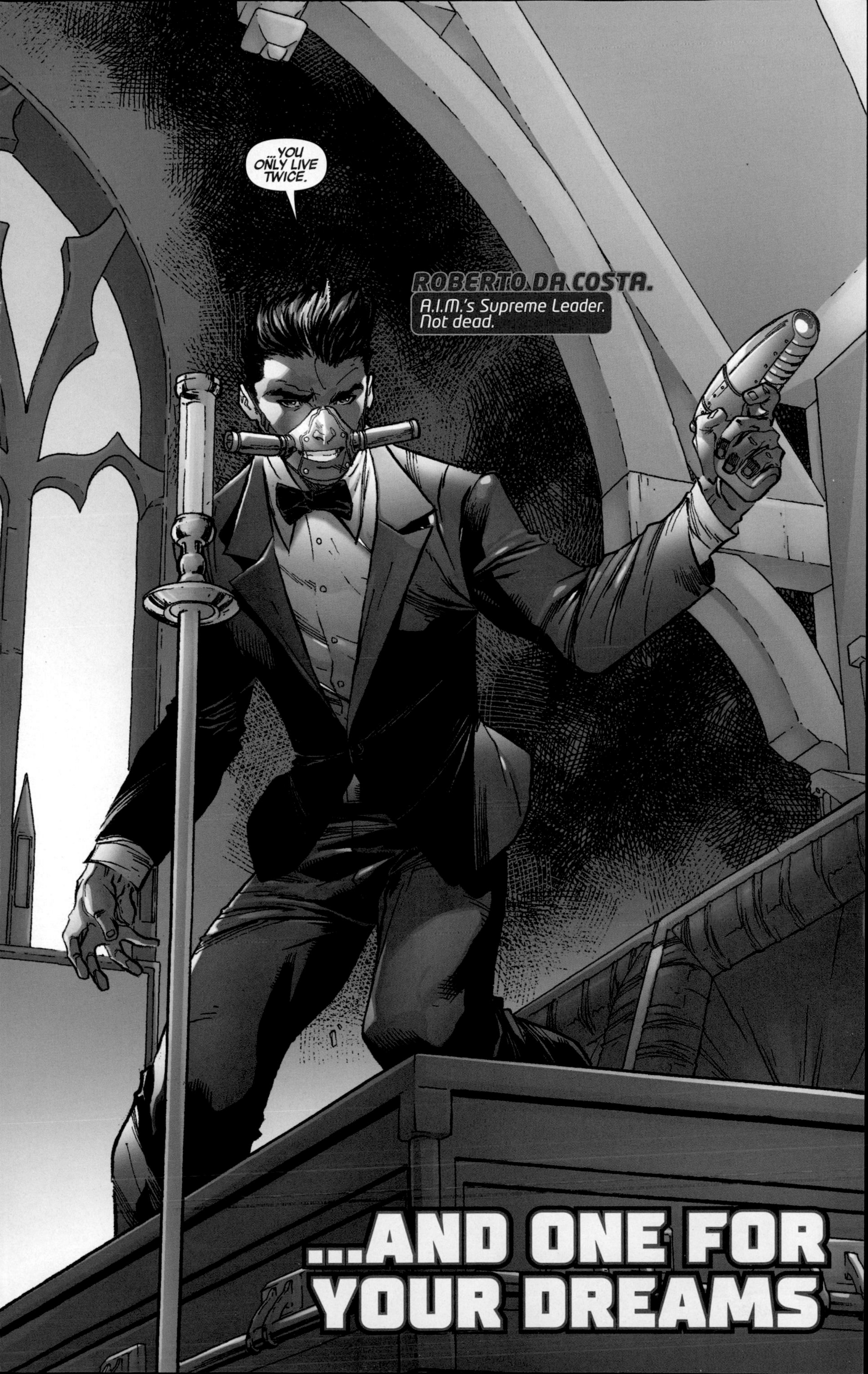
...YOU ONLY LIVE TWICE.
ROBERTO DA COSTA.
A.I.M.'s Supreme Leader. Not dead.
...AND ONE FOR YOUR DREAMS

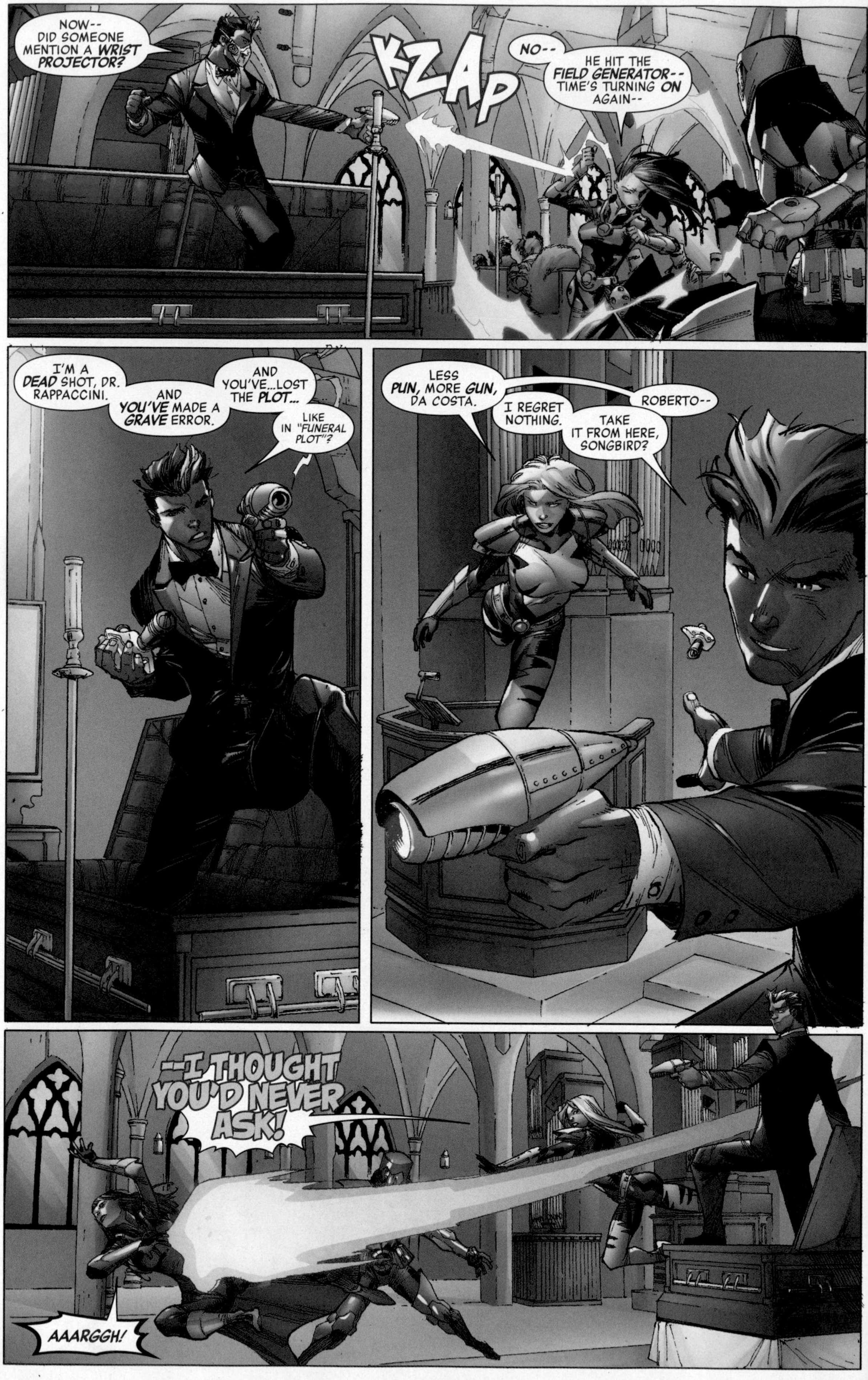
NOW-- DID SOMEONE MENTION A WRIST PROJECTOR?
KZAP
NO--
HE HIT THE FIELD GENERATOR-- TIME'S TURNING ON AGAIN--
I'M A DEAD SHOT, DR. RAPPACCINI.
AND YOU'VE MADE A GRAVE ERROR.
AND YOU'VE...LOST THE PLOT...
LIKE IN "FUNERAL PLOT"?
LESS PUN, MORE GUN, DA COSTA.
I REGRET NOTHING.
ROBERTO--
TAKE IT FROM HERE, SONGBIRD?
--I THOUGHT YOU'D NEVER ASK!
AAARGGH!

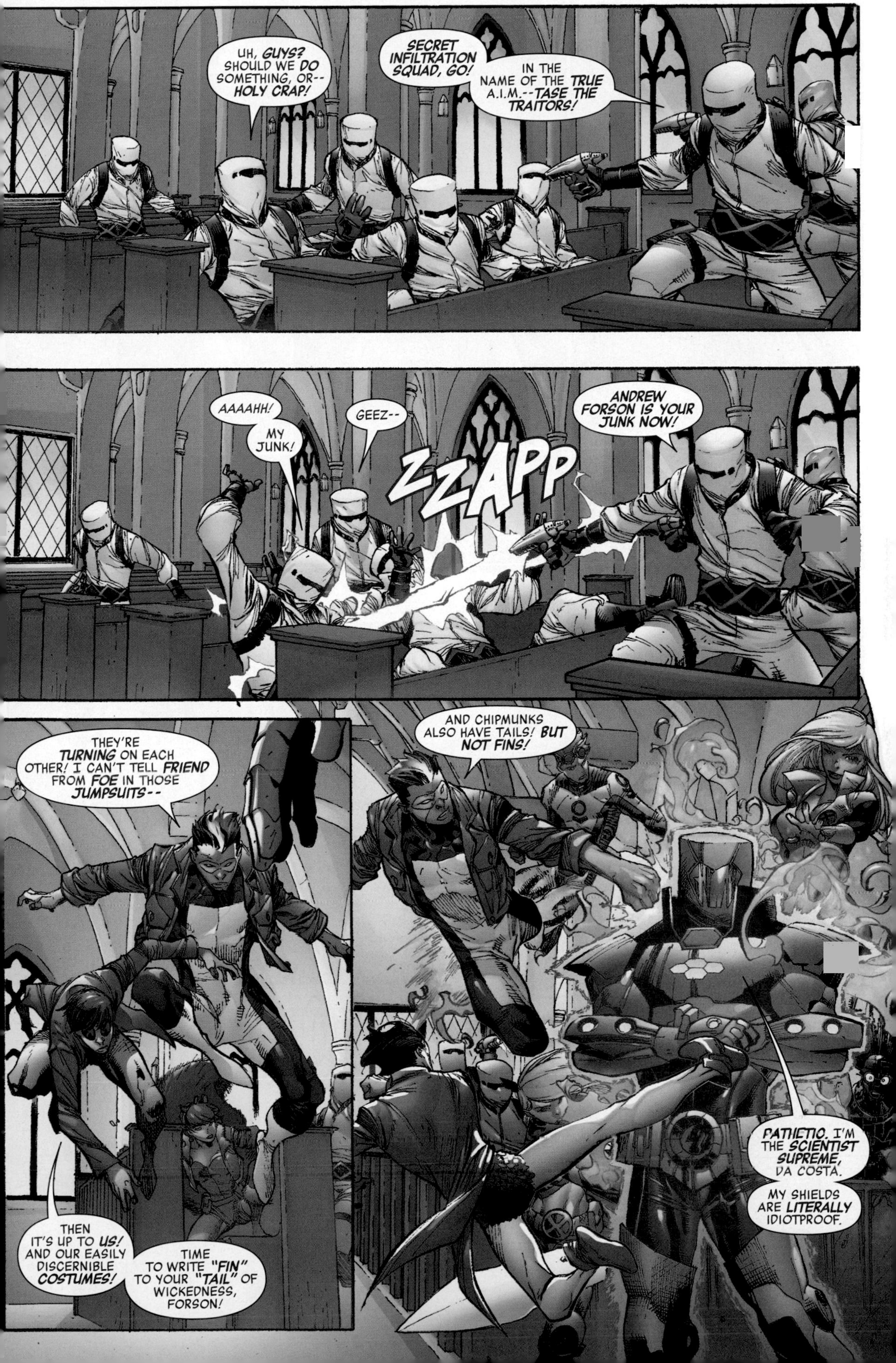
UH, GUYS? SHOULD WE DO SOMETHING, OR-- HOLY CRAP!
SECRET INFILTRATION SQUAD, GO!
IN THE NAME OF THE TRUE A.I.M.--TASE THE TRAITORS!
AAAAHH!
MY JUNK!
GEEZ--
ANDREW FORSON IS YOUR JUNK NOW!
ZZAPP
THEY'RE TURNING ON EACH OTHER! I CAN'T TELL FRIEND FROM FOE IN THOSE JUMPSUITS--
THEN IT'S UP TO US! AND OUR EASILY DISCERNIBLE COSTUMES!
TIME TO WRITE "FIN" TO YOUR "TAIL" OF WICKEDNESS, FORSON!
AND CHIPMUNKS ALSO HAVE TAILS! BUT NOT FINS!
PATHETIC. I'M THE SCIENTIST SUPREME, DA COSTA.
MY SHIELDS ARE LITERALLY IDIOTPROOF.

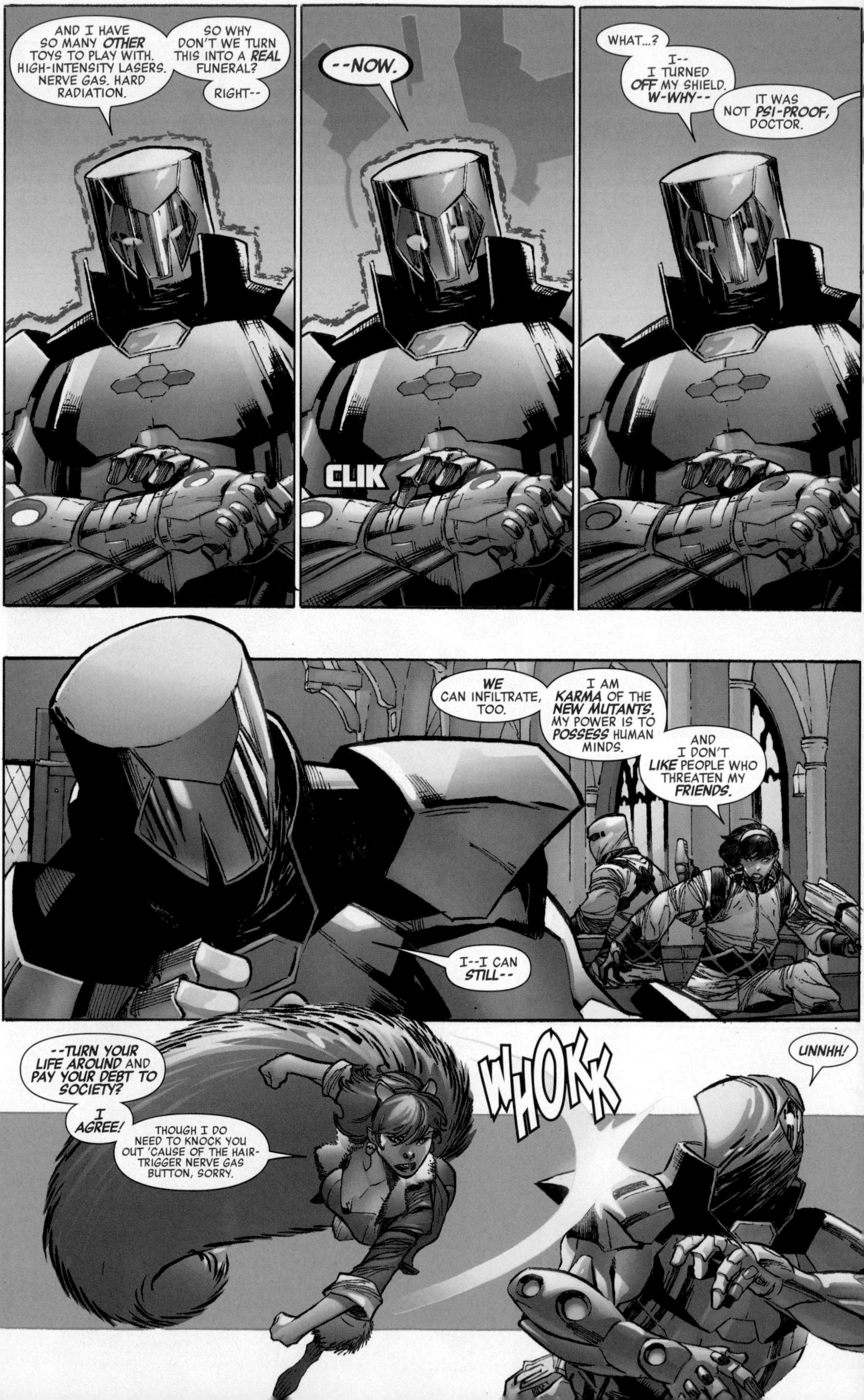
AND I HAVE SO MANY OTHER TOYS TO PLAY WITH. HIGH-INTENSITY LASERS. NERVE GAS. HARD RADIATION.
SO WHY DON'T WE TURN THIS INTO A REAL FUNERAL?
RIGHT--
--NOW.
CLIK
WHAT...?
I-- I TURNED OFF MY SHIELD. W-WHY--
IT WAS NOT PSI-PROOF, DOCTOR.
WE CAN INFILTRATE, TOO.
I AM KARMA OF THE NEW MUTANTS. MY POWER IS TO POSSESS HUMAN MINDS.
AND I DON'T LIKE PEOPLE WHO THREATEN MY FRIENDS.
I--I CAN STILL--
--TURN YOUR LIFE AROUND AND PAY YOUR DEBT TO SOCIETY?
I AGREE!
THOUGH I DO NEED TO KNOCK YOU OUT 'CAUSE OF THE HAIR-TRIGGER NERVE GAS BUTTON, SORRY.
WHOKK
UNNHH!

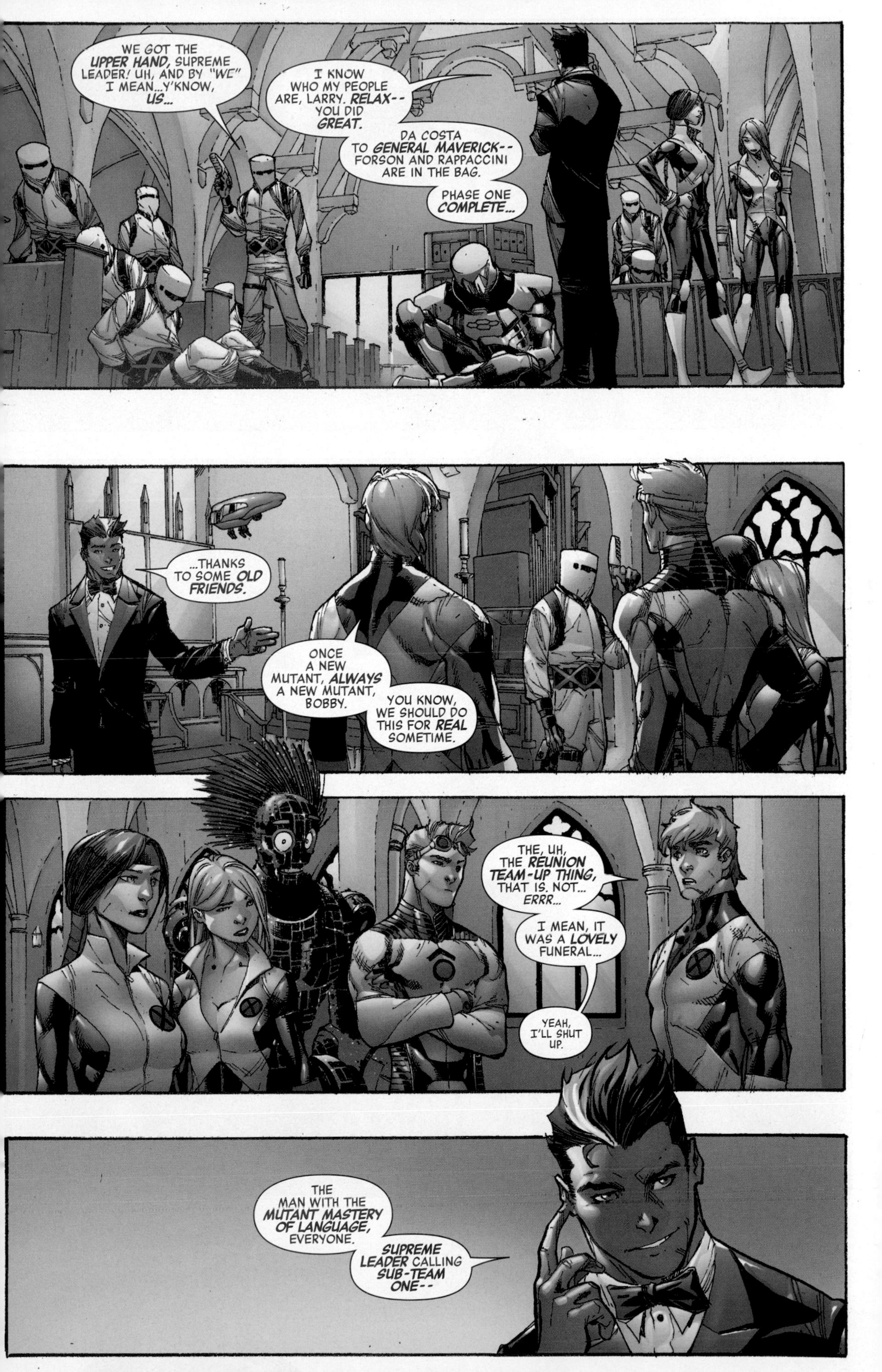

WE GOT THE UPPER HAND, SUPREME LEADER! UH, AND BY "WE" I MEAN...Y'KNOW, US...
I KNOW WHO MY PEOPLE ARE, LARRY. RELAX-- YOU DID GREAT.
DA COSTA TO GENERAL MAVERICK-- FORSON AND RAPPACCINI ARE IN THE BAG.
PHASE ONE COMPLETE...
...THANKS TO SOME OLD FRIENDS.
ONCE A NEW MUTANT, ALWAYS A NEW MUTANT, BOBBY.
YOU KNOW, WE SHOULD DO THIS FOR REAL SOMETIME.
THE, UH, THE REUNION TEAM-UP THING, THAT IS. NOT... ERRR...
I MEAN, IT WAS A LOVELY FUNERAL...
YEAH, I'LL SHUT UP.
THE MAN WITH THE MUTANT MASTERY OF LANGUAGE, EVERYONE.
SUPREME LEADER CALLING SUB-TEAM ONE--

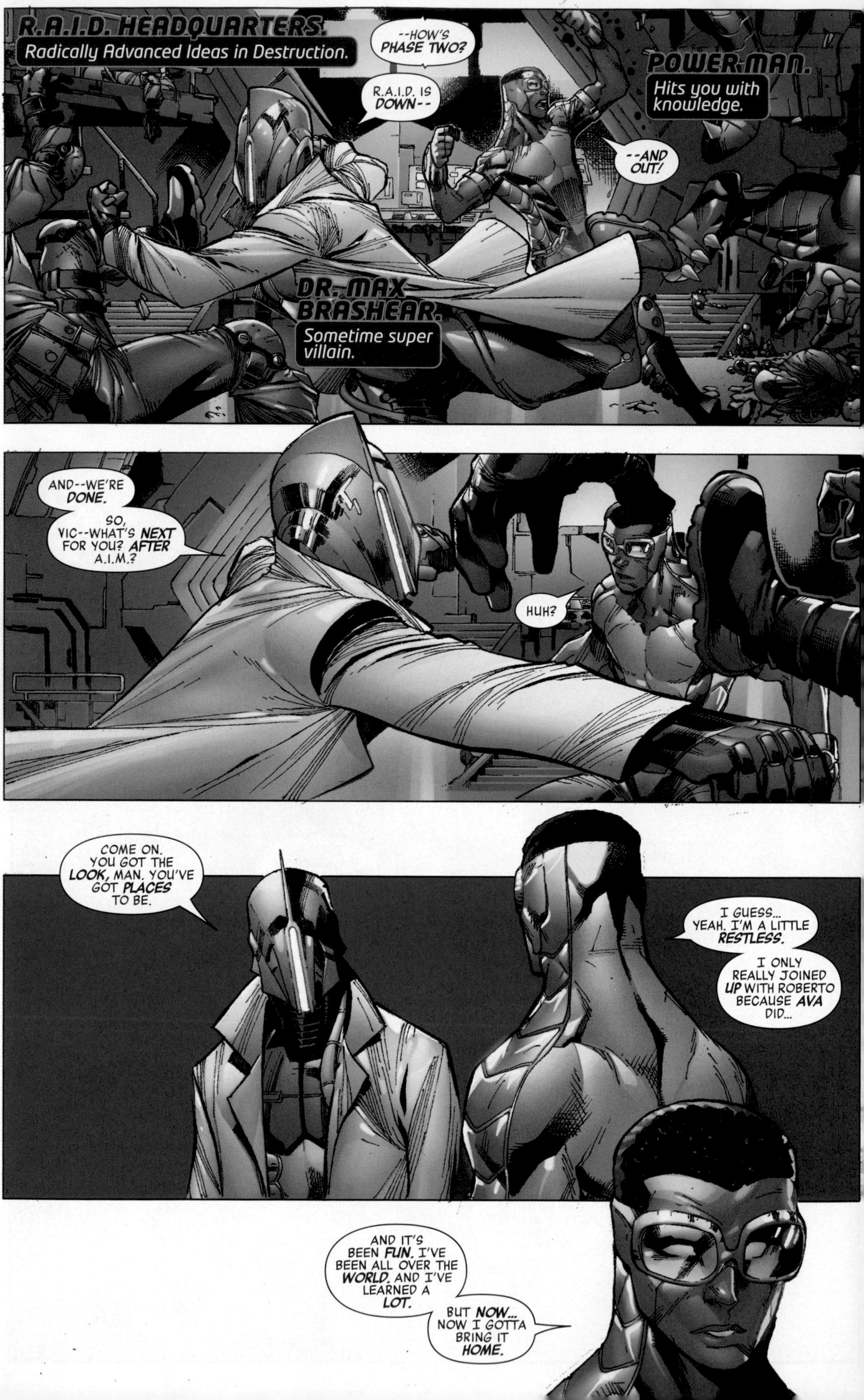

R.A.I.D. HEADQUARTERS.
Radically Advanced Ideas in Destruction.
--HOW'S PHASE TWO?
R.A.I.D. IS DOWN--
POWER MAN.
Hits you with knowledge.
--AND OUT!
DR. MAX BRASHEAR.
Sometime super villain.
AND--WE'RE DONE.
SO, VIC--WHAT'S NEXT FOR YOU? AFTER A.I.M.?
HUH?
COME ON. YOU GOT THE LOOK, MAN. YOU'VE GOT PLACES TO BE.
I GUESS... YEAH. I'M A LITTLE RESTLESS.
I ONLY REALLY JOINED UP WITH ROBERTO BECAUSE AVA DID...
AND IT'S BEEN FUN. I'VE BEEN ALL OVER THE WORLD. AND I'VE LEARNED A LOT.
BUT NOW... NOW I GOTTA BRING IT HOME.

TAKE IT BACK TO THE PEOPLE I STARTED *OUT* PROTECTING. SPANISH HARLEM, NEW YORK CITY...

I'VE BEEN AWAY *TOO LONG*, YOU KNOW?

COOL.

MIND IF I *JOIN* YOU?

UHH...

I'M RESTLESS MYSELF. HELL, I'M *BORED*. AND IT'S NOT LIKE *TONI* NEEDS ME GETTING IN HER WAY.

I'VE NEVER BEEN A FULL-ON *SUPER HERO* BEFORE...

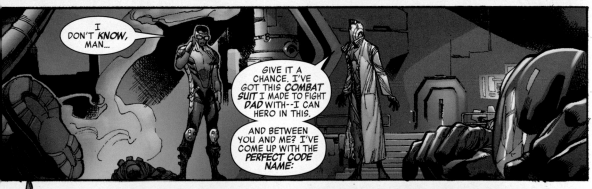

I DON'T *KNOW*, MAN...

GIVE IT A CHANCE. I'VE GOT THIS *COMBAT SUIT* I MADE TO FIGHT *DAD* WITH--I CAN HERO IN THIS.

AND BETWEEN YOU AND ME? I'VE COME UP WITH THE *PERFECT CODE NAME:*

IRON FIST!

... %/0$E@ IT.

FOR THE LOOK ON THEIR FACES *ALONE...*

RIGHT?

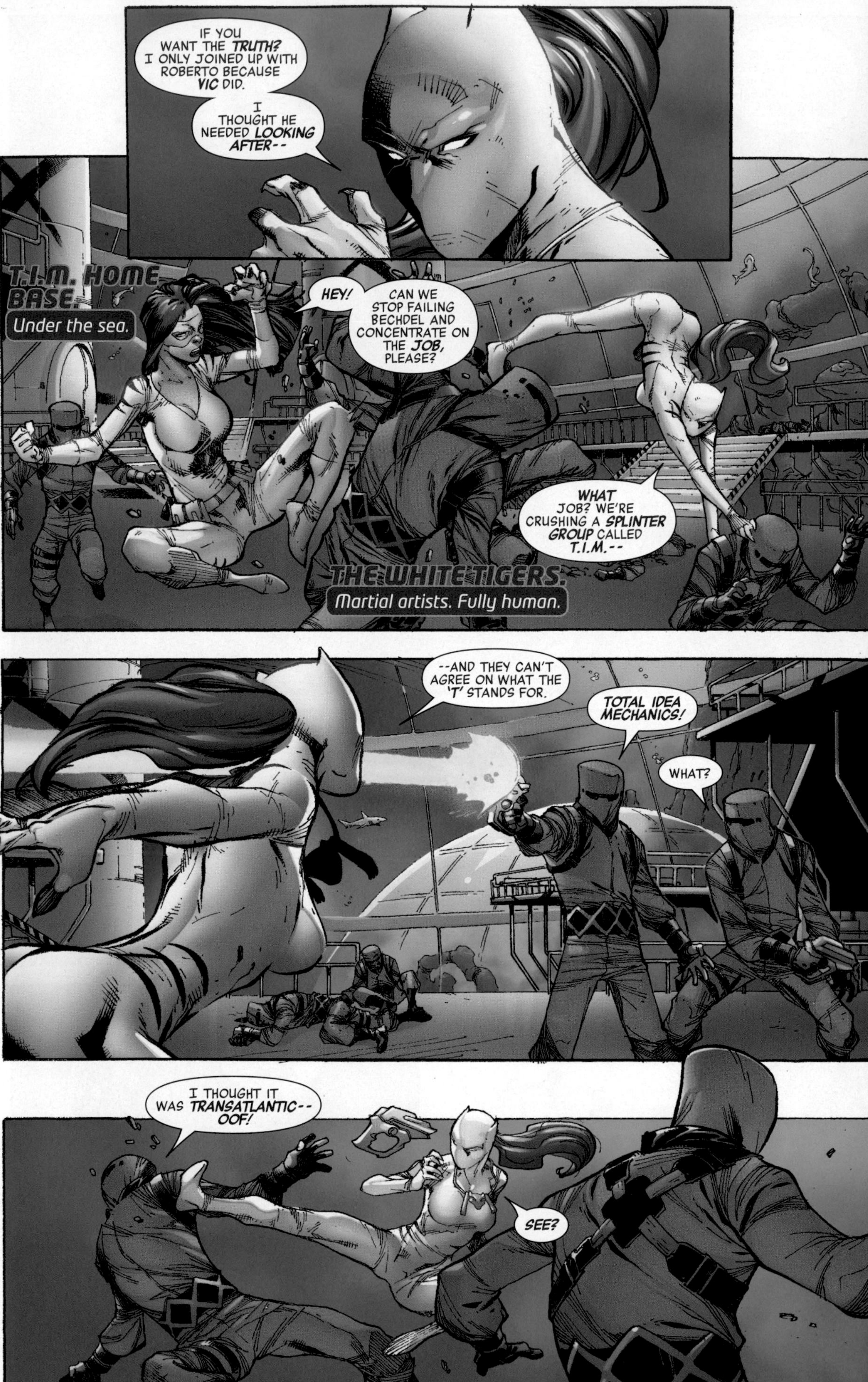
IF YOU WANT THE TRUTH? I ONLY JOINED UP WITH ROBERTO BECAUSE VIC DID.
I THOUGHT HE NEEDED LOOKING AFTER--
T.I.M. HOME BASE.
Under the sea.
HEY!
CAN WE STOP FAILING BECHDEL AND CONCENTRATE ON THE JOB, PLEASE?
WHAT JOB? WE'RE CRUSHING A SPLINTER GROUP CALLED T.I.M.--
THE WHITE TIGERS.
Martial artists. Fully human.
--AND THEY CAN'T AGREE ON WHAT THE 'T' STANDS FOR.
TOTAL IDEA MECHANICS!
WHAT?
I THOUGHT IT WAS TRANSATLANTIC-- OOF!
SEE?

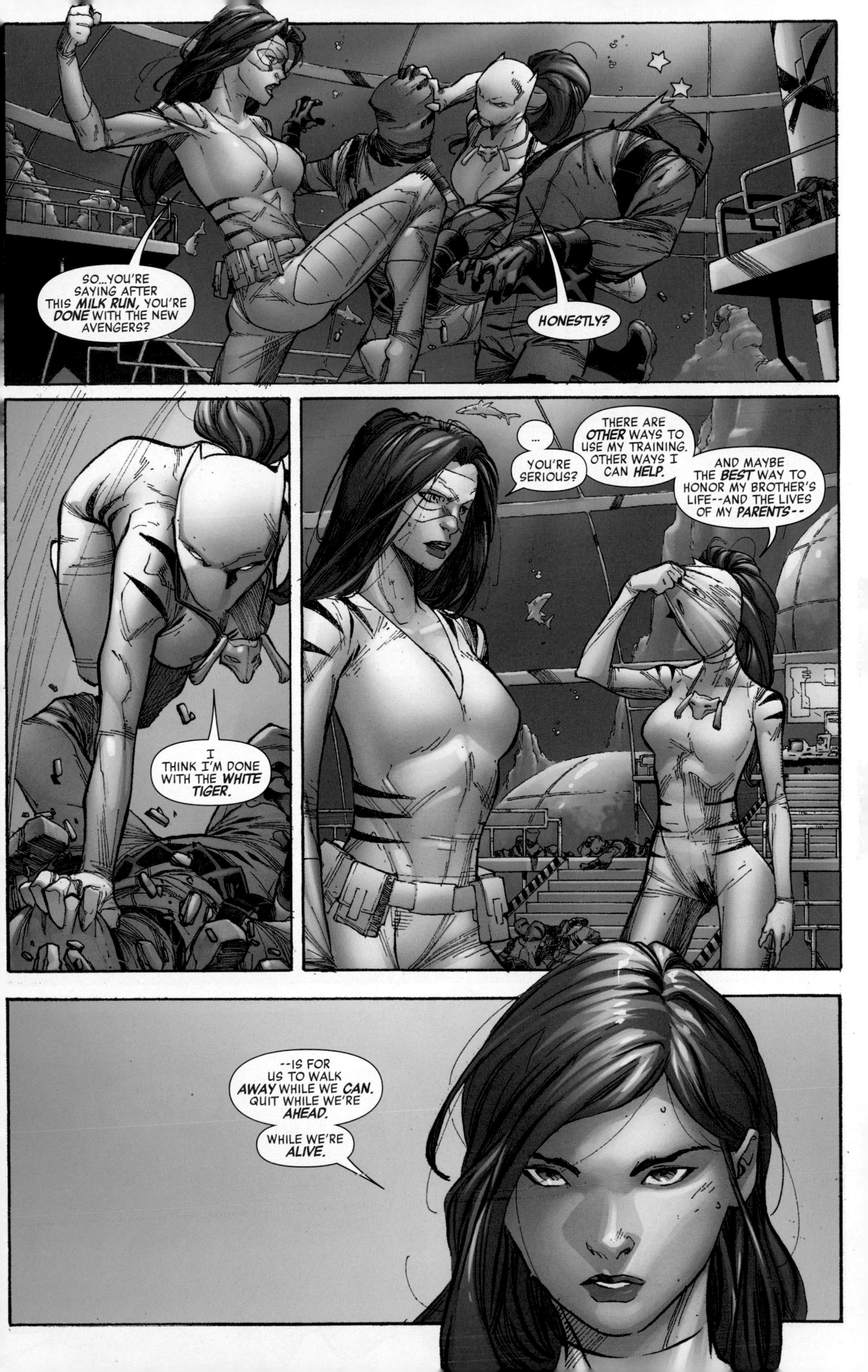
SO...YOU'RE SAYING AFTER THIS MILK RUN, YOU'RE DONE WITH THE NEW AVENGERS?
HONESTLY?
I THINK I'M DONE WITH THE WHITE TIGER.
...
YOU'RE SERIOUS?
THERE ARE OTHER WAYS TO USE MY TRAINING. OTHER WAYS I CAN HELP.
AND MAYBE THE BEST WAY TO HONOR MY BROTHER'S LIFE--AND THE LIVES OF MY PARENTS--
--IS FOR US TO WALK AWAY WHILE WE CAN. QUIT WHILE WE'RE AHEAD.
WHILE WE'RE ALIVE.

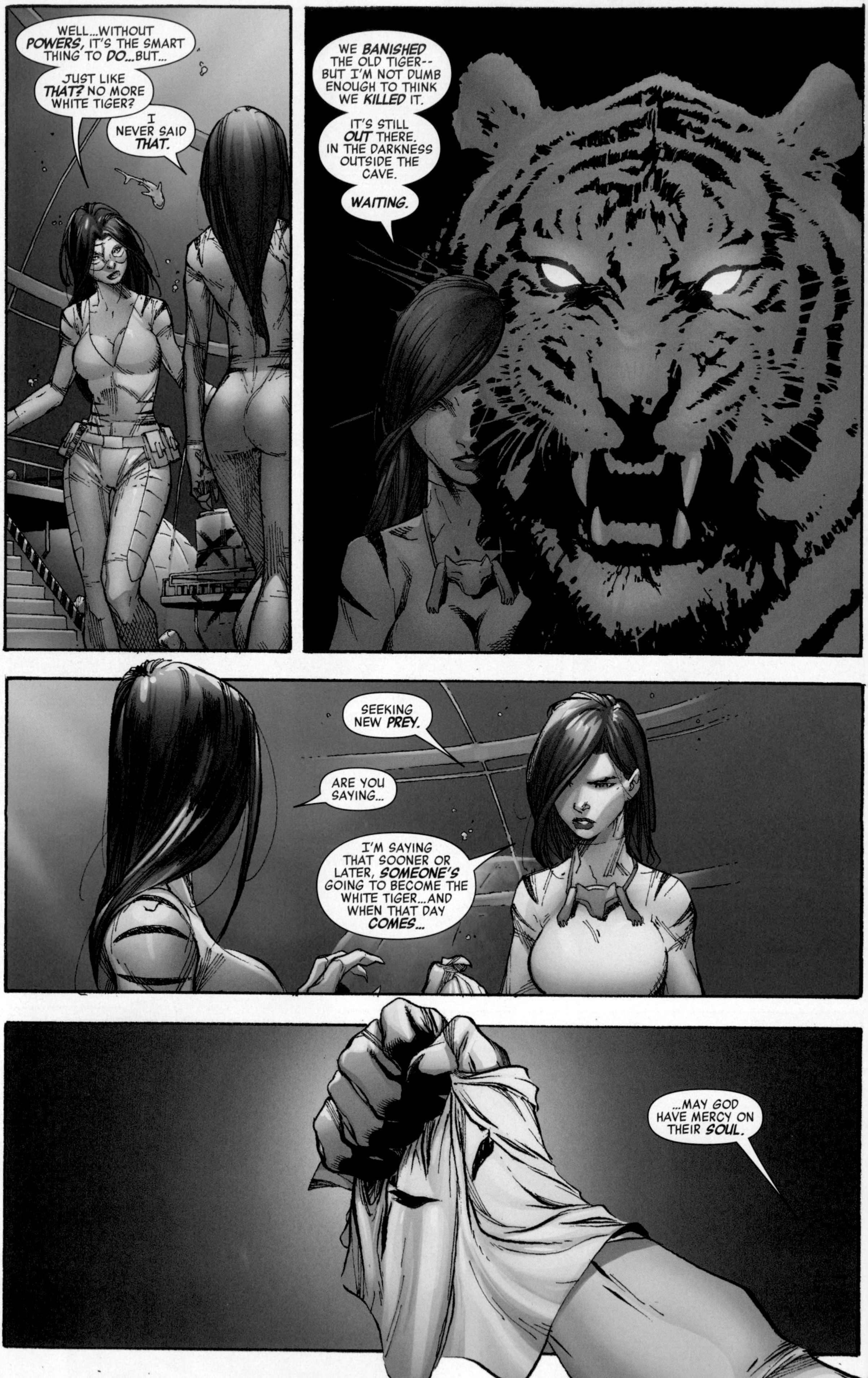
WELL...WITHOUT POWERS, IT'S THE SMART THING TO DO...BUT...
JUST LIKE THAT? NO MORE WHITE TIGER?
I NEVER SAID THAT.
WE BANISHED THE OLD TIGER-- BUT I'M NOT DUMB ENOUGH TO THINK WE KILLED IT.
IT'S STILL OUT THERE. IN THE DARKNESS OUTSIDE THE CAVE.
WAITING.
SEEKING NEW PREY.
ARE YOU SAYING...
I'M SAYING THAT SOONER OR LATER, SOMEONE'S GOING TO BECOME THE WHITE TIGER...AND WHEN THAT DAY COMES...
...MAY GOD HAVE MERCY ON THEIR SOUL.

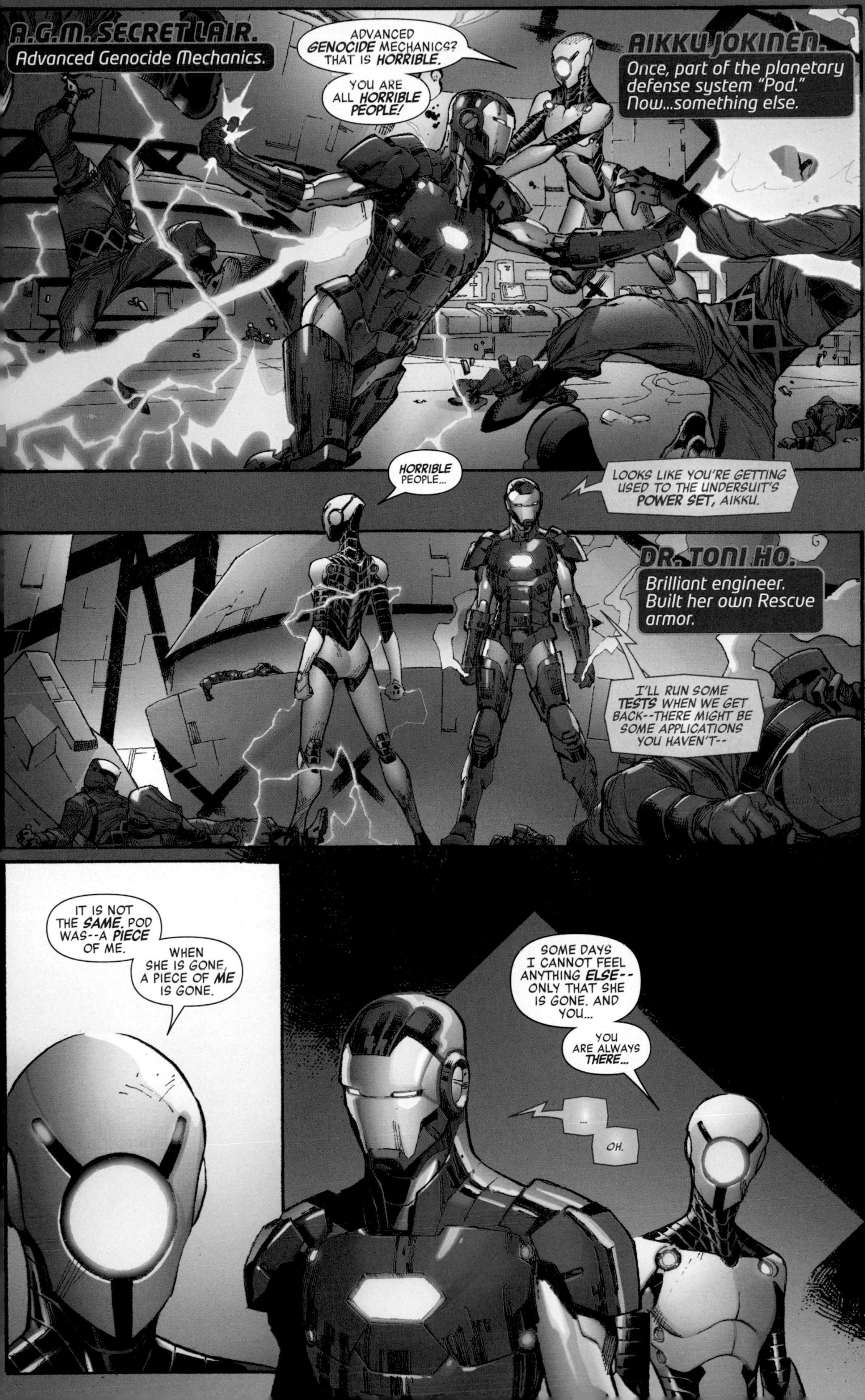
A.G.M. SECRET LAIR.
Advanced Genocide Mechanics.
ADVANCED GENOCIDE MECHANICS? THAT IS HORRIBLE.
YOU ARE ALL HORRIBLE PEOPLE!
AIKKU JOKINEN.
Once, part of the planetary defense system "Pod." Now...something else.
HORRIBLE PEOPLE...
LOOKS LIKE YOU'RE GETTING USED TO THE UNDERSUIT'S POWER SET, AIKKU.
DR. TONI HO.
Brilliant engineer. Built her own Rescue armor.
I'LL RUN SOME TESTS WHEN WE GET BACK--THERE MIGHT BE SOME APPLICATIONS YOU HAVEN'T--
IT IS NOT THE SAME. POD WAS--A PIECE OF ME.
WHEN SHE IS GONE, A PIECE OF ME IS GONE.
SOME DAYS I CANNOT FEEL ANYTHING ELSE--ONLY THAT SHE IS GONE. AND YOU...
YOU ARE ALWAYS THERE...
...
OH.

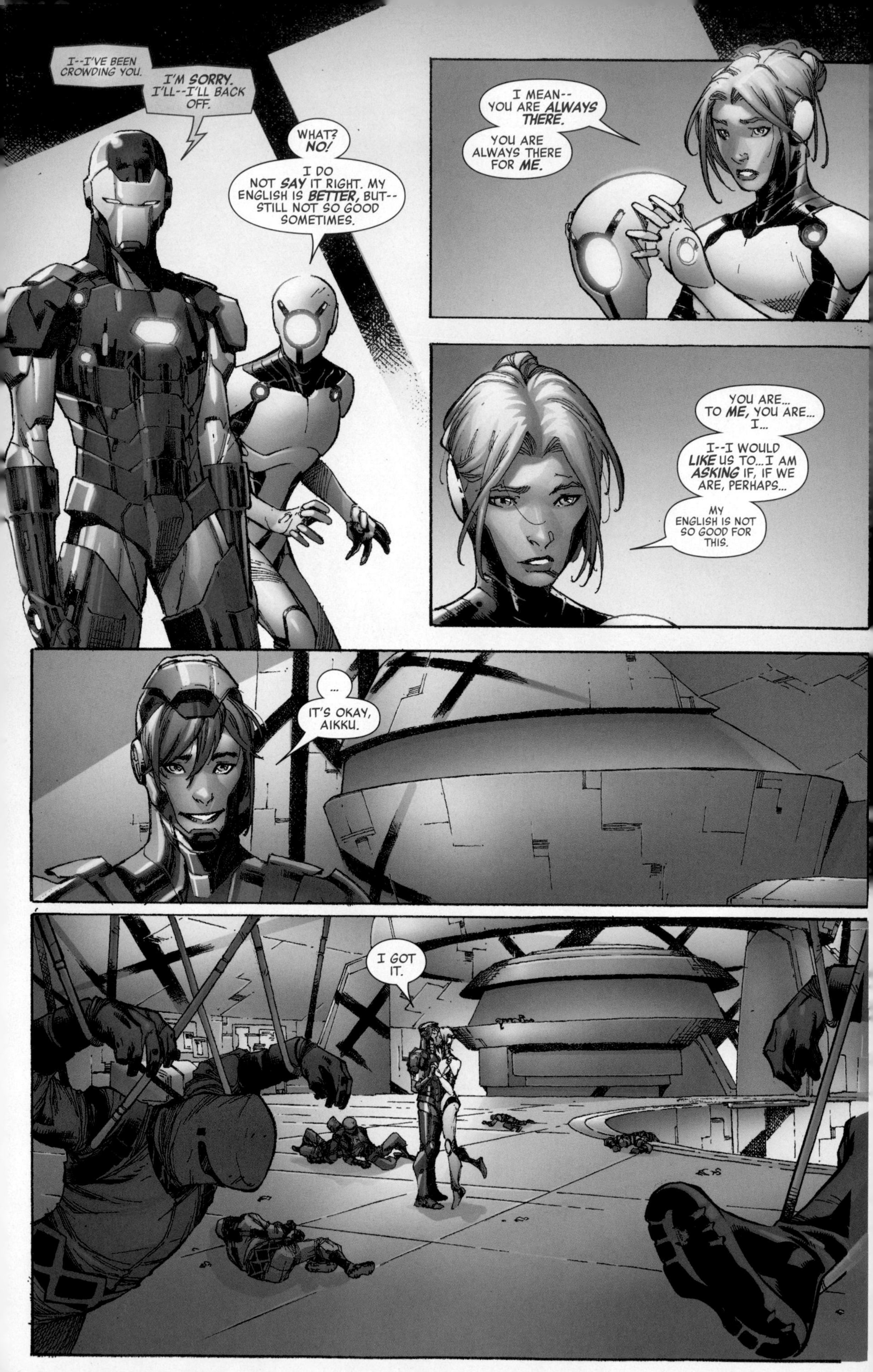

I--I'VE BEEN CROWDING YOU.
I'M SORRY. I'LL--I'LL BACK OFF.
WHAT? NO!
I DO NOT SAY IT RIGHT. MY ENGLISH IS BETTER, BUT-- STILL NOT SO GOOD SOMETIMES.
I MEAN-- YOU ARE ALWAYS THERE.
YOU ARE ALWAYS THERE FOR ME.
YOU ARE... TO ME, YOU ARE... I...
I--I WOULD LIKE US TO...I AM ASKING IF, IF WE ARE, PERHAPS...
MY ENGLISH IS NOT SO GOOD FOR THIS.
...
IT'S OKAY, AIKKU.
I GOT IT.

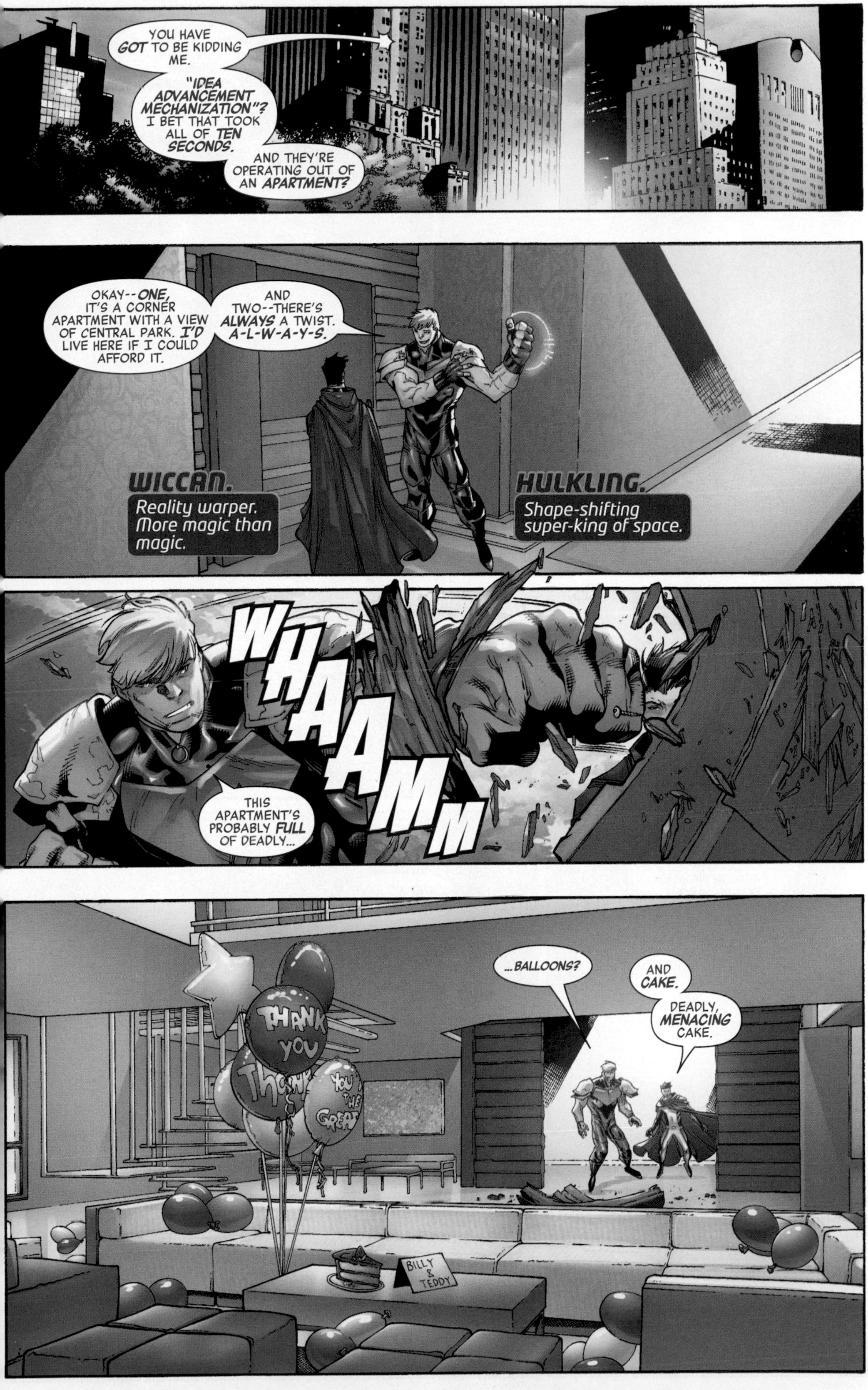
YOU HAVE GOT TO BE KIDDING ME.
"IDEA ADVANCEMENT MECHANIZATION"? I BET THAT TOOK ALL OF TEN SECONDS.
AND THEY'RE OPERATING OUT OF AN APARTMENT?
OKAY--ONE, IT'S A CORNER APARTMENT WITH A VIEW OF CENTRAL PARK. I'D LIVE HERE IF I COULD AFFORD IT.
AND TWO--THERE'S ALWAYS A TWIST. A-L-W-A-Y-S.
WICCAN.
Reality warper. More magic than magic.
HULKLING.
Shape-shifting super-king of space.
WHAAAMM
THIS APARTMENT'S PROBABLY FULL OF DEADLY...
THANK YOU
THANK
YOU THE GREAT
...BALLOONS?
AND CAKE.
DEADLY, MENACING CAKE.
BILLY & TEDDY

"DEAR BILLY AND TEDDY--SURPRISE! NO MISSION. I KNOW YOU TWO WERE GETTING ITCHY FEET..."

"...SO IN LIEU OF THE ASSETS S.H.I.E.L.D. FROZE, I FIGURED I'D GET YOU TWO YOUR OWN PLACE."

WE LIVE HERE?

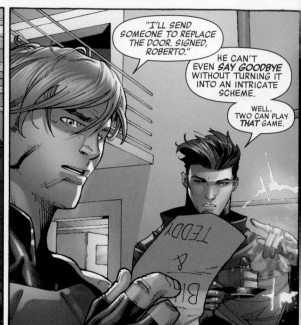

"I'LL SEND SOMEONE TO REPLACE THE DOOR. SIGNED, ROBERTO."

HE CAN'T EVEN SAY GOODBYE WITHOUT TURNING IT INTO AN INTRICATE SCHEME.

WELL, TWO CAN PLAY THAT GAME.

FLY, SLICE OF CAKE! FLY TO ROBERTO'S MOUTH!

TELL HIM HE'S THE BEST!

HEH.

SO NOW WHAT? DO WE KEEP NEW AVENGERING?

BECAUSE I THINK IF WE DID... IT'D JUST BE US. I KNOW DOREEN WANTS TO KEEP AN EYE ON BOBBY.

WELL, MAYBE IT'S TIME FOR THAT YOUNG AVENGERS REUNION WE KEEP TALKING ABOUT.

BUT...YOU KNOW WHAT? THE SUN'S SETTING OVER CENTRAL PARK...WE'VE GOT THE BEST VIEW IN THE CITY...

...AND WE HAVE BALLOONS.

SO IT'S A PRETTY GOOD NIGHT TO JUST BE WICCAN AND HULKLING.

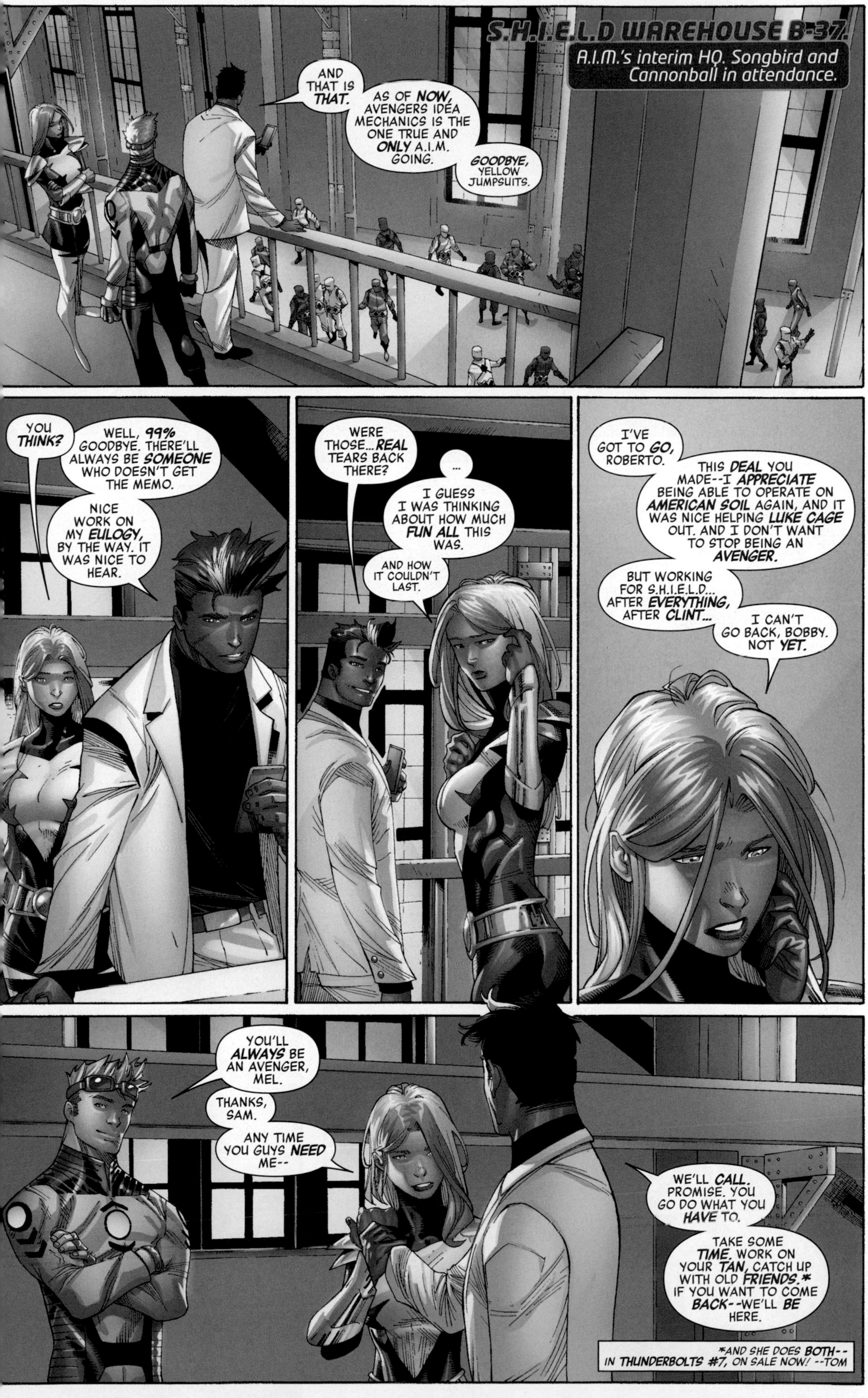
S.H.I.E.L.D WAREHOUSE B-37.
A.I.M.'s interim HQ. Songbird and Cannonball in attendance.
AND THAT IS THAT.
AS OF NOW, AVENGERS IDEA MECHANICS IS THE ONE TRUE AND ONLY A.I.M. GOING.
GOODBYE, YELLOW JUMPSUITS.
YOU THINK?
WELL, 99% GOODBYE. THERE'LL ALWAYS BE SOMEONE WHO DOESN'T GET THE MEMO.
NICE WORK ON MY EULOGY, BY THE WAY. IT WAS NICE TO HEAR.
WERE THOSE...REAL TEARS BACK THERE?
...
I GUESS I WAS THINKING ABOUT HOW MUCH FUN ALL THIS WAS.
AND HOW IT COULDN'T LAST.
I'VE GOT TO GO, ROBERTO.
THIS DEAL YOU MADE--I APPRECIATE BEING ABLE TO OPERATE ON AMERICAN SOIL AGAIN, AND IT WAS NICE HELPING LUKE CAGE OUT. AND I DON'T WANT TO STOP BEING AN AVENGER.
BUT WORKING FOR S.H.I.E.L.D... AFTER EVERYTHING, AFTER CLINT...
I CAN'T GO BACK, BOBBY. NOT YET.
YOU'LL ALWAYS BE AN AVENGER, MEL.
THANKS, SAM.
ANY TIME YOU GUYS NEED ME--
WE'LL CALL. PROMISE. YOU GO DO WHAT YOU HAVE TO.
TAKE SOME TIME. WORK ON YOUR TAN, CATCH UP WITH OLD FRIENDS.* IF YOU WANT TO COME BACK--WE'LL BE HERE.
*AND SHE DOES BOTH-- IN THUNDERBOLTS #7, ON SALE NOW! --TOM

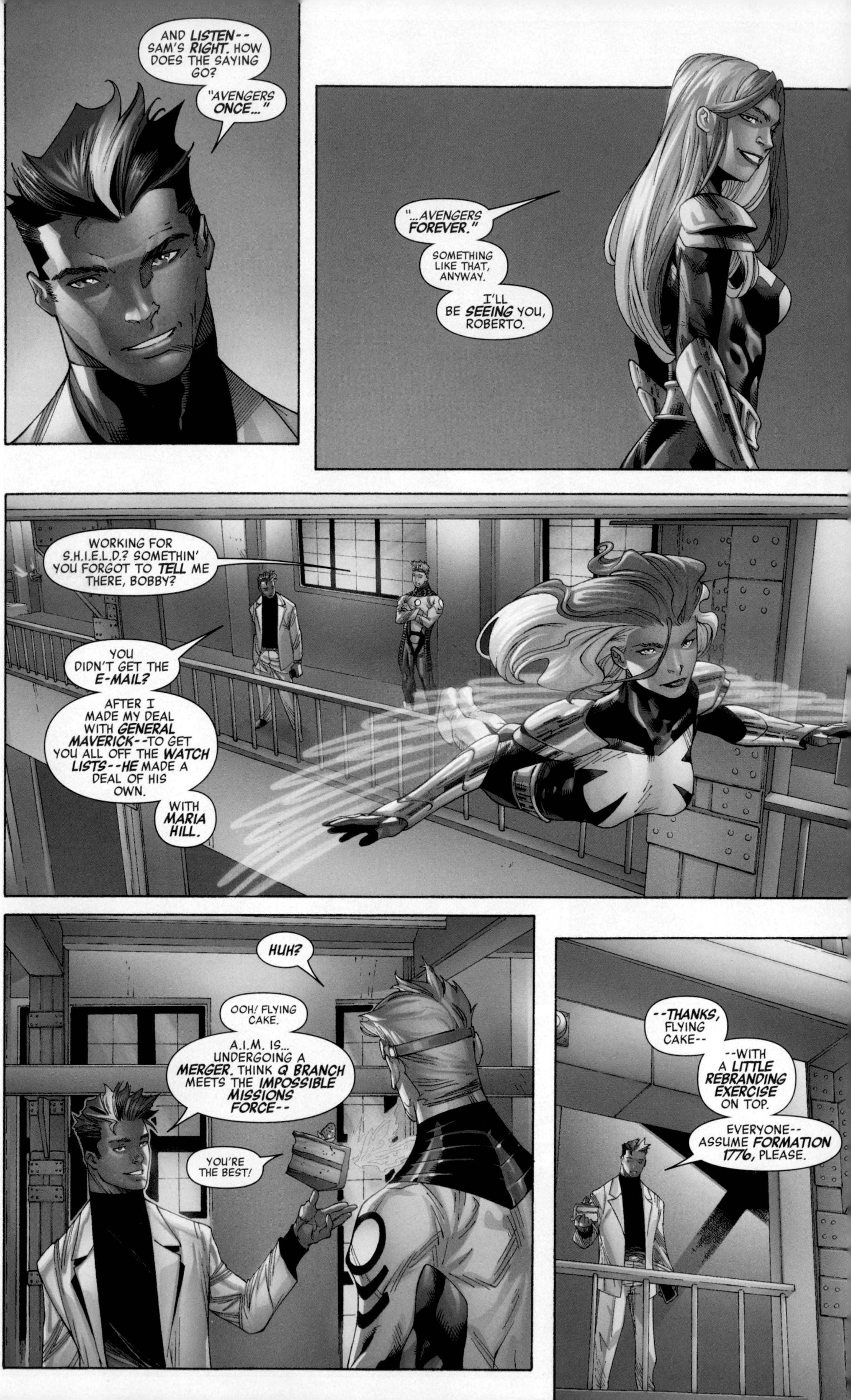
AND LISTEN-- SAM'S RIGHT. HOW DOES THE SAYING GO?
"AVENGERS ONCE..."
"...AVENGERS FOREVER."
SOMETHING LIKE THAT, ANYWAY.
I'LL BE SEEING YOU, ROBERTO.
WORKING FOR S.H.I.E.L.D.? SOMETHIN' YOU FORGOT TO TELL ME THERE, BOBBY?
YOU DIDN'T GET THE E-MAIL?
AFTER I MADE MY DEAL WITH GENERAL MAVERICK--TO GET YOU ALL OFF THE WATCH LISTS--HE MADE A DEAL OF HIS OWN.
WITH MARIA HILL.
HUH?
OOH! FLYING CAKE.
A.I.M. IS... UNDERGOING A MERGER. THINK Q BRANCH MEETS THE IMPOSSIBLE MISSIONS FORCE--
YOU'RE THE BEST!
--THANKS, FLYING CAKE--
--WITH A LITTLE REBRANDING EXERCISE ON TOP.
EVERYONE-- ASSUME FORMATION 1776, PLEASE.

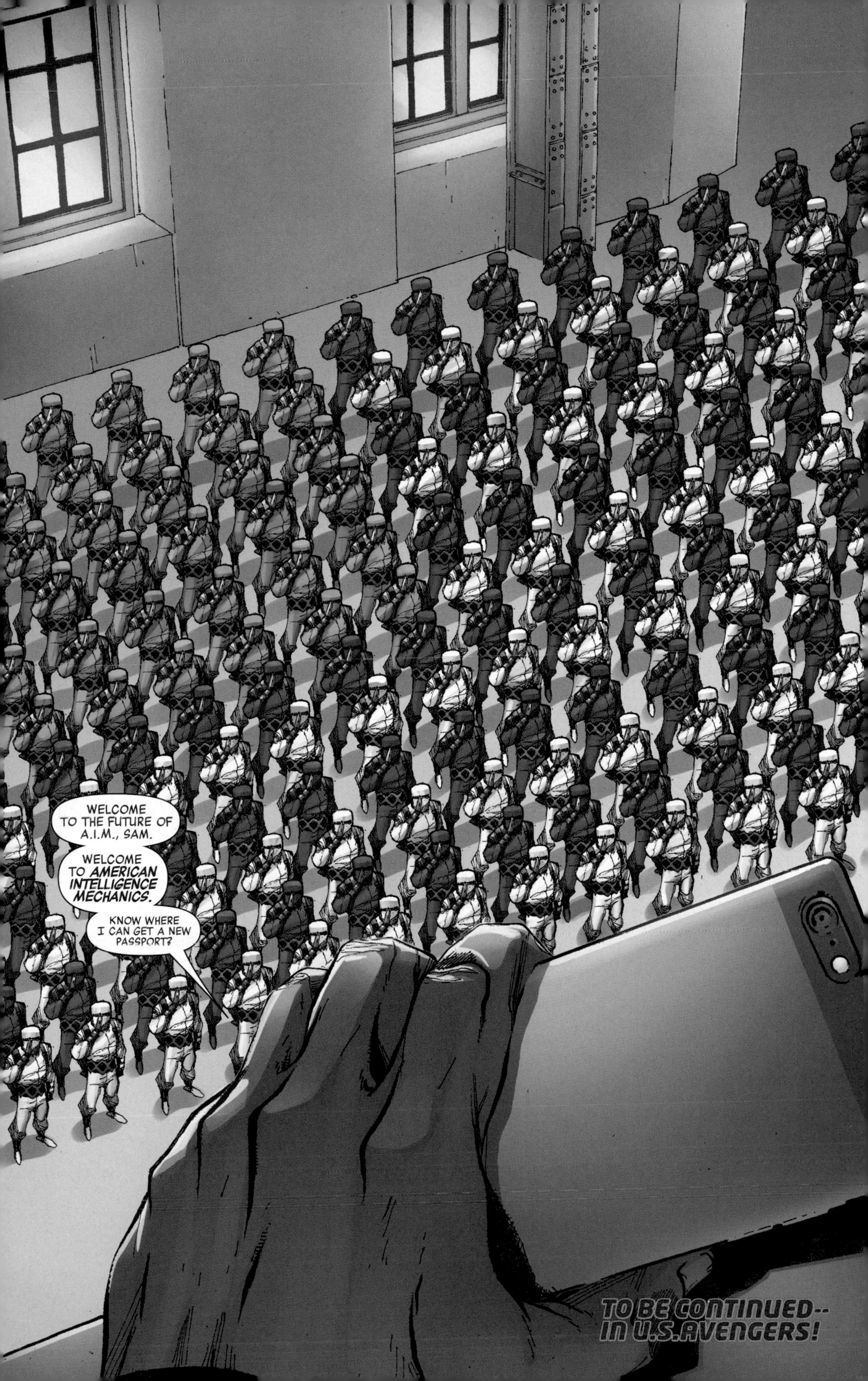
WELCOME TO THE FUTURE OF A.I.M., SAM.
WELCOME TO AMERICAN INTELLIGENCE MECHANICS.
KNOW WHERE I CAN GET A NEW PASSPORT?
TO BE CONTINUED-- IN U.S.AVENGERS!

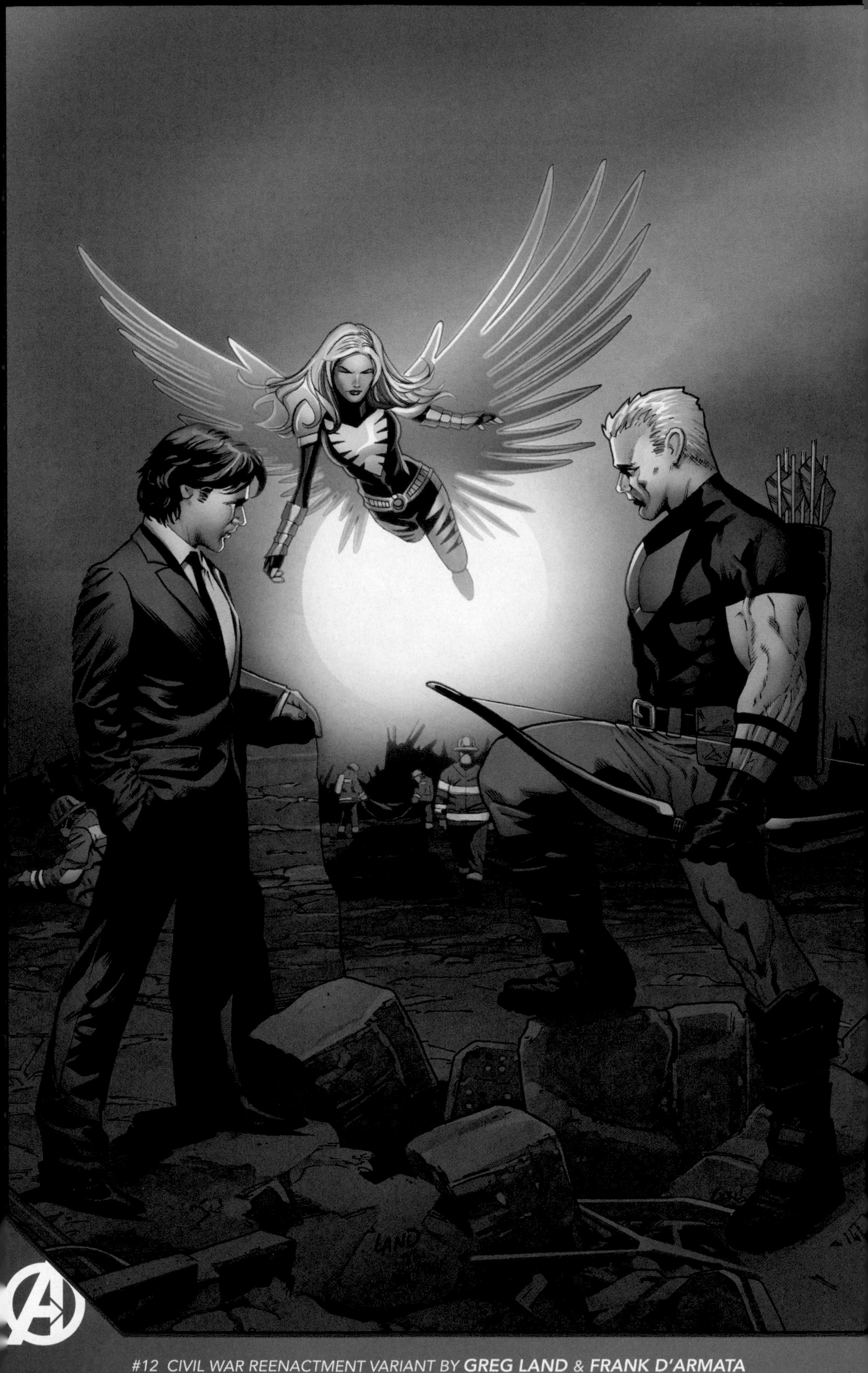

#12 CIVIL WAR REENACTMENT VARIANT BY **GREG LAND** & **FRANK D'ARMATA**

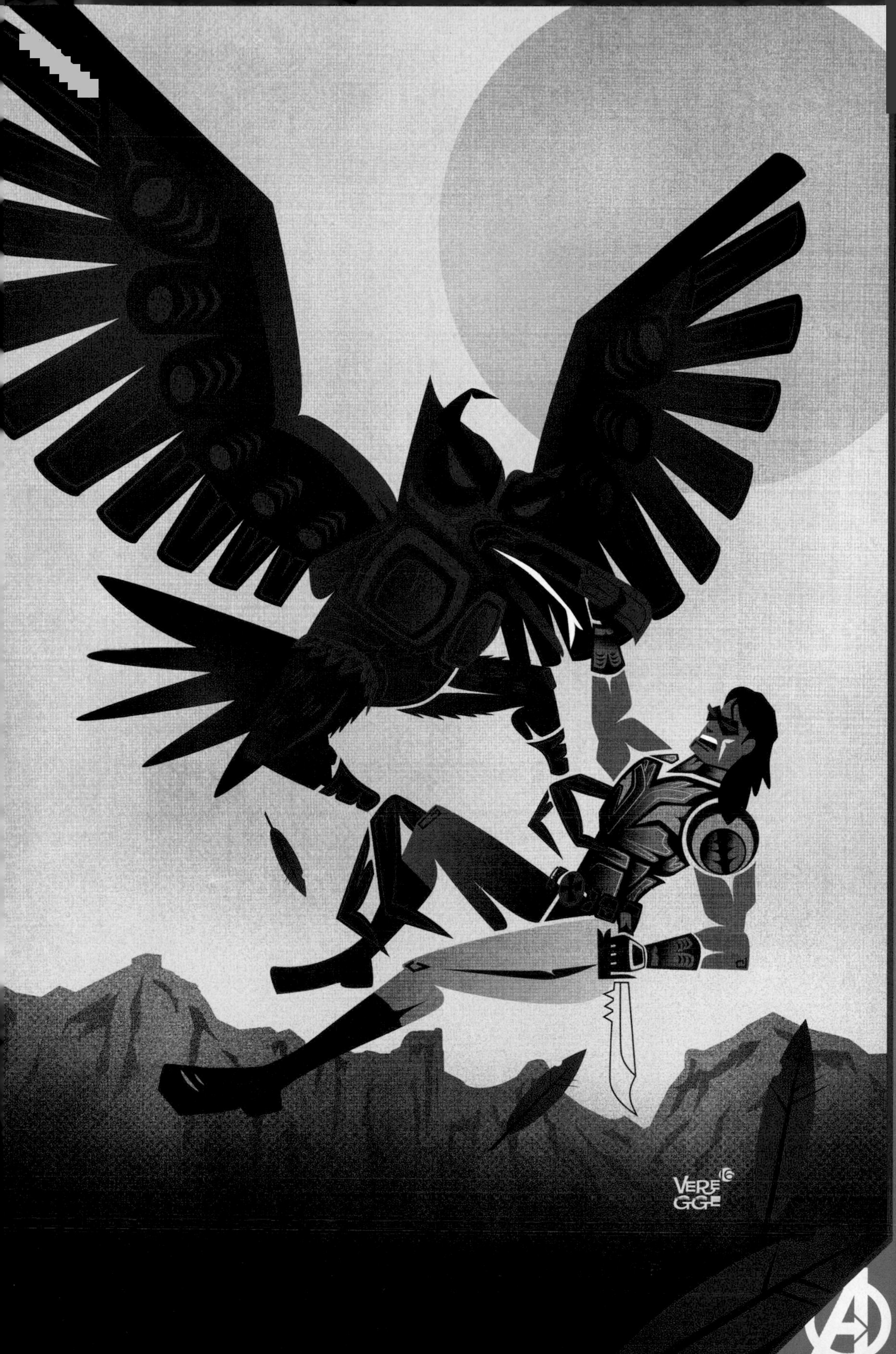
VEREGGE

#13 DEATH OF X VARIANT BY **JEFFREY VEREGGE**

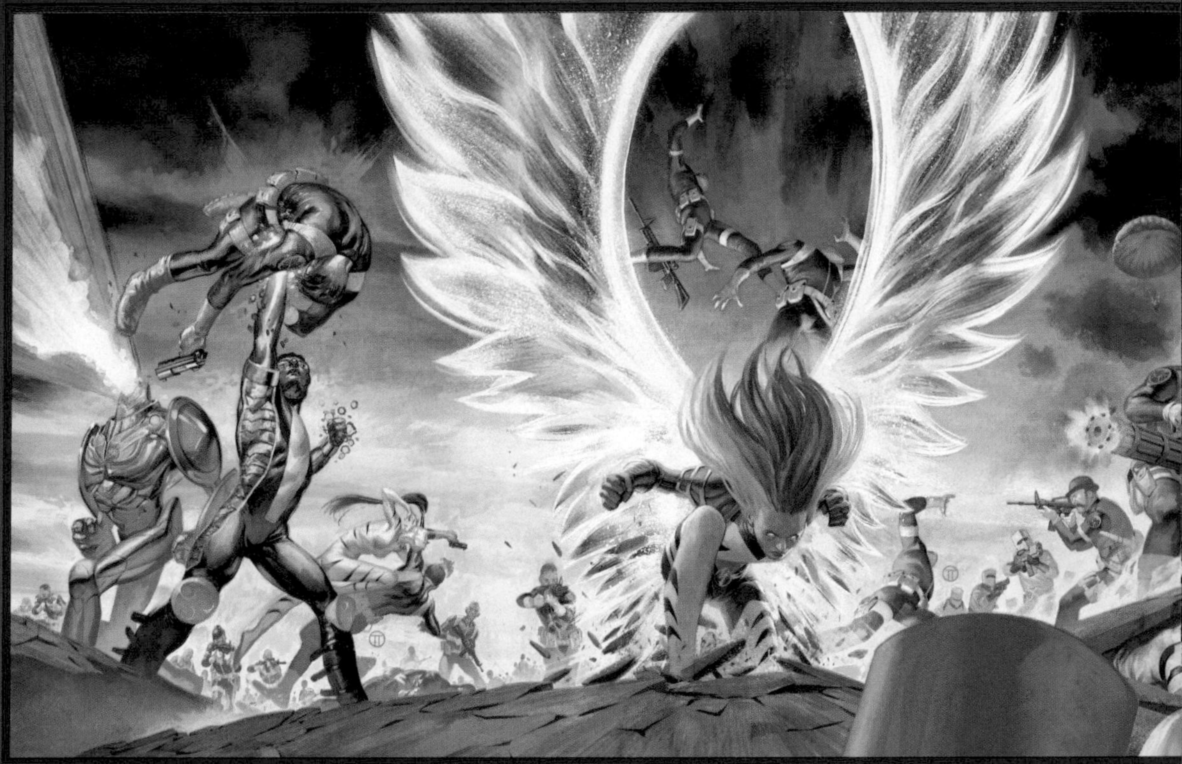

#12-16 CONNECTING COVERS BY **JULIAN TOTINO TEDESCO**

#15, PAGE 2 ART PROCESS BY
PACO MEDINA,
JUAN VLASCO & **JESUS ABURTOV**

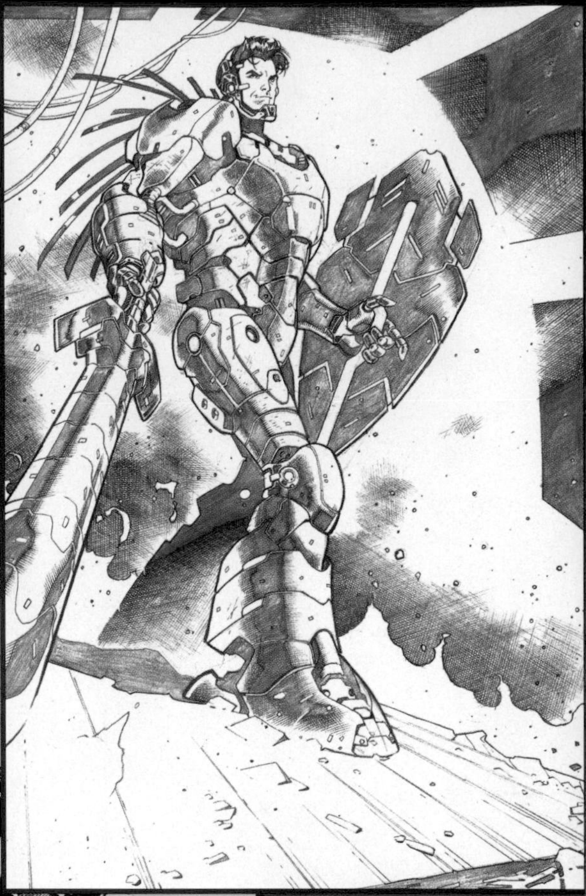

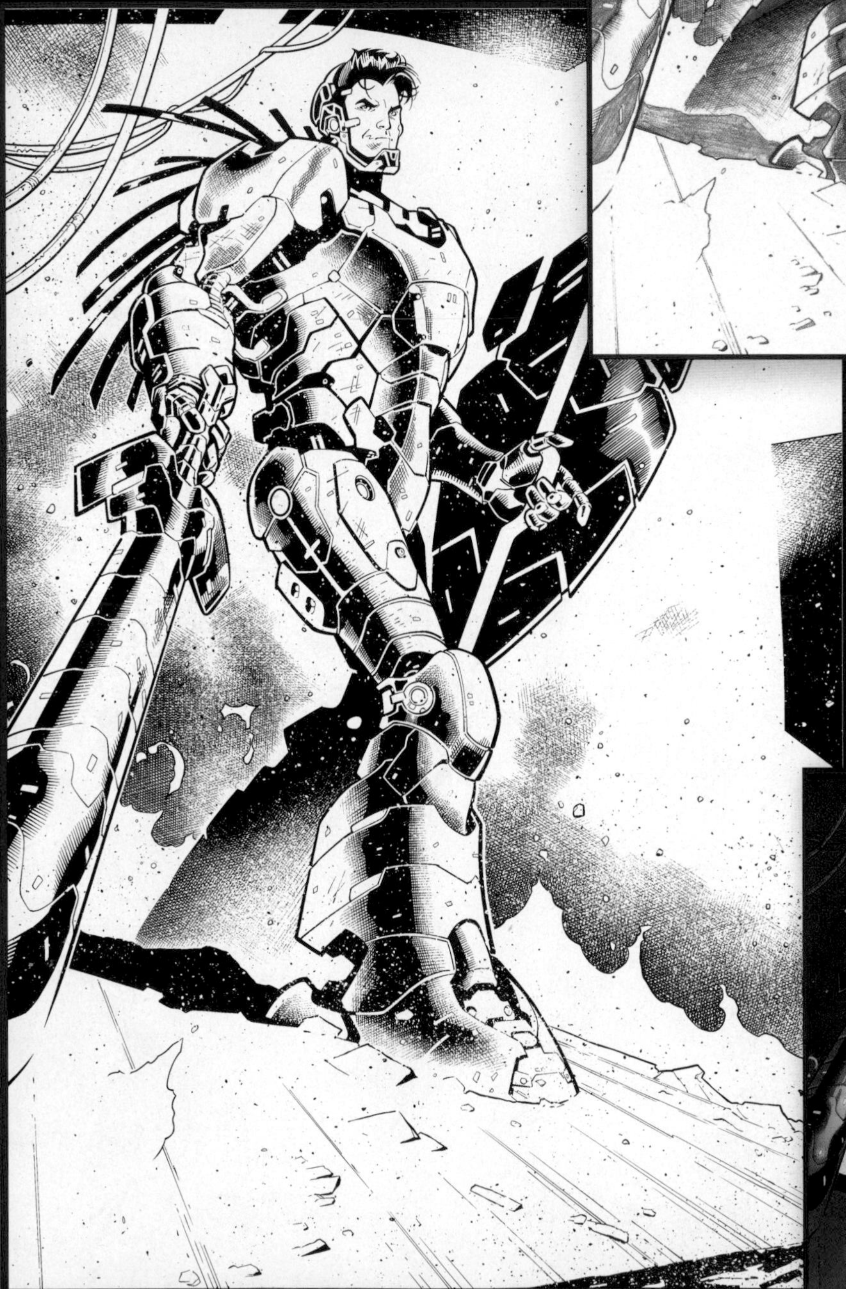

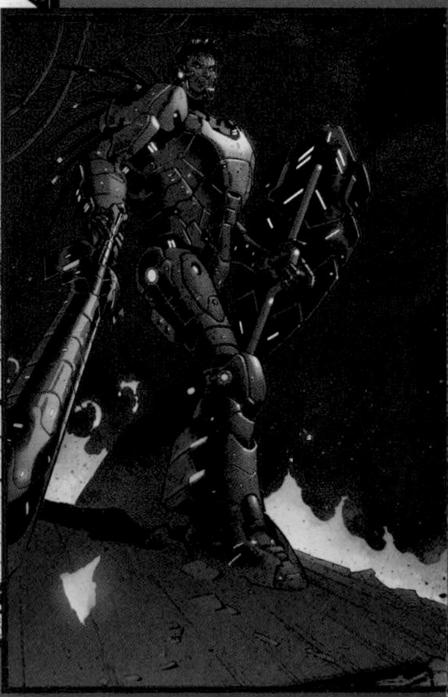

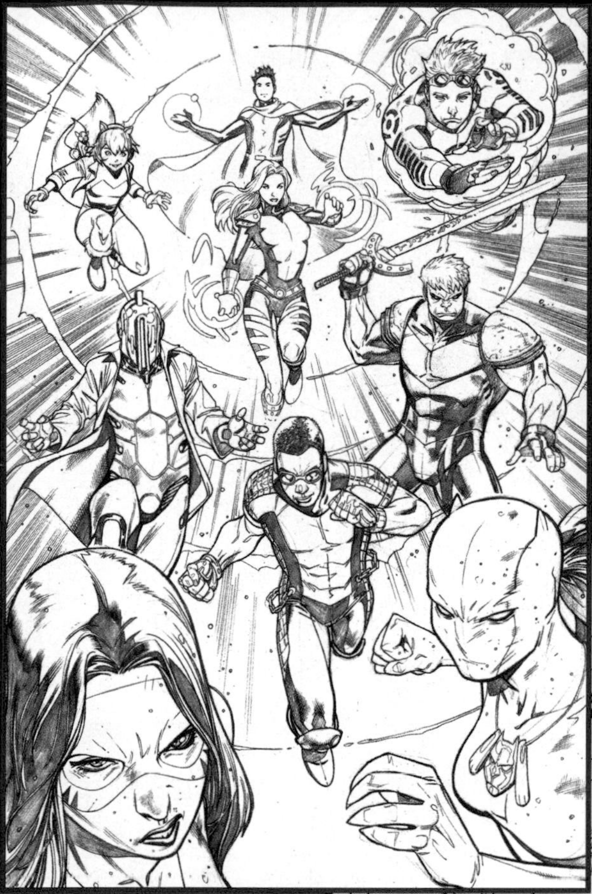

#16, PAGE 2 ART PROCESS BY
PACO MEDINA,
JUAN VLASCO* & *JESUS ABURTOV

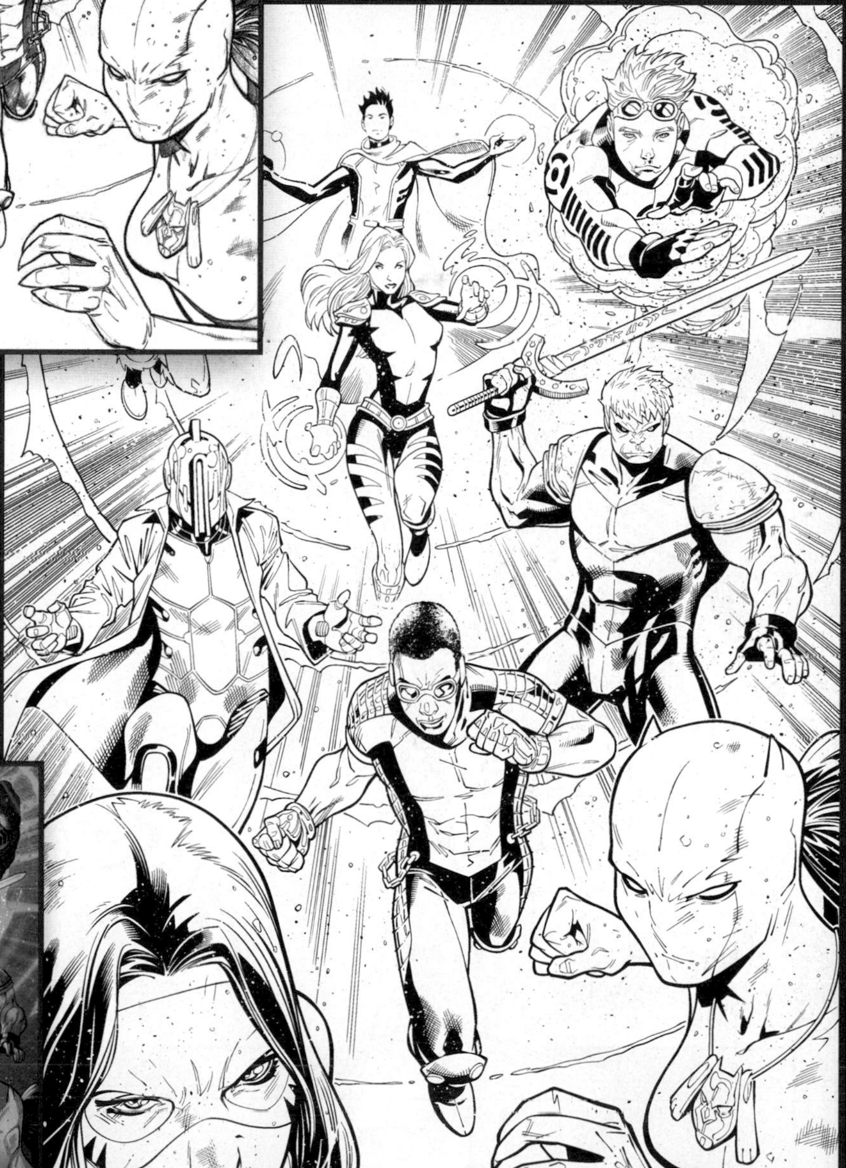

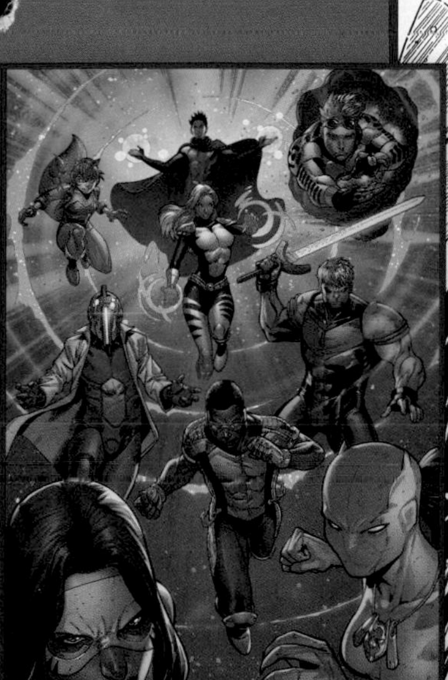

#17, PAGE 2 ART PROCESS BY
PACO MEDINA,
JUAN VLASCO & JESUS ABURTOV

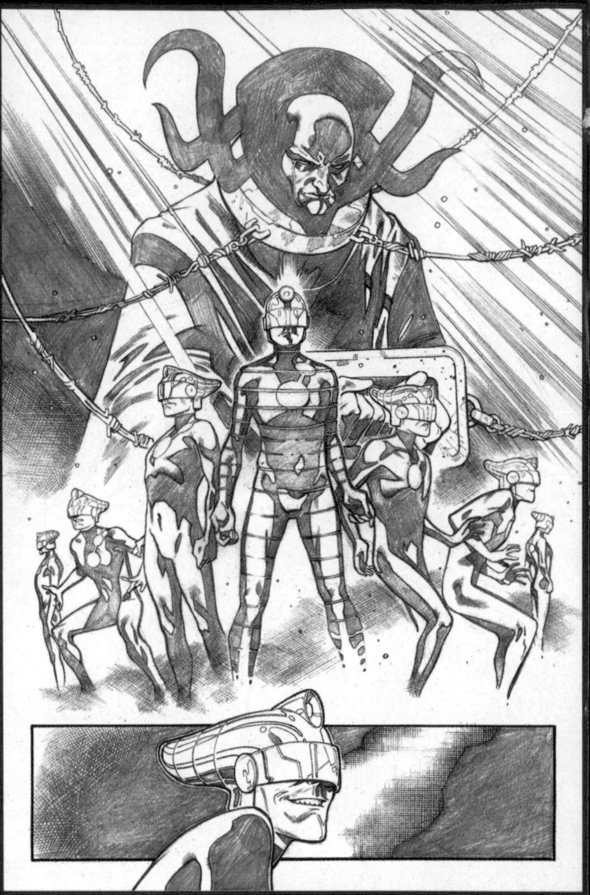

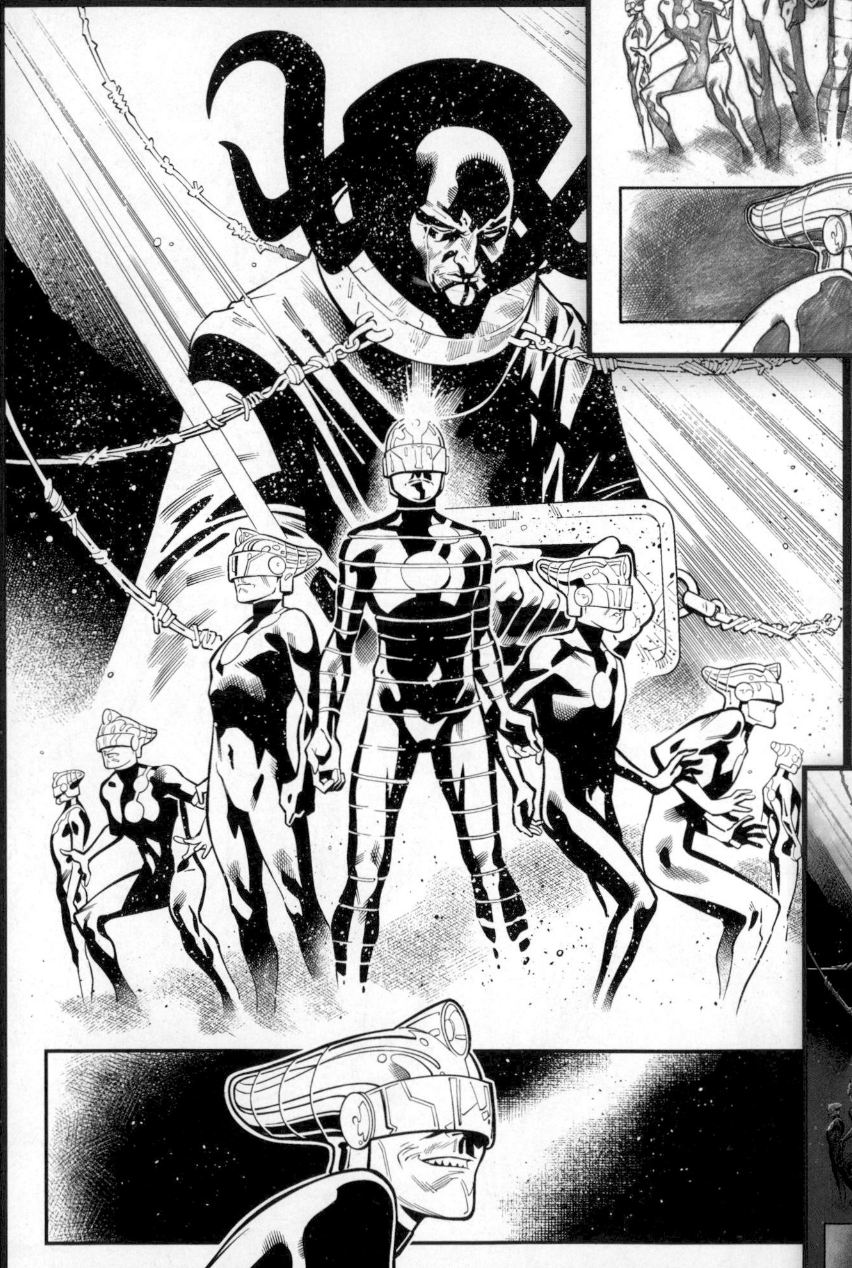

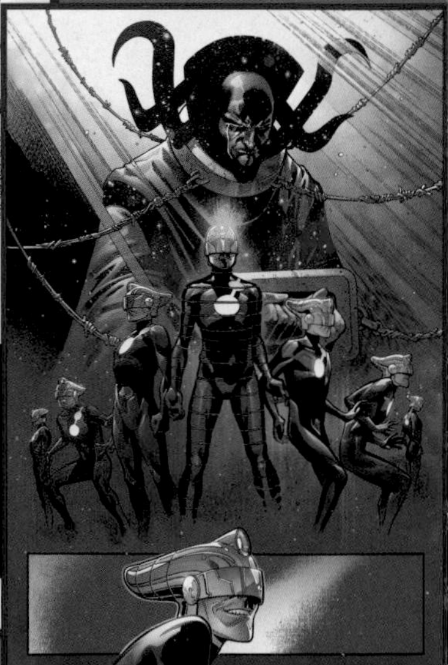